RESEARCH ABSTRACTS IN PHYSICAL EDUCATION AND SPORTS SCIENCES

RESEARCH ABSTRACTS IN PHYSICAL EDUCATION AND SPORTS SCIENCES

(In Two Volumes)

(Volume-1)

DR. C. ASHOK

KALPAZ PUBLICATIONS

DELHI-110052

Research Abstracts in Physical Education and Sports Sciences

Rs. 1800 (Set)

© Dr. C. Ashok

ISBN: 81-7835-648-1 (Set)
ISBN : 81-7835-649-X (Vol. 1)

Published in 2008 in India by
Kalpaz Publications
C-30, Satyawati Nagar,
Delhi-110052
E-mail: kalpaz@hotmail.com
Phone : 9212729499

Laser Type Setting by: Rudra Computer Graphics, Delhi
Vishal Kaushik Printers Delhi - 110093

Dedicated to
My Wife
For her dedication and devotion towards my family

My daughter
For her love and affection

My son
For making everything fun

Contents

Preface

The book "Research Abstracts in Physical Education and Sports Sciences" is emerged for rectifying the discomforts being faced by the research scholars in the field of Physical Education and Sports Sciences. I tried my level best to enlighten a rough idea for selecting the variables, methodology with which the variable has to be tested and how the data are statistically analysed. I have maximally given my efforts in helping the research scholars, even though it is their duty whether the variable is feasible to them or in our country. I sincerely express my gratitude to our Correspondent and Principal for having provided the opportunity to unlimitedly surf in the web with out their magnanimity, this book would not have been formulated. All the suggestions and criticisms are welcomed.

C. Ashok

1

Anthropometric Variables

1. **A New Paradigm for Type 2 Diabetes Mellitus: Could it be a Disease of the Foregut?**

Annals of Surgery. 227(5):637-644, May 1998.

Hickey, Matthew S. PhD *; Pories, Walter J. MD +; MacDonald, Kenneth G. Jr. MD ++; Cory, Kelly A. PhD +; Dohm, G. Lynis PhD +; Swanson, Melvin S. PhD +; Israel, Richard G. PhD *; Barakat, Hisham A. PhD; Considine, Robert V. PhD +; Caro, Jose F. MD [S]; Houmard, Joseph A. PhD ++.

Abstract:

   Summary Background Data: We previously reported, in a study of 608 patients, that the gastric bypass operation (GB) controls type 2 diabetes mellitus in the morbidly obese patient more effectively than any medical therapy. Further, we showed for the first time that it was possible to reduce the mortality from diabetes; GB reduced the chance of dying from 4.5 per cent per year to 1 per cent per year. This control of diabetes has been ascribed to the weight loss induced by the operation. These studies, in weight-stable women, were designed to determine whether weight loss was really the important factor.

   Methods: Fasting plasma **insulin**, fasting plasma **glucose**, minimal model-derived insulin sensitivity and leptin levels were measured in carefully matched cohorts: six women who had undergone GB and had been stable at their lowered weight 24 to 30 months after surgery versus a control group of six women who did not undergo surgery and were similarly weight-stable. The two groups were matched in age, percentage of fat, **body mass index, waist circumference**, and aerobic capacity.

   Results: Even though the two groups of patients were closely matched in weight, age, percentage of fat, and even aerobic capacity, and with both groups maintaining stable weights, the surgical group demonstrated significantly lower levels of serum leptin, fasting plasma insulin, and fasting plasma glucose compared to the control group. Similarly, minimal model-derived insulin sensitivity was significantly higher in the surgical group. Finally, self-reported food intake was significantly lower in the surgiçal group.

Conclusions: Weight loss is not the reason why GB controls diabetes mellitus. Instead, bypassing the foregut and reducing food intake produce the profound long-term alterations in glucose metabolism and insulin action. These findings suggest that our current paradigms of type 2 diabetes mellitus deserve review. The critical lesion may lie in abnormal signals from the gut.

2.   **Cardiorespiratory fitness, body composition, and all-cause and cardiovascular disease mortality in men**

American Journal of Clinical Nutrition, Vol. 69, No. 3, 373-380, March 1999.

Chong Do Lee, Steven N Blair and Andrew S Jackson

Background: Cardiorespiratory fitness and body fatness are both related to health, but their interrelation to all-cause and cardiovascular disease (CVD) mortality is unknown.

Objective: We examined the health benefits of leanness and the hazards of obesity while simultaneously considering cardiorespiratory fitness.

Design: This was an observational cohort study. We followed 21925 men, aged 30–83 y, who had a body-composition assessment and a maximal treadmill exercise test. There were 428 deaths (144 from CVD, 143 from cancer, and 141 from other causes) in an average of 8 y of follow-up (176742 man-years).

Results: After adjustment for age, examination year, cigarette smoking, alcohol intake, and parental history of ischemic heart disease, unfit (low cardiorespiratory fitness as determined by maximal exercise testing), lean men had double the risk of all-cause mortality of fit, lean men (relative risk: 2.07; 95 per cent CI: 1.16, 3.69; $P = 0.01$). Unfit, lean men also had a higher risk of all-cause and CVD mortality than did men who were fit and obese. We observed similar results for fat and fat-free mass in relation to mortality. Unfit men had a higher risk of all-cause and CVD mortality than did fit men in all fat and fat-free mass categories. Similarly, unfit men with low waist girths (< 87 cm) had greater risk of all-cause mortality than did fit men with high waist girths (< 99 cm).

Conclusions: The health benefits of leanness are limited to fit men, and being fit may reduce the hazards of obesity.

Key Words: Body composition • cardiorespiratory fitness • epidemiology • mortality • cardiovascular disease mortality • all-cause mortality • fat mass • fat-free mass • waist girth • men.

3.   The Association between Cardiorespiratory Fitness and Impaired
      Fasting Glucose and Type 2 Diabetes Mellitus in Men
      Annals of Internal Medicine, **Volume 130 Issue 2, 19 January 1999,
      Pages 89-96.**

Ming Wei, MD; Larry W. Gibbons, MD; Tedd L. Mitchell, MD; James
B. Kampert, PhD; Chong D. Lee, EdD; and Steven N. Blair, PED

Background: Several studies show an inverse association between
self-reported physical activity and type 2 diabetes. It is not known whether
physical activity or cardiorespiratory fitness is associated with the onset of
objectively determined impaired fasting glucose and type 2 diabetes.

Objective: To determine whether cardiorespiratory fitness, an objective
marker of physical activity, is associated with risk for impaired fasting glucose
and type 2 diabetes.

Design: Population-based prospective study.

Setting: Preventive medicine clinic.

Patients: 8633 **nondiabetic** men (of whom 7511 did not have impaired
fasting glucose) who were examined at least twice.

Measurements: Cardiorespiratory fitness (determined by a maximal
exercise test on a treadmill), fasting plasma **glucose** level, and other clinical
and personal characteristics and incidence of impaired fasting glucose and
type 2 diabetes.

Results: During an average follow-up of 6 years, 149 patients developed
type 2 diabetes and 593 patients developed impaired fasting glucose. After
age, **cigarette smoking, alcohol** consumption, and parental diabetes were
considered, men in the low-fitness group (the least fit 20 per cent of the cohort)
at baseline had a 1.9-fold risk (95 per cent CI, 1.5- to 2.4-fold) for impaired
fasting glucose and a 3.7-fold risk (CI, 2.4- to 5.8-fold) for diabetes compared
with those in the high-fitness group (the most fit 40 per cent of the cohort).
The risk for impaired fasting glucose was elevated in older men and those with
a higher body mass index. Age, body mass index, blood pressure, triglyceride
level, and a history of parental diabetes were also directly related to risk for
type 2 diabetes.

Conclusions: Low cardiorespiratory fitness was associated with
increased risk for impaired fasting glucose and type 2 diabetes. A sedentary
lifestyle may contribute to the progression from normal fasting glucose to
impaired fasting glucose and diabetes. Risk for type 2 diabetes was elevated
in older persons and those with higher body mass index, blood pressure, and
triglyceride levels and a parental history of diabetes.

4.   **Combined aerobic and resistance exercise training improves functional capacity and strength in CHF**

J Appl Physiol, Vol. 88, Issue 5, 1565-1570, May 2000

Andrew Maiorana[1,2], Gerard O'Driscoll[2,3], Craig Cheetham[1], Julie Collis[1], Carmel Goodman[1], Sarah Rankin[1,2], Roger Taylor[3,4], and Daniel Green[1,2,3]

[1] Departments of Human Movement and Exercise Science and [4] Medicine, The University of Western Australia, Nedlands 6907; and [2] Cardiac Transplant Unit, [3] Department of Cardiology and West Australian Heart Research Institute, Royal Perth Hospital, Perth 6000, Western Australia, Australia.

This study examined the effect of a novel **circuit weight training** (CWT) program on cardiorespiratory fitness, muscular strength, and body composition in 13 patients with **chronic heart failure** (CHF), using a prospective randomized crossover protocol. Peak exercise **oxygen uptake** ($CO_{2\,peak}$) increased after the 8-wk CWT program (19.5 ± 1.2 vs. 22.0 ± 1.5 ml · kg^{-1} · min^1, $P < 0.01$), as did exercise test duration (15.2 ± 0.9 vs. 18.0 ± 1.1 min, $P < 0.001$). Submaximal exercise heart rate was lower after training at 60 and 80 W (121 ± 3 vs. 134 ± 5 beats/min, $P < 0.01$) as was rate pressure product, whereas ventilatory threshold increased, from 52 ± 3 to 58 ± 3 per cent of $O_{2\,peak}$ ($P < 0.05$). CWT also increased maximal isotonic voluntary contractile strength for seven different muscle groups, from 392 to 462 kg ($P = 0.001$). CWT, an exercise prescription specifically targeting peripheral abnormalities in CHF, improves functional capacity and muscular strength in these patients.

Key Words: chronic heart failure; exercise training; peak oxygen uptake; maximal voluntary contraction; anthropometry.

5.   **Effect of Diet and Exercise Intervention on Blood Pressure, Insulin, Oxidative Stress, and Nitric Oxide Availability**

Circulation. 2002;106:2530

Christian K. Roberts, PhD; Nosratola D. Vaziri, MD; R. James Barnard, PhD

From the Department of Physiological Science, University of California, Los Angeles (C.K.R., R.J.B.), and the Division of Nephrology and Hypertension, Department of Medicine, University of California, Irvine (C.K.R., N.D.V.).

Correspondence to R. James Barnard, Department of Physiological Science, UCLA, P.O. 951527, Los Angeles, CA 90095-1527. E-mail jbarnard@physci.ucla.edu.

Background— Diet and exercise can affect **blood pressure** and atherosclerotic risk.

Methods and Results— The present study was designed to examine the effects of a short-term, rigorous diet and exercise intervention on blood pressure, **hyperinsulinemia**, and **nitric oxide** (NO) availability. Men (n=11) were placed on a low-fat, high-fiber diet combined with daily exercise for 45 to 60 minutes for 3 weeks. Pre- and post fasting blood was drawn for serum lipid, insulin, 8-isoprostaglandin F_2 (8-iso-PGF$_2$), and glucose measurements. Anthropometric parameters, blood pressure (BP), and 24-hour urinary NO metabolite excretion (NO_x), a marker of NO bioavailability, were measured. Systolic ($P<0.01$) and diastolic BP ($P<0.01$) and 8-iso-PGF$_2$ decreased ($P<0.05$), whereas urinary NO_x increased ($P<0.05$). There was a significant reduction in fasting **insulin** ($P<0.01$) and a significant correlation between the decrease in serum insulin and the increase in urinary NO_x ($r^2=0.68$, $P<0.05$). All fasting lipids decreased significantly, and the total cholesterol to high-density lipoprotein cholesterol ratio improved. Although body weight and **body mass index** ($P<0.01$) decreased, obesity was still present and there were no correlations between the change in body mass index and the change in insulin, BP, or urinary NO_x.

Conclusions : This intervention resulted in dramatic improvements in BP, oxidative stress, NO availability, and the metabolic profile within 3 weeks, mitigating the risk for atherosclerosis progression and its clinical sequelae.

Key Words: hypertension • free radicals • oxygen • insulin.

6. **Anthropometric and hormone effects of an eight-week exercise-diet intervention in breast cancer patients: results of a pilot study**
Cancer Epidemiology Biomarkers and Prevention, Vol. 7, Issue 6 477-481.

A McTiernan, C Ulrich, C Kumai, D Bean, R Schwartz, J Mahloch, R Hastings, J Gralow and JD Potter

Cancer Prevention Research Program, Fred Hutchinson Cancer Research Center, Seattle, Washington 98104, USA.

To assess the feasibility of an exercise-**diet** intervention in sedentary, overweight **breast cancer** patients, we conducted a pilot 8-week intervention. Recruitment letters and interest surveys were sent to 99 stage 1 or 2 breast cancer patients, ages 25-75 years, who were identified through two Seattle breast surgery practices and the University of Washington Breast Clinic. Ten patients were eligible and interested and were enrolled in the intervention, which consisted of thrice-weekly monitored aerobic exercise sessions and a low-fat (20 per cent of calories from fat) diet. Nine patients completed the program; all adhered well to the intervention and data collection protocol. The patients, ages 40-74 years, lost, on average, 2.6 pounds of body weight, 3.4 cm in waist circumference, 4.6 cm in hip circumference, 2.3 per cent body fat, 3.3 systolic blood pressure points, 0.67 diastolic blood pressure points, and 4.0 pulse beats/min, and they gained an average of 2.3 per cent lean mass. Slight, nonsignificant decreases were observed in serum concentration of total and free **estradiol, estrone sulfate,** total **testosterone, androstenedione,** and **dehydroepiandrosterone.** These pilot data indicate that breast cancer patients are highly motivated to join and adhere to an intense exercise-diet intervention and can experience significant measurable changes in anthropometric and fat mass measures.

7.   **Physiological and anthropometric characteristics of amateur rugby league players**
Br J Sports Med 2000; *34*:303-307
Tim J Gabbett

School of Physiotherapy and Exercise Science, Faculty of Health Sciences, Griffith University Gold Coast, Queensland, Australia
Correspondence to: T J Gabbett, School of Physiotherapy and Exercise Science, Faculty of Health Sciences, Griffith University Gold Coast, PMB50 Gold Coast Mail Centre, Queensland, Australia 9726 email: t.gabbett@mailbox.gu.edu.au

Objectives : To investigate the physiological and anthropometric characteristics of amateur rugby league players.

Methods : Thirty five amateur rugby league players (19 forwards and 16 backs) were measured for height, **body mass,** percentage **body fat** (sum of four skinfolds), muscular **power** (vertical jump), **speed** (10 m and 40 m sprint), and maximal **aerobic power** (multistage fitness test). Data were also collected on match frequency, training status, playing experience, and employment related physical activity levels.

Results : The 10 m and 40 m sprint, vertical jump, percentage body fat, and multistage fitness test results were 20–42 per cent poorer than previously reported for professional rugby league players. Compared with forwards, backs had significantly (p<0.01) lower body mass (79.7 (74.7–84.7) kg *v* 90.8 (86.2–95.4) kg) and significantly (p<0.01) greater speed during the 40 m sprint (6.45 (6.35–6.55) *v* 6.79 (6.69–6.89) seconds). Values for percentage body fat, vertical jump, 10 m sprint, and maximal aerobic power were not significantly different (p>0.05) between forwards and backs. When compared with professional rugby league players, the training status of amateur rugby league players was 30–53 per cent lower, with players devoting less than three hours a week to team training sessions and about 30 minutes a week to individual training sessions.

The training time devoted to the development of muscular power (about 13 minutes a week), speed (about eight minutes a week), and aerobic fitness (about 34 minutes a week) did not differ significantly (p>0.05) between forwards and backs. At the time of the field testing, players had participated, on average, in one 60 minute match every eight days.

Conclusions : The physiological and anthropometric characteristics of amateur rugby league players are poorly developed. These findings suggest that position specific training does not occur in amateur rugby league. The poor fitness of non-elite players may be due to a low playing intensity, infrequent matches of short duration, and/or an inappropriate training stimulus.

Key Words: conditioning; fitness; non-elite; training; rugby.

8.   **Effects of a controlled trial of a school-based exercise program on the obesity indexes of preschool children**
American Journal of Clinical Nutrition, Vol. 68, 1006-1011.
L Mo-suwan, S Pongprapai, C Junjana and A Puetpaiboon
Department of Pediatrics, Faculty of Medicine, Prince of Songkla University, Songkhla, Thailand. mladda@ratree.psu.ac.th

Exercise has been found to be effective for prevention of weight gain and maintenance of a stable weight in adults. The objective of this study was to evaluate the effect of a school-based aerobic exercise program on the **obesity** indexes of preschool children. Subjects were 292 second-year elementary school pupils from 2 kindergartens in Hat Yai municipality, Songkhla province, southern Thailand. A specially designed exercise program, including a 15-min walk before beginning the morning class and a 20-min aerobic dance session after the afternoon nap, 3 times a week, was conducted for 29.6 wk. Weight, height, and triceps **skinfold** thickness were measured 4 times. At the end of the study, the prevalence of obesity, using 95th percentile National Center for Health Statistics triceps-skinfold-thickness cutoffs, of both the exercise and control groups decreased. That of the exercise group decreased from 12.2 per cent at baseline to 8.8 per cent (Wilcoxon signed-rank test, P = 0.058), whereas that of the control group decreased from 11.7 per cent to 9.7 per cent (Wilcoxon signed-rank test, P = 0.179). A sex difference in the response of body mass index (BMI) to exercise was observed. Girls in the exercise group had a lower likelihood of having an increasing BMI slope than the control girls did (odds ratio: 0.32; 95 per cent CI: 0.18, 0.56). In conclusion, our study suggests that a 29.6-wk school-based exercise program can prevent BMI gain in girls and may induce a remission of obesity in preschool-age children.

9.   **Bone mineral density in mother-daughter pairs: relations to lifetime exercise, lifetime milk consumption, and calcium supplements**
      American Journal of Clinical Nutrition, Vol. 63, 72-79.
      CM Ulrich, CC Georgiou, CM Snow-Harter and DE Gillis
      Department of Epidemiology, University of Washington, Seattle 98195, USA.

This study investigated associations between lifetime milk consumption, calcium intake from supplements, lifetime weight-bearing exercise, and bone mineral density (BMD) among 25 elderly women (mean age 72 y) and their premenopausal daughters (mean age 41 y). The BMD of the total, axial, and peripheral skeleton was measured by dual-energy X-ray absorptiometry. Lifetime milk consumption, supplemental calcium intake, and weight-bearing exercise were estimated retrospectively by questionnaire and interview. In multiple-linear-regression analyses, mothers' total and peripheral BMD were positively associated with supplemental calcium intake after age 60 y, body weight, current estrogen replacement therapy (ERT), and past oral contraceptive (OC) use, and negatively associated with age and height (all P < 0.05). Mothers' axial BMD was positively correlated with body weight and past OC use. Among daughters, lifetime weight-bearing exercise was a predictor of total and peripheral BMD, whereas total lean mass was a predictor of axial BMD. Mothers' lifetime milk consumption was positively associated with that of their daughters. Mothers' and daughters' peripheral BMD values were positively correlated after adjustment for daughters' exercise, and mothers' age, body weight, and ERT. These results suggest that calcium supplementation and exogenous estrogen positively influence bone mass in postmenopausal years. Our findings lend support to recommendations for physical activity as a means of osteoporosis prevention. In the age groups studied, the effects of behavioral and hormonal factors on BMD appeared to dominate over familial similarity, which suggests that women may successfully enhance their genetically determined bone mass through weight-bearing exercise, post-menopausal ERT, and adequate calcium intake.

10.   **Exercise Training and Nutritional Supplementation for Physical Frailty in Very Elderly People**
      The New England Jpurnal of Medicine, Volume 330:1769-1775, Number 25, June 23, 1994.
      Maria A. Fiatarone, Evelyn F. O'Neill, Nancy Doyle Ryan, Karen M. Clements, Guido R. Solares, Miriam E. Nelson, Susan B. Roberts, Joseph J. Kehayias, Lewis A. Lipsitz, and William J. Evans

Abstract

Background : Although disuse of skeletal muscle and undernutrition are often cited as potentially reversible causes of frailty in elderly people, the efficacy of interventions targeted specifically at these deficits has not been carefully studied.

Methods : We conducted a randomized, placebo-controlled trial comparing progressive resistance exercise training, multinutrient supplementation, both interventions, and neither in 100 frail nursing home residents over a 10-week period.

Results : The mean (±SE) age of the 63 women and 37 men enrolled in the study was 87.1 ±0.6 years (range, 72 to 98); 94 per cent of the subjects completed the study. Muscle strength increased by 113 ±8 per cent in the subjects who underwent exercise training, as compared with 3 ±9 per cent in the nonexercising subjects (P<0.001). Gait velocity increased by 11.8 ±3.8 percent in the exercisers but declined by 1.0 ±3.8 per cent in the nonexercisers (P = 0.02). Stair-climbing power also improved in the exercisers as compared with the nonexercisers (by 28.4 ±6.6 per cent vs. 3.6 ±6.7 per cent, P = 0.01), as did the level of spontaneous physical activity. Cross-sectional thigh-muscle area increased by 2.7 ±1.8 per cent in the exercisers but declined by 1.8 ±2.0 percent in the nonexercisers (P = 0.11). The nutritional supplement had no effect on any primary outcome measure. Total energy intake was significantly increased only in the exercising subjects who also received nutritional supplementation.

Conclusions : High-intensity resistance exercise training is a feasible and effective means of counteracting muscle weakness and physical frailty in very elderly people. In contrast, multinutrient supplementation without concomitant exercise does not reduce muscle weakness or physical frailty.

Address reprint requests to Dr. Fiatarone at the Human Nutrition Research Center on Aging, 711 Washington St., Boston, MA 02111.

11. **Relationship of Physical Fitness vs Body Mass Index With Coronary Artery Disease and Cardiovascular Events in Women**
JAMA. 2004;292:1179-1187.

Timothy R. Wessel, MD; Christopher B. Arant, MD; Marian B. Olson, MS; B. Delia Johnson, PhD; Steven E. Reis, MD; Barry L. Sharaf, MD; Leslee J. Shaw, PhD; Eileen Handberg, PhD; George Sopko, MD; Sheryl F. Kelsey, PhD; Carl J. Pepine, MD; C. Noel Bairey Merz, MD

Context : Individual contributions of obesity and physical fitness (physical activity and functional capacity) to risk of coronary heart disease in women remain unclear.

Objective : To investigate the relationships of measures of obesity (body mass index [BMI], waist circumference, waist-hip ratio, and waist-height ratio) and physical fitness (self-reported Duke Activity Status Index [DASI] and Postmenopausal Estrogen-Progestin Intervention questionnaire [PEPI-Q] scores) with coronary artery disease (CAD) risk factors, angiographic CAD, and adverse cardiovascular (CV) events in women evaluated for suspected myocardial ischemia.

Design, Setting, and Participants : The National Heart, Lung, and Blood Institute–sponsored Women's Ischemia Syndrome Evaluation (WISE) is a multicenter prospective cohort study. From 1996-2000, 936 women were enrolled at 4 US academic medical centers at the time of clinically indicated coronary angiography and then assessed (mean follow-up, 3.9 [SD, 1.8] years) for adverse outcomes.

Main Outcome Measures : Prevalence of obstructive CAD (any angiographic stenosis 50 per cent) and incidence of adverse CV events (all-cause death or hospitalization for nonfatal myocardial infarction, stroke, congestive heart failure, unstable angina, or other vascular events) during follow-up.

Results : Of 906 women (mean age, 58 [SD, 12] years) with complete data, 19 per cent were of nonwhite race, 76 per cent were overweight (BMI 25), 70 per cent had low functional capacity (DASI scores <25, equivalent to 7 metabolic equivalents [METs]), and 39 per cent had obstructive CAD. During follow-up, 337 (38 per cent) women had a first adverse event, 118 (13 per cent) had a major adverse event, and 68 (8 per cent) died. Overweight women were more likely than normal weight women to have CAD risk factors, but neither BMI nor abdominal obesity measures were significantly associated with obstructive CAD or adverse CV events after adjusting for other risk factors (P = .05 to .88). Conversely, women with lower DASI scores were significantly more likely to have CAD risk factors and obstructive CAD (44 per cent vs 26 per cent, $P<.001$) at baseline, and each 1-MET increase in DASI score was independently associated with an 8 per cent (hazard ratio, 0.92; 95 per cent confidence interval, 0.85-0.99; P = .02) decrease in risk of major adverse CV events during follow-up.

Conclusions : Among women undergoing coronary angiography for suspected ischemia, higher self-reported physical fitness scores were independently associated with fewer CAD risk factors, less angiographic CAD, and lower risk for adverse CV events. Measures of obesity were not independently associated with these outcomes.

Author Affiliations: Division of Cardiovascular Medicine, University of Florida College of Medicine, Gainesville (Drs Wessel, Arant, Handberg, and Pepine); Cardiovascular Institute and Department of Epidemiology, University of Pittsburgh Medical Center, Pittsburgh, Pa (Ms Olson and Drs

Johnson, Reis, and Kelsey); Division of Cardiology, Rhode Island Hospital, Providence (Dr Sharaf); Atlanta Cardiovascular Research Institute, Atlanta, Ga (Dr Shaw); Division of Heart and Vascular Disease, National Heart, Lung, and Blood Institute, National Institutes of Health, Bethesda, Md (Dr Sopko); Division of Cardiology, Department of Medicine, Cedars-Sinai Research Institute, Cedars-Sinai Medical Center, Los Angeles, Calif (Dr Bairey Merz).

12. Nutritional Support for Individuals With COPD* A Meta-analysis

Chest. 2000;117:672-678.

Ivone M. Ferreira, MD, PhD; Dina Brooks, PhD, MSc, BSc(PT); Yves Lacasse, MD, MSc and Roger S. Goldstein, MB, ChB, FCCP
* From the Departments of Medicine (Dr. Goldstein) and Physical Therapy (Dr. Brooks), University of Toronto; the Respiratory Medicine Program (Dr. Ferreira), West Park Hospital, Toronto, Ontario; and Centre de Pneumologie (Dr. Lacasse), Hopital Laval, Ste-Foy, Quebec.

Correspondence to: Ivone M. Ferreira, MD, PhD, Respiratory Medicine Program, West Park Hospital, 82 Buttonwood Ave, Toronto, Ontario, M6M 2J5, Canada; e-mail: ivoneferreira@hotmail.com

Rationale : Malnutrition in patients with COPD is associated with an **impaired pulmonary status**, reduced diaphragmatic mass, lower exercise capacity, and higher **mortality** rate when compared to adequately nourished individuals with COPD. Nutritional support may therefore be a useful part of their comprehensive care.

Purpose : To conduct a meta-analysis of randomized controlled trials (RCTs) to clarify whether nutritional supplementation (caloric supplementation for at least 2 weeks) improved anthropometric measures, pulmonary function, respiratory muscle strength, and functional exercise capacity in patients with stable COPD.

Methods : RCTs were identified from several sources, including the Cochrane Airways Group register of RCTs, a hand search of abstracts presented at international meetings, and consultation with experts. Two reviewers independently selected trials for inclusion, assessed quality, and extracted the data. Within each trial and for each outcome, we calculated an effect size. The effect sizes were then pooled by a random-effects model. Homogeneity among the effect sizes was also tested.

Results : From 272 references, nine RCTs were ultimately included. Six articles were considered as high quality. Only two studies were double blinded. For each of the outcomes studied, the effect of nutritional support was small: the 95 per cent confidence intervals around the pooled effect sizes all included zero. The effect of nutritional support was homogeneous across studies.

Conclusion: Nutritional support had no effect on improving anthropometric measures, lung function, or functional exercise capacity among patients with stable COPD.

Key Words : COPD • meta-analysis • nutrition • respiratory rehabilitation • systematic review.

13.   Distribution of Muscle Weakness in Patients With Stable Chronic Obstructive Pulmonary Disease.

Journal of Cardiopulmonary Rehabilitation. 20(6):353-360, November/ December 2000.

Gosselink, Rik PhD, PT; Troosters, Thierry PhD, PT; Decramer, Marc PhD, MD

Abstract:

Purpose : The authors determined the degree of respiratory and peripheral muscle weakness in patients with moderate to severe chronic obstructive pulmonary disease (COPD). Differences in severity of muscle weakness among muscle groups may provide treatment options, such as selective muscle training, to adapt the exercise prescription in pulmonary rehabilitation programs. In addition, this information may add to the knowledge on the mechanisms of muscle weakness.

Methods : Respiratory and peripheral muscle force were quantified in 22 healthy elderly subjects and 40 consecutive COPD patients (forced expiratory volume in 1 second, percent of predicted value [per cent pred] 41 +/ - 19; transfer factor for carbon monoxide, per cent pred 47 +/- 26) admitted to a pulmonary rehabilitation program. Lung function, diffusing capacity, isometric force of four peripheral muscle groups (handgrip, elbow flexion, shoulder abduction, and knee extension), neck flexion force, and maximal inspiratory and expiratory pressures were measured.

Results: Patients had reduced respiratory muscle strength (mean 64 per cent of control subjects' value [per cent control] and peripheral muscle strength (mean 75 per cent control) compared to normal subjects. Inspiratory **muscle strength** (59 +/- 18 per cent control) was significantly lower than expiratory muscle strength (69 +/- 25 per cent control) and peripheral muscle strength ($P < 0.01$). Neck flexion force (80 +/- 19 per cent control) was better preserved than maximal inspiratory pressure and shoulder abduction force (70 +/- 15 per cent control, $P < 0.01$). Handgrip force (78 +/- 16 per cent control) and elbow flexion force (78 +/- 14 per cent control) were significantly less affected than shoulder abduction force (70 +/- 15 per cent control, $P < 0.01$). Finally, shoulder abduction force and knee-extension force (72 +/- 24 per cent control) were not significantly different.

Conclusions: Muscle weakness in stable COPD patients does not affect all muscles to a similar extent. Inspiratory muscle force is affected more than peripheral muscle force, whereas proximal upper limb muscle strength was impaired more than distal upper limb muscle strength.

14. **Marginal iron deficiency without anemia impairs aerobic adaptation among previously untrained women**

American Journal of Clinical Nutrition, Vol. 75, No. 4, 734-742, April 2002

Thomas Brownlie, IV, Virginia Utermohlen, Pamela S Hinton, Christina Giordano and Jere D Haas

The Division of Nutritional Sciences, Cornell University, Ithaca, NY.

Background: Iron deficiency without anemia has been shown to reduce both muscle-tissue oxidative capacity and endurance in animals. However, the consequences of iron deficiency in humans remain unclear.

Objective : We investigated the effects of iron supplementation on adaptation to aerobic training among marginally iron-depleted women. We hypothesized that iron supplementation for 6 wk would significantly improve iron status and maximal oxygen uptake (O_2max) after 4 wk of concurrent aerobic training.

Design : Forty-one untrained, iron-depleted, nonanemic women were randomly assigned to receive either 50 mg $FeSO_4$ or a placebo twice daily for 6 wk in a double-blind trial. All subjects trained on **cycle ergometers** 5 d/wk for 4 wk, beginning on week 3 of the study.

Results : Six weeks of iron supplementation significantly improved serum **ferritin** and serum transferrin receptor (sTfR) concentrations and transferrin saturation without affecting hemoglobin concentrations or hematocrit. Average O_2max and maximal respiratory exchange ratio improved in both the placebo and iron groups after training; however, the iron group experienced significantly greater improvements in O_2max. Both iron-status and fitness outcomes were analyzed after stratifying by baseline sTfR concentration (> and 8.0 mg/L), which showed that the previously observed treatment effects were due to iron-status and fitness improvements among subjects with poor baseline iron status.

Conclusions : Our findings strongly suggest that iron deficiency without anemia but with elevated sTfR status impairs aerobic adaptation among previously untrained women and that this can be corrected with iron supplementation.

Key Words: Iron deficiency without anemia • iron depletion • women • aerobic training • O_2max • maximal oxygen uptake • serum transferrin receptors • serum ferritin.

15.   Gender differences in glucoregulatory responses to intense exercise
       J Appl Physiol, Vol. 88, Issue 2, 457-466, February 2000
       **Errol B. Marliss[1], Stuart H. Kreisman[1], Anthony Manzon[1], Jeffrey B.
       Halter[2], Mladen Vranic[3], and Sharon J. Nessim[1]**
       [1] McGill Nutrition and Food Science Centre, Royal Victoria Hospital,
Montreal, Quebec, Canada H3A 1A1; [2] Department of Internal Medicine and
Institute of Gerontology, University of Michigan and Veterans Affairs Medical
Center, Ann Arbor, Michigan 48109; and [3] Departments of Physiology and
Medicine, University of Toronto, Toronto, Ontario, Canada M5S 1A8.

We compared glucoregulatory responses to intense exercise (14 min at
88 per cent maximum O_2 uptake) between genders (16 men, 12 women). Analysis
of covariance of maximum O_2 uptake showed no gender effect, with 82 per cent
of variance due to fat-free mass (FFM). **Glycemia** rose comparably during
exercise but was higher in women during recovery ($P = 0.02$). Glucose
production [rate of appearance (R_a); in mg/min] increased markedly in both;
stepwise multiple regression and analysis of covariance of R_a (peak and
incremental area under the curve) showed no effect of gender, body weight, or
FFM. Glucose uptake [rate of disappearance (R_d)] increased less than R_a and
slower in women. R_d area under the curve related to FFM ($P = 0.01$) but not
gender or body weight. Norepinephrine and epinephrine responses (13-18×
baseline) were the same and correlated significantly with R_a. Exercise insulin
and glucagon changes were slight, but postexercise hyperinsulinemia was
greater in women ($P = 0.018$), along with higher R_d. Therefore, intense exercise
glucoregulation is qualitatively similar between genders, with a "feed-forward"
regulation of R_a (consistent with catecholamine mediation). However, women
have a lesser R_d response, related to FFM. This combination leads to greater
recovery-period hyperglycemia and hyperinsulinemia.
       Key Words: female; male; catecholamines; glucose turnover; insulin;
glucagons.

16.   **A 30-Year Follow-Up of the Dallas Bed Rest and Training Study I.
       Effect of Age on the Cardiovascular Response to Exercise**
       Circulation. 2001;104:1350.
       **Darren K. McGuire, MD, MHSc; Benjamin D. Levine, MD; Jon W.
       Williamson, PhD; Peter G. Snell, PhD; C. Gunnar Blomqvist, MD, PhD;
       Bengt Saltin, MD; Jere H. Mitchell, MD**
       From the Pauline and Adolph Weinberger Laboratory for
Cardiopulmonary Research, University of Texas Southwestern Medical Center,
Dallas, Tex (D.K.M., B.D.L., J.W.W., P.G.S., C.G.B., J.H.M.); Institute for Exercise
and Environmental Medicine, Presbyterian Hospital, Dallas, Tex (B.D.L.); and

Copenhagen Muscle Research Center, University of Copenhagen, Copenhagen, Denmark (B.S.).
Correspondence to Darren K. McGuire, MD, MHSc, UT Southwestern Medical Center, 5323 Harry Hines Blvd, Dallas, TX 75390-9047.
E-mail darren.mcguire@utsouthwestern.edu

Background : Cardiovascular capacity declines with aging, as evidenced by declining maximal **oxygen uptake** (O_2max), with little known about the specific mechanisms of this decline. Our study objective was to assess the effect of a 30-year interval on body composition and cardiovascular response to acute exercise in 5 healthy subjects originally evaluated in 1966.

    Methods and Results : Anthropometric parameters and the cardiovascular response to acute maximal exercise were assessed with noninvasive techniques. On average, body weight increased 25 per cent (77 versus 100 kg) and percent body fat increased 100 per cent (14 per cent versus 28 per cent), with little change in fat-free mass (66 versus 72 kg). On average, O_2max decreased 11 per cent (3.30 versus 2.90 L/min). Likewise, O_2max decreased when indexed to total body mass (43 versus 31 mL · kg^{-1} · min^{-1}) or fat-free mass (50 versus 43 mL/kg fat-free mass per minute). Maximal heart rate declined 6 per cent (193 versus 181 bpm) and maximal stroke volume increased 16 per cent (104 versus 121 mL), with no difference observed in maximal cardiac output (20.0 versus 21.4 L/min). Maximal AV oxygen difference declined 15 per cent (16.2 versus 13.8 vol per cent) and accounted for the entire decrease in cardiovascular capacity.

    Conclusions : Cardiovascular capacity declined over the 30-year study interval in these 5 middle-aged men primarily because of an impaired efficiency of maximal peripheral oxygen extraction. Maximal cardiac output was maintained with a decline in maximal heart rate compensated for by an increased maximal stroke volume. Most notably, 3 weeks of bedrest in these same men at 20 years of age (1966) had a more profound impact on physical work capacity than did 3 decades of aging.

    Key Words : aging • oxygen • exercise • body composition.

17. **Ginseng Supplementation Does Not Enhance Healthy Young Adults' Peak Aerobic Exercise Performance**

Journal of the American College of Nutrition, Vol. 17, No. 5, 462-466 (1998)

Jason D. Allen, MEd·, Jeff McLung, PhD, Arnold G Nelson, PhD and Michael Welsch, PhD
Department of Health and Human Performance (J.D.A., J.M.) Louisiana State University, Baton Rouge, Louisiana.

Western Carolina University and Department of Kinesiology (J.D.A., A.G.N., M.W.) Louisiana State University, Baton Rouge, Louisiana.

Address reprint requests to: Jason D. Allen, Department of Kinesiology, H. P. Long Field House, Louisiana State University, Baton Rouge, LA 70803-7101.

Objective: To determine the short term effects (21 days) of 200 mg (7 per cent standardized) Panax ginseng supplementation vs. placebo on peak aerobic exercise performance in healthy young adults, with unrestricted diets.

Methods: Twenty men and eight women (age=23.2±3.2 years, height=175.8±8.6 cm; weight=75.2±15.3 kg) were randomly assigned to either a Panax ginseng or placebo group for a period of 3 weeks in a double blind design. Prior to and following treatment the subjects performed a symptom limited graded exercise test on a Schwinn Airdyne ergometer. The data were analyzed using an analysis of variance.

Results: No significant treatment effect was observed for the dependent variables of VO_2, exercise time, workload, plasma lactate and hematocrit at peak levels, or for heart rate and rate of perceived exertion at 150 watts, 200 watts and peak.

Conclusions: The results of this study do not support an ergogenic effect on peak aerobic exercise performance following a 3-week supplementation period of 200 mg 7 per cent Panax ginseng in healthy young adults with moderate exercise capacities and unrestricted diets.

Key Words: ginseng, VO_{2max}, aerobic, performance, supplement, ergogenic aid.

18. **Influence of diet and exercise on skeletal muscle and visceral adipose tissue in men**

Journal of Applied Physiology, Vol. *81,* No. 6, pp. 2445-2455, December 1996

Robert Ross, John Rissanen, Heather Pedwell, Jennifer Clifford, and Peter Shragge

School of Physical and Health Education, Queen's University, and Department of Radiology, Kingston General Hospital, Kingston, Ontario, Canada K7L 3N6.

Ross, Robert, John Rissanen, Heather Pedwell, Jennifer Clifford, and Peter Shragge.

The effects of **diet** only (DO) and diet combined with either aerobic (DA) or resistance (DR) exercise on subcutaneous **adipose tissue** (SAT), visceral adipose tissue (VAT), **lean tissue** (LT), and skeletal muscle (SM) tissue were evaluated in 33 obese men (DO, $n = 11$; DA, $n = 11$; DR, $n = 11$). All tissues were measured by using a whole body multislice **magnetic resonance imaging** (MRI) model. Within each group, significant reductions were observed for body weight, SAT, and VAT ($P < 0.05$). The reductions in body weight (~10 per cent) and SAT (~25 per cent) and VAT volume (~35 per cent) were not different between groups ($P > 0.05$). For all treatments, the relative reduction in VAT was greater than in SAT ($P < 0.05$). For the DA and DR groups only, the reduction in abdominal SAT (~27 per cent) was greater ($P < 0.05$) than that observed for the gluteal-femoral region (~20 per cent). Conversely, the reduction in VAT was uniform throughout the abdomen regardless of treatment ($P > 0.05$). MRI-LT and MRI-SM decreased both in the upper and lower body regions for the DO group alone ($P < 0.05$). Peak O_2 uptake (liters) was significantly improved (~14 per cent) in the DA group as was muscular strength (~20 per cent) in the DR group ($P < 0.01$). These findings indicate that DA and DR result in a greater preservation of MRI-SM, mobilization of SAT from the abdominal region, by comparison with the gluteal-femoral region, and improved functional capacity when compared with DO in obese men.

Key Words: obesity; magnetic resonance imaging; lean tissue; weight loss.

19. **Clinical research: Metabolic syndrome, dyslipidemia, and vascular abnormalities**

J Am Coll Cardiol, 2004; 43:1823-1827.

Exercise training normalizes vascular dysfunction and improves central adiposity in obese adolescents

Katie Watts, BSc(Hons)[*], Petra Beye, MD, Aris Siafarikas, MD, Elizabeth A. Davis, FRACP, Timothy W. Jones, FRACP, Gerard O'Driscoll, FRACP[*] and Daniel J. Green, PhD[*·*]

· Human Movement and Exercise Science, University of Western Australia, Crawley, Australia.

Endocrinology and Diabetes, Princess Margaret Hospital, Subiaco, Australia.

Telethon Institute Child Health Research, Western Australian Institute Medical Research, Subiaco, Australia.

Cardiac Transplant Unit, Royal Perth Hospital, Perth, Western Australia.

[*] Reprint requests and correspondence: Dr. Daniel J. Green, School of Human Movement, University of Western Australia, Crawley 6009, Western Australia.

brevis@cyllene.uwa.edu.au

Objectives: We sought to characterize the impact of obesity on vascular function in adolescents and to determine whether an exercise program reverses abnormalities in endothelial function.

Background: Obesity, a major modifiable risk factor for cardiovascular disease, is epidemic in Western societies, with rapid rates of increase in the young. Atherosclerosis begins in childhood, and endothelial dysfunction is its earliest detectable manifestation.

Methods: The influence of eight weeks of **circuit training** (CT) was examined in 19 obese subjects (14.3 ± 1.5 years), using a randomized, crossover protocol. Functional capacity and muscular strength were assessed by standard techniques. Body composition was examined using anthropometric measures and dual-energy X-ray absorptiometry. Conduit vessel endothelial function was assessed using high-resolution ultrasound and flow-mediated dilation (FMD) of the brachial artery.

Results: Circuit training decreased abdominal and trunk fat and significantly improved fitness and muscular strength ($p < 0.05$). In the obese group, FMD was significantly impaired relative to control subjects ($n = 20$) at entry (5.3 ± 0.9 per cent vs. 8.9 ± 1.5 per cent, $p < 0.05$) and was normalized after CT (8.8 ± 0.8 per cent, $p < 0.05$).

Conclusions: Circuit training improved functional capacity, muscular strength, and body composition in obese adolescents. Furthermore, conduit vessel function was normalized after exercise training. If vascular dysfunction is an integral component of the pathogenesis of vascular disease, this study supports the value of an exercise program in the management of obese adolescents.

20.   **Bone mass at lumbar spine and tibia in young males—impact of physical fitness, exercise, and anthropometric parameters: a prospective study in a cohort of military recruits.**

Bone. 1995 Sep;17(3):211-9.

Casez JP, Fischer S, Stussi E, Stalder H, Gerber A, Delmas PD, Colombo JP, Jaeger P.

Policlinic of Medicine, University Hospital, Berne, Switzerland.

Bone mineral density (BMD) and **bone mineral content** (BMC) were measured using DXA at lumbar spine and tibial diaphyses at the beginning and at the end of a 15-week training period in 151 military recruits of the Swiss army belonging to 5 different troop categories (infantry grenadiers, tank drivers, tank gunners, signalmen, and privates) who each were exposed to physical training of various intensity. At baseline, height, **body mass index**, and degree of physical fitness independently correlated with vertebral and tibial BMD. Over the 15 weeks of physical training BMD at tibial diaphyses increased by $2.2 +/- 0.3$ per cent at the left leg ($p = 0.0001$) and by 1.1 per cent at the right leg ($p = 0.002$) with differences between troop categories. At lumbar spine, BMD decreased significantly in tank drivers (-1.2 +/- 0.4 per cent, p = 0.001) and particularly in infantry grenadiers (-2.1 +/- 0.4 per cent) who had the most strenuous weight-bearing training, but not in other troop categories. This decrease was twice as large at the center of the vertebra than for the whole vertebra. These BMD changes were associated with increments in serum levels of osteocalcin and alkaline phosphatase activity. From the initial cohort, 48 subjects volunteered for a third investigation carried out 2 years after the end of the military training period. At this time, lumbar BMD and BMC had risen back to baseline, whereas at tibial diaphyses bone width and BMC but not BMD increased by 5.8 +/- 1.1 per cent and 6.2 +/- 0.9 per cent, respectively, vs. baseline (p = 0.0001 for both).

21. **Overweight among children and adolescents in a Native Canadian community: prevalence and associated factors[1,2,3]**
     American Journal of Clinical Nutrition, Vol. 71, No. 3, 693-700, March 2000

Anthony JG Hanley, Stewart B Harris, Joel Gittelsohn, Thomas MS Wolever, Brit Saksvig and Bernard Zinman
From the Samuel Lunenfeld Research Institute, Mount Sinai Hospital, Toronto; the Departments of Public Health Sciences and Nutritional Sciences, University of Toronto; the Thames Valley Family Practice Research Unit, University of Western Ontario, London, Canada; the Department of Nutrition, School of Public Health, Johns Hopkins University, Baltimore; and the Banting and Best Diabetes Centre, University of Toronto.

Background: The prevalence of pediatric obesity in North America is increasing. Native American children are at especially high risk.

Objectives: The objective was to evaluate the prevalence of pediatric overweight and associated behavioral factors in a Native Canadian community with high rates of adult obesity and type 2 diabetes mellitus.

Design: Height and weight were measured in 445 children and adolescents aged 2–19 y. Fitness level, television viewing, body image concepts, and dietary intake were assessed in 242 subjects aged 10–19 y. Overweight was defined as a body mass index 85th percentile value for age- and sex-specific reference data from the third National Health and Nutrition Examination Survey (NHANES III). Multiple logistic regression was used to examine factors associated with overweight, with adjustment for age and sex.

Results: The overall prevalence of overweight in subjects aged 2–19 y was significantly higher than NHANES III reference data [boys: 27.7 per cent (95 per cent CI: 21.8, 34.5); girls: 33.7 per cent (95 per cent CI: 27.9, 40.1)]. In the subset aged 10–19 y, 5 h television viewing/d was associated with a significantly higher risk of overweight than was 2 h/d [odds ratio (OR) = 2.52; 95 per cent CI: 1.06, 5.98]. Subjects in the third and fourth quartiles of fitness had a substantially lower risk of overweight than did those in the first quartile [third quartile compared with first quartile: OR = 0.24 (95 per cent CI: 0.09, 0.66); fourth quartile compared with first quartile: OR = 0.13 (95 per cent CI: 0.03, 0.48)]. Fiber consumption on the previous day was associated with a decreased risk of overweight (OR = 0.69; 95 per cent CI: 0.47, 0.99 for each 0.77 g/MJ increase in fiber intake).

Conclusions: Pediatric overweight is a harbinger of future diabetes risk and indicates a need for programs targeting primary prevention of obesity in children and adolescents.

Key Words: Obesity • overweight • children • adolescence • Native Canadians • North America • diet • physical activity • epidemiology.

22.   **The effect of exercise training on leptin levels in obese males**
       Am J Physiol Endocrinol Metab, Vol. 274, Issue 2, E280-E286, February 1998

W. J. Pasman[1], M. S. Westerterp-Plantenga[2], and W. H. M. Saris[1]
[1] Maastricht University, Department of Human Biology, 6200 MD Maastricht; and [2] Open University, 6401 DL Heerlen, The Netherlands.

The effect of endurance training on plasma **leptin** levels was investigated in 15 obese male subjects (age 37.3 ± 5.2 yr, body weight 96.5 ± 13.6 kg, and body mass index 29.8 ± 3.0 kg/m^2) in a weight loss and exercise program. After 4 mo of treatment consisting of a very low energy **diet** (VLED) and endurance exercise training (3-4 times weekly, 1 h sessions, moderate intensity), two groups were formed. One group continued the exercise sessions (trained subjects, $n = 7$) and the other group stopped with the exercise program (control, $n = 8$). Measurements of anthropometry, aerobic power, and fasted blood samples were executed at fixed time points (0, 2, 4, 10, and 16 mo). With partial regression analysis, keeping the changes in insulin and body fat percentage constant, it was shown that the number of hours of exercise training was significantly correlated with changes in leptin levels, during the 16-mo period ($r = 0.56$, $P < 0.05$). Changes in insulin levels were significantly related to the changes in leptin levels ($r = 0.47$, $P < 0.05$), which were less for changes in body fat percentage ($r = 0.42$, $P = 0.07$). During the VLED, the change in insulin concentration affected leptin levels significantly ($r = 0.79$) but changes in body fat percentage were not noted. It is concluded that endurance exercise training decreased plasma leptin levels independently of changes in plasma insulin levels and body fat percentage.

Key Words: endurance training; insulin; obesity.

23. **Aging, physical conditioning, and exercise-induced changes in hemostatic factors and reaction products**

J Appl Physiol, Vol. 88, Issue 5, 1558-1564, May 2000

P. J. M. van den Burg[1], J. E. H. Hospers[1], W. L. Mosterd[1], B. N. Bouma[2], and I. A. Huisveld[1]

[1] Department of Medical Physiology and Sports Medicine and [2] Department of Hematology, University of Utrecht, 3508 TA Utrecht, The Netherlands.

The influence of age on training-induced changes in resting and stimulated hemostatic potential was studied in three age categories (Cat I-III; 20-30 yr, 35-45 yr, and 50-60 yr, respectively) of sedentary men before and after 12 wk of training. Coagulation, fibrinolytic activity, and activation markers (reflecting fibrin formation and degradation) were determined. Physical conditioning resulted in a more pronounced increase in von Willebrand factor (vWF) and factor VIII clotting activity (FVIII:c) in Cat I and II and a more pronounced shortening of the activated partial **thromboplastin** time in all categories at maximal exertion and during recovery. Enhanced increases in tissue-type plasminogen activator (t-PA) antigen and activity and single-chain (sc) urokinase-type plasminogen activator (u-PA) at maximal exercise and 5 min of recovery were observed in all age groups after training. The effects on FVIII:c, vWF, and scu-PA were most pronounced in the youngest age group (Cat I). Increases in the marker of thrombin generation were highest in Cat III; no effect was seen on thrombin-antithrombin complex, plasmin-antiplasmin complex, and D-dimer in any of the age groups. We concluded that training enhances both coagulation and fibrinolytic potential during strenuous exercise. The effect on FVIII/vWF and t-PA/u-PA is most pronounced in younger individuals, whereas thrombin formation is most pronounced in older individuals.

Key Words: activation markers; coagulation; fibrinolysis.

24. **Total-body skeletal muscle mass: development and cross-validation of anthropometric prediction models[1,2,3]**

American Journal of Clinical Nutrition, Vol. 72, No. 3, 796-803, September 2000.

Robert C Lee, ZiMian Wang, Moonseong Heo, Robert Ross, Ian Janssen and Steven B Heymsfield

[1] From the Obesity Research Center, St Luke's–Roosevelt Hospital Center, Columbia University, College of Physicians and Surgeons, New York, and the School of Physical and Health Education, Queen's University, Kingston, Canada.

Background: Skeletal muscle (SM) is a large body compartment of biological importance, but it remains difficult to quantify SM with affordable and practical methods that can be applied in clinical and field settings.

Objective: The objective of this study was to develop and cross-validate anthropometric SM mass prediction models in healthy adults.

Design : SM mass, measured by using whole-body multislice magnetic resonance imaging, was set as the dependent variable in prediction models. Independent variables were organized into 2 separate formulas. One formula included mainly limb circumferences and skinfold thicknesses [model 1: height (in m) and **skinfold**-corrected upperarm, thigh, and calf girths (CAG, CTG, and CCG, respectively; in cm)]. The other formula included mainly body weight (in kg) and height (model 2). The models were developed and cross-validated in nonobese adults [body mass index (in kg/m^2) < 30].

Results : Two SM (in kg) models for nonobese subjects ($n = 244$) were developed as follows: SM = Ht x (0.00744 x $CAG^2 + 0.00088$ x $CTG^2 + 0.00441$ x CCG^2) + 2.4 x sex - 0.048 x age + race + 7.8, where $R^2 = 0.91$, $P < 0.0001$, and SEE = 2.2 kg; sex = 0 for female and 1 for male, race = -2.0 for Asian, 1.1 for African American, and 0 for white and Hispanic, and SM = 0.244 x BW + 7.80 x Ht + 6.6 x sex - 0.098 x age + race - 3.3, where $R^2 = 0.86$, $P < 0.0001$, and SEE = 2.8 kg; sex = 0 for female and 1 for male, race = -1.2 for Asian, 1.4 for African American, and 0 for white and Hispanic.

Conclusion : These 2 anthropometric prediction models, the first developed in vivo by using state-of-the-art body-composition methods, are likely to prove useful in clinical evaluations and field studies of SM mass in nonobese adults.

Key Words: Limb circumference • skinfold thickness • body composition • skeletal muscle • nonobese adults.

25.   **Exercise elevates plasma levels but not gene expression of IL-1, IL-6, and TNF- in blood mononuclear cells**

J Appl Physiol, Vol. 89, Issue 4, 1499-1504, October 2000

Andrei I. Moldoveanu[1], Roy J. Shephard[1,2,3], and Pang N. Shek[2,3]

[1]Graduate Department of Community Health, Faculty of Medicine, [2] Graduate Department of Exercise Sciences, Faculty of Physical Education and Health, University of Toronto, Toronto M5S 2W6; and [3] Biomedical Sciences Section, Defence and Civil Institute of Environmental Medicine, Toronto, Ontario, Canada M3M 3B9.

Physical activity induces a subclinical inflammatory response, mediated in part by **leukocytes,** and manifested by elevated concentrations of circulating proinflammatory cytokines, including interleukin (IL)-1, IL-6, and tumor necrosis factor- (TNF-). However, the source of the cytokines that appear during exercise remains unknown. In this study, we examined exercise-induced changes in plasma cytokine concentrations and their corresponding mRNA expression in peripheral blood mononuclear cells. Ten healthy [peak oxygen uptake = 48.8 ± 6.5 (SD) ml · kg^1 · min^1] but untrained men [age = 25 ± 5 (SD) yr] undertook 3 h of exercise (cycling and inclined walking) at 60-65 per cent peak oxygen uptake. Circulating leukocyte subset counts were elevated during and 2 h postexercise but returned to normal within 24 h. Plasma concentrations of IL-1, IL-6, and TNF- peaked at the end of exercise and remained elevated at 2 h (IL-6) and up to 24 h (IL-1 and TNF-) postexercise. Cytokine gene expression in circulating mononuclear cells was measured by using the reverse transcriptase-polymerase chain reaction; mRNA accumulation did not change with exercise. In conclusion, mRNA accumulation of IL-1, IL-6, and TNF- in circulating mononuclear cells is not affected by 3 h of moderate endurance exercise and does not seem to account for the observed increases in plasma cytokines.

Key Words: physical exertion; immune; messenger RNA; peripheral blood.

26. **Overweight and obese anovulatory patients with polycystic ovaries: parallel improvements in anthropometric indices, ovarian physiology and fertility rate induced by diet**

Human Reproduction, Vol. 18, No. 9, 1928-1932, September 2003

Pier Giorgio Crosignani[1], Michela Colombo, Walter Vegetti, Edgardo Somigliana, Alessio Gessati and Guido Ragni

Infertility Unit of the First Department Obstetrics and Gynecology, University of Milan, Via della Commenda 12, 20122 Milan, Italy

[1] To whom correspondence should be addressed. e-mail: piergiorgio.crosignani@unimi.it

Background: This prospective study evaluated the effect of weight reduction on anthropometric indices and ovarian morphology in anovulatory overweight patients with **polycystic ovary syndrome** (PCOS).

Methods: Thirty-three anovulatory overweight patients with PCOS were enrolled in the study. All had patent Fallopian tubes and chronic anovulation: 27 of them were oligo-amenorrhoeic. The partners were normospermic. Patients were prescribed a 1200 kcal/day diet, and physical exercise was recommended. Anthropometric indices and ovarian imaging parameters were assessed at baseline and after weight loss of 5 and 10 per cent.

Results: Twenty-five patients (76 per cent) lost at least 5 per cent of their body weight. Eleven of these patients (33 per cent) reached a 10 per cent decrease in weight. Waist circumference at the umbilical level, hip circumference, four **skin folds, body mass index** and **fatty mass ratio** were significantly reduced after 5 and 10 per cent weight loss. Ovarian morphology changed during the diet: we observed a significant reduction in ovarian volume and in the number of microfollicles per ovary. Among the 27 patients with oligo-amenorrhoea, 18 had a resumption of regular cycles and 15 experienced spontaneous ovulation; 10 spontaneous pregnancies occurred in patients who lost at least 5 per cent of their weight.

Conclusions: Weight loss through a controlled low-calorie diet improves anthropometric indices in obese PCOS patients, reduces ovarian volume and microfollicle number and can restore ovulatory cycles, allowing spontaneous pregnancy.

Key Words: diet/fertility/ovarian morphology/PCOS

27.   **Intramyocellular Lipids: Anthropometric Determinants and Relationships with Maximal Aerobic Capacity and Insulin Sensitivity**
The Journal of Clinical Endocrinology & Metabolism, Vol. 88, No. 4 1785-1791

Claus Thamer, Jürgen Machann, Oliver Bachmann, Michael Haap, Dominik Dahl, Beate Wietek, Otto Tschritter, Andreas Niess, Klaus Brechtel, Andreas Fritsche, Claus Claussen, Stephan Jacob, Fritz Schick, Hans-Ulrich Häring and Michael Stumvoll

Department of Endocrinology and Metabolism (C.T., O.B., M.H., D.D., O.T., A.F., S.J., H.-U.H., M.S.) and Section on Experimental Radiology (J.M., B.W., K.B., C.C., F.S.), Department of Diagnostic Radiology, Eberhard-Karls-University, D-72076 Tübingen, Germany; and Medical Clinic (A.N.), Department of Sports Medicine, University of Freiburg, D-79106 Freiburg, Germany

Address all correspondence and requests for reprints to: Dr. Michael Stumvoll, Medizinische Universitätsklinik, Otfried-Müller-Strasse 10, D-72076 Tübingen, Germany. E-mail: michael.stumvoll@med.uni-tuebingen.de .

The existence of metabolically relevant **intramyocellular lipids** (IMCL) as assessed by the noninvasive ^{1}H-magnetic resonance spectroscopy (MRS) has been established. In the present studies, we analyzed the relationships between IMCL in two muscle types [the predominantly nonoxidative tibialis muscle (tib) and the predominantly oxidative soleus muscle (sol)] and anthropometric data, aerobic capacity (VO_2max, **bicycle ergometry**, n = 77) and insulin sensitivity (hyperinsulinemic euglycemic clamp, n = 105) using regression analysis.

In univariate regression, IMCL (tib) was weakly but significantly correlated with percentage of body fat ($r = 0.28$, $P = 0.01$), whereas IMCL (sol) was better correlated with waist-to-hip ratio ($r = 0.41$, $P < 0.0001$). No significant univariate correlation with age or maximal aerobic power was observed. After adjusting for adiposity, IMCL (tib) was positively correlated with measures of aerobic fitness. A significant interaction term between VO_2max and percentage of body fat on IMCL (tib) ($P = 0.04$) existed (whole model $r^2 = 0.26$, $P = 0.001$). In contrast, aerobic fitness did not influence IMCL (sol). No correlation between insulin sensitivity as such and IMCL (tib) ($r = -0.13$, $P = 0.2$) or IMCL (sol) ($r = 0.03$, $P = 0.72$) was observed. Nevertheless, a significant interaction term between VO_2max and IMCL on insulin sensitivity existed [$P = 0.04$ (tib) and $P = 0.02$ (sol)]; [whole model (sol) $r^2 = 0.61$, $P < 0.0001$, (tib) $r^2 = 0.60$, $P < 0.0001$].

In conclusion, **obesity** and aerobic fitness are important determinants of IMCL. IMCL and insulin sensitivity are negatively correlated in untrained subjects. The correlation between the two parameters is modified by the extent of aerobic fitness and cannot be found in endurance trained subjects. Thus, measurements of aerobic fitness and body fat are indispensable for the interpretation of IMCL and its relationship with insulin sensitivity.

This work was supported by a grant from the Deutsche Forschungsgemeinschaft (DFG No. JA-1005/1-1, DFG Stu-192/9-1), the Federal Ministry of Education and Research (Fö. 01KS9602), a grant from the European Community (QLRT-1999-00674) and the Interdisciplinary Center of Clinical Research Tübingen (IZKF).

Abbreviations: EMCL, Extramyocellular lipids; IMCL, intramyocellular lipids; ISI, insulin sensitivity index; MRS, magnetic resonance spectroscopy; sol, soleus muscle; tib, tibialis muscle; WHR, waist to hip ratio; VO_2max, maximal aerobic capacity.

28. **Regional chest wall volumes during exercise in chronic obstructive pulmonary disease**

Thorax 2004;59:210-216

A Aliverti[1], N Stevenson[2], R L Dellacà[1], A Lo Mauro[1], A Pedotti[1] and P M A Calverley[2]

[1] Dipartimento di Bioingegneria, Politecnico di Milano, Italy
[2] University Department of Medicine, University Hospital Aintree, Liverpool, UK

Correspondence to:
Dr A Aliverti
Dipartimento di Bioingegneria, Politecnico di Milano, Piazza Leonardo da Vinci 32, 20133 Milano, Italy; andrea.aliverti@polimi.it

Background: Dynamic hyperinflation of the lungs impairs exercise performance in chronic obstructive pulmonary disease (COPD). However, it is unclear which patients are affected by dynamic hyperinflation and how the respiratory muscles respond to the change in lung volume.

Methods: Using optoelectronic plethysmography, total and regional chest wall volumes were measured non-invasively in 20 stable patients with COPD (mean (SD) forced expiratory volume in 1 second 43.6 (11.6) per cent predicted) and dynamic hyperinflation was tracked breath by breath to test if this was the mechanism of exercise limitation. Resting ventilation, breathing pattern, symptoms, rib cage and abdominal volumes were recorded at rest and during symptom limited cycle ergometry. Pleural, abdominal, and transdiaphragmatic pressures were measured in eight patients.

Results: End expiratory chest wall volume increased by a mean (SE) of 592 (80) ml in 12 patients (hyperinflators) but decreased by 462 (103) ml in eight (euvolumics). During exercise, tidal volume increased in euvolumic patients by reducing end expiratory abdominal volume while in hyperinflators tidal volume increased by increasing end inspiratory abdominal and rib cage volumes. The maximal abdominal pressure was 22.1 (9.0) cm H_2O in euvolumic patients and 7.6 (2.6) cm H_2O in hyperinflators. Euvolumic patients were as breathless as hyperinflators but exercised for less time and reached lower maximum workloads ($p<0.05$) despite having better spirometric parameters and a greater expiratory flow reserve.

Conclusions: Dynamic hyperinflation is not the only mechanism limiting exercise performance in patients with stable COPD. Accurate measurement of chest wall volume can identify the different patterns of respiratory muscle activation during exercise.

Keywords: chronic obstructive pulmonary disease; exercise; lung volume; dynamic hyperinflation.

Abbreviations: BMI, body mass index; COPD, chronic obstructive pulmonary disease; EELV, end expiratory lung volume; EEVcw, end expiratory chest wall volume; FEF, forced expiratory flow at a percentage of FVC; FEV_1, forced expiratory volume in 1 second; FRC, functional residual capacity; FVC, forced vital capacity; IC, inspiratory capacity; OEP, optoelectronic plethysmography; Pab, abdominal pressure; Pdi, transdiaphragmatic pressure; Pga, gastric pressure; Poes, oesophageal pressure; Ppl, pleural pressure; RV, residual volume; TLC, total lung capacity; Vab, abdominal volume; Vcw, total chest wall volume; Vrc, rib cage volume.

29. **Race, Visceral Adipose Tissue, Plasma Lipids, and Lipoprotein Lipase Activity in Men and Women**

Arteriosclerosis, Thrombosis, and Vascular Biology. 2000;20:1932

Jean-Pierre Després; Charles Couillard; Jacques Gagnon; Jean Bergeron; Arthur S. Leon; D. C. Rao; James S. Skinner; Jack H. Wilmore; Claude Bouchard

From the Lipid Research Center (J.-P.D., C.C., J.B.), CHUQ Research Center, CHUL Pavilion, Sainte-Foy, Québec, Canada; the Division of Kinesiology (J.-P.D., J.G.), Laval University School of Medecine, Sainte-Foy, Québec, Canada; the School of Kinesiology and Leisure Studies (A.S.L.), University of Minnesota, Minneapolis; the Division of Biostatistics (D.C.R.), Washington University Medical School, St Louis, Mo; the Department of Kinesiology (J.S.S.), Indiana University, Bloomington; the Department of Health and Kinesiology (J.H.W.) Texas A&M University, College Station; and the Pennington Biomedical Research Center (C.B.), Louisiana State University, Baton Rouge.

Correspondence to Jean-Pierre Després, PhD, Scientific Director and Professor, Lipid Research Center, CHUQ Research Center, CHUL Pavilion, 2705, boulevard Laurier, Room TR-93, Sainte-Foy, Québec, Canada G1V 4G2. E-mail Jean-Pierre.Despres@crchul.ulaval.ca

Abstract : Abdominal **obesity :** is associated with numerous metabolic alterations, such as hypertriglyceridemia and low levels of **high density lipoprotein** (HDL) cholesterol. However, compared with abdominally obese white individuals, abdominally obese black individuals have been characterized by higher plasma HDL cholesterol levels, suggesting that the impact of abdominal fat accumulation on the lipoprotein-lipid profile may differ among ethnic groups. Therefore, we have compared the associations between body fatness, visceral **adipose tissue** (AT) accumulation, and metabolic risk variables in a sample of 247 **white men** and 240 white women versus a sample of 93 black men and 143 black women. Although no difference in mean total body fatness was found between the 2 race groups, white men had higher levels of visceral AT than did **black men** ($P<0.001$). Despite the fact that black women had a greater body fat content than did **white women, black women** had levels of visceral AT that were similar to those of white women, suggesting a lower susceptibility to visceral obesity in black women. This lower accumulation of visceral AT in blacks was accompanied by significantly reduced apolipoprotein B concentrations and ratios of total cholesterol to HDL cholesterol as well as higher plasma HDL cholesterol levels ($P<0.05$) compared with those values in whites. Irrespective of sex, higher postheparin plasma hepatic lipase (HL) and lower lipoprotein lipase (LPL) activities were found in whites, resulting in an HL/LPL ratio that was twice as high in whites as in blacks ($P<0.005$). Although differences in lipoprotein-lipid levels were noted between whites and blacks, results from multiple regression analyses revealed that after control for morphometric and metabolic variables of the study (body fat mass, visceral AT, LPL, HL, and age), ethnicity had, per se, only a minor contribution to the variance in plasma lipoprotein levels. Thus, our results suggest that the higher plasma HDL cholesterol levels and the generally more cardioprotective plasma lipoprotein profile found in abdominally obese black versus white individuals are explained, at least to a certain extent, by a lower visceral AT deposition and a higher plasma LPL activity in black individuals.

Key Words: race • sex • visceral adipose tissue • lipase activities • lipoproteins

30.   **Reduced Alveolar–Capillary Membrane Diffusing Capacity in Chronic Heart Failure**
Its Pathophysiological Relevance and Relationship to Exercise Performance
Circulation. 1995;91:2769-2774.

Sundeep Puri, MB, Mrcp; B. Leigh Baker, BSc; David P. Dutka, MB, MRCP; Celia M. Oakley, MD, FRCP, FACC; J. Michael B. Hughes, DM, Frcp; John g. F. Cleland, MD, FRCP, FACC

From the Department of Medicine (Clinical Cardiology and Respiratory Medicine), Royal Postgraduate Medical School, Hammersmith Hospital, London.

Correspondence to Dr J.G.F. Cleland, British Heart Foundation Senior Research Fellow, MRC Clinical Research Initiative in Heart Failure, West Medical Building, Glasgow University, Glasgow, Scotland, UK.

Background : The pulmonary diffusing capacity for carbon monoxide (DLCO) is reduced in **chronic heart failure** (CHF) and is an independent predictor of peak exercise oxygen uptake. The pathophysiological basis for this remains unknown. The aim of this study was to partition DLCO into its membrane conductance (D_M) and capillary blood volume components (Vc) and to assess if alveolar–capillary membrane function correlated with functional status, exercise capacity, and pulmonary vascular resistance.

Methods and Results : The classic Roughton and Forster method of measuring single-breath DLCO at varying alveolar oxygen concentrations was used to determine D_M and Vc in 15 normal subjects and 50 patients with CHF. All performed symptom-limited maximal bicycle exercise tests with respiratory gas analysis; 15 CHF patients underwent right heart catheterization. DLCO was significantly reduced in CHF patients compared with normal subjects, predominantly because of a reduction in D_M (7.0 ± 2.6 versus 12.9 ± 3.8 versus 20.0 ± 6.1 mmol · min^{-1} · kPa^{-1} in New York Heart Association class III, class II, and normal subjects, respectively, $P<.0001$), even when the reduction in lung volumes was accounted for by the division of D_M by the effective alveolar volume. The Vc component of DLCO was not impaired. D_M significantly correlated with maximal exercise oxygen uptake ($r=.72$, $P<.0001$) and inversely correlated with pulmonary vascular resistance ($r=.65$, $P<.01$) in CHF.

Conclusions : Reduced alveolar–capillary membrane diffusing capacity is the major component of impaired pulmonary gas transfer in CHF, correlating with maximal exercise capacity and functional status. D_M may be a useful marker for the alveolar–capillary barrier damage induced by raised pulmonary capillary pressure.

Key Words: circulation • lung • oxygen

31. **Peripheral Muscle Weakness and Exercise Capacity in Children with Cystic Fibrosis**
    Am. J. Respir. Crit. Care Med., Volume 159, Number 3, March 1999, 748-754

    Kees De Meer, Vincent A. M. Gulmans, and Johan Van Der Laag

Departments of Gastroenterology, Physiotherapy, and Respiratory Diseases, University Children's Hospital "Het Wilhelmina Kinderziekenhuis", Utrecht, The Netherlands

Exercise intolerance in **cystic fibrosis** (CF) is attributed to diminished nutritional and pulmonary function. We studied the pathophysiology of such intolerance in relation to muscle force and **fat-free mass** (FFM), in 15 children with moderately severe symptoms of CF (FEV$_1$ < 80 per cent predicted and/or weight for age < 1 SD of reference median), 13 children with mild symptoms of CF (FEV$_1$ and weight above these thresholds), and 13 healthy controls. Cycle maximal workload (Wmax) and O$_2$max were assessed. Maximal peripheral muscle force was measured, and FFM was calculated from skinfolds. Patients with mild CF, as compared with matched controls, had lower values of Wmax per kilogram of FFM (3.9 ± 0.5 versus 4.6 ± 0.3 W/kg [mean ± SD], respectively; difference = 0.7 [95 per cent CI = 0.4 to 1.1]), and diminished maximal muscle force (2.7 ± 0.4 kN versus 3.1 ± 0.7 kN; difference = 0.44 [95 per cent CI = 0.03 to 0.87]), but similar O$_2$max. Patients with moderate CF had lower FFM, muscle force, and exercise tolerance than did the other groups. Oxygen cost of work was elevated in both groups of CF patients. Muscle force showed a strong positive correlation with Wmax in patients and controls, with disproportionately lower regression slopes in the CF patients. In children with CF, muscle force is decreased and associated with diminished maximal work load, even in the absence of diminished pulmonary or nutritional status.

32. **Effects of four different single exercise sessions on lipids, lipoproteins, and lipoprotein lipase**
    J Appl Physiol Vol. 85, Issue 3, 1169-1174, September 1998

    Michael A. Ferguson[1,2], Nathan L. Alderson[1], Stewart G. Trost[1], David A. Essig[1], Jeanmarie R. Burke[1], and J. Larry Durstine[1]

[1] Department of Exercise Science, University of South Carolina, Columbia, South Carolina 29208; and [2] Georgia Prevention Institute, Medical College of Georgia, Augusta, Georgia 30912

The purpose of this study was to determine the threshold of exercise energy expenditure necessary to change blood lipid and lipoprotein concentrations and **lipoprotein lipase activity** (LPLA) in healthy, trained men. On different days, 11 men (age, 26.7 ± 6.1 yr; body fat, 11.0 ± 1.5 per cent) completed four separate, randomly assigned, submaximal treadmill sessions at 70 per cent maximal O_2 consumption. During each session 800, 1,100, 1,300, or 1,500 kcal were expended. Compared with immediately before exercise, high-density lipoprotein cholesterol (HDL-C) concentration was significantly elevated 24 h after exercise ($P < 0.05$) in the 1,100-, 1,300-, and 1,500-kcal sessions. HDL-C concentration was also elevated ($P < 0.05$) immediately after and 48 h after exercise in the 1,500-kcal session. Compared with values 24 h before exercise, LPLA was significantly greater ($P < 0.05$) 24 h after exercise in the 1,100-, 1,300-, and 1,500-kcal sessions and remained elevated 48 h after exercise in the 1,500-kcal session. These data indicate that, in healthy, trained men, 1,100 kcal of energy expenditure are necessary to elicit increased HDL-C concentrations. These HDL-C changes coincided with increased LPLA.

Key Words : energy expenditure; lipase; triglyceride; high-density lipoprotein cholesterol; kilocalories.

33.   Fitness, Acute Exercise, and Anabolic and Catabolic Mediators in Cystic Fibrosis

Am. J. Respir. Crit. Care Med., Volume 164, Number 8, October 2001, 1432-1437

Pornchai Tirakitsoontorn, Eliezer Nussbaum, Chuanpit Moser, Maryann Hill, and Dan M. Cooper

Department of Pediatrics, University of California Irvine Medical Center, Irvine; and Division of Pediatric Pulmonology, Miller Children's Hospital at Long Beach Memorial Medical Center, Long Beach, California.

Exercise can stimulate catabolic inflammatory cytokines even in healthy children. For patients with cystic fibrosis (CF), this may be problematic because CF is characterized by increased inflammation and suppressed growth. We examined fitness and the response to brief exercise of interleukin-6 (IL-6), tumor necrosis factor- (TNF-), insulinlike growth factor-I (IGF-I), and IGF binding protein-1 (IGFBP-1) in 14 subjects with CF (10.5 ± 0.8 yr of age), 9 of whom were treated with ibuprofen, and 14 healthy control subjects (11.6 ± 0.5 yr of age, NS). Subjects performed brief intermittent, constant work rate protocol (scaled to each individual's exercise capacity) with blood and urine sampling.

Peak O_2 was correlated with IGF-I (r = 0.68, p < 0.01) in control subjects but not in subjects with CF. In subjects with CF, baseline IL-6 was 79 per cent greater (p < 0.05) and IGF-I was 47 per cent lower than in control subjects (p < 0.05). *Post hoc* analysis revealed a progressive increase in the IL-6 response to exercise, with the lowest increase observed in control subjects (11.8 ± 4.6 pg/L/kJ), higher increases in patients with CF treated with ibuprofen (23.4 ± 7.7 pg/L/kJ), and highest in subjects with CF not receiving ibuprofen (29.2 ± 7.5 pg/L/kJ). Qualitatively similar results were observed for TNF-. Exercise also significantly increased IGFBP-1 in both control subjects and subjects with CF. Brief exercise can increase even chronically elevated inflammatory mediators in CF, and this response may be attenuated by ibuprofen.

34. Anticipatory Blood Pressure Response to Exercise Predicts Future High Blood Pressure in Middle-aged Men

Hypertension. 1996;27:1059-1064.

Susan A. Everson; George A. Kaplan; Debbie E. Goldberg; Jukka T. Salonen

From the Human Population Laboratory, Western Consortium for Public Health (S.A.E., D.E.G.); the Human Population Laboratory, California Department of Health Services (G.A.K.), Berkeley, Calif; and the Research Institute of Public Health and Department of Community Health and General Practice, University of Kuopio (Finland) (J.T.S.).

Abstract : Increases in **blood pressure** during the period of emotional arousal attendant to impending exertion are well documented, yet the etiologic significance of these elevations is unknown. Research suggests that exaggerated cardiovascular responses to psychological stress may be importantly related to hypertension. We examined blood pressure reactivity in anticipation of an exercise stress test in relation to future hypertension in the Kuopio Ischemic Heart Disease Risk Factor Study, a population-based study of middle-aged men from Eastern Finland. Subjects were 508 unmedicated men with resting blood pressure less than 165/95 mm Hg who completed a bicycle ergometer stress test at baseline and whose hypertensive status was assessed at 4 years of follow-up. Systolic and diastolic reactivity were calculated as the difference between blood pressure measured after seated rest on the **bicycle ergometer** before initiation of exercise and mean seated resting blood pressure measured 1 week earlier. Logistic regression models adjusted for age and resting blood pressure revealed a graded association between quartiles of reactivity and risk of subsequent hypertension (165/95 mm Hg), with men showing systolic responses greater than or equal to 30 mm Hg or diastolic responses greater than 15 mm Hg at nearly four times the risk of becoming hypertensive (odds ratios, 3.80 [95 per cent confidence interval, 1.90 to 7.63] and 3.65 [95 per cent confidence interval, 1.86 to 7.17], respectively) relative to the least-reactive groups (systolic response, <10 mm Hg; diastolic response, <5 mm Hg). Adjustments for traditional risk factors for hypertension did not alter these associations. Results demonstrate the clinical significance of the pressor response in anticipation of exercise and support the hypothesis that cardiovascular reactivity to psychological challenge plays a role in the etiology of hypertension.

Key Words: cardiovascular system • hypertension • exercise • blood pressure • risk factors.

35.   **Peripheral Muscle Weakness in Patients with Chronic Obstructive Pulmonary Disease**

Am. J. Respir. Crit. Care Med., Volume 158, Number 2, August 1998, 629-634

Sarah Bernard, Pierre Leblanc, François Whittom, Guy Carrier, Jean Jobin, Roger Belleau, and François Maltais

Unité de Recherche, Institut de Cardiologie et de Pneumologie de Québec, Université Laval, Ste-Foy, Québec, Canada

Peripheral muscle weakness is commonly found in patients with **chronic obstructive pulmonary disease** (COPD) and may play a role in reducing exercise capacity. The purposes of this study were to evaluate, in patients with COPD: (1) the relationship between muscle strength and cross-sectional area (CSA), (2) the distribution of peripheral muscle weakness, and (3) the relationship between muscle strength and the severity of lung disease. Thirty-four patients with COPD and 16 normal subjects of similar age and body mass index were evaluated. Compared with normal subjects, the strength of three muscle groups ($p < 0.05$) and the right thigh muscle CSA, evaluated by computed tomography (83.4 ± 16.4 versus 109.6 ± 15.6 cm^2, $p < 0.0001$), were reduced in COPD. The quadriceps strength/thigh muscle CSA ratio was similar for the two groups. The reduction in quadriceps strength was proportionally greater than that of the shoulder girdle muscles ($p < 0.05$). Similar observations were made whether or not patients had been exposed to systemic corticosteroids in the 6-mo period preceding the study, although there was a tendency for the quadriceps strength/thigh muscle CSA ratio to be lower in patients who had received corticosteroids. In COPD, quadriceps strength and muscle CSA correlated positively with the FEV$_1$ expressed in percentage of predicted value ($r = 0.55$ and $r = 0.66$, respectively, $p < 0.0005$). In summary, the strength/muscle cross-sectional area ratio was not different between the two groups, suggesting that weakness in COPD is due to muscle atrophy. In COPD, the distribution of peripheral muscle weakness and the correlation between quadriceps strength and the degree of airflow obstruction suggests that chronic inactivity and muscle deconditioning are important factors in the loss in muscle mass and strength.

36. **Effects of Endurance Exercise Training on Plasma HDL Cholesterol Levels Depend on Levels of Triglycerides**
     Evidence From Men of the Health, Risk Factors, Exercise Training and Genetics (HERITAGE) Family Study
     Arteriosclerosis, Thrombosis, and Vascular Biology. 2001;21:1226.

Charles Couillard; Jean-Pierre Després; Benoît Lamarche; Jean Bergeron; Jacques Gagnon; Arthur S. Leon; D. C. Rao; James S. Skinner; Jack H. Wilmore; Claude Bouchard

From the Lipid Research Center (C.C., J.-P.D., B.L., J.B.) and the Laboratory of Molecular Endocrinology (J.G.), Laval University Medical Research Center, CHUL Pavilion, Sainte-Foy, Québec, Canada; the Physical Activity Sciences Laboratory (J.G.), Department of Kinesiology, and the Department of Food Sciences and Nutrition (J.-P.D., B.L.), Laval University, Sainte-Foy, Québec, Canada; the Québec Heart Institute (J.-P.D.), Laval Hospital Research Center, Sainte-Foy, Québec, Canada; the School of Kinesiology and Leisure Studies (A.S.L.), University of Minnesota, Minneapolis; the Division of Biostatistics (D.C.R.), Washington University Medical School, St. Louis, Mo; the Department of Kinesiology (J.S.S.), Indiana University, Bloomington; the Department of Health and Kinesiology (J.H.W.), Texas A & M University, College Station; and the Pennington Biomedical Research Center (C.B.), Louisiana State University, Baton Rouge.

Correspondence to Jean-Pierre Després, PhD, Québec Heart Institute, Pavilion Mallet, 2nd Floor, 2725 chemin Sainte-Foy, Sainte-Foy, Québec, Canada G1V 4G5. E-mail Jean-Pierre.Despres@crchul.ulaval.ca

Abstract : High density lipoprotein (HDL) cholesterol concentrations have been shown to increase with regular endurance exercise and, therefore, can contribute to a lower risk of coronary heart disease in physically active individuals compared with sedentary subjects. Although low HDL cholesterol levels are frequently observed in combination with hypertriglyceridemia, some individuals may be characterized by isolated hypoalphalipoproteinemia, i.e., low HDL cholesterol levels in the absence of elevated triglyceride (TG) concentrations. The present study compared the responses of numerous lipoprotein-lipid variables to a 20-week endurance exercise training program in men categorized on the basis of baseline TG and HDL cholesterol concentrations: (1) low TG and high HDL cholesterol (normolipidemia), (2) low TG and low HDL cholesterol (isolated low HDL cholesterol), (3) high TG and high HDL cholesterol (isolated high TGs), and (4) high TGs and low HDL cholesterol (high TG/low HDL cholesterol). A series of physical and metabolic variables was measured before and after the training program in a sample of 200 men enrolled in the Health, Risk Factors, Exercise Training and Genetics (HERITAGE) Family Study. At baseline, men with high TG/low HDL cholesterol had more visceral adipose tissue than did men with isolated low HDL cholesterol and men with normolipidemia. The 0.4 per cent (not significant) exercise-induced increase in HDL cholesterol levels in men with isolated low HDL cholesterol suggests that they did not benefit from the "HDL-raising" effect of exercise. In contrast, men with high TG/low HDL cholesterol showed a significant increase in HDL cholesterol levels (4.9 per cent, $P<0.005$). Whereas both subgroups of men with elevated TG levels showed reductions in plasma TGs (-15.0 per cent, $P<0.005$), onsly those with high TG/low HDL cholesterol showed significantly reduced apolipoprotein B levels at the end of the study (-6.0 per cent, $P<0.005$). Multiple regression analyses revealed that the exercise-induced change in abdominal subcutaneous adipose tissue (10.6 per cent, $P<0.01$) was the only significant correlate of the increase in plasma HDL cholesterol with training in men with high TG/low HDL cholesterol. Results of the present study suggest that regular endurance exercise training may be particularly helpful in men with low HDL cholesterol, elevated TGs, and abdominal obesity.

Key Words: HDL cholesterol • triglycerides • exercise training • coronary heart disease

37.   **Anthropometric and Behavioral Correlates of Insulin-like Growth Factor I and Insulin-like Growth Factor Binding Protein 3 in Middle-aged Japanese Men**
Am J Epidemiol 2002; 156:344-348.
    Satoshi Teramukai[1], Thomas Rohan[2], Hiroyuki Eguchi[3], Takashi Oda[4], Koichi Shinchi[4] and Suminori Kono[1]
    [1] Department of Preventive Medicine, Faculty of Medical Sciences, Kyushu University, Fukuoka, Japan.
    [2] Department of Epidemiology and Social Medicine, Albert Einstein College of Medicine, Bronx, NY.
    [3] Self Defense Forces Fukuoka Hospital, Kasuga, Fukuoka, Japan.
    [4] Self Defense Forces Kumamoto Hospital, Kumamoto, Japan.

    High levels of plasma insulin-like growth factor I (IGF-I) and low levels of insulin-like growth factor binding protein 3 (IGFBP-3) have been related to increased risk of several cancers. Little is known about the behavioral determinants of these biologic markers. The authors examined the relation of anthropometric and behavioral factors to plasma concentrations of IGF-I and IGFBP-3 in a cross-sectional study of 616 Japanese men aged 45–55 years in 1995–1996. In univariate analyses, body mass index was strongly, positively associated with both IGF-I and IGFBP-3. The waist/hip ratio was also linearly related to IGF-I and IGFBP-3 up to the third quartile level. Height was weakly, positively associated with IGF-I and IGFBP-3. Smoking was inversely associated with IGF-I and IGFBP-3. Alcohol use was associated inversely with IGF-I and positively with IGFBP-3. Neither IGF-I nor IGFBP-3 was related to physical activity. Results of the multivariate analysis were essentially the same as those of the univariate analyses. The findings regarding body mass index are in contrast to those of previous studies showing null or inverse associations, and they suggest that the relation of body mass index to IGF-I or IGFBP-3 may vary among populations. The study also indicates that smoking and alcohol use might affect plasma IGF-I and IGFBP-3.

Key Words: alcohol drinking; body constitution; body mass index; insulin-like growth factor I; insulin-like growth factor binding protein 3; smoking

Abbreviations: Abbreviations: IGF-I, insulin-like growth factor I; IGFBP-3, insulin-like growth factor binding protein 3; MET, metabolic equivalent.

38. **Glucose infusion partially attenuates glucose production and increases uptake during intense exercise**

J Appl Physiol Vol. 85, Issue 2, 511-524, August 1998

Anthony Manzon[1], Simon J. Fisher[2], José A. Morais[1], Lorraine Lipscombe[1], Marie-Claude Guimond[1], Sharon J. Nessim[1], Ronald J. Sigal[1], Jeffrey B. Halter[3], Mladen Vranic[2], and Errol B. Marliss[1]

[1] McGill Nutrition and Food Science Centre, Royal Victoria Hospital, Montreal, Quebec, Canada H3A 1A1; [2] Departments of Physiology and Medicine, University of Toronto, Toronto, Ontario, Canada 5S 1A8; and [3] Department of Internal Medicine and Institute of Gerontology, University of Michigan, Veterans Affairs Medical Center, Ann Arbor, Michigan 48109

Glucose infusion can prevent the increase in glucose production (R_a) and increase glucose uptake (R_d) during exercise of moderate intensity. We postulated that *1*) because in postabsorptive intense exercise (>80 per cent maximal O_2 uptake) the eightfold increase in R_a may be mediated by catecholamines rather than by glucagon and insulin, exogenous glucose infusion would not prevent the R_a increment, and 2) such infusion would cause greater R_d. Fit young men were exercised at >85 per cent maximal O_2 uptake for 14 min in the postabsorptive state [controls (Con), $n = 12$] or at *minute 210* of a 285-min glucose infusion. In seven subjects, the infusion was constant (CI; $4 \text{ mg} \cdot \text{kg}^1 \cdot \text{min}^1$), and in seven subjects it was varied (VI) to mimic the exercise R_a response in Con. Although glucose suppressed R_a to zero (with glycemia ~6 mM and insulin ~150 pM), an endogenous R_a response to exercise occurred, to peak increments two-thirds those in Con, in both CI and VI. Glucagon was unchanged, and very small increases in the glucagon-to-insulin ratio occurred in all three groups. **Catecholamine** responses were similar in all three groups, and correlation coefficients of R_a with plasma norepinephrine and epinephrine were significant in all. In all CI and VI, R_d at rest was 2× Con, increased earlier in exercise, and was higher for the 1 h of recovery with glucose infusion. Thus the R_a response was only partly attenuated, and the catecholamines are likely to be the regulators. This suggests that an acute endogenous R_a rise is possible even in the postprandial state. Furthermore, the fact that more circulating glucose is used by muscle during exercise and early recovery suggests that muscle glycogen is spared.

Key Words: norepinephrine; epinephrine; glucose turnover; insulin; glucagon

39.   **Physical Fitness and Physical Activity in Obese and Nonobese Flemish Youth**

Obesity Research 11:434-441 (2003)

Benedicte Deforche*, Johan Lefevre, Ilse De Bourdeaudhuij*, Andrew P. Hills, William Duquet and Jacques Bouckaert*

* Department of Movement and Sport Sciences, Ghent University, Ghent, Belgium;

Department of Sport and Movement Sciences, Faculty of Physical Education and Physiotherapy, Catholic University Leuven, Leuven, Belgium;

School of Human Movement Studies, Queensland University of Technology, Brisbane, Australia; and

Faculty of Physical Education and Physiotherapy, Free University Brussels, Brussels, Belgium.

Address correspondence to Benedicte Deforche, Ghent University, Department of Movement and Sport Sciences, Watersportlaan 2, B-9000 Ghent, Belgium. E-mail: benedicte.deforche@rug.ac.be

Objective: To assess different aspects of physical fitness and physical activity in obese and nonobese Flemish youth.

Research Methods and Procedures: A random sample of 3214 Flemish schoolchildren was selected and divided into an "**obese**" and "nonobese" group based on body mass index and sum of **skinfolds**. Physical fitness was assessed by the **European physical fitness test battery**. Physical activity was estimated by a modified version of the **Baecke Questionnaire**.

Results: Obese subjects had inferior performances on all tests requiring propulsion or lifting of the **body mass** (standing-broad jump, sit-ups, bent-arm hang, speed shuttle run, and endurance shuttle run) compared with their nonobese counterparts ($p < 0.001$). In contrast, the obese subjects showed greater strength on handgrip ($p < 0.001$). Both groups had similar levels of leisure-time physical activity; however, nonobese boys had a higher sport index than their obese counterparts ($p < 0.05$).

Discussion: Results of this study show that obese subjects had poorer performances on weight-bearing tasks, but did not have lower scores on all fitness components. To encourage adherence to physical activity in obese youth, it is important that activities are tailored to their capabilities. Results suggest that weight-bearing activities should be limited at the start of an intervention with obese participants and alternative activities that rely more on static strength used.

Key Words: physical fitness • physical activity • adiposity • children • youth

40. **Insulin Sensitivity Index, Acute Insulin Response, and Glucose Effectiveness in a Population-based Sample of 380 Young Healthy Caucasians**
   Analysis of the Impact of Gender, Body Fat, Physical Fitness, and Life-Style Factors

J. Clin. Invest. Volume 98, Number 5, September 1996, 1195-1209

Jesper O. Clausen[***]**, Knut Borch-Johnsen**[*]**, Hans Ibsen**[*]**, Richard N. Bergman, Philip Hougaard**[§]**, Kaj Winther**[¶]**, and Oluf Pedersen**[**]
[*] The Glostrup Population Studies, Medical Department C, Glostrup Hospital, University of Copenhagen, 2600 Glostrup, Denmark; Department of Physiology and Biophysics, University of Southern California Medical School, Los Angeles, California 90007; [§] Statistics HRT, CNS, GH, Novo Nordisk A/S, 2880 Bagsvaerd, Denmark; Department of Clinical Chemistry, Glostrup Hospital, University of Copenhagen, 2600 Glostrup, Copenhagen, Denmark; [¶] Department of Clinical Chemistry, Kolding Hospital, 6000 Kolding; and [**] Steno Diabetes Center 2820, Gentofte, Copenhagen, Denmark

Background : Insulin sensitivity and insulin secretion are traits that are both genetically and environmentally determined.

Aim : The aim of this study was to describe the distribution of the insulin sensitivity index (Si), the acute insulin response, and glucose effectiveness (Sg) in young healthy Caucasians and to estimate the relative impact of anthropometric and environmental determinants on these variables.

Methods : The material included 380 unrelated Caucasian subjects (18-32 yr) with measurement of Si, Sg and insulin secretion during a combined intravenous **glucose** (0.3 grams/kg body weight) and **tolbutamide** (3 mg/kg body weight) tolerance test.

Results : The distributions of Si and acute **insulin** response were skewed to the right, whereas the distribution of Sg was Gaussian distributed. Sg was 15 per cent higher in women compared with men ($P < 0.001$). Waist circumference, body mass index, maximal aerobic capacity, and women's use of oral contraceptives were the most important determinants of Si. Approximately one-third of the variation of Si could be explained by these factors. Compared with individuals in the upper four-fifths of the distribution of Si, subjects with Si in the lowest fifth had higher waist circumference, higher blood pressure, lower VO_2max, and lower glucose tolerance and fasting dyslipidemia and dysfibrinolysis. Only 10 per cent of the variation in acute insulin response could be explained by measured determinants.

Conclusion : Estimates of body fat, maximal aerobic capacity, and women's use of oral contraceptives explain about one-third of the variation in Si in a population-based sample of young healthy Caucasians. (*J. Clin. Invest.* 1996. 98:1195-1209.)

Key Words: insulin sensitivity; insulin secretion; glucose effectiveness; body fat; life-style factors.

41.   **Exercise training, vascular function, and functional capacity in middle-aged subjects.**

Medicine and Science in Sports and Exercise. 33(12):2022-2028, December 2001.

Maiorana, Andrew; O'driscoll, Gerard; Dembo, Lawrence; Goodman, Carmel; Taylor, Roger; Green, Daniel

Abstract:

Purpose: The aim of this study was to investigate the effect of 8 wk of exercise training on functional capacity, muscular strength, body composition, and vascular function in sedentary but healthy subjects by using a randomized, crossover protocol.

Methods: After familiarization sessions, 19 subjects aged 47 +/- 2 yr (mean +/- SE) undertook a randomized, crossover design study of the effect of 8 wk of supervised circuit training consisting of combined aerobic and resistance exercise. Peak oxygen uptake (&OV03122peak), sum of 7 maximal voluntary contractions and the sum of 8 skinfolds and 5 segment girths were determined at entry, crossover, and 16 wk. Endothelium-dependent and -

independent vascular function were determined by forearm strain-gauge plethysmography and intrabrachial infusions of acetylcholine (ACh) and sodium nitroprusside (SNP) in 16 subjects.

Results: Training did not alter ACh or SNP responses. & OV03122peak (28.6 +/- 1.1 to 32.6 +/- 1.3 mL[middle dot]kg-1[middle dot]min-1, P < 0.001), exercise test duration (17.4 +/- 1.1 to 22.1 +/- 1.2 min, P < 0.001), and muscular strength (465 +/- 27 to 535 +/- 27 kg, P < 0.001) significantly increased after the exercise program, whereas **skinfolds** decreased (144 +/- 10 vs 134 +/- 9 mm, P < 0.001).

Conclusion: These results suggest that moderate intensity **circuit training** designed to minimize the involvement of the arms improves functional capacity, body composition, and strength in healthy, middle-aged subjects without significantly influencing upper limb vascular function. This finding contrasts with previous studies in subjects with type 2 diabetes and heart failure that employed an identical training program.

42. **Mobilization of visceral and subcutaneous adipose tissue in response to energy restriction and exercise**
   American Journal of Clinical Nutrition, Vol. 60, 695-703.

   R Ross and J Rissanen
   School of Physical and Health Education, Queen's University, Ontario, Canada.

   The effects of energy restriction (diet) in combination with either aerobic (DA) or resistance exercise (DR) on adipose tissue (AT) distribution were evaluated in 24 obese women (DA, n = 10; DR, n = 14). AT distribution was measured by magnetic resonance imaging (MRI). Comparison between groups demonstrated that the relative losses observed for body weight, subcutaneous AT (SAT), and visceral AT (VAT) volume were not significantly different (P > 0.05). A significant reduction in the volume ratio of VAT to SAT was observed for both groups (P < 0.01). Comparison of arm, abdomen and torso, and lower-body regions revealed that the regional mobilization of SAT was not significantly different between groups (P > 0.05) and that for both groups there was a preferential mobilization of SAT from the abdominal region (P < 0.05). Within the VAT depot, significant reductions were observed for both intraperitoneal and extraperitoneal AT (P < 0.01). These findings suggest that the combination of moderate energy restriction and either resistance or aerobic exercise induces significant reductions in VAT and SAT, with a preferential loss of VAT, and are thus effective means of reducing total and upper-body obesity in obese women.

43.   Effect of aging on response to exercise training in humans: skeletal muscle GLUT-4 and insulin sensitivity

J Appl Physiol Vol. 86, Issue 6, 2019-2025, June 1999

Julie H. Cox[1], Ronald N. Cortright[1], G. Lynis Dohm[2], and Joseph A. Houmard[1]

[1] Human Performance Laboratory, Department of Exercise and Sport Science and [2] Department of Biochemistry, School of Medicine, East Carolina University, Greenville, North Carolina 27858

The purpose of this study was to compare the effects of short-term exercise training on insulin-responsive glucose transporter (GLUT-4) concentration and insulin sensitivity in young and older individuals. Young and older women [22.4 ± 0.8 (SE) yr, n = 9; and 60.9 ± 1.0 yr, n = 10] and men (20.9 ± 0.9, n = 9; 56.5 ± 1.9 yr, n = 8), respectively, were studied before and after 7 consecutive days of exercise training (1 h/day, 75 per cent maximal oxygen uptake). The older groups had more adipose tissue, increased central adiposity, and a lower maximal oxygen uptake. Despite these differences, increases in whole body insulin action (insulin sensitivity index, determined with an intravenous glucose tolerance test and minimal-model analysis) with training were similar regardless of age, in both the women and men (mean increase of 2.2 ± 0.3-fold). This was accompanied by similar relative increases in muscle (**vastus lateralis**) GLUT-4 protein concentration, irrespective of age (mean increase of 3.1 ± 0.7-fold). Body mass did not change with training in any of the groups. These data suggest that older human skeletal muscle retains the ability to rapidly increase muscle GLUT-4 and improve insulin action with endurance training.

Key Words: insulin action; glucose transport; men; women.

44.   Clinical and anthropometric correlates of bone mineral acquisition in healthy adolescent girls

Journal of Clinical Endocrinology and Metabolism, Vol. 73, 1332-1339.

DK Katzman, LK Bachrach, DR Carter and R Marcus

Musculoskeletal Research Laboratory, Veterans Administration Medical Center, Palo Alto, California 94304.

We studied the acquisition of bone mineral in 45 healthy prepubertal and pubertal girls and related changes in **bone mass** to age, **body mass**, pubertal status, **calcium intake**, and exercise. A subgroup of 12 girls was followed longitudinally. **Bone mineral content** (BMC) of the lumbar spine, whole body, and femoral neck was measured by dual energy x-ray absorptiometry and that at the midradius by single photon absorptiometry. For comparison, spine and whole body mineral contents were also measured by dual photon absorptiometry. Bone mass was expressed in conventional terms of BMC and area density (BMD). However, we show that BMD fails to account for differences in bone thickness. Since bone size increases during adolescence, we present a new expression, **bone mineral apparent density** (BMAD), which is BMC normalized to a derived bone reference volume. This term minimizes the effect of bone geometry and allows comparisons of mineral status among bones of similar shape but different size. BMC increased with age at all sites. These increases were most rapid in the early teens and plateaued after 16 yr of age. When bone mineral values at all sites were regressed against age, height, weight, or pubertal stage, consistent relationships emerged, in which BMC was most strongly correlated, BMD was correlated to an intermediate degree, and BMAD correlated only modestly or without significance. Dietary calcium and exercise level did not correlate significantly with bone mass. From these relationships, we attribute 50 per cent of the pubertal increase in spine mineral and 99 per cent of the change in whole body mineral to bone expansion rather than to an increase in bone mineral per unit volume. In multiple regressions, pubertal stage most consistently predicted mineral status. This study emphasizes the importance of pubertal development and body size as determinants of bone acquisition in girls. BMAD may prove to be particularly useful in studies of bone acquisition during periods of rapid skeletal growth.

45.   **A 30-Year Follow-Up of the Dallas Bed Rest and Training Study II. Effect of Age on Cardiovascular Adaptation to Exercise Training**
Circulation. 2001;104:1358.

Darren K. McGuire, MD, MHSc; Benjamin D. Levine, MD; Jon W. Williamson, PhD; **Peter G. Snell, PhD; C. Gunnar Blomqvist, MD, PhD; Bengt Saltin, MD; Jere H. Mitchell, MD**

From the Pauline and Adolph Weinberger Laboratory for Cardiopulmonary Research (D.K.M., B.D.L., J.W.W., P.G.S., C.G.B., J.H.M.), University of Texas Southwestern Medical Center, Dallas, Tex; the Institute for Exercise and Environmental Medicine (B.D.L.), Presbyterian Hospital, Dallas, Tex; and Copenhagen Muscle Research Center (B.S.), University of Copenhagen, Denmark.

Correspondence to Darren K. McGuire, MD, MHSc, UT Southwestern Medical Center, 5323 Harry Hines Blvd, Dallas, TX 75390-9047.

E-mail darren.mcguire@utsouthwestern.edu

Background : Aerobic power declines with age. The degree to which this decline is reversible remains unclear. In a 30-year longitudinal follow-up study, the cardiovascular adaptations to exercise training in 5 middle-aged men previously trained in 1966 were evaluated to assess the degree to which the age-associated decline in aerobic power is attributable to deconditioning and to gain insight into the specific mechanisms involved.

Methods and Results : The cardiovascular response to acute submaximal and maximal exercise were assessed before and after a 6-month endurance training program. On average, O_{2max} increased 14 per cent (2.9 versus 3.3 L/min), achieving the level observed at the baseline evaluations 30 years before. Likewise, O_{2max} increased 16 per cent when indexed to total body mass (31 versus 36 mL/kg per minute) or fat-free mass (44 versus 51 mL/kg fat-free mass per minute). Maximal heart rate declined (181 versus 171 beats/min) and maximal stroke volume increased (121 versus 129 mL) after training, with no change in maximal cardiac output (21.4 versus 21.7 L/min); submaximal heart rates also declined to a similar degree. Maximal $AVDO_2$ increased by 10 per cent (13.8 versus 15.2 vol per cent) and accounted for the entire improvement of aerobic power associated with training.

Conclusions : One hundred percent of the age-related decline in aerobic power among these 5 middle-aged men occurring over 30 years was reversed by a 6-month endurance training program. However, no subject achieved the same maximal O_2 attained after training 30 years earlier, despite a similar relative training load. The improved aerobic power after training was primarily the result of peripheral adaptation, with no effective improvement in maximal oxygen delivery.

Key Words: aging • oxygen • exercise • cardiac output • heart rate.

46.   **Physical fitness and clustering of risk factors associated with the metabolic syndrome.**
Medicine and Science in Sports and Exercise. 31(2):287-293, February 1999.

WHALEY, MITCHELL H.; KAMPERT, JAMES B.; KOHL, HAROLD W. III; BLAIR, STEVEN N.

Abstract:

Purpose: The purposes of this study were to 1) assess the prevalence of clustering of metabolic markers of the MS in a defined population and 2) determine the association between CRF and such clustering in a large group of adult men (N = 15,537) and women (N = 3,899).

Methods: Metabolic markers of the MS included systolic **blood pressure** (BP) >= 140 mm Hg, serum triglycerides >= 150 mg [middle dot]dL-1, fasting blood glucose >= 110 mg[middle dot]dL-1, and elevated central adiposity (waist circumference > 100 cm). Cardiorespiratory fitness was defined as total time on a maximal treadmill exercise test. The cohort was grouped by the number of metabolic abnormalities and level of CRF. Associations between CRF and the number of metabolic abnormalities were assessed using proportional odds logit models.

Results: Among men, the age-adjusted cumulative odds ratio for abnormal markers of the MS was 3.0 (95 per cent C.I. 2.7-3.4; P < 0.001) for the least-fit men when compared with moderately-fit ones, and 10.1 (95 per cent C.I. 9.1-11.2; P < 0.001) when compared with the most-fit men. Among women, the age-adjusted cumulative odds ratio was 2.7 (95 per cent C.I. 2.1-3.5; P < 0.001) for the least-fit women when compared with moderately-fit ones, and 4.9 (95 per cent C.I. 3.8-6.3; P < 0.001) when compared with the most-fit women.

Conclusions: These cross-sectional results suggest that low CRF is associated with an increased clustering of the metabolic abnormalities associated with the MS in both adult men and women and support the need for future prospective analyses.

47. Physiological and anthropometric determinants of sport climbing performance

Br J Sports Med 2000; *34*:359-365

Christine M Mermier[1], Jeffrey M Janot[1], Daryl L Parker[1] and Jacob G Swan[1]

[1] Center for Exercise and Applied Human Physiology, University of New Mexico, Albuquerque, New Mexico, USA

Correspondence to: C M Mermier, University of New Mexico, Center for Exercise and Applied Human Physiology, Johnson Center, B143, Albuquerque, NM 87131-1251, USA email: cmermier@unm.edu

Objective : To identify the physiological and anthropometric determinants of sport climbing performance.

Methods: Forty four **climbers** (24 men, 20 women) of various skill levels (self reported rating 5.6–5.13c on the Yosemite decimal scale) and years of experience (0.10–44 years) served as subjects. They climbed two routes on separate days to assess climbing performance. The routes (11 and 30 m in distance) were set on two artificial climbing walls and were designed to become progressively more difficult from start to finish. Performance was scored according to the system used in sport climbing competitions where each successive handhold increases by one in point value. Results from each route were combined for a total climbing performance score. Measured variables for each subject included anthropometric (height, weight, leg length, arm span, per cent body fat), demographic (self reported climbing rating, years of climbing experience, weekly hours of training), and physiological (knee and shoulder extension, knee flexion, grip, and finger pincer strength, bent arm hang, grip endurance, hip and shoulder flexibility, and upper and lower body anaerobic power). These variables were combined into components using a principal components analysis procedure. These components were then used in a simultaneous multiple regression procedure to determine which components best explain the variance in sport rock climbing performance.

Results : The principal components analysis procedure extracted three components. These were labelled training, anthropometric, and flexibility on the basis of the measured variables that were the most influential in forming each component. The results of the multiple regression procedure indicated that the training component uniquely explained 58.9 per cent of the total variance in climbing performance. The anthropometric and flexibility components explained 0.3 per cent and 1.8 per cent of the total variance in climbing performance respectively.

Conclusions : The variance in climbing performance can be explained by a component consisting of trainable variables. More importantly, the findings do not support the belief that a climber must necessarily possess specific anthropometric characteristics to excel in sport rock climbing.

Key Words: rock climbing; strength; muscular endurance; training; anthropometric determinants.

48. **Relation of Age, Exercise, Anthropometric Measurements, and Diet with Glucose and Insulin Levels in a Population Aged 70 Years and Over**

American Journal of Epidemiology Vol. 138, No. 9: 688-696

A. John Campbell[1,], Wendy J. Busby[1], Caroline C. Horwath[2] and M. Clare Robertson[1]

[1]Department of Medicine, Otago University Medical School Dunedin, New Zealand

[2]Department of Human Nutrition, Otago University Medical School Dunedin, New Zealand

Reprint requests to Professor A. J. Campbell, Department of Medicine, Otago University Medical School, P. O. Box 913, Dunedin, New Zealand

A community-based sample of people 70 years from Mosgiel, New Zealand, was investigated to determine the relation of age, diet, exercise, drugs, and anthropometric measurements with glucose and insulin. From an initial sample of 856 subjects on August 1, 1988, 782 (91.4 per cent) completed the questionnaires and physical examination. Glucose was estimated in 726 subjects and insulin in 607 subjects 2 hours after a standardized meal. In the multivariate analysis for women, glucose was related to age and exercise, and insulin was related to **glucose** levels, triceps **skinfold** thickness, and **waist/hip ratios**. In the multivariate analysis for men, none of the variables was related to glucose levels; insulin levels were related to glucose and waist/hip ratio. Impaired glucose tolerance in women was associated with high body mass index, waist/hip ratio, lower exercise levels, and the taking of thiazide drugs or oral steroids. In men, no significant model to identify those with impaired glucose tolerance could be developed. Glucose and insulin levels in women were related to age and external factors, particularly exercise and anthropometric measurements. In men, external factors were less clearly related to glucose and insulin levels, but this lack of association in men may be due to the smaller number of men in the sample, their younger age, and the narrower range of values found in the men.

Key Words: aged; anthropometry; diet; exercise; glucose; insulin.

49. **Growth, development, and physical fitness of Flemish vegetarian children, adolescents, and young adults[1,2]**

American Journal of Clinical Nutrition, Vol. 70, No. 3, 579S-585S, September 1999

Marcel Hebbelinck, Peter Clarys and Ann De Malsche

[1] From the Laboratories of Human Biometry and Biological Chemistry, Faculty of Physical Education and Physical Therapy, Vrije Universiteit Brussel, Brussels.

This study was designed to assess average daily dietary intakes of energy in 82 vegetarian children (group A: 6– 9-y-old girls and 6–11-y-old boys), adolescents (group B: 10– 15-y-old girls and 12–17-y-old boys), and young adults (group C: 16–30-y-old females and 18–30-y-old males) and included determination of height and weight; triceps, suprailiac, and calf skinfold thicknesses; puberty ratings; and physical fitness. Dietary energy intake was lower than recommended values in all 3 groups. Height and weight did not differ significantly from the reference data except in group B, which had significantly lower heights and weights and lower body mass indexes (P <0.05). Triceps and suprailiac skinfold thicknesses were lower in all age groups, whereas the calf skinfold thickness was only significantly lower in the 10–15-y-old girls ($P < 0.05$). The vegetarian children were as physically fit as the reference group. The vegetarian adolescent boys and girls and the young adults scored significantly lower on the standing long jump and 30-s sit-up ($P < 0.05$). The vegetarian subjects of groups B and C recovered significantly faster from the step test ($P < 0.05$). Puberty ratings plotted on percentile graphs showed that all vegetarian subjects, except for 1 girl, were within the normal developmental range. We conclude that, within the limits of this study, vegetarian subjects have lower relative body weights and skinfold thicknesses in adolescence than do nonvegetarians. They scored lower on the strength tests and better on the cardiorespiratory test when compared with reference values. The growth and maturation status of the vegetarian population were within the normal range.

Key Words: Growth • development • physical fitness • vegetarian children • adolescents • young adults • Belgium.

50. **The effects of a health education intervention initiated at first grade over a 3 year period: physical activity and fitness indices**
Health Education Research, Vol. 13, No. 4, 593-606, 1998
Yannis Manios, Anthony Kafatos and George Mamalakis
Department of Social Medicine, Preventive Medicine and Nutrition Clinic, School of Medicine, University of Crete PO Box 1393, Iraklion, Crete, Greece.

A health education intervention was carried out for three consecutive years on primary school Cretan children. Baseline measures were obtained from 962 pupils (509 boys and 453 girls) registered in first grade in 1992. The health education intervention programme was directed at both the children of the intervention group and their parents, and has a projected duration of 6 years. After the completion of the 3 years of intervention and while pupils were in fourth grade, measures were obtained for evaluation purposes on a random subsample of 393 pupils of the original cohort. Statistically greater improvements in the intervention, as opposed to the control group, were observed for both children's and parents' health knowledge, and children's standing broad jump, sit-ups (SUP), sit-and-reach, handgrip and endurance run test (ERT). Furthermore, time spent on moderate to vigorous physical activities out of school significantly increased for intervention group children compared to the control group. Statistically smaller increases in the intervention as opposed to the control group were observed in suprailiac **skinfold** and body mass index. The degree of improvement in both SUP and ERT related positively to parent's baseline physical activity score. Finally, the parental attitude of health-related hedonism related negatively to SUP improvement.

51. **Detection of expiratory flow limitation during exercise in COPD patients**
Journal of Applied Physiology, Vol. 82, No. 3, pp. 723-731, March 1997
Nickolaos G. Koulouris, Ioanna Dimopoulou, Päivi Valta, Richard Finkelstein, Manuel G. Cosio, and J. Milic-Emili
Meakins-Christie Laboratories and Respiratory Division, Royal Victoria Hospital, McGill University, Montreal, Quebec, Canada H2X 2P2.

The negative expiratory pressure (NEP) method was used to detect expiratory flow limitation at rest and at different exercise levels in 4 normal subjects and 14 patients with **chronic obstructive pulmonary disease** (COPD). This method does not require performance of forced expirations, nor does it require use of body plethysmography. It consists in applying negative pressure (5 cm H_2O) at the mouth during early expiration and comparing the flow-volume curve of the ensuing expiration with that of the preceding control breath. Subjects in whom application of NEP does not elicit an increase in flow during part or all of the tidal expiration are considered flow limited. The four normal subjects were not flow limited up to 90 per cent of maximal exercise power output (max). Five COPD patients were flow limited at rest, 9 were flow limited at one-third$_{max}$, and 12 were flow limited at two-thirds$_{max}$. Whereas in all patients who were flow limited at rest the maximal O_2 uptake was below the normal limits, this was not the case in most of the other patients. In conclusion, NEP provides a rapid and reliable method to detect expiratory flow limitation at rest and during exercise.

Key Words: negative expiratory pressure; chronic obstructive pulmonary disease; exercise performance; dynamic hyperinflation.

52. **Effects of exercise and stress on body fat distribution in male cynomolgus monkeys.**
Int J Obes Relat Metab Disord. 1993 Oct;17(10):597-604
Jayo JM, Shively CA, Kaplan JR, Manuck SB.
Department of Comparative Medicine, Bowman Gray School of Medicine of Wake Forest University, Winston-Salem, North Carolina 27157.

The effects of exercise and stress on regional and whole body adiposity were examined in an established animal model of diet-induced coronary artery atherosclerosis, the cynomolgus monkey (Macaca fascicularis). A total of 79 adult male monkeys were assigned to four experimental groups after baseline stabilization and training: (i) exercise, stress, (n = 20); (ii) exercise, no stress (n = 20); (iii) sedentary, stress (n = 20); and (iv) sedentary, no stress (n = 19). The monkeys consumed an ad libitum diet containing 188 mg cholesterol per day with 43 per cent of calories as saturated fat. Anthropometric measurements of regional and whole body adiposity were collected throughout the study. A subset (n = 40) of animals representing all four groups underwent computerized tomography (CT) scans at the end of the study to determine amounts of total abdominal, intra-abdominal and subcutaneous abdominal adipose tissue. Results indicate that, in general, stress interacted with exercise to affect anthropometric measurements of regional adiposity. In contrast, stress had independent and significant effects on the amount and distribution of abdominal fat as measured using CT. Stressed monkeys in both the exercise and sedentary groups had more intra-abdominal fat (and thus greater intra-abdominal-:subcutaneous abdominal fat ratios) than their nonstressed counterparts. There were no significant interactions between exercise and stress or exercise effects on abdominal fat distribution as measured by CT. These results support the belief that an arousal syndrome caused by chronic stress, and resulting in increased activity along the hypothalamo-adrenal axis, may play a role in the preferential deposition of fat in the abdomen.

53.   Physical fitness and vegetarian diets: is there a relation?[1,2]
American Journal of Clinical Nutrition, Vol. 70, No. 3, 570S-575S, September 1999

David C Nieman

[1]From the Department of Health, Leisure, and Exercise Science, Appalachian State University, Boone, NC.

The available evidence supports neither a beneficial nor a detrimental effect of a **vegetarian diet** on physical performance capacity, especially when carbohydrate intake is controlled for. Concerns have been raised that an emphasis on plant foods to enhance carbohydrate intake and optimize body glycogen stores may lead to increases in dietary fiber and phytic acid intake to concentrations that reduce the bioavailability of several nutrients, including zinc, iron, and some other trace minerals. There is no convincing evidence, however, that vegetarian athletes suffer impaired nutrient status from the interactive effect of their heavy exertion and plant-food based dietary practices to the extent that performance, health, or both are impaired. Although there has been some concern about protein intake for vegetarian athletes, data indicate that all essential and nonessential amino acids can be supplied by plant food sources alone as long as a variety of foods is consumed and the energy intake is adequate. There has been some concern that vegetarian female athletes are at increased risk for **oligoamenorrhea**, but evidence suggests that low energy intake, not dietary quality, is the major cause. In conclusion, a vegetarian diet per se is not associated with improved aerobic endurance performance. Although some concerns have been raised about the nutrient status of vegetarian athletes, a varied and well-planned vegetarian diet is compatible with successful athletic endeavor.

Key Words: Exercise • endurance • athlete • carbohydrate • meat • iron • protein • creatine • vegetarian diet • humans.

54.   Anthropometry in Body Composition: An Overview

Annals of the New York Academy of Sciences 904:317-326 (2000)

J. Wang[a], J. C. Thornton, S. Kolesnik and R. N. Pierson, J1r.

Body Composition Unit, St. Luke's/Roosevelt Hospital, Columbia University, New York, New York 10025, USA

[a]Address for correspondence: Jack Wang, Body Composition Unit, St. Luke's/Roosevelt Hospital, 1111 Amsterdam Avenue, New York, NY 10025. Voice: 212-523-3395; fax: 212-523-3416.

jw9@columbia.edu

Anthropometry is a simple reliable method for quantifying body size and proportions by measuring body length, width, circumference (C), and **skinfold** thickness (SF). More than 19 sites for SF, 17 for C, 11 for width, and 9 for length have been included in equations to predict body fat percent with a standard error of estimate (SEE) range of ± 3 per cent to ± 11 per cent of the mean of the criterion measurement. Recent studies indicate that not only total **body fat**, but also regional fat and skeletal muscle, can be predicted from anthropometrics. Our Rosetta database supports the thesis that sex, age, **ethnicity**, and site influence anthropometric predictions; the prediction reliabilities are consistently higher for Whites than for other ethnic groups, and also by axial than by peripheral sites (biceps and calf). The reliability of anthropometrics depends on standardizing the caliper and site of measurement, and upon the measuring skill of the anthropometrist. A reproducibility of ± 2 per cent for C and ± 10 per cent for SF measurements usually is required to certify the anthropometrist.

55.   Effect of endurance training and seasonal fluctuation on coagulation and fibrinolysis in young sedentary men

Journal of Applied Physiology, *Vol. 82, No. 2, pp. 613-620, February 1997*

P. J. M. Van Den Burg, J. E. H. Hospers, M. Van Vliet, W. L. Mosterd, B. N. Bouma, and I. A. Huisveld

Departments of Medical Physiology and Sports Medicine and of Haematology, University of Utrecht, 3508 TA Utrecht, The Netherlands.

The effect of 12 wk of submaximal training on hemostatic variables was studied in 20 young sedentary men (Tr) and 19 nontraining matched controls (Con). After training, a more pronounced increase in factor VIII coagulant activity ($P < 0.01$), reflected in a decrease in activated partial thromboplastin time ($P < 0.01$) during maximal exercise, was seen. Both basal plasminogen activator inhibitor 1 antigen (PAI-1 Ag) and activity (PAI-1 Act; $P < 0.05$), as well as basal and exercise-induced tissue-type plasminogen activator antigen (t-PA Ag; $P < 0.05$), were decreased after training. The overall effect on fibrinolysis was reflected in an increase in the t-PA Act/t-PA Ag ratio in the Tr group. In contrast, during the same period (February-June), the Con group demonstrated an increase in basal PAI-1 Ag and PAI-1 Act ($P < 0.05$), together with an increase in basal and exercise-induced t-PA Ag ($P < 0.05$). Both basal and exercise-induced t-PA Act were unchanged, but t-PA Act/t-PA Ag was decreased ($P < 0.05$) in the Con group. We conclude that physical training promotes both coagulation and fibrinolytic potential during exercise and may reverse unfavorable seasonal effects on fibrinolysis.

Key Words: exercise; training; season; hemostasis.

56.   The Influence of Personal Variables on Work-Related Low-Back Disorders and Implications for Future Research.
Original Article
Journal of Occupational and Environmental Medicine. 39(8):748-759, August 1997.

Dempsey, Patrick G. PhD; Burdorf, Alex PhD; Webster, Barbara S. BSPT, PA

Abstract:
Work-related low-back disorders (LBDs) continue to be one of the single largest sources of compensation costs. The relative contributions of personal, workplace, organizational, and environmental variables to the development and severity of LBDs are not completely understood. The inclusion of personal variables in epidemiologic studies of LBDs has been inconsistent, and different authors have different opinions concerning the importance of such variables. Personal variables either known or suspected to influence outcomes are discussed to elucidate the importance of these variables with respect to understanding LBDs and conducting epidemiological studies in industry. The authors suggest that age, **gender**, injury history, relative strength, **smoking**, and psychosocial variables be studied further, and that height, weight, pathologies, genetic factors, maximum oxygen uptake, and absolute strength are unlikely to produce significant effects in industrial populations.

57.   Exercise-Induced Reduction in Obesity and Insulin Resistance in Women: a Randomized Controlled Trial
Obesity Research 12:789-798 (2004)

Robert Ross*·, Ian Janssen*·, Jody Dawson*, Ann-Marie Kungl*, Jennifer L. Kuk*, Suzy L. Wong*, Thanh-Binh Nguyen-Duy*, SoJung Lee*, Katherine Kilpatrick* and Robert Hudson

* School of Physical and Health Education and Departments of Medicine, Division of Endocrinology and Metabolism and Community Health and Epidemiology, Queen's University, Kingston, Ontario, Canada.

Address correspondence to Robert Ross, School of Physical and Health Education, Queen's University, Kingston, Ontario, Canada K7L 3N6. E-mail: rossr@post.queensu.ca

Objectives: To determine the effects of equivalent diet- or exercise-induced weight loss and exercise without weight loss on subcutaneous fat, visceral fat, and insulin sensitivity in obese women.

Research Methods and Procedures: Fifty-four premenopausal women with abdominal **obesity** [waist circumference 110.1 ± 5.8 cm (mean ± SD)] (BMI 31.3 ± 2.0 kg/m²) were randomly assigned to one of four groups: diet weight loss (n = 15), exercise **weight loss** (n = 17), exercise without weight loss (n = 12), and a weight-stable control group (n = 10). All groups underwent a 14-week intervention.

Results: Body weight decreased by 6.5 per cent within both weight loss groups and was unchanged in the exercise without weight loss and control groups. In comparison with controls, cardiorespiratory fitness improved within the exercise groups only ($p < 0.01$). Reduction in total, abdominal, and abdominal subcutaneous fat within the exercise weight loss group was greater ($p < 0.001$) than within all other groups. The reduction in total and abdominal fat within the diet weight loss and exercise without weight loss groups was greater than within controls ($p < 0.001$) but not different from each other ($p > 0.05$). Visceral fat decreased within all treatment groups ($p < 0.008$), and these changes were not different from each other. In comparison with the control group, insulin sensitivity improved within the exercise weight loss group alone ($p < 0.001$).

Discussion: Daily exercise without caloric restriction was associated with substantial reductions in total fat, abdominal fat, visceral fat, and insulin resistance in women. Exercise without weight loss was also associated with a substantial reduction in total and abdominal obesity.

Key Words: weight loss • exercise • visceral fat • abdominal fat • insulin resistance.

58. **Substrate metabolism during different exercise intensities in endurance-trained women**

J Appl Physiol Vol. 88, Issue 5, 1707-1714, May 2000

J. A. Romijn[1], E. F. Coyle[2], L. S. Sidossis[3,4], J. Rosenblatt[3,4], and R. R. Wolfe[3,4]

[1] Department of Endocrinology and Metabolism, Leiden University Medical Center, 2300 RC Leiden, The Netherlands; [2] Human Performance Laboratory, Department of Kinesiology and Health, The University of Texas at Austin, Austin 78712; [3] Metabolism Unit, Shriners Burns Institute, and [4] Departments of Anesthesiology and Surgery, University of Texas Medical Branch, Galveston, Texas 77550.

We have studied eight endurance-trained women at rest and during exercise at 25, 65, and 85 per cent of maximal oxygen uptake. The rate of appearance (R_a) of free fatty acids (FFA) was determined by infusion of [$^2H_2$]palmitate, and fat oxidation rates were determined by indirect calorimetry. Glucose kinetics were assessed with [6,6-$^2H_2$] glucose. Glucose R_a increased in relation to exercise intensity. In contrast, whereas FFA R_a was significantly increased to the same extent in low- and moderate-intensity exercise, during high-intensity exercise, FFA R_a was reduced compared with the other exercise values. Carbohydrate oxidation increased progressively with exercise intensity, whereas the highest rate of fat oxidation was during exercise at 65 per cent of maximal oxygen uptake. After correction for differences in lean body mass, there were no differences between these results and previously reported data in endurance-trained men studied under the same conditions, except for slight differences in glucose metabolism during low-intensity exercise (Romijn JA, Coyle EF, Sidossis LS, Gastaldelli A, Horowitz JF, Endert E, and Wolfe RR. *Am J Physiol Endocrinol Metab* 265: E380-E391, 1993). We conclude that the patterns of changes in substrate kinetics during moderate- and high-intensity exercise are similar in trained men and women.

Key Words : stable isotopes; body composition; glucose; glycogen; fatty acids.

59.   Insulin Sensitivity, Cardiorespiratory Fitness, and Physical Activity in Overweight Hispanic Youth

Obesity Research 12:77-85 (2004)

Geoff D.C. Ball*, Gabriel Q. Shaibi, Martha L. Cruz*, Michael P. Watkins*, Marc J. Weigensberg and Michael I. Goran*,

Departments of Preventive Medicine, Biokinesiology and Physical Therapy, and

Pediatrics, Los Angeles County/University of Southern California Medical Center and

Physiology and Biophysics, University of Southern California, Los Angeles, California.

Address correspondence to Michael I. Goran, Departments of Preventive Medicine and Physiology and Biophysics, University of Southern California, Health Sciences Campus, 1540 Alcazar Street, CHP-208D, Los Angeles, CA 90089. E-mail: goran@usc.edu

Objective: To determine whether cardiorespiratory fitness and/or physical activity (PA) were related to measures of insulin sensitivity and secretion independent of body composition in overweight Hispanic children.

Research Methods and Procedures: Ninety-five Hispanic children (n = 55 boys; n = 40 girls; 8 to 13 years old) participated in this investigation. The frequently sampled intravenous glucose tolerance test was used to determine the **insulin sensitivity index** (SI), the **acute insulin response**, and the disposition index. Cardiorespiratory fitness [maximal oxygen uptake (VO_{2max})] was evaluated using a **treadmill** protocol, and PA was determined by an interviewer-administered questionnaire. Body composition was measured using DXA.

Results: Unadjusted correlations indicated that VO_{2max} (milliliters of O_2 per minute) was negatively related to SI (r = -0.46, $p < 0.05$) and disposition index (r = -0.31, $p < 0.05$) and positively associated with fasting insulin (r = 0.29, $p < 0.05$), but these relationships were no longer significant once gender, Tanner stage, fat mass, and soft lean tissue mass were included as covariates (all $p > 0.05$). Multivariate linear regression analysis showed that body fat mass explained 53 per cent of the variance in SI and that VO_{2max} (milliliters of O_2 per minute) was not independently related to SI. Cardiorespiratory fitness was positively related to both fat mass (r = 0.43, $p < 0.001$) and soft lean tissue mass (r = 0.89, $p < 0.001$). PA was not related to any measure of insulin sensitivity and secretion.

Discussion: Cardiorespiratory fitness, as determined by VO_{2max} (milliliters of O_2 per minute), was not independently related to insulin sensitivity or secretion, suggesting that VO_{2max} influences insulin dynamics indirectly through fat mass.

Key Words: Hispanic • children • physical fitness • body composition

60. **Is abdominal fat preferentially reduced in response to exercise-induced weight loss?**
Roundtable Consensus Statement
Medicine and Science in Sports and Exercise. 31(11) Supplement 1:S568, November 1999.
Ross, Robert; Janssen, Ian

Abstract:

Purpose: It is known that a preferential deposition of fat in the abdominal region is the obesity phenotype that conveys the greatest health risk. Although physical activity is commonly prescribed to reduce obesity, the influence of exercise-induced weight loss on abdominal fat is unclear. This review was undertaken to clarify whether abdominal fat is preferentially reduced consequent to weight loss induced by regular exercise.

Methods: A literature search (Medline, 1966-1998) was performed using appropriate keywords to identify studies reporting changes in both whole body and abdominal fat in response to exercise.

Results: At present there are no randomized controlled trails (RCT) wherein it was clear that exercise alone induced weight loss. For the four RCT within which regular exercise was not associated with weight loss, abdominal fat measured by waist circumference was unchanged. A similar trend is observed for the nonrandomized studies. Abdominal obesity as measured by **waist circumference** is unchanged for those studies reporting no loss in weight or fat; however, a modest reduction (~3 cm) is observed in response to exercise-induced weight loss of about 3 kg. Without exception, these studies were not designed to determine whether abdominal obesity was preferentially reduced. Absent from the literature are RCT that employ imaging techniques (e.g., computerized tomography or magnetic resonance imaging) to determine whether exercise-induced weight loss is associated with reductions in either visceral or abdominal subcutaneous fat. However, the findings from four nonrandomized or controlled studies report that exercise with or without **weight loss** is associated with reductions in both visceral and subcutaneous fat.

Conclusions: There is insufficient evidence to determine whether exercise-induced weight loss is associated with reductions in abdominal fat. Clearly there is a need for carefully controlled studies wherein the primary aim is to determine the influence of regular exercise on total and abdominal adiposity.

61.   **Exercise training and energy restriction decrease neutrophil phagocytic activity in judoists**
CLINICAL SCIENCES
Medicine and Science in Sports and Exercise. 33(4):519-524, April 2001.
Kowatari, Kenji; Umeda, Takashi; Shimoyama, Tadashi; Nakaji, Shigeyuki; Yamamoto, Yousuke; Sugawara, Kazuo

Abstract:

Purpose: To investigate the effects of weight reduction as the result of exercise training and energy restriction on neutrophil function.

Methods: Eighteen male competitive college judoists participated in the study. In a whole blood assay, oxidative burst activity, phagocytic activity, expressions of Fc gamma receptor 3 (CD16), and complement receptor 3 (CD11b) of neutrophils were measured on a per cell basis by flow cytometry at day 20, 5, and 1 before and at day 7 after the competition.

Results: The rate of **neutrophil** producing reactive oxygen species decreased before the competition, whereas the oxidative burst activity per cell increased significantly in all subjects, which resulted in a significant increase of the total oxidative burst activity. However, there were no significant effect of energy restriction on oxidative burst activity. The rate of neutrophils incorporating opsonized zymosan decreased significantly with energy restriction. The total phagocytic activity of 10000 neutrophils and the phagocytic activity per cell also decreased significantly by severe energy restriction. The surface antigen expressions of CD11b and CD16 were unaffected by weight reduction.

Conclusions: The results suggest that with respect to the management of health conditions, weight reduction for judoists should be composed of exercise training and energy restriction should be moderate.

62. Reduction in C-reactive protein through cardiac rehabilitation and exercise training

J Am Coll Cardiol, 2004; 43:1056-1061.

Richard V. Milani, MD, FACC·*, **Carl J. Lavie, MD, FACC*** and **Mandeep R. Mehra, MD, FACC***

* Cardiovascular Health Center, Department of Cardiology, Ochsner Clinic Foundation, New Orleans, Louisiana, USA

Manuscript received July 15, 2003; revised manuscript received September 26, 2003, accepted October 6, 2003.

· **Reprint requests and correspondence:** Dr. Richard V. Milani, Department of Cardiology, Ochsner Clinic Foundation, 1514 Jefferson Highway, New Orleans, Louisiana 70121, USA.

· rmilani@ochsner.org

Presented in part at the 74th Annual Scientific Sessions of the American Heart Association, Anaheim, California, November 11 to 14, 2001.

Objectives: This study was designed to assess the effects of three-month formal phase II cardiac rehabilitation and exercise training programs on high-sensitivity C-reactive protein (HSCRP) levels in patients with **coronary heart disease** (CHD).

Background: High-sensitivity C-reactive protein is associated with abdominal adiposity and other CHD risk factors and is a potent independent predictor of CHD events. Although weight reduction and statin therapy reduce HSCRP levels, the independent effects of cardiac rehabilitation programs on HSCRP are not well established.

Methods: We analyzed plasma levels of HSCRP in 277 patients with CHD (235 consecutive patients before and after formal phase II cardiac rehabilitation and exercise training programs and 42 "control" patients who did not attend cardiac rehabilitation). Additionally, we determined the effects of cardiac rehabilitation on HSCRP independent of statin therapy and weight loss.

Results: Rehabilitation patients improved significantly in body fat, obesity indices, exercise capacity, and other cardiac risk factors. Mean (5.9 ± 7.7 to 3.8 ± 5.8 mg/l; -36 per cent; $p < 0.0001$) and median levels of HSCRP (-41 per cent; $p = 0.002$) decreased significantly in the rehabilitation group but not in the control population. Similar significant reductions in HSCRP occurred in the rehabilitation patients regardless of whether they received statin therapy or lost weight.

Conclusions: Therapeutic lifestyle changes effected through a three-month cardiac rehabilitation program significantly improved numerous cardiac risk factors. Through this holistic approach to secondary prevention, we observed significant reductions in HSCRP levels. These findings identify another clinical modality of reducing HSCRP beyond use of statin drugs and suggest an additional benefit of formal phase II cardiac rehabilitation and exercise training programs.

63. **Adult Female Hip Bone Density Reflects Teenage Sports-Exercise Patterns But Not Teenage Calcium Intake**
Pediatrics Vol. 106 No. 1 July 2000, pp. 40-44

Tom Lloyd*, Vernon M. Chinchilli*, Nan Johnson-Rollings*, Kessey Kieselhorst, Douglas F. Eggli§, and Robert Marcus

From the Departments of * Health Evaluation Sciences, Clinical Nutrition, and § Radiology, Pennsylvania State University, College of Medicine, Hershey, Pennsylvania; and Department of Medicine, Stanford University and Veterans Affairs Medical Center, Palo Alto, California.

Objective : To examine how cumulative teenage sports histories and time-averaged teenage calcium intake are related to total body bone mineral gain between ages 12 and 18 years and to proximal femur bone mineral density (BMD) at age 18 years.

Design : Longitudinal.

Setting : University Hospital and local suburban community in Central Pennsylvania.

Study Participants : Eighty-one white females in the ongoing Penn State Young Women's Health Study.

Outcome Measures : Total body and proximal femur (hip) bone measurements by dual energy radiograph absorptiometry; nutrient intakes, including calcium, from 33 days of prospective food records collected at regular intervals between ages 12 and 18 years; and self-reported sports-**exercise** scores between ages 12 and 18 years.

Results : Cumulative sports-**exercise** scores between ages 12 and 18 years were associated with hip BMD at age 18 years ($r = .42$) but were not related to total body bone mineral gain. Time-averaged daily **calcium intake**, which ranged from 500 to 1500 mg/day in this cohort was not associated with hip BMD at age 18 years, or with total body bone mineral gain at age 12 through 18 years.

Conclusions : The amount of physical activity that distinguishes a primarily sedentary teenager from one who engages in some form of **exercise** on a nearly daily basis is related to a significant increase in peak hip BMD.

Key Words: peak hip bone density, teenage sport histories, osteoporosis prevention.

64. Range of tricuspid regurgitation velocity at rest and during exercise in normal adult men: implications for the diagnosis of pulmonary hypertension

J Am Coll Cardiol, 1999; 33:1662-1666

Eduardo Bossone, MD, PhD[a], Melvyn Rubenfire, MD, FACC[a], David S. Bach, MD, FACC[a], Mark Ricciardi, MD[a] and William F. Armstrong, MD, FACC[a]

[a] Division of Cardiology, Department of Internal Medicine, University of Michigan, Ann Arbor, Michigan, USA

Reprint requests and correspondence: Dr. William F. Armstrong, University of Michigan Hospital, Division of Cardiology, Women's L3119, 1500 E. Medical Center Drive, Ann Arbor, Michigan 48109-0273

WFA@umich.edu

Objectives

The aim of this study was to explore the full range of **tricuspid valve regurgitation velocity** (TRV) at rest and with exercise in disease free individuals. Additionally we examined the relationship of stroke volume (SV), cardiac output (CO) and TRV to exercise capacity.

Background

Doppler evaluation of TRV can be used to estimate pulmonary artery systolic pressure (PASP). Most studies have assumed TRV 2.5 m/s as the upper limits of normal. The full range of TRV with exercise has been incompletely defined.

Methods

Highly conditioned athletes (n = 26) and healthy, active, young male volunteers (n = 14) underwent standardized recumbent bicycle exercise. Exercise parameters included: TRV, SV, CO, systolic (SBP) and diastolic (DBP) systemic **blood pressure**.

Results

Tricuspid valve regurgitation, SV, HR and CO were significantly higher in athletes than in nonathletes over all workloads, including rest. Systolic blood pressure and DBP did not show significant differences between the two groups.

Conclusions

This study defines the upper physiologic limits of TRV at rest and during exercise in normals and provides a noninvasive standard for the diagnosis of pulmonary hypertension.

65.   **Determinants of axial and peripheral bone mass in Chinese adolescents**
Arch Dis Child 1998;78:524-530 (June)

J C Y Cheng,[a] S S S F Leung,[b] W T K Lee,[a] J T F Lau,[c] N Maffulli,[d] A Y K Cheung,[c] K M Chan[a]

[a] Department of Orthopaedics and Traumatology, Chinese University of Hong Kong, Prince of Wales Hospital, Hong Kong, [b] Department of Paediatrics, Chinese University of Hong Kong, [c] Centre for Clinical Trials and Epidemiological Research, Chinese University of Hong Kong, [d] Department of Orthopaedic Surgery, University of Aberdeen Medical School, Polwarth Building, Foresterhill, Aberdeen AB25 2ZD, UK

Correspondence to: Dr Maffulli.

Objective : To determine the relation of puberty, physical activity, physical fitness, and calcium intake with **bone mineral content** (BMC) of the distal radius, and on **bone mineral density** (BMD) of the L2 to L4 vertebrae in a group of healthy Chinese adolescents.

Design : Cross sectional survey.

Subjects : A group of 179 healthy Chinese adolescents (92 boys and 87 girls) aged 12 to 13 years enrolled in the first year of the Tii Junior High School in Shatin, Hong Kong. Ninety four of the pupils enrolled were in the physical education major class (PE), and the other 85 were in the art major class (ARTS).

Main Outcome Measures : Correlation of BMC of the distal radius and BMD of the L2 to L4 vertebrae with level of physical activity, physical fitness (isometric and isokinetic), muscle strength of the upper and lower limb, and calcium intake.

Results: BMC of the distal radius and BMD of the L2 to L4 vertebrae were significantly positively correlated. Univariate and regression analysis showed that age, pubertal staging, physical fitness, and muscle strength were significantly associated with bone mass in a positive way. Calcium intake and type of sport practised did not exert a significant influence on BMC of the distal radius and BMD of the L2 to L4 vertebrae in boys. The results for the BMD of the L2 to L4 vertebrae were similar in girls and boys; however, in girls, the BMC of the distal radius had a negative correlation with calcium intake. Physical fitness was a significant positive predictor of BMD of the L2 to L4 vertebrae.

Conclusions: Among Chinese adolescents bone mass was positively influenced by certain measures of physical fitness as well as by age, weight, and pubertal stage.

Key Words: physical activity; muscle strength; bone mass.

66. **Prior exercise and postprandial substrate extraction across the human leg**

Am J Physiol Endocrinol Metab, Vol. 279, Issue 5, E1020-E1028, November 2000

D. Malkova[1], R. D. Evans[3], K. N. Frayn[3], S. M. Humphreys[3], P. R. M. Jones[2], and A. E. Hardman[1]

[1] Human Muscle Metabolism Research Group, Department of Physical Education, Sports Science and Recreation Management, [2] Human Biology Research Group, Department of Human Sciences, Loughborough University, Loughborough, Leicestershire LE11 3TU; and [3] Oxford Lipid Metabolism Group, Sheikh Rashid Laboratory, The Radcliffe Infirmary, Oxford OX2 6HE, United Kingdom

Prior exercise decreases postprandial plasma triacylglycerol (TG) concentrations, possibly through changes to skeletal muscle TG extraction. We measured postprandial substrate extraction across the leg in eight normolipidemic men aged 21-46 yr. On the afternoon preceding one trial, subjects ran for 2 h at 64 ± 1 per cent of maximal oxygen uptake (exercise); before the control trial, subjects had refrained from exercise. Samples of femoral arterial and venous blood were obtained, and leg blood flow was measured in the fasting state and for 6 h after a meal (1.2 g fat, 1.2 g carbohydrate/kg body mass). Prior exercise increased time averaged postprandial TG clearance across the leg (total TG: control, 0.079 ± 0.014 ml $\cdot$ 100 ml tissue[1] $\cdot$ min[1]; exercise, 0.158 ± 0.023 ml $\cdot$ 100 ml tissue[1] $\cdot$ min[1], P <0.01), particularly in the chylomicron fraction, so that absolute TG uptake was maintained despite lower plasma TG concentrations (control, 1.53 ± 0.13 mmol/l; exercise, 1.01 ± 0.16 mmol/l, $P < 0.001$). Prior exercise increased postprandial leg blood flow and glucose uptake (both $P < 0.05$). Mechanisms other than increased leg TG uptake must account for the effect of prior exercise on postprandial lipemia.

Key Words: triacylglycerol; glucose; arteriovenous differences; leg blood flow.

67. **Relationship between activity levels, aerobic fitness, and body fat in 8- to 10-yr-old children**

J Appl Physiol Vol. 86, Issue 4, 1428-1435, April 1999

Ann V. Rowlands, Roger G. Eston, and David K. Ingledew

School of Sport, Health, and Physical Education Sciences, University of Wales, Bangor LL57 2EN, Wales, United Kingdom

The relationships between children's activity, aerobic fitness, and fatness are unclear. Indirect estimates of activity, e.g., **heart rate** (HR) and recall, may mask any associations. The purpose of this study was to assess these relationships by using the Tritrac-R3D, a pedometer, and heart rate. Thirty-four children, ages 8-10 yr, participated in the study. The Tritrac and pedometer were worn for up to 6 days. HR was measured for 1 day. Activity measured by Tritrac or pedometer correlated positively to fitness in the whole group (Tritrac, $r = 0.66$; pedometer, $r = 0.59$; $P < 0.01$) and in boys and girls separately ($P < 0.05$) and correlated negatively to fatness in the whole group ($r = 0.42$, $P < 0.05$). In contrast, HR did not correlate significantly to fitness, and HR of >139 beats/min correlated positively to fatness in girls ($r = 0.64$, $P < 0.05$). This suggests that HR is misleading as a measure of activity. This study supports a positive relationship between activity and fitness and suggests a negative relationship between fatness and activity.

Key Words: physical activity; accelerometry; pedometry; heart rate.

68. **Exhaled Nitric Oxide and Exercise in Stable COPD Patients***

Chest. 2000;117:702-707.

Enrico Clini, MD, FCCP; Luca Bianchi, MD; Michele Vitacca, MD; Roberto Porta, MD; Katia Foglio, MD and Nicolino Ambrosino, MD, FCCP

* From the Pulmonary Division, Lung Function Unit, Fondazione S. Maugeri IRCCS, Gussago (Brescia), Italy.

Correspondence to: Enrico Clini, MD, FCCP, Fondazione Maugeri IRCCS, Via Pinidolo 23, 25064 Gussago (Bs). Italy; e-mail fsm.g2@numerica.it

Study objective: To evaluate exhaled nitric oxide (eNO) during exercise in patients with stable COPD.

Setting: Outpatient evaluation in a rehabilitation center.

Patients: Eleven consecutive male patients with stable COPD (age, 65 ± 6 years; FEV_1, 56 ± 10 per cent predicted). Eight healthy (six men; age, 51 ± 16 years) nonsmoking, nonatopic volunteers served as control subjects.

Methods: In each subject, a symptom-limited cycle ergometry test was performed by monitoring eNO with the tidal-breath method to assess eNO concentration (FENO) and output (NO) at rest, peak exercise, and recovery time.

Results: Resting FENO (9.8 ± 5.1 and 14.1 ± 6.3 parts per billion, respectively) and NO (4.2 ± 2.0 and 5.9 ± 3.4 nmol/min, respectively) were lower, although not significantly, in COPD patients than in control subjects. In both groups, FENO significantly decreased whereas NO significantly increased during exercise. Both variables returned to baseline during the recovery time. Peak exercise NO, but not FENO, was significantly lower in COPD patients than in control subjects (7.9 ± 5.4 and 12.7 ± 6.0 nmol/min, respectively, p < 0.05). The rise in NO was weakly correlated to oxygen consumption (O_2) both in control subjects (r = 0.31, p = 0.002) and in COPD patients (r = 0.22, p = 0.03). FENO showed an inverse correlation to O_2 in both groups (r = -0.53, p = 0.000; r = -0.31, p = 0.003 in control subjects and COPD patients, respectively).

Conclusions: In patients with mild and moderate COPD, eNO during exercise parallels that observed in normal control subjects. NO, but not FENO, is significantly reduced at peak exercise in COPD patients as compared with control subjects. The long-term effects of exercise training on eNO has to be evaluated by further studies.

Key Words: chemiluminescence analyzer • chronic respiratory diseases • respiration.

69. Dairy Calcium is Related to Changes in Body Composition during a Two-Year Exercise Intervention in Young Women

Journal of the American College of Nutrition, Vol. 19, No. 6, 754-760 (2000)

Yi-Chin Lin, MS, PhD, Roseann M. Lyle, PhD, Linda D. McCabe, MS, George P. McCabe, PhD, Connie M. Weaver, PhD and Dorothy Teegarden, PhD

Department of Foods and Nutrition (Y.-C.L., L.D.M., C.M.W., D.T.), Purdue University, West Lafayette, Indiana.

Department of Health, Kinesiology and Leisure Studies (R.M.L.), Purdue University, West Lafayette, Indiana.

Department of Statistics (G.P.M.), Purdue University, West Lafayette, Indiana

Address reprint requests to: Dorothy Teegarden, Ph.D., Department of Foods and Nutrition, Stone Hall 1264, Purdue University, West Lafayette IN 47907. E-mail: Teegarden@CFS.Purdue.edu

Objective: Relationships between micronutrients and dairy product intake and changes in body weight and composition over two years were investigated.

Design: Two year prospective non-concurrent analysis of the effect of calcium intake on changes in body composition during a two year exercise intervention.

Subjects: 54 normal weight young women, 18 to 31 years of age.

Measures of Outcome: Mean intakes of nutrients of interest were determined from three-day diet records completed at baseline and every six months for two years. The change in total body weight and body composition (assessed by dual x-ray absorptiometry) from baseline to two years was also determined.

Results: Total calcium/kilocalories and vitamin A together predicted (negatively and positively, respectively) changes in body weight ($R^2 = 0.19$) and body fat ($R^2 = 0.27$). Further, there was an interaction of calcium and energy intake in predicting changes in body weight, such that, only at lower energy intakes, **calcium intake** (not adjusted for energy) predicted changes in body weight.

Conclusions: Regardless of exercise group assignment, calcium adjusted for energy intake had a negative relationship and vitamin A intake a positive relationship with two year changes in total body weight and body fat in young women aged 18 to 31 years. Thus, subjects with high calcium intake, corrected by total energy intake, and lower vitamin A intake gained less weight and body fat over two years in this randomized exercise intervention trial.

Key Words: body composition, diet, premenopausal women, calcium, milk, dairy.

70. **Myoglobin O2 desaturation during exercise. Evidence of limited O2 transport.**

J Clin Invest. 1995 October; 96(4): 1916–1926.

R S Richardson, E A Noyszewski, K F Kendrick, J S Leigh, and P D Wagner

Department of Medicine, University of California, La Jolla 92093-0623, USA.

Abstract

The assumption that cellular **oxygen pressure** (PO2) is close to zero in maximally exercising muscle is essential for the hypothesis that O2 transport between blood and mitochondria has a finite conductance that determines maximum O2 consumption. The unique combination of isolated human quadriceps exercise, direct measures of arterial, femoral venous PO2, and 1H nuclear magnetic resonance spectroscopy to detect myoglobin desaturation enabled this assumption to be tested in six trained men while breathing room air (normoxic, N) and 12 per cent O2 (hypoxic, H). Within 20 s of exercise onset partial myoglobin desaturation was evident even at 50 per cent of maximum O2 consumption, was significantly greater in H than N, and was then constant at an average of 51 +/- 3 per cent (N) and 60 +/- 3 per cent (H) throughout the incremental exercise protocol to maximum work rate. Assuming a myoglobin PO2 where 50 per cent of myoglobin binding sites are bound with O2 of 3.2 mmHg, myoglobin-associated PO2 averaged 3.1 +/- .3 (N) and 2.1 +/- .2 mmHg (H). At maximal exercise, measurements of arterial PO2 (115 +/- 4 [N] and 46 +/- 1 mmHg [H]) and femoral venous PO2 (22 +/- 1.6 [N] and 17 +/- 1.3 mmHg [H]) resulted in calculated mean capillary PO2 values of 38 +/- 2 (N) and 30 +/- 2 mmHg(H). Thus, for the first time, large differences in PO2 between blood and intracellular tissue have been demonstrated in intact normal human muscle and are found over a wide range of exercise intensities. These data are consistent with an O2 diffusion limitation across the 1-5-microns path-length from red cell to the sarcolemma that plays a role in determining maximal muscle O2 uptake in normal humans.

Full text.

71. **Coagulation and fibrinolysis after moderate and very heavy exercise in healthy male subjects.**

Basic Sciences

Medicine & Science in Sports & Exercise. 30(2):246-251, February 1998.

Weiss, Claus; Seitel, Gunther; Bartsch, Peter

Abstract:

To examine the relationship between exercise intensity and activation of coagulation and fibrinolysis, we measured markers of thrombin, fibrin, and plasmin formation in 12 male subjects (mean 24 +/- 4 yr (SD)) before and after running on a treadmill for 1 h at two different intensities corresponding to moderate (82 per cent maximal heart rate (HR), 68 per cent [spacing dot above]VO2max) and very heavy (94 per cent maximal HR, 83 per cent [spacing dot above]VO2max) exercise. During moderate exercise plasma levels of tissue plasminogen activator (t-PA) antigen rose from 3.7 +/- 0.5 (mean +/- SE) to 14.6+/- 1.8 ng[middle dot]mL-1 (P < 0.01) and of plasmin-[alpha]-antiplasmin (PAP) complexes from 2.1 +/- 0.3 to 4.2+/- 0.7 nmol[middle dot]L-1 (P < 0.01), whereas prothrombin fragment 1+2 (PTF1+2), thrombin-antithrombin III (TAT) complexes and fibrinopeptide A (FPA) did not change significantly. In response to very heavy exercise, mean plasma levels of t-PA antigen and PAP complexes exceeded the upper limit of normal values 2.5- (P < 0.01) and two-fold(P < 0.01), respectively, while significant increases of plasma levels of PTF1+2 (P < 0.01), TAT (P < 0.05), and FPA(P < 0.01) occurred within the range of normal. We conclude that in healthy young individuals, exercise-induced activation of coagulation is well balanced by activation of the fibrinolytic system, since moderate exercise results in increased plasmin formation only, while at very heavy exercise generation of plasmin seems to exceed that of thrombin and fibrin.

72.   Fitness Alters the Associations of BMI and Waist Circumference with Total and Abdominal Fat

Obesity Research 12:525-537 (2004)

Ian Janssen*, Peter T. Katzmarzyk*·, Robert Ross·, Arthur S. Leon, James S. Skinner¶, D.C. Rao‖, Jack H. Wilmore**, Tuomo Rankinen and Claude Bouchard

·   Department of Community Health and Epidemiology and
·   School of Physical and Health Education
      Department of Medicine, Division of Endocrinology and Metabolism, Queen's University, Kingston, Ontario, Canada;
      School of Kinesiology and Leisure Studies, University of Minnesota, Minneapolis, Minnesota;
·   ¶ Department of Kinesiology, Indiana University, Bloomington, Indiana;
      ‖ Division of Biostatistics, Departments of Genetics and Psychiatry, Washington University, St. Louis, Missouri;
·   ** Department of Health and Kinesiology, Texas A&M University, College Station, Texas; and
·   Human Genomics Laboratory, Pennington Biomedical Research Center, Baton Rouge, Louisiana.

      Address correspondence to Peter T. Katzmarzyk, School of Physical and Health Education, Queen's University, Kingston, Ontario, Canada K7L 3N6. E-mail: katzmarz@post.queensu.ca

Objective: We tested the following hypotheses in black and white men and women: 1) for a given BMI or **waist circumference** (WC), individuals with moderate **cardiorespiratory fitness** (CRF) have lower amounts of total fat mass and abdominal subcutaneous and visceral fat compared with individuals with low CRF; and 2) exercise training is associated with significant reductions in total adiposity and abdominal fat independent of changes in BMI or WC.

Research Methods and Procedures: The sample included 366 sedentary male (111 blacks and 255 whites) and 462 sedentary female (203 blacks and 259 whites) participants in the HERITAGE Family Study. The relationships between BMI and WC with total fat mass (determined by underwater weighing) and abdominal subcutaneous and visceral fat (determined by computed tomography) were compared in subjects with low (lower 50 per cent) and moderate (upper 50 per cent) CRF. The effects of a 20-week aerobic exercise training program on changes in these adiposity variables were examined in 86 per cent of the subjects.

Results: Individuals with moderate CRF had lower levels of total fat mass and abdominal subcutaneous and visceral fat than individuals with low CRF for a given BMI or WC value. The 20-week aerobic exercise program was associated with significant reductions in total adiposity and abdominal fat, even after controlling for reductions in BMI and WC. With few exceptions, these observations were true for both men and women and blacks and whites.

Discussion: These findings suggest that a reduction in total adiposity and abdominal fat may be a means by which CRF attenuates the health risk attributable to obesity as determined by BMI and WC.

Key Words: visceral fat • subcutaneous fat • exercise • HERITAGE Family Study.

73. Time course of hemorheological alterations after heavy anaerobic exercise in untrained human subjects

J Appl Physiol, Vol. 94, Issue 3, 997-1002, March 2003

Ozlem Yalcin[1], Alpaslan Erman[2], Sedat Muratli[2], Melek Bor-Kucukatay[1], and Oguz K. Baskurt[1]

[1]Department of Physiology, Akdeniz University School of Medicine, and [2]School of Physical Education and Sports, Akdeniz University, Antalya, Turkey 07070

The time course of hemorheological alterations was investigated after heavy anaerobic exercise in untrained male human subjects. The Wingate protocol was performed by each subject, and blood lactate, red blood cell (RBC) deformability and aggregation, white blood cell (WBC) activation, and several hematological parameters were investigated during 24 h after the exercise and compared with preexercise values. Compared with the preexercise value, **blood lactate** level was found to be ~10-fold higher immediately after the exercise. There was a transient, significant increment of RBC and WBC counts immediately after exercise that was followed by a decrement of RBC count. There was a second increase of WBC count, accompanied with increased percentages of granulocytes and granulocyte activation, starting 45 min after exercise. RBC deformability was found to be impaired immediately after exercise and remained reduced for at least 12 h; RBC aggregation was also found to be decreased after exercise, with the onset of this decrease delayed by 30 min. The results of this study indicate that a single bout of heavy anaerobic exercise may induce significant hemorheological deterioration lasting for up to 12 h and thus suggest the need to consider such effects in individuals with impaired cardiovascular function.

Key Words: Wingate test; erythrocyte deformability; erythrocyte aggregation; granulocyte activation.

74. **Physical Fitness and C-Reactive Protein Level in Children and Young Adults: The Columbia University BioMarkers Study**
PEDIATRICS Vol. 111 No. 2 February 2003, pp. 332-338

Carmen R. Isasi, MD, PhD*, Richard J. Deckelbaum, MD, Russell P. Tracy, PhD‖, Thomas J. Starc, MD¶, Lars Berglund, MD, PhD# and Steven Shea, MD, MS*

· Division of General Medicine, Department of Medicine, Columbia University College of Physicians and Surgeons, New York, New York
Department of Epidemiology, Joseph Mailman School of Public Health, Columbia University, New York, New York
Institute of Human Nutrition and Department of Pediatrics, Columbia University, New York, New York
‖ Departments of Pathology and Biochemistry, University of Vermont, Colchester, Vermont
¶ Division of Pediatric Cardiology, Department of Pediatrics, Columbia University College of Physicians and Surgeons, New York, New York
# Division of Endocrinology, Clinical Nutrition, and Vascular Medicine, Department of Medicine, University of California Davis, Sacramento, California

Objective : To examine the association of physical fitness with C-reactive protein (CRP) level in children and young adults.

Methods : Subjects ($N = 205$) aged 6 to 24 years were enrolled in the Columbia University BioMarkers Study (1994–1998). Physical fitness was assessed using a non-effort-dependent **treadmill** testing protocol (physical work capacity at heart rate of 170 beats per minute). CRP level was measured using a high-sensitivity assay.

Results : Subjects were 54 per cent female and 65 per cent of Hispanic origin. Mean fitness level was higher in boys than in girls, but CRP levels did not differ by gender. Fitness level was inversely correlated with CRP ($r = -0.22$). This relationship was significant in boys ($r = -0.32$) but not in girls ($r = -0.15$). After multivariate regression adjustment for age, race/ethnicity, body mass index, and family history of early-onset ischemic heart disease, physical fitness remained inversely associated with CRP level in boys (ß = -0.02; standard error = 0.01).

Conclusions. These findings indicate that physical fitness is inversely related to CRP level in children and that this relationship is more pronounced in boys than in girls.

Key Words: children • C-reactive protein • fitness • obesity • physical fitness.

Abbreviations: CRP, C-reactive protein • IL-6, interleukin-6 • PWC_{170}, physical work capacity at heart rate of 170 beats per minute • BMI, body mass index • SE, standard error.

75. Body Composition Analysis by Dual Energy X-ray Absorptiometry and Exercise Performance in Underweight Patients with COPD[*]
Chest. 1999; 115:371-375.

Masanori Yoshikawa, MD; Takahiro Yoneda, MD; Atsushi Kobayashi, MD; Akihiro Fu, MD; Hideaki Takenaka, MD; Nobuhiro Narita, MD and Kunimoto Nezu, MD, FCCP

[*] From the Second Department of Internal Medicine and Department of Surgery III, Nara Medical University, Nara, Japan.

Study objectives: The aim of this study was to examine the effect of body composition on maximal exercise performance in patients with COPD.

Methods: The study was carried out on 27 patients with COPD and was confirmed by pulmonary function testing. Body composition was measured by **dual energy x-ray absorptiometry** (DXA). Exercise performance was conducted on a cycle ergometer and was measured as **maximal work rate** (WRmax) and maximal **oxygen uptake** (O_2max). **Bone mineral content** (BMC), **lean mass** (LEAN), and fat mass (FAT) were assessed by DXA and were expressed as a percentage of ideal body weight, BMC, LEAN, and FAT.

Results: LEAN per cent correlated significantly with O_2max ($r = 0.66$, p = 0.0002) and WRmax ($r = 0.70$, p < 0.0001). No significant correlation was found between FAT per cent and exercise performance. By stepwise regression analysis, variables significantly contributing to WRmax and O_2max were LEAN per cent and the maximal voluntary ventilation. Total variance explained in these models was 81 per cent for WRmax and 82 per cent for O_2max.

Conclusion: Lean mass was an important determinant of maximal exercise performance in patients with COPD.

Key Words: body composition analysis • COPD • dual energy x-ray absorptiometry • exercise performance • lean body mass • malnutrition.

76.   **Doubly labeled water measurement of human energy expenditure during strenuous exercise**
      Journal of Applied Physiology, Vol 71, Issue 1 16-22.
      R. W. Hoyt, T. E. Jones, T. P. Stein, G. W. McAninch, H. R. Lieberman, E. W. Askew and A. Cymerman

US Army Research Institute of Environmental Medicine, Natick, Massachusetts 01760.

The energy expenditures (EE) of 23 adult male Marines were measured during a strenuous 11-day cold-weather field exercise at 2,200- to 2,550-m elevation by both doubly labeled water (2H2 18O, DLW) and intake balance methods. The DLW EE calculations were corrected for changes in baseline isotopic abundances in a control group that did not receive 2H2 18O. Intake balance EE was estimated from the change in body energy stores and food intake. Body energy-store changes were calculated from anthropometric [-1,574 +/- 144 (SE) kcal/day] and isotope dilution (-1,872 +/- 293 kcal/day) measurements made before and after the field exercise. The subjects kept daily logbook records of ration consumption (3,132 +/- 165 kcal/day). Mean DLW EE (4,919 +/- 190 kcal/day) did not differ significantly from intake balance EE estimated from food intake and either anthropometric (4,705 +/- 181 kcal/day) or isotope dilution (5,004 +/- 240 kcal/day) estimates of the change in body energy stores. The DLW method can be used with at least the same degree of confidence as the intake balance method to measure the EE of active free-living humans.

77.   **Dehydroepiandrosterone Replacement in Women with Adrenal Insufficiency: Effects on Body Composition, Serum Leptin, Bone Turnover, and Exercise Capacity**
      The Journal of Clinical Endocrinology & Metabolism Vol. 86, No. 5 1968-1972

Frank Callies, Martin Fassnacht, Jan Christoph van Vlijmen, Ines Koehler, Doris Huebler, Markus J. Seibel, Wiebke Arlt and Bruno Allolio
Department of Endocrinology, Medical University Hospital Wuerzburg (F.C., M.F., J.C.v.V., I.K., W.A., B.A.), 97080 Wuerzburg; Jenapharm (D.H.), 07745 Jena; and Department of Internal Medicine I, University of Heidelberg (M.J.S.), 69 M5 Heidelberg, Germany.

Address all correspondence and requests for reprints to: Dr. Frank Callies, Department of Endocrinology, Medical University Hospital, Josef Schneider Strasse 2, 97080 Wuerzburg, Germany.

Studies in animals and humans using supraphysiological doses of **dehydroepiandrosterone** (DHEA) reported significant changes in body composition and carbohydrate metabolism. To investigate the metabolic action of a physiological DHEA replacement dose, we studied 24 women with adrenal insufficiency (AI; mean ± SD age, 42.3 ± 9.3 yr; duration of disease, 9.2 ± 8.4 yr; body mass index, 23.4 ± 4.0 kg/m²) in a double blind, placebo-controlled, randomized, cross-over design. They received 50 mg DHEA/day and placebo orally for 4 months each, with a 1 -month washout period. Measurements included fasting serum glucose, insulin, leptin, bone markers, anthropometric parameters determined by bioimpedance analysis, and exercise capacity as assessed by an incremental cycling test. DHEA did not induce any change in body mass index (placebo *vs.* DHEA, 23.3 ± 4.1 *vs.* 23.2 ± 3.9 kg/m²; $P = 0.39$), parameters of body composition, or exercise capacity. However, compared with placebo, DHEA replacement led to a significant decrease in serum leptin (absolute change after 4 months, DHEA *vs.* placebo, -5.3 ± 8.0 *vs.* 1.1 ± 5.7 ng/ mL; $P = 0.01$). This is most likely the result of the DHEA-induced normalization of circulating androgens. DHEA had no effect on fasting glucose, insulin, or the glucose/insulin ratio. Compared with placebo, serum osteocalcin increased slightly, but significantly, during DHEA treatment (absolute change after 4 months DHEA *vs.* placebo, +1.6 ± 5.3 *vs.* -1.2 ± 6.2 ng/mL; $P = 0.02$). However, urinary cross-links excretion did not change. In conclusion, replacement of DHEA in a physiological dose in patients with pathological DHEA deficiency does not have a significant effect on carbohydrate metabolism, body composition, or exercise capacity. The biological relevance of the changes in leptin and osteocalcin levels remains to be determined.

78. Effects of Diet and Exercise on Obesity-Related Vascular Dysfunction in Children

Circulation. 2004;109:1981-1986.

Kam S. Woo, MD; Ping Chook, MD; Chung W. Yu, PhD; Rita Y.T. Sung, MD; Mu Qiao, MS; Sophie S.F. Leung, MD; Christopher W.K. Lam, PhD; Con Metreweli, MD; David S. Celermajer, PhD

From the Department of Medicine and Therapeutics (K.S.W., P.C., M.Q.), the Department of Pediatrics (C.W.Y., R.Y.T.S., S.S.F.L.), the Department of Chemical Pathology (C.W.K.L.), and the Department of Diagnostic Radiology and Organ Imaging (C.M.), Prince of Wales Hospital, The Chinese University of Hong Kong; and the Department of Medicine (D.S.C.), The Royal Prince Alfred Hospital, University of Sydney, Sydney, Australia.

Correspondence to Prof K.S. Woo, Department of Medicine and Therapeutics, Prince of Wales Hospital, Shatin, Hong Kong. E-mail kamsangwoo@cuhk.edu.hk

Background : The prevalence of obesity in both adults and children is increasing rapidly. Obesity in children is independently associated with arterial endothelial dysfunction and wall thickening, key early events in atherogenesis that precede plaque formation.

Methods and Results : To evaluate the reversibility of obesity-related arterial dysfunction and carotid intima-media thickening by dietary and/or exercise intervention programs, 82 overweight children (**body mass index,** 25±3), 9 to 12 years of age, were randomly assigned to dietary modification only or diet plus a supervised structured exercise program for 6 weeks and subsequently for 1 year. The prospectively defined primary end points were ultrasound-derived arterial endothelial function (endothelium-dependent dilation) of the brachial artery and intima-media thickness of common carotid artery. At 6 weeks, both interventions were associated with decreased waist-hip ratio ($P<0.02$) and cholesterol level ($P<0.05$) as well as improved arterial endothelial function. **Diet** and exercise together were associated with a significantly greater improvement in endothelial function than diet alone ($P=0.01$). At 1 year, there was significantly less thickening of the carotid wall ($P<0.001$) as well as persistent improvements in body fat content and lipid profiles in the group continuing an exercise program. Vascular function was significantly better in those children continuing exercise (n=22) compared with children who withdrew from the exercise program (n=19) ($P<0.05$).

Conclusions : Obesity-related vascular dysfunction in otherwise healthy young children is partially reversible with diet alone or particularly diet combined with exercise training at 6 weeks, with sustained improvements at 1 year in those persisting with diet plus regular exercise.

Key Words: endothelium • exercise • atherosclerosis • lifestyle • obesity.

79. **Right Ventricular Diastolic Function 15 to 35 Years After Repair of Tetralogy of Fallot**
    Restrictive Physiology Predicts Superior Exercise Performance
    Circulation. 1995;91:1775-1781.

Michael A. Gatzoulis, MD; Andrew L. Clark, MRCP; Seamus Cullen, MRCP; Claus G. H. Newman, FRCP; Andrew N. Redington, FRCP

From the Royal Brompton Hospital and the National Heart and Lung Institute (M.A.G., A.L.C., S.C., A.N.R.), London, and Chelsea and Westminster Hospital (C.G.H.N.), London.

Correspondence to Dr Andrew N. Redington, Department of Paediatric Cardiology, Royal Brompton Hospital and the National Heart and Lung Institute, Sydney St, London SW3 6NP, England.

Background : We have shown previously that transient right ventricular restriction after tetralogy of Fallot repair prolongs postoperative course. This is a prospective study of right ventricular diastolic performance in late follow-up patients.

Methods and Results : We studied biventricular function, using Doppler echocardiographic examination. Pulmonary arterial, tricuspid, and mitral valves and superior vena cava Doppler spectrals were obtained in 41 patients (mean age, 28.8 years), 15 to 35 years (mean, 23.6) after complete repair of tetralogy of Fallot. Patients were considered to have evidence of right ventricular restriction if antegrade diastolic flow was detected in the main pulmonary artery, coinciding with atrial systole (A wave), throughout the respiratory cycle. Exercise function was measured by graded treadmill testing with respiratory mass spectrometry. Three patients were excluded because of pulmonary outflow obstruction (Doppler gradient >40 mm Hg) or residual intracardiac shunts. Of the 38 patients, 37 were in sinus rhythm. Twenty (52.6 per cent) had definite evidence of restriction with an A wave in the pulmonary artery, augmented during inspiration. In all 20 cases, there was superior vena caval flow reversal with atrial systole. Both inspiratory and expiratory transtricuspid E-wave deceleration time was significantly shorter in the restrictive group ($P<.003$ and $P<.03$, respectively). All patients had Doppler evidence of pulmonary regurgitation, but its duration was shorter in the restrictive group ($P<.01$) during inspiration. Cardiothoracic ratio was significantly lower in the restrictive group ($P<.01$), suggesting less severe pulmonary regurgitation. Both restrictive and nonrestrictive groups had reduced exercise MO_2 compared with healthy age- and sex-matched control subjects, but those with restrictive physiology had significantly better maximum oxygen uptake than the nonrestrictive group ($P<.001$).

Conclusions : Isolated right ventricular restriction late after tetralogy of Fallot repair is common. Although it reflects abnormal hemodynamics, the A wave contributes to forward pulmonary arterial flow and shortens the duration of pulmonary regurgitation. Consequently, there is less cardiomegaly and improved exercise performance in those patients.

Key Words: tetralogy of Fallot • echocardiography • exercise • ventricles.

80. **Heart Rate Recovery Following Maximal Exercise Testing as a Predictor of Cardiovascular Disease and All-Cause Mortality in Men With Diabetes**
Diabetes Care 26:2052-2057, 2003
Yiling J. Cheng, MD, PHD[1], Michael S. Lauer, MD[2], Conrad P. Earnest, PHD[1], Timothy S. Church, MD, MPH, PHD[1], James B. Kampert, PHD[1], Larry W. Gibbons, MD, MPH[3] and Steven N. Blair, PED[1]

[1] Cooper Institute, Center for Epidemiological Research, Dallas, Texas
[2] Cleveland Clinic Foundation, Cleveland, Ohio
[3] The Cooper Clinic, Dallas, Texas
Address correspondence and reprint requests to Yiling J. Cheng, MD, PhD, The Cooper Institute, Center for Epidemiological Research, 12330 Preston Rd., Dallas, TX 75230. E-mail: ycheng@cooperinst.org.

Objective : Heart rate recovery (HRR) is an independent prognostic indicator for cardiovascular disease (CVD) and all-cause mortality in healthy men. We examined the association of HRR to CVD-related and all-cause mortality in men with diabetes.

Research Design and Methods : In this cohort study we examined 2,333 men with documented **diabetes** (mean age 49.4 years) that had baseline 5-min HRR measurement following maximal exercise (heart rate$_{peak}$ - heart rate$_{5 min of recovery}$) at The Cooper Clinic, Dallas, TX. We identified HRR quartiles as quartile 1 <55, quartile 2 55–66, quartile 3 67–75, and quartile 4 >75 bpm. Hazard ratios (HRs) for cardiovascular and all-cause death were adjusted for age, cardiorespiratory fitness, resting heart rate, fasting blood glucose, BMI, **smoking** habit, **alcohol** consumption, total cholesterol, triglyceride, and history of CVD at baseline.

Results : During a median of 14.9 years follow-up, there were 142 deaths that were considered CVD related and 287 total deaths. Compared with men in the highest quartile of HRR, adjusted HRs in the first, second, and third quartiles were 2.0 (95 [per cent] CI 1.1–3.8), 1.5 (0.8–2.7), and 1.5 (0.9–2.8), respectively, for cardiovascular death (*P* for trend < 0.001). Similarly, for all-cause death, adjusted HRs in the first, second, and third quartiles were 2.0 (1.3–3.2), 1.5 (1.0–2.3), and 1.5 (1.1–2.3) (*P* for trend < 0.001).

Conclusions : Among men with diabetes, a decreased HRR, even measured as long as 5 min after recovery, was independently predictive of cardiovascular and all-cause death.

ACLS, Aerobics Center Longitudinal Study • CVD, cardiovascular disease • ECG, electrocardiogram • HR, hazard ratio • HRR, heart rate recovery • MET, maximal metabolic equivalent

81. **Effects of long-term exercise of moderate intensity on anthropometric values and serum lipids and lipoproteins.**
Eur J Clin Chem Clin Biochem. 1995 Mar;33(3):121-6.
Ponjee GA, Janssen EM, Hermans J, van Wersch JW.
Diagnostisch Centrum SSDZ, Delft, The Netherlands.

The influence of endurance training on serum lipids and lipoproteins was investigated in 20 sedentary males and 14 sedentary females. The total group was trained 3 to 4 times a week for 9 months. After 24 weeks all subjects ran a 15 km-race and after 36 weeks a half-marathon (21 km) race. Anthropometric values were determined before and after the training programme. Blood samples were drawn before the start of the training programme and, in order to avoid the measurement of acute effects, 5 days before both races. In the male group, median body weight and **body mass** were significantly decreased (p < 0.01) after nine months of training, while in the female group body weight and body mass index remained essentially unchanged. Percentage body fat, measured by **skinfold** thickness was significantly decreased in both groups at the end of the training programme. During the training period, median serum total cholesterol, low density lipid cholesterol and triacylglycerol concentrations decreased significantly (p < 0.01) in the male group, while in the female population the median serum lipid- and **lipoprotein** concentrations did not differ from pre-training values. The changes in serum lipids or lipoproteins did not correlate significantly with changes in body weight, body mass index or percentage body fat. Stepwise multiple regression showed that these changes were mostly dependent on initial concentrations in serum. Finally, no significant increase in median high density lipid cholesterol was observed in either the male or female group.

82. **Influence of Cardiac Functional Capacity on Gender Differences in Maximal Oxygen Uptake in Children***

Chest. 2000;117:629-635.

Thomas Rowland, MD; Donna Goff, MS; Leslie Martel, MEd and Lisa Ferrone, MS

* From the Department of Pediatrics (Dr. Rowland, and Mss. Martel and Ferrone), Baystate Medical Center, Springfield, MA; and the Department of Exercise Science (Ms. Goff), University of Massachusetts, Amherst, MA.

Correspondence to: Thomas Rowland, MD, Department of Pediatrics, Baystate Medical Center, Springfield, MA 01199.

Objective: To examine the role of gender differences in cardiac functional capacity in explaining higher mean values for maximal oxygen uptake (O_2max) in boys than in girls.

Design: Comparative group exercise testing.

Setting: Pediatric exercise testing laboratory.

Subjects: Twenty-five prepubertal boys (mean [± SD] age, 12 ± 0.4 years) and 24 premenarcheal girls (mean age, 11.7 ± 0.5 years)..

Interventions: Maximal incremental upright cycle exercise.

Measurements and results: Mean values for O_2max were the following: boys, 47.2 ± 6.1 mL/kg/min; and girls, 40.4 ± 5.8 mL/kg/min (16.8 per cent difference; $p < 0.05$). The average maximal stroke index with **Doppler echocardiography** was 62 ± 9 mL/m^2 for boys and 55 ± 9 mL/m^2 for girls (12.7 per cent difference; $p < 0.05$). No significant gender differences were seen in maximal heart rate or arterial venous oxygen difference. When O_2max and maximal stroke volume (SV) were expressed relative to lean body mass, gender differences declined but persisted, falling to 6.2 per cent and 5.2 per cent, respectively.

Conclusions: These findings indicate that differences in SV as well as in body composition contribute to gender-related variations in O_2max during childhood. Whether this reflects small gender differences in relative heart size or dynamic factors influencing ventricular preload and contractility during exercise is unknown.

Key Words: cardiac output • children • exercise testing.

83. **Responses of total and free insulin-like growth factor-I and insulin-like growth factor binding protein-3 after resistance exercise and training in elderly subjects**
*Acta Physiologica Scandinavica,*Volume 165 Page 51 January 1999
Bermon, Ferrari, Bernard, Altare and Dolisi
To investigate the effects of an acute bout of exercise on total and free insulin-like growth factor-I and insulin-like growth factor binding protein-3 plasma concentrations, 32 healthy elderly subjects (67–80 years, 16 men) performed a strength test, which consisted of two sets of 12 repetitions at 12-repetition maximum and four sets of 5 repetitions at 5-repetition maximum for horizontal leg press, seated chest press, and bilateral leg extension movements. Ten out of the 32 subjects served as time controls. Blood samples were drawn prior (08.30 h), immediately (10.30 h), and 6 h (16.30 hours) after the strength test in exercising and resting subjects. The 32 subjects were then randomly assigned to habitual physical activity or to an 8-week strength training program. After 8 weeks, both sedentary and trained groups underwent blood samplings under the above-mentioned conditions. The exercising group showed increased total and free insulin-like growth factor-I concentrations immediately (+17.7 and +93.8 per cent, respectively), and 6 h (+7.5 and +31.2 per cent, respectively) after the test, whereas no significant changes in insulin-like growth factor binding protein-3 concentrations were observed in either exercising or resting control groups. Strength training induced no significant changes in baseline insulin-like growth factor-I and insulin-like growth factor binding protein-3 concentrations. Trained and sedentary groups showed similar hormonal response pattern to the strength test, which consisted of increased total and free insulin-like growth factor-I concentrations. The data indicated that strength exercise can induce an early and sustained insulin-like growth factor-I release, in elderly subjects, regardless of their training status.

84.   **Regular Aerobic Exercise Prevents and Restores Age-Related Declines in Endothelium-Dependent Vasodilation in Healthy Men**
Circulation. 2000;102:1351.

Christopher A. DeSouza, PhD; Linda F. Shapiro, MD; Christopher M. Clevenger, PhD; Frank A. Dinenno, PhD; Kevin D. Monahan, MS; Hirofumi Tanaka, PhD; Douglas R. Seals, PhD

From the Human Cardiovascular Research Laboratory, Center for Physical Activity, Disease Prevention, and Aging, Department of Kinesiology and Applied Physiology, University of Colorado, Boulder (C.A.D., L.F.S., C.M.C., F.A.D., K.D.M., H.T., D.R.S.); and the Department of Medicine, Divisions of Cardiology and Geriatric Medicine, University of Colorado, Health Sciences Center, Denver (D.R.S.).

Correspondence to Christopher DeSouza, PhD, Department of Kinesiology and Applied Physiology, University of Colorado, Campus Box 354, Boulder, CO 80309. E-mail desouzac@stripe.colorado.edu

Background : In sedentary humans endothelium-dependent vasodilation is impaired with advancing age contributing to their increased cardiovascular risk, whereas endurance-trained adults demonstrate lower age-related risk. We determined the influence of regular aerobic exercise on the age-related decline in endothelium-dependent vasodilation.

Methods and Results : In a cross-sectional study, 68 healthy men 22 to 35 or 50 to 76 years of age who were either sedentary or endurance exercise–trained were studied. Forearm blood flow (FBF) responses to intra-arterial infusions of acetylcholine and sodium nitroprusside were measured by strain-gauge plethysmography. Among the sedentary men, the maximum FBF response to acetylcholine was 25 per cent lower in the middle aged and older compared with the young group ($P<0.01$). In contrast, there was no age-related difference in the vasodilatory response to acetylcholine among the endurance-trained men. FBF at the highest acetylcholine dose was almost identical in the middle aged and older (17.3 ± 1.3 mL/100 mL tissue per minute) and young (17.7 ± 1.4 mL/100 mL tissue per minute) endurance-trained groups. There were no differences in the FBF responses to sodium nitroprusside among the sedentary and endurance- trained groups. In an exercise intervention study, 13 previously sedentary middle aged and older healthy men completed a 3-month, home-based aerobic exercise intervention (primarily walking). After the exercise intervention, acetylcholine-mediated vasodilation increased 30 per cent ($P<0.01$) to levels similar to those in young adults and middle aged and older endurance-trained men.

Conclusions : Our results indicate that regular aerobic exercise can prevent the age-associated loss in endothelium-dependent vasodilation and restore levels in previously sedentary middle aged and older healthy men. This may represent an important mechanism by which regular aerobic exercise lowers the risk of cardiovascular disease in this population.

Key Words: exercise • endothelium • vasodilation • nitric oxide • blood flow.

85. **Tricarboxylic acid cycle intermediate pool size and estimated cycle flux in human muscle during exercise**

Am J Physiol Endocrinol Metab, Vol. 275, Issue 2, E235-E242, August 1998

Martin J. Gibala[1], Dave A. MacLean[1], Terry E. Graham[2], and Bengt Saltin[1]

[1] Copenhagen Muscle Research Centre, Rigshospitalet, DK-2200 Copenhagen N, Denmark; and [2] Department of Human Biology and Nutritional Sciences, University of Guelph, Guelph, Ontario, Canada N1G 2W1

We examined the relationship between **tricarboxylic acid** (TCA) cycle intermediate (TCAI) pool size, TCA cycle flux (calculated from leg O_2 uptake), and **pyruvate dehydrogenase activity** (PDH_a) in human skeletal muscle. Six males performed moderate leg extensor exercise for 10 min, followed immediately by intense exercise until exhaustion (3.8 ± 0.5 min). The sum of seven measured TCAI (TCAI) increased (P 0.05) from 1.39 ± 0.11 at rest to 2.88 ± 0.31 after 10 min and to 5.38 ± 0.31 mmol/kg dry wt at exhaustion. TCA cycle flux increased $\sim$70-fold during submaximal exercise and was $\sim$100-fold higher than rest at exhaustion. PDH_a corresponded to 77 and 90 per cent of TCA cycle flux during submaximal and maximal exercise, respectively. The present data demonstrate that a tremendous increase in TCA cycle flux can occur in skeletal muscle despite a relatively small change in TCAI pool size. It is suggested that the increase in TCAI during exercise may primarily reflect an imbalance between the rate of pyruvate production and its rate of oxidation in the TCA cycle.

Key Words: pyruvate dehydrogenase complex; muscle oxygen uptake; amino acids; metabolism.

86. **High prevalence of arrhythmias in elderly male athletes with a lifelong history of regular strenuous exercise**

Heart 1998;79:161-164 (February)

K Jensen-Urstad,[a] F Bouvier,[a] B Saltin,[b] M Jensen-Urstad[c]

[a] Department of Clinical Physiology, Söder Hospital, Karolinska Institute, Stockholm, Sweden, [b] Department of Physiology and Pharmacology III, Karolinska Institute, [c] Department of Cardiology, Huddinge University Hospital, Karolinska Institute

Correspondence to: Dr Jensen-Urstad, Department of Cardiology, Huddinge University Hospital, S-141 86 Huddinge, Sweden.

Abstract

Objective : To characterise cardiac arrhythmias and cardiac autonomic function in 11 elderly men (mean (SD) age 73.2 (2.8) years) with a lifelong history of regular very strenuous exercise. A control group of 12 healthy sedentary or moderately physically active men (74.5 (2.7) years) was also studied.

Design : 48 hour ambulatory electrocardiograms were recorded. Cardiac autonomic function was estimated from power spectral analysis of **heart rate** variability. Maximal oxygen uptake during **treadmill** exercise testing was 2.91 (0.52) l (41 (7) ml/kg).

Results : Nine of 11 athletes had complex ventricular arrhythmias compared with five of 12 controls. Seven athletes but none of the controls had episodes of heart rate below 40 beats/min and two athletes had RR intervals longer than two seconds. Heart rate variability in the athletes was higher than in the controls.

Conclusions : Elderly athletes with a lifelong training history seem to have more complex arrhythmias and profound bradyarrhythmias than do healthy elderly controls, which may increase the risk of sudden cardiac death. In contrast, the age related decrease in heart rate variability seems to be retarded, which has a positive prognostic value and may decrease the risk of life threatening ventricular arrhythmias.

Key Words: arrhythmias; heart rate variability; athletes; exercise; elderly men.

87. **Determinants of Aerobic and Anaerobic Exercise Performance in Cystic Fibrosis**

Am. J. Respir. Crit. Care Med., Volume 157, Number 4, April 1998, 1145-1150

Ashish R. Shah, David Gozal, and Thomas G. Keens

Division of Pediatric Pulmonology, Childrens Hospital Los Angeles; Department of Pediatrics, University of Southern California School of Medicine, Los Angeles, California; and Constance S. Kaufman Pediatric Pulmonary Research Laboratory, Departments of Pediatrics and Physiology, Tulane University School of Medicine, New Orleans, Louisiana

We examined aerobic and anaerobic exercise performance in 17 subjects with cystic fibrosis (CF) (age 25 ± 10 [SD] yr; 47 per cent females; FEV_1 62 ± 21 per cent pred) and 17 age- and sex-matched control subjects (age 25 ± 8 [SD]

yr; 41 per cent females; FEV_1 112 ± 15 per cent pred) in relation to pulmonary function and nutritional status. Aerobic capacity was determined as maximal oxygen consumption (O_2max) (ml/kg/min) and anaerobic threshold (AT; ml o $_2$/kg/min) from a graded exercise stress test on an electronically braked **bicycle ergometer.** Anaerobic performance was assessed from the average work of two bouts of pedaling to exhaustion at a load corresponding to 130 per cent o $_2$max from graded exercise. Both aerobic and anaerobic performances were decreased in subjects with CF (p < 0.001). The duration of anaerobic exercise in subjects with CF was similar to control subjects. In control subjects, pulmonary function did not correlate to aerobic or anaerobic exercise. In subjects with CF significant relationships between FEV_1, vital capacity, and FEF_{25-75} per cent to AT were found, suggesting the pulmonary limitation to aerobic capacity. In both patients with CF and control subjects, lean body mass and arm muscle area significantly correlated with anaerobic performance but not with o $_2$max or AT. We conclude that nutritional status, rather than pulmonary function, is the major determinant of anaerobic exercise capacity in CF. The preserved duration of anaerobic exercise at equivalent workloads (corresponding to 130 per cent of o $_2$max from graded exercise) suggests that readily available energy stores in muscle may be similar in CF and normal individuals.

88. **Diaphragm Activation during Exercise in Chronic Obstructive Pulmonary Disease**

Am. J. Respir. Crit. Care Med., Volume 163, Number 7, June 2001, 1637-1641

Christer Sinderby, Jadranka Spahija, Jennifer Beck, Darek Kaminski, Sheng Yan, Norman Comtois, and Pawel Sliwinski

Guy-Bernier Research Center, Maisonneuve-Rosemont Hospital, Department of Medicine, and Ste Justine Research Center, Ste Justine Hospital, Department of Pediatrics, University of Montreal, and Meakins-Christie Laboratories, McGill University, Montreal, Quebec, Canada; and Institute of Tuberculosis & Lung Diseases, Warsaw, Poland

Although it has been postulated that central inhibition of respiratory drive may prevent development of diaphragm fatigue in patients with chronic obstructive pulmonary disease (COPD) during exercise, this premise has not been validated. We evaluated **diaphragm electrical activation** (EAdi) relative to maximum in 10 patients with moderately severe COPD at rest and during incremental exhaustive bicycle exercise. Flow was measured with a pneumotachograph and volume by integration of flow. EAdi and transdiaphragmatic pressures (Pdi) were measured using an esophageal catheter. **End-expiratory lung volume** (EELV) was assessed by inspiratory capacity (IC) maneuvers, and maximal voluntary EAdi was obtained during these maneuvers. **Minute ventilation** (E) was 12.2 ± 1.9 L/min (mean ± SD) at rest, and increased progressively (p < 0.001) to 31.0 ± 7.8 L/min at end-exercise. EELV increased during exercise (p < 0.001) causing end-inspiratory lung volume to attain 97 ± 3 per cent of TLC at end-exercise. Pdi at rest was 9.4 ± 3.2 cm H_2O and increased during the first two thirds of exercise (p < 0.001) to plateau at about 13 cm H_2O. EAdi was 24 ± 6 per cent of voluntary maximal at rest and increased progressively during exercise (p < 0.001) to reach 81 ± 7 per cent at end-exercise. In conclusion, dynamic hyperinflation during exhaustive exercise in patients with COPD reduces diaphragm pressure-generating capacity, promoting high levels of diaphragm activation.

89.   Nutritional Intervention in COPD*
A Systematic Overview

Chest. 2001;119:353-363.

Ivone M. Ferreira, MD, PhD; Dina Brooks, PhD, MSc (PT); Yves Lacasse, MD, MSc and Roger S. Goldstein, MB, ChB, FCCP

* From the Departments of Medicine (Drs. Ferreira and Goldstein) and Physical Therapy (Dr. Brooks), the University of Toronto and Respiratory Medicine, West Park Hospital, Toronto, Ontario; and Centre de Pneumologie (Dr. Lacasse), Hopital Laval, Ste-Foy, Quebec, Canada.

Correspondence to: Ivone M. Ferreira, MD, PhD, C/o Dr. Roger Goldstein, West Park Hospital, 82 Buttonwood Ave, Toronto, Canada M6M 215;

e-mail: ivoneferreira@hotmail.com

Objective: We conducted a systematic overview of randomized controlled trials (RCTs) to clarify the contribution of nutritional supplementation for patients with stable COPD.

Methods: RCTs were identified from several sources, including the Cochrane Airways Group register of RCTs, a hand search of abstracts presented at international meetings, and consultation with experts. Two reviewers independently selected trials for inclusion, assessed quality, and extracted the data.

Results: Twenty-one reports were classified according to the type, duration of supplementation, and the presence of anabolic substances. High carbohydrate meals were associated with an increase in carbon dioxide production and a decrease in exercise capacity. Short-term crossover studies in which diets of various compositions were administered supported the notion that high carbohydrate loads increase the stress on the ventilatory system. The influence of longer-term supplementation (> 2 weeks) on weight, anthropometry, and exercise capacity varied, without there being a consistent effect. Lean body weight was only occasionally reported and health-related quality of life too rarely to be included as an outcome. The influence of recombinant human growth hormone was disappointing. Anabolic steroids increased body weight and **lean body mass**, but had little influence on exercise capacity.

Conclusion: This systematic overview in patients with COPD supports the notion that those with marginal ventilatory reserve might benefit from a dietary regimen in which a high percentage of calories are supplied by fat. Although there are reports of the benefits of nutritional repletion, trials of > 2 weeks failed to show consistent benefit on body weight. Evaluating nutritional repletion is hampered by the absence of information regarding body composition, exercise, and health-related quality of life. Growth hormone has not been shown to be useful. Further studies are needed to refine the beneficial effects of anabolic steroids as adjunctive agents together with nutritional support and exercise.

Key Words: anabolic steroids • COPD • growth hormone • nutrition • respiratory rehabilitation • systematic overview.

90.   **Oxidation rate of exogenous carbohydrate during exercise is higher in boys than in men**
J Appl Physiol Vol. 94, Issue 1, 278-284, January 2003
Brian W. Timmons[1], Oded Bar-Or[1], and Michael C. Riddell[2]
[1] Children's Exercise and Nutrition Centre, McMaster University, Hamilton L8N 3Z5; and [2] Department of Kinesiology and Health Science, Faculty of Pure and Applied Sciences, York University, Toronto, Ontario, Canada M3J 1P3

To determine whether the relative utilization of **exogenous carbohydrate** (CHO_{exo}) differs between children and adults, substrate utilization during 60 min of cycling at 70 per cent peak O_2 uptake was studied in 12 pre- and early pubertal boys (9.8 ± 0.1 yr) and 10 men (22.1 ± 0.5 yr) on two occasions. Subjects consumed either a placebo or a ^{13}C-enriched 6 per cent CHO_{exo} beverage (total volume per trial: 24 ml/kg). Substrate utilization was calculated for the final 30 min of exercise. During both trials, total fat oxidation was higher (5.4 ± 0.5 vs. 3.0 ± 0.4 mg $\cdot$ kg[1] $\cdot$ min[1], $P < 0.001$) and total CHO oxidation lower (27.4 ± 1.5 vs. 34.8 ± 1.2 mg $\cdot$ kg[1] $\cdot$ min[1], $P < 0.001$) in boys than in men, respectively. During the CHO_{exo} trial, CHO_{exo} oxidation was higher ($P < 0.001$) in boys (8.8 ± 0.5 mg $\cdot$ kg[1] $\cdot$ min[1]) than in men (6.2 ± 0.5 mg $\cdot$ kg[1] $\cdot$ min[1]) and provided a greater ($P < 0.001$) relative proportion of total energy in boys (21.8 ± 1.4 per cent) than in men (14.6 ± 0.9 per cent). These results suggest that, although endogenous CHO utilization during exercise is lower, the relative oxidation of ingested CHO is considerably higher in boys than in men. The greater reliance on CHO_{exo} in boys may be important in preserving endogenous fuels and may be related to pubertal status.

Key Words: children; adults; carbon-13 isotope; substrate utilization.

91. **Prostate Cancer Risk in Relation to Anthropometry and Physical Activity: The National Health and Nutrition Examination Survey I Epidemiological Follow-Up Study**

Cancer Epidemiology Biomarkers and Prevention Vol. 9, 875-881, September 2000

Geraldine Clarke and Alice S. Whittemore[1]

Department of Health Research and Policy, Stanford University School of Medicine, Stanford, California 94305-5405

We studied the relationship of prostate cancer to anthropometry and self-reported physical activity among 5377 African-American and Caucasian participants in the National Health and Nutrition Examination Survey I cohort. The cohort was first examined between 1971 and 1975 and then followed prospectively through the Epidemiologic Follow-up Study in 1982–1984, 1986, 1987, and 1992. Men who reported low levels of nonrecreational physical activity had increased risk of prostate cancer compared with very active men. These findings were unchanged after adjustment for potential confounders and were stronger for African-Americans (relative risk, 3.7; 95 per cent confidence interval, 1.7–8.4) than for Caucasians (relative risk, 1.7; confidence interval, 0.8–2.3). Lower levels of recreational activity were weakly associated with increased prostate cancer risk among African-Americans but not among Caucasians. Prostate cancer risk was unrelated to a variety of anthropometric variables. These results suggest that inactive men are at increased risk of prostate cancer.

92. **A Randomized Study of the Effects of Aerobic Exercise by Lactating Women on Breast-Milk Volume and Composition**

The New England Journal of Medicine, Volume 330:449-453, Number 7, February 17, 1994

Kathryn G. Dewey, Cheryl A. Lovelady, Laurie A. Nommsen-Rivers, Megan A. McCrory, and Bo Lonnerdal

Abstract

Background : The potential risks and benefits of regular exercise during lactation have not been adequately evaluated. We investigated whether regular aerobic exercise had any effects on the volume or composition of breast milk.

Methods : Six to eight weeks post partum, 33 sedentary women whose infants were being exclusively breast-fed were randomly assigned to an exercise group (18 women) or a control group (15 women). The exercise program consisted of supervised aerobic exercise (at a level of 60 to 70 percent of the heart-rate reserve) for 45 minutes per day, 5 days per week, for 12 weeks. Energy expenditure, dietary intake, body composition, and the volume and composition of breast milk were assessed at 6 to 8, 12 to 14, and 18 to 20 weeks post partum. Maximal oxygen uptake and the plasma **prolactin** response to nursing were assessed at 6 to 8 and 18 to 20 weeks.

Results : The women in the exercise group expended about 400 kcal per day during the exercise sessions but compensated for this energy expenditure with a higher energy intake than that recorded by the control women (mean [±SD] intake, 2497 ±436 vs. 2168 ±328 kcal per day at 18 to 20 weeks; P<0.05). Maximal oxygen uptake increased by 25 percent in the exercising women but by only 5 percent in the control women (P<0.001). There were no significant differences between the two groups in maternal body weight or fat loss, the volume or composition of the breast milk, the infant's weight gain, or maternal prolactin levels during the 12-week study.

Conclusions : In this study, aerobic exercise performed four or five times per week beginning six to eight weeks post partum had no adverse effect on lactation and significantly improved the cardiovascular fitness of the mothers.

Source Information

From the Department of Nutrition, University of California, Davis (K.G.D., L.A.N., M.A.M., B.L.), and the Department of Food, Nutrition and Food Service Management, University of North Carolina, Greensboro (C.A.L.).

Address reprint requests to Dr. Dewey at the Department of Nutrition, University of California, Davis, CA 95616-8669.

93. **Vascular and metabolic response to cycle exercise in sedentary humans: effect of age**

Am J Physiol Heart Circ Physiol, Vol. 284, Issue 4, H1251-H1259, April 2003

J. G. Poole, L. Lawrenson, J. Kim, C. Brown, and R. S. Richardson

Department of Medicine, University of California, La Jolla, California 92093.

We measured leg blood flow (LBF), drew arterial-venous (A-V) blood samples, and calculated muscle O_2 consumption (O_2) during incremental cycle ergometry exercise [15, 30, and 99 W and maximal effort (maximal work rate,

WR$_{max}$)] in nine sedentary young (20 ± 1 yr) and nine sedentary old (70 ± 2 yr) males. LBF was preserved in the old subjects at 15 and 30 W. However, at 99 W and at WR$_{max}$, leg vascular conductance was attenuated because of a reduced LBF (young: 4.1 ± 0.2 l/min and old: 3.1 ± 0.3 l/min) and an elevated mean arterial blood pressure (young: 112 ± 3 mmHg and old: 132 ± 3 mmHg) in the old subjects. Leg A-V O$_2$ difference changed little with increasing WR in the old group but was elevated compared with the young subjects. Muscle maximal O$_2$ and cycle WR$_{max}$ were significantly lower in the old subjects (young: 0.8 ± 0.05 l/min and 193 ± 7 W; old: 0.5 ± 0.03 l/min and 117 ± 10 W). The submaximally unchanged and maximally reduced cardiac output associated with aging coupled with its potential maldistiribution are candidates for the limited LBF during moderate to heavy exercise in older sedentary subjects.

O$_{2 max}$; vascular conductance; skeletal muscle.

94. Stress Fractures in Female Army Recruits: Implications of Bone Density, Calcium Intake, and Exercise

Journal of the American College of Nutrition, Vol. 17, No. 2, 128-135 (1998)

Alana D. Cline, PhD, RD, G. Richard Jansen, PhD and Christopher L. Melby, PhD

Department of Food Science and Human Nutrition, Colorado State University, Ft. Collins.

Address reprint requests to: Alana D. Cline, PhD, RD, Pennington Biomedical Research Center, Louisiana State University, 6400 Perkins Road, Baton Rouge, LA 70808-4124.

Objective: To identify characteristics and factors associated with increased risk for stress fractures in military women.

Design: Case-control study to retrospectively examine physical activity, prior calcium intake, and bone density as predictors of stress fractures.

Setting: A military training installation which incorporates physical training for women.

Subjects: Forty-nine female soldiers with confirmed stress fractures (cases) and 78 female soldiers with no orthopedic injuries (controls), aged 18 to 33 years.

Measures: Retrospective self-reports of habitual exercise, sports participation, and food intake; current height, weight, and **body mass index** (BMI); demographic variables (age, ethnicity, menstrual patterns, smoking habits); and bone density on radiologically defined stress fractures.

Results: Cases and controls were similar in height, weight, and BMI. Measurements of **bone density** (g/cm^2) at the trochanter (cases, 0.77±0.09;

controls, 0.77±0.08); femoral neck (cases, 0.94±0.10; controls, 0.94±0.09); Ward's triangle (cases, 0.91±0.11; controls, 0.93±0.11); lumbar spine (cases, 1.21±0.12; controls, 1.24±0.10); and radius shaft (cases, 0.67±0.09; controls, 0.68±0.05) were not different between groups. **Calcium intake** was not different between groups (cases, 1154±751 mg/day; controls, 944±513 mg/day) and did not correlate with bone density (r=0.01 to -0.06 at four sites). Sports participation positively correlated with bone density in the hip (r=0.49). Leisure activity energy expenditure (kcal/day) tended toward association with lower stress fracture risk as expenditure level increased (p=0.06).

Conclusion: Stress fracture in female Army recruits was not correlated with bone density or calcium intake during adolescence, although a weak relationship to prior physical activity was observed.

Key Words: stress fracture, bone density, physical activity, calcium, exercise.

95. **Effects of testosterone and exercise on muscle leanness in eugonadal men with AIDS wasting**

J Appl Physiol, Vol. 90, Issue 6, 2166-2171, June 2001

Wesley P. Fairfield[1], Michael Treat[2], Daniel I. Rosenthal[2], Walter Frontera[5], Takara Stanley[1], Colleen Corcoran[1], Madeline Costello[3], Kristin Parlman[3], David Schoenfeld[4], Anne Klibanski[1], and Steven Grinspoon[1]

[1] Neuroendocrine Unit, [2] Department of Radiology, [3] Physical Therapy, and [4] General Clinical Research Center, Massachusetts General Hospital and Harvard Medical School, and [5] Department of Physical Medicine and Rehabilitation, Spaulding Rehabilitation Hospital and Harvard Medical School, Boston, Massachusetts 02114.

Loss of lean body and muscle mass characterizes the **acquired immunodeficiency syndrome** (AIDS) **wasting syndrome** (AWS). Testosterone and exercise increase muscle mass in men with AWS, with unclear effects on muscle composition. We examined muscle composition in 54 eugonadal men with AWS who were randomized to *1)* testosterone (200 mg im weekly) or placebo and simultaneously to *2)* resistance training or no training in a 2 × 2 factorial design. At baseline and after 12 wk, we performed assessments of whole body composition by dual-energy X-ray absorptiometry and single-slice computed tomography for midthigh cross-sectional area and muscle composition. Leaner muscle has greater attenuation. Baseline muscle attenuation correlated inversely with whole body fat mass ($r = 0.52, P = 0.0001$). This relationship persisted in a model including age, body mass index, testosterone level, viral load, lean body mass, and thigh muscle cross-sectional area ($P = 0.02$). Testosterone ($P = 0.03$) and training ($P = 0.03$) increased muscle attenuation. These data demonstrate that thigh muscle attenuation by computed tomography varies inversely with whole body fat and increases with testosterone and training. Anabolic therapy in these patients increases muscle leanness.

Key Words: resistance exercise training; muscle attenuation; acquired immunodeficiency syndrome.

96. **Expiratory flow limitation during exercise in competition cyclists**
J Appl Physiol, Vol. 86, Issue 2, 611-616, February 1999
Susana Mota[1], Pere Casan[1], Franchek Drobnic[2], Jordi Giner[1], Olga Ruiz[2], Joaquín Sanchis[1], and Joseph Milic-Emili[3]
[1] Departament de Pneumologia, Hospital de la Santa Creu i de Sant Pau, Universitat Autònoma and [2] Centre d'Alt Rendiment, Sant Cugat del Vallès, 08025 Barcelona, Spain; and [3] Meakins-Christie Laboratories, McGill University, Montreal, Quebec, Canada H2X 2P2

In some trained athletes, maximal exercise ventilation is believed to be constrained by **expiratory flow limitation** (FL). Using the negative expiratory pressure method, we assessed whether FL was reached during a progressive maximal exercise test in 10 male competition cyclists. The cyclists reached an average maximal O_2 consumption of 72 ml $\cdot$ kg^1 $\cdot$ min^1 (range: 67-82 ml $\cdot$ kg^1 $\cdot$ min^1) and ventilation of 147 l/min (range: 122-180 l/min) (88 per cent of preexercise maximal voluntary ventilation in 15 s). In nine subjects, FL was absent at all levels of exercise (i.e., expiratory flow increased with negative expiratory pressure over the entire tidal volume range). One subject, the oldest in the group, exhibited FL during peak exercise. The group end-expiratory lung volume (EELV) decreased during light-to-moderate exercise by 13 per cent (range: 5-33 per cent) of forced vital capacity but increased as maximal exercise was approached. EELV at peak exercise and at rest were not significantly different. The end-inspiratory lung volume increased progressively throughout the exercise test. The conclusions reached are as follows: *1*) most well-trained young cyclists do not reach FL even during maximal exercise, and, hence, mechanical ventilatory constraint does not limit their aerobic exercise capacity, and *2*) in absence of FL, EELV decreases initially but increases during heavy exercise.

Key Words: negative expiratory pressure; exercise performance; dynamic hyperinflation.

97. **Tryptophan Levels, Excessive Exercise, and Nutritional Status in Anorexia Nervosa**
Psychosomatic Medicine 62:535-538 (2000)
Angela Favaro, MD, PhD, Lorenza Caregaro, MD, Alberto B. Burlina, MD and Paolo Santonastaso, MD

From the Departments of Neurologic and Psychiatric Sciences (A.F., P.S.), Clinical Medicine (L.C.), and Pediatrics (A.B.), University of Padua, Padua, Italy.
Address reprint requests to: Prof. Paolo Santonastaso, Clinica Psichiatrica, Dip. Scienze Neurologiche e Psichiatriche, Via Giustiniani, 3 35128 Padova, Italy. Email: santopla@ux1.unipd.it

Objective: It has been hypothesized that reduced dietary availability of tryptophan may be the cause of impaired serotonin activity in underweight anorexics. The study reported here evaluated the relationship between tryptophan availability in the blood and nutritional status in anorexia nervosa.

Methods: The total amount of tryptophan and the ratio between tryptophan and other large neutral amino acids (TRP/LNAA) were assessed in a sample of 16 starving anorexic patients. Body weight and composition and energy intake were evaluated in all patients. All subjects also completed self-reported questionnaires such as the **Hopkins Symptom Checklist** and **Eating Disorders Inventory** (EDI).

Results: The TRP/LNAA ratio seems to be higher in patients with a more severe catabolic status. It is, in fact, significantly inversely correlated with body mass index, body fat, muscle mass, daily energy intake, and daily tryptophan intake. The TRP/LNAA ratio also correlates with growth hormone and the EDI drive for thinness. Patients who exercise excessively had significantly higher TRP/LNAA ratios.

Conclusions: In starving anorexic patients, the TRP/LNAA ratio does not seem to be determined by the content of tryptophan in the diet, but it correlates with measures of catabolism. The relationship of the TRP/LNAA ratio to excessive exercise and starvation indicates the importance of further investigations exploring the role of tryptophan availability in maintaining anorexia nervosa.

Key Words: anorexia nervosa • tryptophan • serotonin • hyperactivity • starvation.

Abbreviations: AN = anorexia nervosa; BMI = body mass index; DSM-IV= *Diagnostic and Statistical Manual of Mental Disorders*,fourth edition; EDI = Eating Disorders Inventory; GH = growthhormone; HSCL = Hopkins Symptom Checklist; LNAA = largeneutral amino acids; MAC = mid-upper arm circumference; MAMC= midarm muscle circumference; TRP = tryptophan; TSF =triceps skinfold; 5-HT = 5-hydroxytryptamine.

98. **National physical education curriculum: motor and cardiovascular health related fitness in Greek adolescents**
Br J Sports Med 2003;37:311-314
Y Koutedakis[1] and C Bouziotas[2]

[1] Department of Sports and Exercise Science, Thessaly University, Trikala, Greece

[2] School of Sport, Performing Arts and Leisure, University of Wolverhampton, UK

Correspondence to:

Professor Koutedakis, Department of Sport and Exercise Science, University of Thessaly, Karies, 42100 Trikala, Greece;

y.koutedakis@uth.gr

Background: State school physical education (PE) programmes are common throughout Greece. However, it is not known if the main objectives of the Greek PE curriculum are achieved.

Objective: To assess the current national PE curriculum in relation to selected motor and cardiovascular health related fitness parameters.

Methods: A sample of 84 Greek schoolboys (mean (SD) age 13.6 (0.3) years, height 160.7 (8.6) cm, weight 50 (10.8) kg) volunteered. Forty three indicated participation only in school PE classes and habitual free play (PE group). The remaining 41 were involved in extracurricular organised physical activities in addition to school PE and habitual free play (PE+ group). The subjects underwent anthropometric, motor (flexibility, balance, standing broad jump, hand grip, sit ups, and plate tapping), and cardiovascular health related (percentage body fat, aerobic fitness, and physical activity) fitness assessments.

Results: Children in the PE group had inferior motor and cardiovascular health related fitness profiles compared with those in the PE+ group. Body fat (20.3 (8.8) *v* 13.9 (3.5); $p<0.001$), aerobic fitness (34.7 (3.7) *v* 43.9 (4.2); $p<0.001$), and time spent in intensive physical activity (0.2 (0.2) *v* 0.7 (0.3); $p<0.001$) showed the greatest differences between the two groups. In the pupils in the PE group, these were lower than the levels proposed to be necessary to combat future health risks. Adjustments for confounding variables showed a decrease in the significance of motor fitness, but not in cardiovascular health related parameters.

Conclusions: The national PE curriculum for Greek secondary schools does not achieve the required levels of motor and cardiovascular health related fitness and should be reconsidered.

Key Words: aerobic fitness; body fat; coronary heart disease; physical activity; adolescents

Abbreviations: PE, physical education; MET, metabolic equivalent.

99.   **Percentage of Body Fat and Body Mass Index Are Associated with Mobility Limitations in People Aged 70 and Older from NHANES III**

Journal of the American Geriatrics Society ,Volume 50 Page 1802 - November 2002.

Kirsten Krahnstoever Davison, PhD,* Earl S. Ford, MD, Mary E. Cogswell, DrPH, William H. Dietz, MD, PhD

Objectives : To assess the association between functional limitations and body composition indices, including percentage of body fat, muscle mass, and body mass index (BMI).

Design : A cross-sectional, population-representative sample.

Setting : All noninstitutionalized people living in the United States (National Health and Nutrition Examination Survey). Data were collected between 1988 and 1994.

Participants : One thousand five hundred twenty-six women and 1,391 men aged 70 and older.

Measurements : Independent variables included **BMI**, muscle mass, and percentage of body fat; the latter two were assessed using predictive equations. The dependent variable, functional limitations, was defined as difficulty in performing at least three of five functional living tasks, such as carrying a 10-pound bag of groceries.

Results : Women in the highest quintile for percentage of body fat and women with a BMI of 30 or greater were two times more likely to report functional limitations than women in the comparison groups. Similar, but weaker, relationships were found among men; men in the highest quintile for body fat and men with a BMI of 35 or greater were 1.5 times more likely to report limitations. Low muscle mass (**sarcopenia**) and sarcopenia in combination with high percentage of body fat (sarcopenic obesity) were not associated with a greater likelihood of reporting functional limitations.

Conclusions : Prevention of excessive accumulation of body fat and maintenance of a BMI in the normal range may reduce the likelihood of functional limitations in old age.

100.   **Arabian Peninsula men tend to insulin resistance and cardiovascular risk seen in South Asians**

*Tropical Medicine & International Health,*Volume 3 Page 89 - February 1998

R. N. H. Pugh[1], M. M. Hossain[1], M. Malik[2], I. T. El Mugamer[3] & M. A. White[4]

Summary

Objective : To test the hypothesis that peninsular Arabs and South Asians share a tendency to insulin resistance, differing from other ethnic groups living in the United Arab Emirates (UAE).

Methods : A representative sample of 358 apparently healthy men aged 35–49 years drawn from a multi-ethnic office-based workforce in the UAE was tested. The sample included a reference group of expatriate South Asians, in whom insulin resistance has already been described as the cause of high coronary heart disease (CHD) mortality. All subjects were screened for CHD risk factors, including glucose tolerance and 2-h serum insulin determinations.

Results : There was a high prevalence of previously undiagnosed cases of diabetes (10.1 per cent) and **hypertension** (14.2 per cent). South Asian and peninsular Arab men shared the tendency to significantly higher 2-h glucose and insulin levels, lower HDL cholesterol concentrations and abdominal obesity especially compared to Europeans, who were five times less likely to be glucose-intolerant (OR 5.40, P = 0.015). Three other Arab groups were intermediate in most trends.

Conclusion : Susceptibility to insulin resistance in Arabian peninsula men is strongly supported, suggesting that control of obesity and promotion of exercise are the best approach to CHD prevention.

101. Evidence of O_2 supply-dependent $O_{2\,max}$ in the exercise-trained human quadriceps

J Appl Physiol, Vol. 86, Issue 3, 1048-1053, March 1999

R. S. Richardson, B. Grassi, T. P. Gavin, L. J. Haseler, K. Tagore, J. Roca, and P. D. Wagner

Department of Medicine, University of California San Diego, La Jolla, California 92093

Maximal O_2 delivery and O_2 uptake (O_2) per 100 g of active muscle mass are far greater during knee extensor (KE) than during cycle exercise: 73 and 60 ml $\cdot$ min^1 $\cdot$ 100 g^1 (2.4 kg of muscle) (R. S. Richardson, D. R. Knight, D. C. Poole, S. S. Kurdak, M. C. Hogan, B. Grassi, and P. D. Wagner. *Am. J. Physiol.* 268 (*Heart Circ. Physiol.* 37): H1453-H1461, 1995) and 28 and 25 ml $\cdot$ min^1 $\cdot$ 100 g^1 (7.5 kg of muscle) (D. R. Knight, W. Schaffartzik, H. J. Guy, R. Predilleto, M. C. Hogan, and P. D. Wagner. *J. Appl. Physiol.* 75: 2586-2593, 1993), respectively. Although this is evidence of muscle O_2 supply dependence in itself, it raises the following question: With such high O_2 delivery in KE, are the quadriceps still O_2 supply dependent at maximal exercise? To answer this question, seven trained subjects performed maximum KE exercise in hypoxia [0.12 inspired O_2 fraction (FI$_{O2}$)], normoxia (0.21 FI$_{O2}$), and **hyperoxia** (1.0 FI$_{O2}$) in a balanced order. The protocol (after warm-up) was a square wave to a previously determined maximum work rate followed by incremental stages to ensure that a true maximum was achieved under each condition. Direct measures of arterial and venous blood O_2 concentration in combination with a thermodilution blood flow technique allowed the determination of O_2 delivery and muscle O_2. Maximal O_2 delivery increased with inspired O_2: 1.3 ± 0.1, 1.6 ± 0.2, and 1.9 ± 0.2 l/min at 0.12, 0.21, and 1.0 FI_{O2}, respectively ($P < 0.05$). Maximal work rate was affected by variations in inspired O_2 (25 and +14 per cent at 0.12 and 1.0 FI_{O2}, respectively, compared with normoxia, $P < 0.05$) as was maximal O_2 ($O_{2\,max}$): 1.04 ± 0.13, 1.24 ± 0.16, and 1.45 ± 0.19 l/min at 0.12, 0.21, and 1.0 FI_{O2}, respectively ($P < 0.05$). Calculated mean capillary PO_2 also varied with FI_{O2} (28.3 ± 1.0, 34.8 ± 2.0, and 40.7 ± 1.9 Torr at 0.12, 0.21, and 1.0 FI_{O2}, respectively, $P < 0.05$) and was proportionally related to changes in $O_{2\,max}$, supporting our previous finding that a decrease in O_2 supply will proportionately decrease muscle $O_{2\,max}$. As even in the isolated quadriceps (where normoxic O_2 delivery is the highest recorded in humans) an increase in O_2 supply by hyperoxia allows the achievement of a greater $O_{2\,max}$, we conclude that, in normoxic conditions of isolated KE exercise, KE $O_{2\,max}$ in trained subjects is not limited by mitochondrial metabolic rate but, rather, by O_2 supply.

102. The influence of 6 months of oral anabolic steroids on body mass and respiratory muscles in undernourished COPD patients

Chest, Vol 114, 19-28.

IM Ferreira, IT Verreschi, LE Nery, RS Goldstein, N Zamel, D Brooks and JR Jardim

Respiratory Division of Federal University of Sao Paulo, Brazil.

Study objective: To evaluate the influence of oral anabolic steroids on body mass index (BMI), lean body mass, anthropometric measures, respiratory muscle strength, and functional exercise capacity among subjects with COPD. DESIGN: Prospective, randomized, controlled, double-blind study. **Setting**: Pulmonary rehabilitation program. **Participants**: Twenty-three undernourished male COPD patients in whom BMI was below 20 kg/m2 and the maximal inspiratory pressure (PImax) was below 60 per cent of the predicted value. **Intervention**: The study group received 250 mg of testosterone i.m. at baseline and 12 mg of oral stanozolol a day for 27 weeks, during which time the control group received placebo. Both groups participated in inspiratory muscle exercises during weeks 9 to 27 and cycle ergometer exercises during weeks 18 to 27. **Measurements and Results**: Seventeen of 23 subjects completed the study. Weight increased in nine of 10 subjects who received anabolic steroids (mean, +1.8+/-0.5 kg; p<0.05), whereas the control group lost weight (-0.4+/-0.2 kg). The study group's increase in BMI differed significantly from that of the control group from weeks 3 to 27 (p<0.05). **Lean body mass** increased in the study group at weeks 9 and 18 (p<0.05). Arm muscle circumference and thigh circumference also differed between groups (p<0.05). Changes in PImax (study group, 41 per cent; control group, 20 per cent) were not statistically significant. No changes in the 6-min walk distance or in maximal exercise capacity were identified in either group. **Conclusion:** The administration of oral anabolic steroids for 27 weeks to malnourished male subjects with COPD was free of clinical or biochemical side effects. It was associated with increases in BMI, lean body mass, and anthropometric measures of arm and thigh circumference, with no significant changes in endurance exercise capacity.

103. **Gender-dependent effects of exercise training on serum leptin levels in humans**
Am J Physiol Endocrinol Metab 272: E562-E566, 1997

M. S. Hickey, J. A. Houmard, R. V. Considine, G. L. Tyndall, J. B. Midgette, K. E. Gavigan, M. L. Weidner, M. R. McCammon, R. G. Israel and J. F. Caro

Human Performance Laboratory, East Carolina University, Greenville, North Carolina 27858, USA.

Leptin, the product of the ob gene, is elevated in obese humans and appears to be closely related to body fat content. The purpose of the present investigation was to determine the effect of aerobic exercise training on systemic leptin levels in humans. Eighteen sedentary middle-aged men (n = 9) and women (n = 9) who did not differ in aerobic capacity (29.4 +/- 1.2 vs. 27.5 +/- 1.2 ml x kg(-1) x min(-1)) or insulin sensitivity index (3.41 +/- 1.12 vs. 4.88 +/- 0.55) were studied. **Fat** mass was significantly lower in females vs. males (21.83 +/- 2.25 vs. 26.99 +/- 2.37 kg, P < 0.05). Despite this, fasting serum leptin was significantly higher in the females vs. males (18.27 +/- 2.55 vs. 9.88 +/- 1.26 ng/ml, P < 0.05). Serum leptin concentration decreased 17.5 per cent in females (P < 0.05) after 12 wk of aerobic exercise training (4 day/wk, 30-45 min/day) but was not significantly reduced in males. Fat mass was not altered after training in either group. In contrast, both aerobic capacity (+13 per cent males, +9.1 per cent females) and insulin sensitivity (+35 per cent males, +82 per cent females) were significantly improved subsequent to training. These data suggest that 1) women have higher circulating leptin concentrations despite lower fat mass and 2) exercise training appears to have a greater effect on systemic leptin levels in females than in males.

104.   Anthropometry of young competitive sport rock climbers
Br J Sports Med 2003;**37**:420-424

P B Watts, L M Joubert, A K Lish, J D Mast and B Wilkins
Northern Michigan University, Marquette, MI 49855, USA
Correspondence to:
Professor Watts, 1401 Presque Isle Avenue, Marquette, MI 49855, USA;
pwatts@nmu.edu

Background: Adult elite competitive rock climbers are small in stature with low body mass and very low body fat percentage. These characteristics have generated concern that young climbers may attempt body mass reduction to extreme levels with adverse consequences for health and performance. No published anthropometry data for young competitive climbers exist.

Objective: To describe the general anthropometric characteristics of junior US competitive rock climbers.

Methods: Ninety subjects (mean (SD) age 13.5 (3.0) years) volunteered to participate. All competed at the Junior Competition Climbers Association US National Championship. Anthropometric variables, including height, mass, body mass index (**BMI**), arm span, biiliocristal and biacromial breadths, **skinfold** thickness at nine anatomical sites, forearm and hand volumes, and handgrip strength, were measured. Selected variables were expressed as ratio values and as normative age and sex matched centile scores where appropriate. A control group (n = 45) of non-climbing children and youths who participated in a variety of sports activities, including basketball, cross country running, cross country skiing, soccer, and swimming, underwent the same testing procedures in the Exercise Science Laboratory of Northern Michigan University.

Results: Mean (SD) self reported climbing ability was 11.80 (1.20), or about 5.11d on the Yosemite decimal system scale. The mean (SD) experience level was 3.2 (1.9) years, and subjects competed in 10 (5) organised competitions over a 12 month period. Despite similarity in age, there were significant differences ($p<0.01$) between climbers and control subjects for height, mass, centile scores for height and mass, ratio of arm span to height ("ape index"), biiliocristal/biacromial ratio, sum of seven and sum of nine skinfolds, estimated body fat percentage, and handgrip/mass ratio. Despite significantly lower skinfold sums and estimated body fat percentage, no differences were found between climbers and controls for absolute BMI or BMI expressed as a centile score.

Conclusions: Young competitive climbers have similar general anthropometric characteristics to elite adult climbers. These include relatively small stature, low body mass, low sums of **skinfold**s, and high handgrip to mass ratio. Relative to age matched athletic non-climbers, climbers appear to be more linear in body type with narrow shoulders relative to hips. Differences in body composition exist between climbers and non-climbing athletes despite similar BMI values.

Key Words: anthropometry; body composition; body mass index; sport rock climbers; young athletes.

Abbreviations: BMI, body mass index; YDS, Yosemite decimal system

105. Evaluation of anthropometric equations to assess body-composition changes in young women[1,2,3]

American Journal of Clinical Nutrition, Vol. 73, No. 2, 268-275, February 2001

Karl E Friedl, Kathleen A Westphal, Louis J Marchitelli, John F Patton, W Cameron Chumlea and Shumei S Guo

[1] From the Occupational Physiology Division, US Army Research Institute of Environmental Medicine, Natick, MA, and the Division of Human Biology, Department of Community Health, Wright State University School of Medicine, Dayton, OH.

Background: Healthy young women who engage in an exercise program may lose fat that is not reflected in body weight changes because of concurrent gains in **fat-free mass** (FFM).

Objective: This study addressed the question of how well anthropometry-based predictive equations can resolve these changes.

Design: Several widely used skinfold-thickness- or circumference-based equations were compared by using dual-energy X-ray absorptiometry to study 150 healthy young women before and after 8 wk of Army basic combat training (average energy expenditure: 11.7 MJ/d).

Results: Women lost 1.2 ± 2.6 kg fat ($\pm$ SD) and gained 2.5 ± 1.5 kg FFM. Fat loss ($r = 0.47$), but not FFM gain ($r = 0.01$), correlated with initial fatness. Thus, for many women who lost fat, body weight did not change or increased. Fat loss was associated with a reduction in abdominal circumference but this alone was not a consistent marker of fat loss. One circumference equation and one **skinfold**-thickness equation yielded the smallest residual SDs (2.0 per cent and 1.9 per cent body fat, respectively) compared with the other equations in predicting body fat. The sensitivity and specificity of the best equations in predicting changes in percentage body fat were not better than 55 per cent and 66 per cent, respectively.

Conclusions: These data suggest that for women, anthropometry can provide better estimates of fatness than body mass index but it is still relatively insensitive to short-term alterations in body composition. Not surprisingly, the circumference equation that includes the most labile sites of female fat deposition (ie, waist and hips instead of upper arm or thigh) proved to be the most reliable.

Key Words: Anthropometry • weight reduction • body composition • dual-energy X-ray absorptiometry • body circumferences • skinfold thicknesses • exercise • generalized equations • women • military personnel • physical training • fitness program.

106.   **Effect of growth hormone on exercise tolerance in children with cystic fibrosis.**
Clinical Sciences
Medicine and Science in Sports & Exercise. 34(4):567-572, April 2002.
    Hutler, matthias; schnabel, dirk; staab, doris; tacke, albrecht; wahn, ulrich; boning, dieter; beneke, ralph

Abstract:

Purpose: The effect of growth hormone (GH) treatment on exercise tolerance in children with cystic fibrosis was investigated.

Methods: 10 prepubertal children (mean +/- SD; age: 12.1 +/- 1.7 yr; height: 137.4 +/- 9.2 cm; body mass: 27.8 +/- 4.2 kg; forced expiratory volume in 1 s (FEV1): 68 +/- 22 per cent predicted) were randomly assigned to either control period (CON, standard therapy) or recombinant human **growth hormone** (GH) period (additional GH treatment, 0.11-0.14 IU[middle dot]kg-1, daily, s.c.) for the first 6 months, and then assigned to the other period for the next 6 months. At study entry and after each period, anthropometric data, pulmonary function, and exercise capacity (peak exercise capacity, O2peak, and isokinetic muscle strength) were measured.

Results: Changes in height (+4.3 +/- 1.0 cm), total body mass (+2.2 +/- 0.8 kg), and lean body mass (LBM, +2.9 +/- 0.7 kg) were significantly higher (P < 0.01) after GH treatment compared with CON. Pulmonary function did not significantly change in either of the periods. In contrast to CON, GH treatment improved absolute O2peak (+19 per cent, P < 0.01), peak ventilation (+14 per cent, P < 0.01), and peak oxygen pulse (+18 per cent, P < 0.01). Analysis of variance revealed that most of the changes (71 per cent) in O2peak could be explained by those in LBM and FEV1 (P = 0.001).

Conclusion: GH treatment clearly improved exercise tolerance, presumably resulting from the combined effects of GH on the muscular, cardiovascular, and pulmonary capacity.

107. Exercise Affects Protein Utilization in Healthy Children[1,2]
Journal of Nutrition. 2001;131:2659-2663.

D.R. Bolster, M.A. Pikosky, L. M. McCarthy and N. R. Rodriguez[3]
Department of Nutritional Sciences, University of Connecticut, Storrs, CT 06269
[3]To whom correspondence should be addressed. E-mail: nrodrigu@canr.uconn.edu.

Although health initiatives promote increased physical activity in children, the physiologic outcomes have not been well characterized. This investigation examined the effects of programmed aerobic exercise on protein metabolism in children ($n = 7$; mean ± SEM: $9.14 ± 0.46$ y old; weight, $32.1 ± 1.6$ kg; height, $138 ± 2.5$ cm; and body mass index, $16.21 ± 0.36$ kg/m^2) using ^{15}N-glycine methodology. Boys ($n = 5$) and girls ($n = 2$) walked (5 d/wk, 3.2–6.4 km/d) for 6 wk. Criterion measures taken at baseline (Pre) and after the exercise program (Post) included anthropometric data, dietary assessment, nitrogen balance, nitrogen flux (Q), protein synthesis (PS), protein breakdown (PB) and net protein balance [(Net) = PS - PB]. After the walking program, there were no significant changes in body weight, fat-free mass or percentage of body fat, whereas height increased ($P < 0.01$). Energy and protein intakes were constant throughout the study. Nitrogen balance was significantly more positive Post than Pre ($P < 0.05$). There was a significant decrease in Q ($P < 0.0001$) with corresponding decreases in PS ($P < 0.001$) and PB ($P < 0.01$). These data provide the first evidence that programmed aerobic exercise alters whole-body protein utilization in healthy, nonobese children. Longitudinal studies are required to further examine changes in protein metabolism associated with increased physical activity in this population. In addition, findings suggest a need to evaluate nutrient requirements for healthy, physically active boys and girls.

Key Words: • metabolism • protein turnover • physical activity • nitrogen balance • humans.

2

Biomechanical Variables

1.   **Biomechanics of the knee-extension exercise. Effect of cutting the anterior cruciate ligament**
The Journal of Bone and Joint Surgery, Vol 66, Issue 5 725-734, 1984.
ES Grood, WJ Suntay, FR Noyes and DL Butler
We conducted this study to determine the effective moment arm of the knee extensor mechanism and the conditions under which the anterior **cruciate ligament** is loaded during knee-extension exercises. The moment arm was calculated from measurement of the quadriceps force required to extend the knee with and without resistive weights placed at the foot, the leg weight, and the location of its center of gravity. Changes in three-dimensional joint motion after the anterior cruciate ligament was removed were considered to be an indication that the ligament was loaded. The quadriceps force rose during the initial phase of knee extension and remained nearly constant at an average value of 177 newtons between 50 and 15 degrees. With extension past 15 degrees it rose rapidly, reaching an average of 350 newtons at zero degrees of extension, and continued to increase with hyperextension. The addition of thirty-one newtons (seven pounds) at the foot approximately doubled the **quadriceps force** that was required to extend the knee. The effective moment arm of the extensor mechanism increased with knee extension, peaked at approximately 20 degrees, and rapidly decreased with further extension. No change was found in the quadriceps force or its effective moment arm when the anterior cruciate ligament was sectioned except in hyperextension, where the quadriceps force decreased in two of five specimens. There was, however, an increased anterior tibial displacement in the range of 30 degrees to full extension, suggesting that the anterior cruciate ligament is loaded in that flexion arc. Clinical Relevance: This study demonstrates that very large quadriceps forces are required to accomplish the last 15 degrees of extension

during leg-raising exercises, typically twice those required to reach 30 degrees of flexion. The large forces that are required to obtain full extension explain why an extensor lag occurs with quadriceps weakness even though a full passive range of motion is possible. Since thirty-one newtons (seven pounds) of resistive weight added at the foot approximately doubles the quadriceps forces required to extend the leg alone, using such weights can produce very large quadriceps forces and concurrent patellofemoral and tibiofemoral contact forces. Because the quadriceps force increases little as the leg is extended from 50 to 15 degrees, in patients with patellofemoral chondroses for whom a full range of joint motion is not desired, quadriceps exercises can be limited to the amount of extension without decreasing quadriceps force.

2. **Biomechanics of the knee during closed kinetic chain and open kinetic chain exercises.**
Medicine and Science in Sports and Exercise. 30(4):556-569, April 1998.
Escamilla, Rafael F.; Fleisig, Glenn S.; Zheng, Nigel; Barrentine, Steven W.; Wilk, Kevin E.; Andrews, James R.

Abstract:
Purpose: Although closed (CKCE) and open (OKCE) kinetic chain exercises are used in athletic training and clinical environments, few studies have compared knee joint biomechanics while these exercises are performed dynamically. The purpose of this study was to quantify **knee force**s and muscle activity in CKCE(squat and leg press) and OKCE (knee extension).

Methods: Ten male subjects performed three repetitions of each exercise at their 12-repetition maximum. Kinematic, kinetic, and electromyographic data were calculated using video cameras (60 Hz), force transducers (960 Hz), and EMG(960 Hz). Mathematical muscle modeling and optimization techniques were employed to estimate internal muscle forces.

Results: Overall, the squat generated approximately twice as much hamstring activity as the leg press and knee extensions. Quadriceps muscle activity was greatest in CKCE when the knee was near full flexion and in OKCE when the knee was near full extension. OKCE produced more rectus femoris activity while CKCE produced more vasti muscle activity. Tibiofemoral compressive force was greatest in CKCE near full flexion and in OKCE near full extension. Peak tension in the posterior cruciate ligament was approximately twice as great in CKCE, and increased with knee flexion. Tension in the anterior cruciate ligament was present only in OKCE, and occurred near full extension. Patellofemoral compressive force was greatest in CKCE near full flexion and in the mid-range of the knee extending phase in OKCE.

3.   The biomechanics of anterior cruciate ligament rehabilitation and reconstruction
American Journal of Sports Medicine, Vol 12, Issue 1 8-18, 1984.
SW Arms, MH Pope, RJ Johnson, RA Fischer, I Arvidsson and E Eriksson

The rehabilitation of knee injuries involving the anterior cruciate ligament (ACL) is controversial. This paper describes strain in the normal and reconstructed ACL during a series of passive and active tests of knee flexion with and without varus, valgus, and axial rotation torques on the tibia. Strain in the human knee ACL was significantly different depending on whether the knee flexion angle was changed passively or via simulated quadriceps contraction. The knee joint capsule was found to be important for strain protection of the ACL. Quadriceps activity did not strain the normal or reconstructed ACL when the knee was flexed beyond 60 degrees, but significantly strained the tissue from 0 to 45 degrees of knee flexion. Immobilization may not protect the ACL if isometric quadriceps contractions are allowed to occur. Properly placed reconstructions exhibited strain behavior which closely followed the anteromedial band of the ACL.

4.   Muscle Exercise After Anterior Cruciate Ligament Reconstruction: Biomechanics of the Simultaneous Isometric Contraction Method of the Quadriceps and the Hamstrings.
Clinical Orthopaedics and Related Research. 220:266-274, July 1987.
YASUDA, KAZUNORI M.D.; SASAKI, TETSUTO M.D.

Biomechanical analysis of two-dimensional models composed from roentgenographic pictures and elec-tromyographic analysis on simultaneous isometric contraction exercises of the quadriceps and hamstrings were conducted in 20 healthy adult males. During simultaneous isometric contraction at 5[degrees] **knee flexion,** an anterior drawer force equivalent to 15 per cent of the tension of the quadriceps was exerted to the tibia, and decreased with increased angle of flexion. The mean angle at which this force became zero was 7.4[degrees], with a standard deviation of 5.0[degrees]. When the angle increased further, a posterior drawer force to the tibia occurred and gradually increased. Each tension of the quadriceps or hamstrings during maximum simultaneous isometric contraction of the quadriceps and hamstrings was estimated as 30 per cent-60 per cent of that during separate isometric contractions of each muscle. In the early stage of the rehabilitation after the anterior cruciate ligament reconstruction, the simultaneous isometric contraction of the quadriceps and the hamstrings is useful as one of the muscle exercise methods because it can be performed safely with the knee position near the full extension and can generate sufficient muscle force to be an effective exercise.

5.   **Electromyographic analysis of the glenohumeral muscles during a baseball rehabilitation program**
American Journal of Sports Medicine, Vol 19, Issue 3 264-272, 1991.
H Townsend, FW Jobe, M Pink and J Perry
Biomechanics Laboratory, Centinela Hospital Medical Center, Inglewood, CA 90301.

Many exercises are used to strengthen the glenohumeral muscles, but there have been limited studies to evaluate the exercises. Thus, the purpose of this study was to decide how the muscles responsible for humeral motion can best be exercised in a rehabilitation program for the throwing athlete. Dynamic, fine wire, intramuscular electromyography was carried out in 15 normal male volunteers performing 17 shoulder exercises derived from a shoulder rehabilitation program used by professional baseball clubs. The four rotator cuff muscles were studied, as well as other positioners of the humerus, including the pectoralis major, latissimus dorsi, and three portions of the deltoid. The electromyographic activity was synchronized with cinematography and averaged over 30 degrees arcs of motion. An exercise was considered to be a significant challenge for a muscle if it generated at least 50 per cent of its predetermined maximum contraction over three consecutive arcs (i.e., a 90 degrees range). Four exercises were consistently found to be among the most challenging exercises for every muscle. These shoulder exercises consisted of 1) elevation in the scapular plane with thumbs down, 2) flexion, 3) horizontal abduction with arms externally rotated, and 4) press-up. This study documents that the minimum for an effective and succinct rehabilitation protocol for the glenohumeral muscles would include these exercises.

6.   **Effects of resistive and balance exercises on isokinetic strength in older persons**
J Am Geriatr Soc. 1994 Sep;42(9):937-46.
Judge JO, Whipple RH, Wolfson LI.
Travelers Center on Aging, University of Connecticut Health Center, Farmington 06030-5215.

Objective: To determine the safety and efficacy of 3 months of resistive training of multiple lower extremity muscle groups compared with balance training in persons over 75 years.

Design: Randomized 3-month clinical trial. Subjects (n = 110, mean age 80) were randomized to 4 groups in a 2 x 2 design (control, resistive, balance, combined resistive/balance).

Interventions: Resistive training involved knee extension and flexion, hip abduction and extension, and plantar and dorsiflexion using simple resistive machines and sandbags. Balance training consisted of exercises to improve postural control. The control group attended 5 health-related discussion sessions.

Measurements: Summed isokinetic moments (N m) of 8 leg movements: hip, knee and ankle flexion/extension, and hip abduction/adduction. Secondary outcomes were gait velocity and chair rise time.

Main results: Summed peak moment increased in both resistive exercise-trained groups (13 per cent increase in the resistive group and 21 per cent in the combined training group, $P < 0.001$). The effect of resistance training was significant (MANOVA $F = 21.1$, $P < 0.001$), but balance training did not improve strength, and there was no interaction (positive or negative) between balance and resistive training. Maximal gait velocity and chair rise time did not improve. Eleven subjects (20 per cent) had musculoskeletal complaints related to resistive training, but all were able to complete the program with modifications.

Conclusion: Resistive training using simple equipment is an effective and acceptable method to increase overall leg strength in older persons. Resistive or balance training did not improve maximal gait velocity or chair rise time in this sample of relatively healthy older persons.

7. **Anterior cruciate ligament strain behavior during rehabilitation exercises in vivo**
    American Journal of Sports Medicine, Vol. 23, Issue 1 24-34, 1995.
    BD Beynnon, BC Fleming, RJ Johnson, CE Nichols, PA Renstrom and MH Pope
    Mc Clure Musculoskeletal Research Center, Department of Orthopaedics and Rehabilitation, University of Vermont, Burlington 05405-0084.

Before studying the biomechanical effects of rehabilitation exercises on the reconstructed knee, it is important to understand their effects on the normal anterior cruciate ligament. The objective of this investigation was to measure the strain behavior of this ligament during rehabilitation activities in vivo. Participants were patient volunteers with normal anterior cruciate ligaments instrumented with the Hall effect transducer. At 10 degrees and 20 degrees of flexion, ligament strain values for active extension of the knee with a weight of 45 N applied to a subject's lower leg were significantly greater than active motion without the weight. Isometric quadriceps muscle contraction at 15 degrees and 30 degrees also produced a significant increase in ligament strain, while at 60 degrees and 90 degrees of knee flexion there was no change in ligament strain relative to relaxed muscle condition. Simultaneous quadriceps and hamstrings muscles contraction at 15 degrees produced a significant increase in ligament strain compared with the relaxed state but did not strain the ligament at 30 degrees, 60 degrees, and 90 degrees of flexion. Isometric contraction of hamstrings muscles did not produce change in ligament strain at any flexion angle. Exercises that produce low or unstrained ligament values, and would not endanger a properly implanted graft, are either dominated by the hamstrings muscle (isometric hamstring), involve quadriceps muscle activity with the knee flexed at 60 degrees or greater (isometric quadriceps, simultaneous quadriceps and hamstrings contraction), or involve active knee motion between 35 degrees and 90 degrees of flexion.

8. **On the biomechanics of cycling. A study of joint and muscle load during exercise on the bicycle ergometer.**
Scand J Rehabil Med Suppl. 1986;16:1-43.
Ericson M.

The aim of the study was to quantify the load induced in the lower limb joints and muscles during exercise on a **bicycle ergometer** and to study how these loads changed with adjustments of the bicycle ergometer or cycling technique. The forces, load moments and muscular power output acting on and about the hip, knee and ankle joints during cycling were determined using cine-film, pedal force measurements and biomechanical calculations based upon static and dynamic mechanics. The muscular activity of eleven lower limb muscles was recorded and quantified using EMG. The load moments acting about the bilateral hip, knee and ankle joint axes were found to be generally lower than those induced during normal level walking. The varus and valgus load moments acting about the antero-posterior knee joint axis were approximately the same as those induced during walking. The tibio-femoral compressive joint force and the anteriorly directed tibio-femoral shear force mainly stressing the anterior cruciate ligament were low. The talocrural joint compressive force and achilles tendon tensile force were low compared to those in level walking. The magnitude of lower limb muscular activity during cycling approximated that obtained during walking, with three major exceptions. M. vastus medialis et lateralis were more activated during cycling than during walking, and tibialis anterior was less activated. The hip extensor muscles produced 27 per cent, hip flexors 4 per cent, knee extensors 39 per cent, knee flexors 10 per cent and ankle plantar flexors 20 per cent of the total positive mechanical work. Of the four parameters studied (workload, pedalling rate, saddle height, pedal foot position) workload was the most important adjustment factor for change of joint load and muscular activity. An increased pedalling rate increased the muscular activity in most of the muscles investigated, generally without changing the joint load. Increased saddle height decreased the maximum flexing knee load moment, but did not significantly change the flexing hip or dorsiflexing ankle load moment. Muscular activity in most of the muscles investigated was not generally changed by different saddle heights. Use of a posterior foot position instead of an anterior decreased the dorsiflexing ankle load moment, increased the gluteus medius and rectus femoris activity, and decreased soleus muscular activity but did not significantly change the hip or knee moments. It is suggested that cycling might be a useful exercise in the rehabilitation of patients with injuries to the anterior cruciate ligament, medial collateral ligament of the knee or achilles tendon.

9.   **Biomechanical considerations in patellofemoral joint rehabilitation**
       American Journal of Sports Medicine, Vol 21, Issue 3 438-444, 1993.
       LA Steinkamp, MF Dillingham, MD Markel, JA Hill and KR Kaufman
       Functional Rehabilitation and Sports Therapy, Palo Alto, CA 94306.

Patellofemoral joint biomechanics during leg press and leg extension exercises were compared in 20 normal subjects (10 men, 10 women) aged 18 to 45 years. Knee moment, patellofemoral joint **reaction force**, and patellofemoral joint stress were calculated for each subject at four knee flexion angles (0 degree, 30 degrees, 60 degrees, and 90 degrees) during leg press and leg extension exercises. All three parameters (knee moment, patellofemoral joint reaction force, and patellofemoral joint stress) were significantly greater in leg extension exercise than leg press exercise at 0 degree and 30 degrees of knee flexion ($P < 0.001$). At 60 degrees and 90 degrees of knee flexion, all three parameters were significantly greater in leg press exercise than leg extension exercise ($P < 0.001$). Patellofemoral joint stresses for leg press and leg extension exercises intersected at 48 degrees of knee flexion. This study demonstrates that patients with patellofemoral joint arthritis may tolerate rehabilitation with leg press exercise better than with leg extension exercise in functional ranges of motion because of lower patellofemoral joint stresses.

10.   **Muscle mechanics: adaptations with exercise-training.**
       Exerc Sport Sci Rev. 1996;24:427-73.
       Fitts RH, Widrick JJ.
       Department of Biology, Marquette University, Milwaukee, Wisconsin, USA.

       Based on the MHC isoform pattern, adult mammalian limb skeletal muscles contain two and, in some species, three types of fast fibers (Type IIa, IIx, and IIb), and one slow fiber (Type I). Slow muscles, such as the soleus, contain primarily the slow Type I fiber, whereas fast-twitch muscles are composed primarily of a mixture of the fast myosin isozymes. Force generation involves cross-bridge interaction and transition from a weakly bound, low-force state (AM-ADP-P(i)) to the strongly bound, high-force state (AM-ADP). This transition is thought to be rate limiting in terms of dP/dt, and the high-force state is the dominant cross-bridge form during a peak isometric contraction. Intact fast and slow skeletal muscles generate approximately the same amount of peak force (Po) of between 200 and 250 kN.m-2. However, the rate of transition from the low- to high-force state shows Ca2+ sensitivity and is 7-fold higher in fast-twitch, as compared to slow-twitch, skeletal muscle fibers. Fiber Vo or the maximal cross-bridge cycle rate is highly correlated with and thought to be dependent on the specific activity of the myosin or myofibrillar ATPase. The hierarchy for Vo is the Type IIb > IIx > IIa > I. This functional difference for the fast fiber types explains the higher Vo observed in the predominantly Type IIb SVL vs. the mixed fast Type IIa and IIb EDL muscle. A plot of Vo vs. species size demonstrates that an inverse relationship exists between Vo and body mass. From the standpoint of work capacity, the important property is power output. An analysis of individual muscles indicates that peak power is obtained at loads considerably below 50 per cent of Po. Individuals with a high percentage of fast-twitch fibers generate a greater torque and higher power at a given velocity than those with predominantly slow-twitch fibers. In humans, mean peak power occurred in a ratio of 10:5:1 for the Type IIb, IIa, and I fibers. The in vivo measurement of the torque-velocity relationship and Vmax in human muscle is difficult because of limitations inherent in the equipment used and the inability to study the large limb muscles independently. Nevertheless, the in vivo torque-velocity relationships are similar to those measured in vitro in animals. This observation suggests that little central nervous system inhibition exists and that healthy subjects are able to achieve maximal activation of their muscles. Although peak isometric tension is not dependent on fiber type distribution, a positive correlation exists between the percentage of fast fibers and peak torque output at moderate-to-high angular isokinetic velocities. Consequently, peak power output is substantially greater in subjects possessing a predominance of fast fibers. The mechanical properties of slow and fast muscles do adapt to programs of regular exercise. Endurance exercise training has been shown to increase the Vo of the slow soleus by 20 per cent. This increase could have been caused by either a small increase in all, or most, of the fibers, or to a conversion of a few fibers from slow to fast. Recently, the increase was shown to be caused by the former, as the individual slow Type I fibers of the **soleus** showed a 20 per cent increase in Vo, but there was little or no change in the percentage of fast fibers. The increased Vo was correlated with, and likely caused by, an increased fiber ATPase. We hypothesize that the increased ATPase and cross-bridge cycling speed might be attributable to an increased expression of fast MLCs in the slow Type I fibers (Fig. 14.10). This hypothesis is based on the fact that light chains have been shown to be involved in the power stroke, and removal of light chains depresses force and velocity. Regular endurance exercise training had no effect on fiber size, but with prolonged durations of daily training it depressed Po and peak power. When the training is maintained over prolonged periods, it may even induce atrophy of the slow Type I and fast Type IIa fibers.

11. **An in vivo strain gage study of elongation of the anterior cruciate ligament**
    American Journal of Sports Medicine, Vol. 13, Issue 1 22-26, 1985.
    CE Henning, MA Lynch and KR Glick Jr

    The purpose of this paper is to study the load-elongation characteristics of a Grade II sprain of the anterior cruciate ligament (ACL) at the time of local anesthesia arthroscopy. The data may be used to increase diagnostic and prognostic accuracy when evaluating Grade II ACL sprains and to structure properly a rehabilitation program following ACL injury. This report is based on the data from two in vivo strain gage studies of Grade II ACL sprains. Following instrumentation of the ligament, several events common to physical examination and rehabilitation programs were tested. The Lachman test produced greater elongation of the anteromedial fibers than did the anterior drawer or pivot shift test. A fairly high force of 80 pounds may be required by the examiner's hands to test satisfactorily the anteromedial fibers in the acutely injured large athlete. The proper order for a rehabilitation program should be crutch walking, cycling, walking, slow running, and faster running. Patients should be cautioned to run on a perfectly level surface. Cycling produced 7 per cent as much elongation as an 80 pound Lachman test, and the one leg half squat 21 per cent as much. Quadriceps rehabilitation can be done more safely using these exercises. Quadriceps exercises by knee extension against a 20 pound weight boot in the range of full extension to 22 degrees flexion created peak elongation of the anteromedial fibers ranging from 87 to 121 per cent of that produced by an 80 pound Lachman test. We recommend that quadriceps exercises and testing by knee extension through a full range of motion not be done during the first year following ACL injury or reconstruction.

12. **Intrinsic risk factors and athletic injuries.**
    Sports Med. 1990 Apr;9(4):205-15.
    Taimela S, Kujala UM, Osterman K.
    Paavo Nurmi Centre, University of Turku, Finland.

    The benefits of physical activity are widely known. However, the risk of a musculoskeletal injury is an unfavourable consequence in physical training.

Age, gender, injury history, body size, local anatomy and biomechanics, aerobic fitness, muscle strength, imbalance and tightness, ligamentous laxity, central motor control, psychological and psychosocial factors as well as general mental ability are factors in the predisposition to injury. Junior (15 to 16 years) and senior athletes seem to be at a higher risk of injury in many types of sport. However, the relationship between age and injuries apparently depends on both the type and intensity of activity practiced. The majority of injured athletes in many studies have been males. Men are, however, more likely to participate in vigorous exercise and sport and it is not known if men are at a generally higher risk of injury when the exposure is taken into account. Certain lesions, such as sprains, strains and dislocations, tend to recur. Previous injuries may necessarily not cause a repetition of injury if treated adequately, but certain individuals may be at a higher risk of injury due to injury-prone biological characteristics. Excessive height and weight have been shown to predispose to stress injuries in physical training. Idiopathic or acquired abnormalities in the anatomy or biomechanics in any joint may lead to a local injury. However, physical requirements vary widely between different types of activity and predisposition to injury due to anatomical or biomechanical factors seems to be characteristic for each type of exercise. Lack of fitness, muscle weakness, joint looseness and poor general flexibility have been suggested as factors in the outcome of athletic injuries but no definite conclusions can be made on the basis of the existing literature. Long simple reaction times to visual stimuli and long choice reaction times to visual stimuli have recently been related to musculoskeletal injuries. No exceptional personality dimension in injury proneness as a whole has been found and the results from specific groups cannot be extrapolated generally. Accumulation of life stress apparently predisposes to an athletic injury. Musculoskeletal injuries seem to be more common in subjects with lower scores in intelligence tests but no causation has been shown yet. Altogether, a complex network of risk factors for athletic injuries has been found. However, no prospective study including all the recognised injury risk factors has been presented in the literature.

13. Knee biomechanics of the dynamic squat exercise

Medicine & Science in Sports & Exercise. 33(1):127-141, January 2001.
Escamilla, Rafael F.

Purpose: Because a strong and stable knee is paramount to an athlete's or patient's success, an understanding of knee biomechanics while performing the squat is helpful to therapists, trainers, sports medicine physicians, researchers, coaches, and athletes who are interested in closed kinetic chain exercises, knee rehabilitation, and training for sport. The purpose of this review was to examine knee biomechanics during the dynamic squat exercise.

Methods: Tibiofemoral shear and compressive forces, patellofemoral compressive force, knee muscle activity, and knee stability were reviewed and discussed relative to athletic performance, injury potential, and rehabilitation.

Results: Low to moderate posterior shear forces, restrained primarily by the posterior cruciate ligament (PCL), were generated throughout the squat for all knee flexion angles. Low anterior shear forces, restrained primarily by the anterior cruciate ligament (ACL), were generated between 0 and 60 [degrees] knee flexion. Patellofemoral compressive forces and tibiofemoral compressive and shear forces progressively increased as the knees flexed and decreased as the knees extended, reaching peak values near maximum knee flexion. Hence, training the squat in the functional range between 0 and 50 [degrees] knee flexion may be appropriate for many knee rehabilitation patients, because knee forces were minimum in the functional range. Quadriceps, hamstrings, and gastrocnemius activity generally increased as knee flexion increased, which supports athletes with healthy knees performing the parallel squat (thighs parallel to ground at maximum knee flexion) between 0 and 100 [degrees] knee flexion. Furthermore, it was demonstrated that the parallel squat was not injurious to the healthy knee.

Conclusions: The squat was shown to be an effective exercise to employ during cruciate ligament or patellofemoral rehabilitation. For athletes with healthy knees, performing the parallel squat is recommended over the deep squat, because injury potential to the menisci and cruciate and collateral ligaments may increase with the deep squat. The squat does not compromise knee stability, and can enhance stability if performed correctly. Finally, the squat can be effective in developing hip, knee, and ankle musculature, because moderate to high quadriceps, hamstrings, and gastrocnemius activity were produced during the squat.

14. Gait biomechanics are not normal after anterior cruciate ligament reconstruction and accelerated rehabilitation

Medicine and Science in Sports and Exercise. 30(10):1481-1488, October 1998.

Devita, Paul; Hortobagyi, Tibor; Barrier, Jason

Purpose: Accelerated rehabilitation for anterior cruciate ligament (ACL) injury and reconstruction surgery is designed to return injured people to athletic activities in approximately 6 months. The small amount of empirical data on this population suggests, however, that the torque at the knee joint may not return until 22 months after surgery during walking and even longer during running. Although the rehabilitation has ended and individuals have returned to preinjury activities, gait mechanics appear to be abnormal at the end of accelerated programs. The purpose of this study was to compare lower extremity joint kinematics, kinetics, and energetics between individuals having undergone ACL reconstruction and accelerated rehabilitation and healthy individuals.

Methods: Eight ACL-injured and 22 healthy subjects were tested. Injured subjects were tested 3 wk and 6 months (the end of rehabilitation) after surgery. **Ground reaction force** and kinematic data were combined with inverse dynamics to predict sagittal plane joint torques and powers from which angular impulse and work were derived.

Results: The difference in all kinematic variables between the two tests for the ACL group averaged 38 per cent (all P < 0.05). The kinematics were not different between the ACL group after rehabilitation and healthy subjects. Angular impulses and work averaged 100 per cent difference for all joints (all P < 0.05) between tests for the ACL group. After rehabilitation, the differences between injured and healthy groups in angular impulse and work at both the hip and knee remained large and averaged 52 per cent (all P < 0.05).

Conclusions: Results indicated that after reconstruction surgery and accelerated rehabilitation for ACL injury, humans walk with normal kinematic patterns but continue to use altered joint torque and power patterns.

15. Comparison of tibiofemoral joint forces during open-kinetic-chain and closed-kinetic-chain exercises

The Journal of Bone and Joint Surgery, Vol 75, Issue 5 732-739, 1993.
GE Lutz, RA Palmitier, KN An and EY Chao
Biomechanics Laboratory, Mayo Clinic, Rochester, Minnesota.

The purpose of this study was to analyze forces at the tibiofemoral joint during open and closed-kinetic-chain exercises. Five healthy subjects performed maximum isometric contractions at 30, 60, and 90 degrees of knee flexion during open-kinetic-chain extension, open-kinetic-chain flexion, and closed-kinetic-chain exercises. Electromyographic activity of the quadriceps and hamstrings, as well as load and torque-cell data, were recorded. Tibiofemoral shear and compression forces were calculated with use of a two-dimensional biomechanical model. The results showed that, during the open-kinetic-chain extension exercise, maximum posterior **shear forces** (the resisting forces to anterior drawer) of 285 +/- 120 newtons (mean and standard deviation) occurred at 30 degrees of knee flexion and maximum anterior shear forces (the resisting forces to posterior drawer) of 1780 +/- 699 newtons occurred at 90 degrees of knee flexion. The closed-kinetic-chain exercise produced significantly less posterior shear force at all angles when compared with the open-kinetic-chain extension exercise. In addition, the closed-kinetic-chain exercise produced significantly less anterior shear force at all angles except 30 degrees when compared with the open-kinetic-chain flexion exercise ($p < 0.05$). Analysis of tibiofemoral compression forces and electromyographic recruitment patterns revealed that the closed-kinetic-chain exercise produced significantly greater compression forces and increased muscular co-contraction at the same angles at which the open-kinetic-chain exercises produced maximum shear forces and minimum muscular co-contraction.

16.   Musculoskeletal adaptations to weightlessness and development of effective countermeasures.
Medicine and Science in Sports and Exercise. 28(10):1247-1253, October 1996.

Baldwin, Kenneth M. (Co-chair); White, Timothy p. (Co-chair); Arnaud, Sara B.; Edgerton, V. Reggie; Kraemer, William J.; Kram, Rodger; Raab-cullen, Diane; Snow, Christine M.

A Research Roundtable, organized by the American College of Sports Medicine with sponsorship from the National Aeronautics and Space Administration, met in November 1995 to define research strategies for effective exercise countermeasures to weightlessness. Exercise was considered both independently of, and in conjunction with, other therapeutic modalities (e.g., pharmacological, nutritional, hormonal, and growth-related factors) that could prevent or minimize the structural and functional deficits involving skeletal muscle and bone in response to chronic exposure to weightlessness, as well as return to Earth baseline function if a degree of loss is inevitable. Musculoskeletal deficits and countermeasures are described with respect to: (1) muscle and connective tissue atrophy and localized bone loss, (2) reductions in motor performance, (3) potential proneness to injury of hard and soft tissues, and (4) probable interaction between **muscle atrophy** and cardiovascular alterations that contribute to the postural hypotension observed immediately upon return from space flight. In spite of a variety of countermeasure protocols utilized previously involving largely endurance types of exercise, there is presently no activity-specific countermeasure(s) that adequately prevent or reduce musculoskeletal deficiencies. It seems apparent that countermeasure exercises that have a greater resistance element, as compared to endurance activities, may prove beneficial to the musculoskeletal system. Many questions remain for scientific investigation to identify efficacious countermeasure protocols, which will be imperative with the emerging era of long-term space flight.

17. **In vivo muscle fibre behaviour during counter-movement exercise in humans reveals a significant role for tendon elasticity**

Journal of Physiology (2002), 540.2, pp. 635-646, 2002

Y. Kawakami, T. Muraoka, S. Ito, H. Kanehisa and T. Fukunaga

Department of Life Science (Sports Science), University of Tokyo, Komaba, Tokyo 153-8902, Japan

Six men performed a single ankle plantar flexion exercise in the supine position with the maximal effort with counter movement (CM, plantar flexion preceded by dorsiflexion) and without counter movement (NoCM, plantar flexion only) produced by a sliding table that controlled applied load to the ankle (40 per cent of the maximal voluntary force). The reaction force at the foot and ankle joint angle were measured using a force plate and a **goniometer**, respectively. From real-time **ultrasonography** of the gastrocnemius medialis muscle during the movement, the fascicle length was determined. The estimated peak force, average power, and work at the Achilles' tendon during the plantar flexion phase in CM were significantly greater than those in NoCM. In CM, in the dorsiflexion phase, fascicle length initially increased with little electromyographic activity, then remained constant while the whole muscle-tendon unit lengthened, before decreasing in the final plantar flexion phase. In NoCM, fascicle length decreased throughout the movement and the fascicle length at the onset of movement was longer than that of the corresponding phase in CM. It was concluded that during CM muscle fibres optimally work almost isometrically, by leaving the task of storing and releasing elastic energy for enhancing exercise performance to the tendon.

18. **Glucose, exercise and insulin: emerging concepts**

Journal of Physiology, 535.2, pp. 313-322, 2001.

Erik A. Richter, Wim Derave * and Jørgen F. P. Wojtaszewski

Copenhagen Muscle Research Centre, Department of Human Physiology, Institute of Exercise and Sports Sciences, University of Copenhagen, DK-2100 Copenhagen, Denmark and * Laboratory of Exercise Physiology and Biomechanics, Faculty of Physical Education and Physiotherapy, Katholieke Universiteit Leuven, B-3001 Leuven, Belgium.

Physical exercise induces a rapid increase in the rate of glucose uptake in the contracting skeletal muscles. The enhanced membrane glucose transport capacity is caused by a recruitment of glucose transporters (GLUT4) to the sarcolemma and t-tubules. This review summarises the recent progress in the understanding of signals that trigger GLUT4 translocation in contracting muscle. The possible involvement of calcium, protein kinase C (PKC), nitric oxide (NO), glycogen and AMP-activated protein kinase (AMPK) are discussed. Furthermore, the possible mechanisms behind the well-described improvement of insulin action on glucose uptake and glycogen synthase activity in the post-exercise period is discussed. It is concluded that both during and following muscle contractions, glycogen emerges as an important modulator of signalling events in glucose metabolism.

19.   **Treadmill Aerobic Exercise Training Reduces the Energy Expenditure and Cardiovascular Demands of Hemiparetic Gait in Chronic Stroke Patients**
Stroke. 1997;28:326-330.

R.F. Macko, MD; C.A. DeSouza, PhD; L.D. Tretter, BS; K.H. Silver, MD; G.V. Smith, PhD; P.A. Anderson, PhD; Naomi Tomoyasu, PhD; P. Gorman, MD D.R. Dengel, PhD

The Neurology and Geriatrics Services and the Geriatrics Research, Education, and Clinical Center, Baltimore (Md) Department of Veterans Affairs Medical Center (R.F.M., L.D.T., K.H.S., N.T.); Departments of Neurology (R.F.M., K.H.S., P.G.), Physical Therapy (G.V.S., P.A.A.), and Medicine, Division of Gerontology (R.F.M., K.H.S.), University of Maryland School of Medicine, Baltimore; Department of Kinesiology, University of Colorado at Boulder (C.A.D.); and Division of Geriatrics and the Geriatrics Research, Education, and Clinical Center, Ann Arbor (Mich) Department of Veterans Affairs Medical Center (D.R.D.).

Correspondence to Richard Macko, MD, Department of Neurology, University of Maryland School of Medicine, 22 N Greene St, Baltimore, MD 21201-1595.

Background and Purpose : Elevated energy costs of hemiparetic gait contribute to functional disability after stroke, particularly in physically deconditioned older patients. We investigated the effects of 6 months of treadmill aerobic exercise training on the energy expenditure and cardiovascular demands of submaximal effort ambulation in stroke patients with chronic hemiparetic gait.

Methods : Nine older stroke patients with chronic hemiparetic gait were enrolled in a 6-month program of low-intensity aerobic exercise using a graded treadmill. Repeated measures of energy expenditure based on steady state oxygen consumption during a standardized 1-mph submaximal effort treadmill walking task were performed before and after training.

Results : Six months of exercise training produced significant reductions in energy expenditure (n=9; 3.40 ± 0.27 versus 2.72 ± 0.25 kcal/min [mean$\pm$SEM]; $P<.005$) during a given submaximal effort treadmill walking task. Repeated measures analysis in the subset of patients (n=8) tested at baseline and after

3 and 6 months revealed that reductions in energy expenditure were progressive (F=11.1; P<.02) and that exercise-mediated declines in both oxygen consumption (F=9.7; P<.02) and respiratory exchange ratio (F=13.4; P<.01) occurred in a strong linear pattern. These stroke patients could perform the same standardized submaximal exercise task at progressively lower heart rates after 3 months (96±4 versus 87±4 beats per minute) and 6 months of training (82±4 beats per minute; F=35.4; P<.002).

Conclusions : Six months of low-intensity **treadmill** endurance training produces substantial and progressive reductions in the energy expenditure and cardiovascular demands of walking in older patients with chronic hemiparetic stroke. This suggests that task-oriented aerobic exercise may improve functional mobility and the cardiovascular fitness profile in this population.

Key Words : cerebrovascular disorders • energy metabolism • exercise • hemiplegia • rehabilitation.

20. **Exercise and balance in aged women: a pilot controlled clinical trial.**
Arch Phys Med Rehabil. 1989 Feb;70(2):138-43.
Lichtenstein MJ, Shields SL, Shiavi RG, Burger C.
Department of Medicine, Vanderbilt University, Nashville, TN.

A pilot controlled trial was conducted to determine the feasibility of testing an exercise program as a means of improving balance in aged women. A random sample of 50 women more than 65 years old was recruited from two apartment buildings. The buildings were randomized to serve as exercise and control sites. The 24 exercisers did not differ significantly from the 26 controls except that they were better educated and had better vision. The median compliance was 85 per cent of requested sessions attended by the exercisers. Follow-up measures were obtained in 92 per cent and 81 per cent of the exercise and control groups, respectively. The outcome variables studied were changes in sway (areas and velocity of the center of force as measured using a biomechanics platform) in four stances with eyes open or closed, on two feet, or on one foot. After 16 weeks, in stances on one foot, exercisers had smaller areas compared to controls with eyes open, but larger areas with eyes closed. Subgroup analysis indicated that compliance with the exercise program was a determinant of degree of change in the area measures. The inconsistent effect of exercise on area measures of sway in this study may be due to (a) lack of statistical power to detect between-group differences, (b) inadequate compliance with the exercise program, (c) baseline differences between the two groups at randomization, and (d) ineffective or inadequate duration of the exercise program. We conclude that controlled clinical trials to study the effect of exercise on balance measures in community-dwelling elderly women are feasible.

21.   Applied Biomechanics of the Patella
Clinical Orthopaedics & Related Research. 389:9-14, August 2001.
Grelsamer, Ronald P. MD; Weinstein, Craig H. MD, MPH
Although numerous prominent orthopaedists of the twentieth century considered the patella to be useless, even detrimental, it now is clear that the patella serves an important biomechanical function. It is a complex lever that magnifies the moment arm of the extensor mechanism. The patellofemoral contact area (the fulcrum of the lever) shifts along a proximodistal axis through the knee's arc of motion. As the knee flexes, the force within the patellar tendon diminishes relative to that of the quadriceps tendon. One's interpretation of patellar tracking is dependent on the choice of coordinates. When assessing tracking by way of anatomic coordinates, patellas are seen to be slightly lateralized at 0[degrees] flexion and to follow similar paths down the trochlea. The tracking pattern is the result of an elaborate interplay between the quadriceps muscles, patellofemoral ligaments, the geometry of the trochlea, and the quadriceps angle. The articular cartilage of the patella is the thickest in the human body and does not follow the contour of the subchondral bone. Patellar cartilage is softer and more permeable than that of the trochlea. It is insensate. In size, nature, and number, the facets of the patellar articulation vary from person to person.

22.   No effects of oral ribose supplementation on repeated maximal exercise and de novo ATP resynthesis
J Appl Physiol, Vol. 91, Issue 5, 2275-2281, November 2001.
B. Op 't Eijnde1, M. Van Leemputte1, F. Brouns2,4, G. J. Van Der Vusse3, V. Labarque1, M. Ramaekers1, R. Van Schuylenberg1, P. Verbessem1, H. Wijnen1, and P. Hespel1
1 Exercise Physiology and Biomechanics Laboratory, Department of Kinesiology, Faculty of Physical Education and Physiotherapy, Katholieke Universiteit Leuven, B-3001 Heverlee; 2 Health and Nutrition Group, Eridania Béghin-Say, Vilvoorde, Belgium; and 3 Department of Physiology, Cardiovascular Research Institute, and 4 Department of Human Biology, Maastricht University, NL-6200 MD, Maastricht, The Netherlands

A double-blind randomized study was performed to evaluate the effect of oral ribose supplementation on repeated maximal exercise and ATP recovery after intermittent maximal muscle contractions. Muscle power output was measured during dynamic knee extensions with the right leg on an isokinetic dynamometer before (pretest) and after (posttest) a 6-day training period in conjunction with ribose (R, 4 doses/day at 4 g/dose, n = 10) or placebo (P, n = 9) intake. The exercise protocol consisted of two bouts (A and B) of maximal contractions, separated by 15 s of rest. Bouts A and B consisted of 15 series of 12 contractions each, separated by a 60-min rest period. During the training period, the subjects performed the same exercise protocol twice per day, with 3-5 h of rest between exercise sessions. Blood samples were collected before and after bouts A and B and 24 h after bout B. Knee-extension power outputs were ~10 per cent higher in the posttest than in the pretest but were similar between P and R for all contraction series. The exercise increased blood lactate and plasma ammonia concentrations ($P < 0.05$), with no significant differences between P and R at any time. After a 6-wk washout period, in a subgroup of subjects (n = 8), needle-biopsy samples were taken from the vastus lateralis before, immediately after, and 24 h after an exercise bout similar to the pretest. ATP and total adenine **nucleotide content** were decreased by ~25 and 20 per cent immediately after and 24 h after exercise in P and R. Oral ribose supplementation with 4-g doses four times a day does not beneficially impact on postexercise muscle ATP recovery and maximal intermittent exercise performance.

Key Words: ergogenics; adenine nucleotides; ATP; ammonia; purine salvage.

23. **Muscle damage from eccentric exercise: mechanism, mechanical signs, adaptation and clinical applications**
Journal of Physiology (2001), 537.2, pp. 333-345, 2001
U. Proske and D. L. Morgan *
Department of Physiology and * Department of Electrical and Computer Systems Engineering, Monash University, Melbourne, Australia

In eccentric exercise the contracting muscle is forcibly lengthened; in concentric exercise it shortens. While concentric contractions initiate movements, eccentric contractions slow or stop them. A unique feature of eccentric exercise is that untrained subjects become stiff and sore the day afterwards because of damage to muscle fibres. This review considers two possible initial events as responsible for the subsequent damage, damage to the excitation-contraction coupling system and disruption at the level of the sarcomeres. Other changes seen after eccentric exercise, a fall in active tension, shift in optimum length for active tension, and rise in passive tension, are seen, on balance, to favour sarcomere disruption as the starting point for the damage. As well as damage to muscle fibres there is evidence of disturbance of muscle sense organs and of proprioception. A second period of exercise, a week after the first, produces much less damage. This is the result of an adaptation process. One proposed mechanism for the adaptation is an increase in sarcomere number in muscle fibres. This leads to a secondary shift in the muscle's optimum length for active tension. The ability of muscle to rapidly adapt following the damage from eccentric exercise raises the possibility of clinical applications of mild eccentric exercise, such as for protecting a muscle against more major injuries.

24.   The biomechanics of adiposity – structural and functional limitations of obesity and implications for movement
*obesity reviews,*Volume 3,Page 35 ,February 2002.
A. P. Hills1, E. M. Hennig2, N. M. Byrne3 and J. R. Steele4

Obesity is a significant health problem and the incidence of the condition is increasing at an alarming rate worldwide. Despite significant advances in the knowledge and understanding of the multifactorial nature of the condition, many questions regarding the specific consequences of the disease remain unanswered. For example, there is a dearth of information pertaining to the structural and functional limitations imposed by overweight and obesity. A limited number of studies to date have considered plantar pressures under the feet of obese vs. non-obese, the influence of foot structure on performance, gait characteristics of obese children and adults, and relationships between obesity and osteoarthritis. A better appreciation of the implications of increased levels of body weight and/or body fat on movement capabilities of the **obese** would provide an enhanced opportunity to offer more meaningful support in the prevention, treatment and management of the condition.

25.   Electromyographic Evaluation of Closed and Open Kinetic Chain Knee Rehabilitation Exercises
Athl Train. 1993 Spring; 28(1): 23, 26, 28-30.
Victoria L. Graham, MS, ATC

Head Athletic Trainer in Women's Athletics at Ball State University, Muncie, IN 47306.

Gale M. Gehlsen, PhD

Gale M. Gehlsen is Professor and Director at Biomechanics Laboratory, Ball State University.

Jennifer A. Edwards, MA

Jennifer A. Edwards is Instructor in Biomechanics and Anatomy at Department of Physical Education, Ball State University.

The use of closed kinetic chain knee rehabilitation exercises has been advocated in recent years. The primary reason cited for employing closed kinetic chain exercises is that these exercises result in less anteroposterior (A/P) shear force at the knee joint, when compared with traditionally used open kinetic chain exercises. The purpose of this study was to determine the electromyographical (EMG) activity ratio of quadriceps to hamstrings occurring in the following exercises: unilateral one quarter squats, leg extensions (N-K Table), lateral step-ups, and movements on the Fitter (Fitter International, Inc), Stair-master 4000 (Randal Sports/Medical Products, Inc), and slideboard. Ten female student-athletes participated in this study. EMG surface electrodes were applied over the rectus femoris and biceps femoris muscles. The subjects completed three maximum isometric contractions for both muscle groups to obtain baseline EMG data. They then performed repetitions of each exercise. These movements were videotaped simultaneously with a stationary shuttered video camera operating at 30 Hz. A computer program was used to analyze the videotaped performances for knee joint range of motion (ROM). Three trials of data were averaged. Baseline EMG activity was used to determine percentage of maximum EMG activity for each exercise. There were significant differences (p.<01) among the exercises for the following dependent variables: ROM, maximum angle, percent of maximum contraction, time of contraction, and total EMG (EMG area under the curve). This study suggests that the five closed kinetic chain exercises studied result in minimal A/P shear forces at the knee joint.

26. Hamstrings—an anterior cruciate ligament protagonist. An in vitro study

American Journal of Sports Medicine, Vol 21, Issue 2 231-237, 1993.
RC More, BT Karras, R Neiman, D Fritschy, SL Woo and DM Daniel
Department of Orthopedic Surgery, Kaiser Hospital, San Diego, California 92120.

A cadaveric model that incorporated quadriceps and hamstrings muscle loads was developed to simulate the squat exercise. The addition of hamstrings load affected knee kinematics in two ways. First, anterior tibial translation during flexion ("femoral roll-back") was significantly reduced (P = 0.003) and second, internal tibial rotation during flexion was reduced (P = 0.008). However, quadriceps force was unaffected by the addition of hamstrings load. Thus, it seems likely that hamstrings muscle activity that has been observed in vivo during a squat probably functions synergistically with the anterior cruciate ligament to provide anterior knee stability. After the ACL was sectioned, anterior tibial translation was significantly increased during the squat (P = 0.04). The anterior cruciate ligament was then reconstructed using a graft instrumented with a load cell. During passive motion, maximal graft tension was at full extension. During simulated squat exercise, the addition of hamstrings caused a significant decrease in graft load (P = 0.006). During the squat, maximal graft tension was at full extension, and was equal to the graft tension at full passive extension. Thus, the squat exercise may be useful in the early stages of anterior cruciate ligament rehabilitation.

27.   Effects of different dropping intensities on fascicle and tendinous tissue behavior during stretch-shortening cycle exercise

J Appl Physiol, 96: 848-852, 2004.

Masaki Ishikawa and Paavo V. Komi

Neuromuscular Research Center, Department of Biology of Physical Activity, University of Jyväskylä, 40100 Jyväskylä, Finland

This study examined whether the elasticity of the tendinous tissues plays an important role in human locomotion by improving the power output and efficiency of skeletal muscle. Ten subjects performed one-leg **drop jump**s (DJ) from different dropping heights with a constant rebound height. The **fascicle length** of the vastus lateralis muscle was measured by using real-time ultrasonography during DJ. In the braking phase of the DJ, fascicle lengthening decreased and the tendinous tissue lengthening increased with increased dropping intensity. In the subsequent push-off phase, the shortening of tendinous tissues increased with higher dropping intensity. The averaged electromyographic activities of the preactivation and braking phases increased and those of the push-off phase decreased as the drop height was increased. With higher dropping height but constant submaximal rebound jump, the stretched tendinous tissue length increased with less stretched fascicle during the braking phase. In the subsequent push-off phase, the recoil of tendinous tissues became greater. These results suggest that the increased prestretch intensity has considerable influence on the process of storage and subsequent recoil of the elastic energy during the stretch-shortening cycle action.

Key Words: elastic recoil; **ultrasonography**; drop jump.

28.   Effects of technique variations on knee biomechanics during the squat and leg press.

Medicine and Science in Sports and Exercise. 33(9):1552-1566, September 2001.

Escamilla, Rafael F.; Fleisig, Glenn s.; Zheng, Naiquan; Lander, Jeffery E.; Barrentine, Steven W.; Andrews, James R.; Bergemann, Brian W.; Moorman, Claude T. Lii

Purpose: The specific aim of this project was to quantify knee forces and muscle activity while performing squat and leg press exercises with technique variations.

Methods: Ten experienced male lifters performed the squat, a high foot placement leg press (LPH), and a low foot placement leg press (LPL) employing a wide stance (WS), narrow stance (NS), and two foot angle positions (feet straight and feet turned out 30[degrees]).

Results: No differences were found in muscle activity or knee forces between foot angle variations. The squat generated greater quadriceps and hamstrings activity than the LPH and LPL, the WS-LPH generated greater hamstrings activity than the NS-LPH, whereas the NS squat produced greater gastrocnemius activity than the WS squat. No ACL forces were produced for any exercise variation. Tibiofemoral (TF) compressive forces, PCL tensile forces, and patellofemoral (PF) compressive forces were generally greater in the squat than the LPH and LPL, and there were no differences in knee forces between the LPH and LPL. For all exercises, the WS generated greater PCL tensile forces than the NS, the NS produced greater TF and PF compressive forces than the WS during the LPH and LPL, whereas the WS generated greater TF and PF compressive forces than the NS during the squat. For all exercises, muscle activity and knee forces were generally greater in the knee extending phase than the knee flexing phase.

Conclusions: The greater muscle activity and knee forces in the squat compared with the LPL and LPH implies the squat may be more effective in muscle development but should be used cautiously in those with PCL and PF disorders, especially at greater knee flexion angles. Because all forces increased with knee flexion, training within the functional 0-50[degrees] range may be efficacious for those whose goal is to minimize knee forces. The lack of ACL forces implies that all exercises may be effective during ACL rehabilitation.

29. Vagal modulation of the heart and central hemodynamics during handgrip exercise

Am J Physiol Heart Circ Physiol, 278: H1648-H1652, 2000.

Heidi A. Kluess, Robert H. Wood, and Michael A. Welsch

Department of Kinesiology, Louisiana State University, Baton Rouge, Louisiana 70813

Blood pressure and continuous electrocardiogram recordings were obtained from 12 participants during spontaneous breathing (SB1), dynamic handgrip exercise at 20 per cent (HG20) of maximal voluntary contraction (MVC), and spontaneous breathing (SB2) and dynamic handgrip exercise at 60 per cent (HG60) of MVC. Repeated-measures ANOVAs were used to examine the effects of the exercise conditions on mean arterial pressure (MAP), on mean standard deviation (SDNN), and on the coefficient of variation of R-R intervals. The mean R-R interval responded to exercise in an intensity-dependent manner. SDNN decreased with exercise but was not intensity dependent. Coefficient of variation decreased during HG20, and MAP increased following HG60. These data are consistent with the notion that changes in cardiovascular function with low-intensity exercise are primarily mediated by parasympathetic withdrawal, and as exercise intensity increases, additional cardiovascular reactivity is mediated by increased sympathetic outflow. The change in the coefficient of variation from rest to exercise was unique in comparison to the changes in SDNN, and this merits further investigation.

Key Words: heart rate variability; autonomic; hemodynamic.

30.   **In vitro modeling of human tibial strains during exercise in micro-gravity.**
J Biomech.;34(5):693-8, May 2001.
Peterman MM, Hamel AJ, Cavanagh PR, Piazza SJ, Sharkey NA.
Center for Locomotion Studies, 29 Recreation Building, Pennsylvania State University, University Park, PA 16802-5702, USA.

Prolonged exposure to micro-gravity causes substantial bone loss (Leblanc et al., Journal of Bone Mineral Research 11 (1996) S323) and treadmill exercise under gravity replacement loads (GRLs) has been advocated as a countermeasure. To date, the magnitudes of GRLs employed for locomotion in space have been substantially less than the loads imposed in the earthbound 1G environment, which may account for the poor performance of locomotion as an intervention. The success of future treadmill interventions will likely require GRLs of greater magnitude. It is widely held that mechanical tissue strain is an important intermediary signal in the transduction pathway linking the external loading environment to bone maintenance and functional adaptation; yet, to our knowledge, no data exist linking alterations in external skeletal loading to alterations in bone strain. In this preliminary study, we used unique cadaver simulations of micro-gravity locomotion to determine relationships between localized tibial bone strains and external loading as a means to better predict the efficacy of future exercise interventions proposed for bone maintenance on orbit. Bone strain magnitudes in the distal tibia were found to be linearly related to ground reaction force magnitude ($R(2)>0.7$). Strain distributions indicated that the primary mode of tibial loading was in bending, with little variation in the neutral axis over the stance phase of gait. The greatest strains, as well as the greatest strain sensitivity to altered external loading, occurred within the anterior crest and posterior aspect of the tibia, the sites furthest removed from the neutral axis of bending. We established a technique for estimating local strain magnitudes from external loads, and equations for predicting strain during simulated micro-gravity walking are presented.

31.   Effects of resistance training on selected indexes of immune function in elderly women

J Appl Physiol, Vol. 86, Issue 6, 1905-1913, June 1999.

M. G. Flynn1, M. Fahlman2, W. A. Braun3, C. P. Lambert3, L. E. Bouillon3, P. G. Brolinson4, and C. W. Armstrong3

1 Wastl Human Performance Laboratory, Purdue University, West Lafayette, Indiana 47907; 2 Wayne State University, Detroit, Michigan 48201; 3 Exercise Physiology and Applied Biomechanics Laboratories, The University of Toledo, Toledo; and 4 Northwest Ohio Center for Sports Medicine, The Toledo Hospital, Toledo, Ohio 43606

Women aged 67-84 yr were randomly assigned to either resistance exercise (RE, n = 15) or control group (C, n = 14). RE group completed 10 wk of resistance training, whereas C group maintained normal activity. Blood samples were obtained from the RE group (at the same time points as for resting C) at rest, immediately after resistance exercise, and 2 h after exercise before (week 0) and after (week 10) training. Mononuclear cell (CD3+, CD3+CD4+, CD3+CD8+, CD19+, and CD3_CD16+CD56+) number, lymphocyte proliferative (LP) response to mitogen, natural cell-mediated cytotoxicity (NCMC), and serum cortisol levels were determined. Strength increased significantly in RE subjects (per centchange 8-repetition maximum = 148 per cent). No significant group, exercise time, or training effects were found for CD3+, CD3+CD4+, or CD3+CD8+ cells, but there was a significant exercise time effect for CD3CD16+CD56+ cells. LP response was not different between groups, across exercise time, or after training. NCMC was increased immediately after exercise for RE subjects at week 0 and for RE and C groups at week 10. The week 0 and week 10 NCMC values were above baseline for both RE and C groups 2 h after exercise. In conclusion, acute resistance exercise did not result in postexercise suppression of NCMC or LP, and 10 wk of resistance training did not influence resting immune measures in women aged 67-84 yr.

Key Words: muscle strength; aging; host defense; natural killer cells.

32.   Kinematic and Electromyographic Analysis of Elbow Flexion During Inertial Exercise

J Athl Train. 1995 September; 30(3): 254–258.

James E. Tracy, MS, PT, ATC, CSCS

Clinical Assistant Professor of Physical Therapy at East Carolina University, Greenville, NC 27858-4353.

Shuchi Obuchi, MS, PT

Shuchi Obuchi is Graduate Student at Department of Physical Therapy, Georgia State University, Atlanta, GA.

Ben Johnson, PhD

Ben Johnson is Assistant Professor of Biomechanics at Georgia State University.

Inertial exercise protocols are currently used clinically to improve and restore normal muscle function even though research to substantiate their effectiveness cannot be cited in the literature. The purpose of this study was to compare simultaneous kinematic and electromyographic (EMG) data obtained from 12 subjects during elbow flexion on the Impulse Inertial Exercise System. Testing sessions consisted of inertial exercise performed using phasic and tonic techniques with loads of: a) 0 kg, b) 2.27 kg, c) 4.54 kg, d) 6.80 kg, e) 9.07 kg. Greater peak angular velocities, peak platform accelerations (change in velocity of platform during elbow flexion), mean and peak triceps brachii muscle EMG activity, and less range of motion were observed during phasic exercise. There was also a general trend for peak angular velocities and peak platform acceleration to increase as the load decreased. No significant difference in mean or peak EMG activity of the biceps brachii muscle was seen between techniques. Clinicians and athletic trainers using inertial exercise should consider both the exercise technique and load characteristics when designing protocols to meet the specific needs of patients.

33. Lower extremity muscle activation during horizontal and uphill running

J Appl Physiol, Vol. 83, Issue 6, 2073-2079, December 1997.

Mark A. Sloniger, Kirk J. Cureton, Barry M. Prior, and Ellen M. Evans

Department of Exercise Science, The University of Georgia, Athens, Georgia 30602-6554.

To provide more comprehensive information on the extent and pattern of muscle activation during running, we determined lower extremity muscle activation by using exercise-induced contrast shifts in magnetic resonance (MR) images during horizontal and uphill high-intensity (115 per cent of peak oxygen uptake) running to exhaustion (2.0-3.9 min) in 12 young women. The mean percentage of muscle volume activated in the right lower extremity was significantly ($P < 0.05$) greater during uphill (73 ± 7 per cent) than during horizontal (67 ± 8 per cent) running. The percentage of 13 individual muscles or groups activated varied from 41 to 90 per cent during horizontal running and from 44 to 83 per cent during uphill running. During horizontal running, the muscles or groups most activated were the adductors (90 ± 5 per cent), semitendinosus (86 ± 13 per cent), gracilis (76 ± 20 per cent), biceps femoris (76 ± 12 per cent), and semimembranosus (75 ± 12 per cent). During **uphill** running, the muscles most activated were the adductors (83 ± 8 per cent), biceps femoris (79 ± 7 per cent), gluteal group (79 ± 11 per cent), gastrocnemius (76 ± 15 per cent), and vastus group (75 ± 13 per cent). Compared with horizontal running, uphill running required considerably greater activation of the vastus group (23 per cent) and soleus (14 per cent) and less activation of the rectus femoris (29 per cent), gracilis (18 per cent), and semitendinosus (17 per cent). We conclude that during high-intensity horizontal and uphill running to exhaustion, lasting 2-3 min, muscles of the lower extremity are not maximally activated, suggesting there is a limit to the extent to which additional muscle mass recruitment can be utilized to meet the demand for force and energy. Greater total muscle activation during exhaustive uphill than during horizontal running is achieved through an altered pattern of muscle activation that involves increased use of some muscles and less use of others.

Key Words: exercise; magnetic resonance imaging; skeletal muscle function.

34. Desmin cytoskeletal modifications after a bout of eccentric exercise in the rat

Am J Physiol Regul Integr Comp Physiol, Vol. 283, Issue 4, R958-R963, October 2002.

Ilona A. Barash1, David Peters1, Jan Fridén2, Gordon J. Lutz1, and Richard L. Lieber1

1 Departments of Orthopaedics and Bioengineering, and the Biomedical Sciences Graduate Group, University of California and Veterans Affairs Medical Centers, San Diego, California 92161; and 2 Department of Hand Surgery, Sahlgrenska University Hospital, SE405 30 Göteborg, Sweden

Desmin content and immunohistochemical appearance were measured in tibialis anterior muscles of rats subjected to a single bout of 30 eccentric contractions (ECs). Ankle torque was measured before EC and at various recovery times, after which immunohistochemical and immunoblot analyses were performed. Torque decreased by ~50 per cent immediately after EC and fully recovered 168 h later (P < 0.001). Loss of desmin staining was maximal 12 h after EC and recovered by 72 h. Immunoblots unexpectedly demonstrated a significant increase in the desmin-to-actin ratio by 72 h after EC (P < 0.01) and was still increasing after 168 h (P < 0.0001). These data demonstrate a relatively rapid qualitative loss of desmin immunostaining immediately after a single EC bout but a tremendous quantitative increase in desmin content 72-168 h later. This dynamic restructuring of the muscle's intermediate filament system may be involved in the mechanism of EC-induced muscle injury and may provide a structural explanation for the protective effects observed in muscle after a single EC bout.

Key Words: intermediate filaments; muscle injury; calpain; cytoskeleton; biomechanics

35. **The effect of exercise and anabolic steroids on the mechanical properties and crimp morphology of the rat tendon**
American Journal of Sports Medicine, Vol 16, Issue 2 153-158, 1988.
TO Wood, PH Cooke and AE Goodship
Comparative Orthopaedic Research Group, University of Bristol, England.

The administration of anabolic steroids is believed to be widespread among athletes, but convincing evidence relating to the beneficial effect of such compounds on collagenous structures of the locomotor system is not available. Since it has not been possible to analyze relevant human tissue, an animal model was used to investigate the change in particular mechanical and morphological properties of rat tendon after a period of controlled exercise, with or without anabolic steroid supplementation. A significant difference (P less than 0.001) was found between the crimp angles and lengths of collagen fibrils and theoretical toe limit strains of the four groups under study. No other significant differences (P greater than 0.05) were observed. Controlled exercise and anabolic steroid administration produced the greatest change in crimp parameters and the largest theoretical toe limit strain. This implies that muscle contraction will be greater for a given stress and thus alter the normal biomechanics of limb movement. Further studies are required to determine more definitively the effects of anabolic steroids on a connective tissue such as tendon.

36. **Designing Exercise Regimens to Increase Bone Strength**
Exercise and Sport Sciences Reviews. 31(1):45-50, January 2003. *Turner, Charles H. 1; **Robling, Alexander G. 2***

Exercise is a very effective way to strengthen bones, particularly during childhood and adolescence. A collection of studies from the clinic and laboratory have provided new insights into how bone building effects of exercise can be maximized. From the available data we have calculated an "osteogenic index" for exercises.

37. **"Leg spring" characteristics and the aerobic demand of running.**
Medicine & Science in Sports & Exercise. 30(5):750-754, May 1998.
Heise, Gary D.; Martin, Philip E.

Purpose: By applying a simple, linear mass-spring model to running, the normalized leg spring stiffness (Kleg), the normalized effective vertical stiffness (Kvert), and the mass-specific mechanical power output of the spring (Psp) were determined and correlated with aerobic demand. The purpose of the study was to determine whether leg spring characteristics explain any of the interindividual variability observed in aerobic demand at a given submaximal running speed.

Methods: Recreational runners (N = 16) ran on a treadmill at 3.35 m[middle dot]s-1 for physiological measures and overground for biomechanical measures. The latter included a sagittal plane video record of the running motion and ground reaction data.

Results: We found no relationship between the aerobic demand of running and Kleg (r = -0.18), an inverse relationship between aerobic demand and Kvert (r = -0.48), and a positive correlation between aerobic demand and Psp (r = 0.45).

Conclusions: The inverse relationship between Kvert and aerobic demand indicates that less economical runners possess a more compliant running style during ground contact. This running style may place greater force demands on extensor musculature.

38. **Intramuscular pressure and electromyography as indexes of force during isokinetic exercise**
Journal of Applied Physiology, Vol. 74, Issue 6 2634-2640, 1993.

M. Aratow, R. E. Ballard, A. G. Crenshaw, J. Styf, D. E. Watenpaugh, N. J. Kahan and A. R. Hargens

Life Science Division, National Aeronautics and Space Administration Ames Research Center, Moffett Field, California 94035-1000.

A direct method for measuring force production of specific muscles during dynamic exercise is presently unavailable. Previous studies indicate that both intramuscular pressure (IMP) and electromyography (EMG) correlate linearly with muscle contraction force during isometric exercise. The objective of this study was to compare IMP and EMG as linear assessors of muscle contraction force during dynamic exercise. IMP and surface EMG activity were recorded during concentric and eccentric isokinetic plantarflexion and dorsiflexion of the ankle joint from the tibialis anterior (TA) and soleus (SOL) muscles of nine male volunteers (28-54 yr). Ankle torque was measured using a dynamometer, and IMP was measured via catheterization. IMP exhibited better linear correlation than EMG with ankle joint torque during concentric contractions of the SOL (IMP R2 = 0.97, EMG R2 = 0.81) and the TA (IMP R2 = 0.97, EMG R2 = 0.90), as well as during eccentric contractions (SOL: IMP R2 = 0.91, EMG R2 = 0.51; TA: IMP R2 = 0.94, EMG R2 = 0.73). IMP provides a better index of muscle contraction force than EMG during concentric and eccentric exercise through the entire range of torque. IMP reflects intrinsic mechanical properties of individual muscles, such as length-tension relationships, which EMG is unable to assess.

39.   Cartilage: from biomechanics to physical therapy
Ann Readapt Med Phys. 2001;44(5):259-67.
Rannou F, Poiraudeau S, Revel M

Objectives: To review the current knowledge about the relationship between physical activities, cartilage biology, osteoarthritis and rehabilitation.

Method: PubMed, Ovid, Cochrane Data base were interrogated for the period 1966-2000. Key words were: chondrocyte, cartilage, osteoarthritis, mechanical stimulation, exercises, physical therapy, rehabilitation. Were reviewed: the mechanical biology of the chondrocytes and the cartilage, the mechanisms of transduction, the me abolic response of the chondrocytes to mechanical stresses; the effects of physical activity and immobilization on the cartilage in animal models, the main studies on the epidemiology of limbs osteoarthritis and clinical trials on rehabilitation.

Results: In vitro studies have demonstrated that some molecules are involved in the transduction of mechanical stress into intracellular biological event. Chondrocytes and cartilage are sensitive to mechanical stress and cartilage extracellular matrix synthesis and degradation can be modulated by mechanical events. Applications of cyclic loads usually lead to an enhanced matrix synthesis while static loads usually decrease matrix production. In animal models, intensive physical activity or immobilization lead to cartilage alteration mimicking osteoarthritis. In human, intensive and prolonged physical activities are probably associated with hip and knee osteoarthritis. However, there is evidence that exercise therapy and continuous passive motion have beneficial effects on patients with knee or hip osteoarthritis. Fundamental and clinical studies are still needed to determine if exercise programs could have an effect on chondromodulation. Continuous passive motion could help, in the future, to better understand the relationship between mechanical stimulation and cartilage homeostasis.

Conclusion: Rehabilitation could be beneficial in the therapeutic management of limbs osteoarthritis. The protocols of rehabilitation should however be more evaluated in controlled trials.

40.   New in Vivo Measurements of Pressures in the Intervertebral Disc in Daily Life.

Spine. 24(8):755-762, April 15, 1999.

Wilke, Hans-Joachim PhD *; Neef, Peter MD +; Caimi, Marco MD ++; Hoogland, Thomas MD [S]; Claes, Lutz E. PhD *

Study Design. We conducted intradiscal pressure measurements with one volunteer performing various activities normally found in daily life, sports, and spinal therapy.

Objectives. The goal of this study was to measure intradiscal pressure to complement earlier data from Nachemson with dynamic and long-term measurements over a broad range of activities.

Summary of Background Data. Loading of the spine still is not well understood. The most important in vivo data are from pioneering intradiscal pressure measurements recorded by Nachemson during the 1960s. Since that time, there have been few data to corroborate or dispute those findings.

Methods. Under sterile surgical conditions, a pressure transducer with a diameter of 1.5 mm was implanted in the nucleus pulposus of a nondegenerated L4-L5 disc of a male volunteer 45-years-old and weighing 70 kg. Pressure was recorded with a telemetry system during a period of approximately 24 hours for various lying positions; sitting positions in a chair, in an armchair, and on a pezziball (ergonomic sitting ball); during sneezing, laughing, walking, jogging, stair climbing, load lifting; during hydration over 7 hours of sleeping, and others.

Results. The following values and more were measured: lying prone, 0.1 MPa; lying laterally, 0.12 MPa; relaxed standing, 0.5 MPa; standing flexed forward, 1.1 MPa; sitting unsupported, 0.46 MPa; sitting with maximum flexion, 0.83 MPa; nonchalant sitting, 0.3 MPa; and lifting a 20-kg weight with round flexed back, 2.3 MPa; with flexed knees, 1.7 MPa; and close to the body, 1.1 MPa. During the night, pressure increased from 0.1 to 0.24 MPa.

Conclusions. Good correlation was found with Nachemson's data during many exercises, with the exception of the comparison of standing and sitting or of the various lying positions. Notwithstanding the limitations related to the single-subject design of this study, these differences may be explained by the different transducers used. It can be cautiously concluded that the intradiscal pressure during sitting may in fact be less than that in erect standing, that muscle activity increases pressure, that constantly changing position is important to promote flow of fluid (nutrition) to the disc, and that many of the physiotherapy methods studied are valid, but a number of them should be re-evaluated.

41.   **Knee injuries in female athletes.**
Sports Med. 1995 Apr;19(4):288-302.
Hutchinson MR, Ireland ML.
Kentucky Sports Medicine, Lexington, USA.

Female athletes are at increased risk for certain sports-related injuries, particularly those involving the knee. Factors that contribute to this increased risk are the differences in sports undertaken and in gender anatomy and structure. Gender differences include baseline level of conditioning, lower extremity alignment, physiological laxity, pelvis width, tibial rotation and foot alignment. Sports like gymnastics and cheerleading create a noncontact environment, but can result in significant knee injuries. In quick stopping and cutting sports, females have an increased incidence of anterior cruciate ligament (ACL) injury by noncontact mechanisms. Patellofemoral (PF) disorders are also very common in female athletes. Awareness of these facts helps the sports medicine professional make an accurate diagnosis and institute earlier treatment-focused rehabilitation with or without surgery. Further prospective and retrospective research is needed in areas of epidemiology, mechanisms, severity and types of knee injuries. The goal is to lessen the severity of certain knee injuries and to prevent others.

42.   **Do high impact exercises produce higher tibial strains than running?**
Br J Sports Med, 34:195-199, 2000
Charles Milgrom1, Aharon Finestone2, Yael Levi1, Ariel Simkin1, Ingrid Ekenman3, Stephen Mendelson1, Michael Millgram1, Meir Nyska1, Nissim Benjuya4 and David Burr5

1.   Department of Orthopaedics, Hadassah University Hospital, Hebrew University Medical School, Jerusalem, Israel
2.   Department of Orthopaedics, Rabin Medical Center, Beilinson Campus, Petach Tikva, Israel
3.   Department of Orthopaedics, Huddinge University Hospital, Huddinge, Sweden
4.   Department of Biomechanics, Kaye College, Beersheva, Israel
5.   Department of Anatomy, Indiana University Medical Center, Indianapolis, Indiana, USA
     Correspondence to: Professor C Milgrom, Department of Orthopaedics, Hadassah University Hospital, Ein Kerem, PO Box 12000, Jerusalem, Israel

Background : Bone must have sufficient strength to withstand both instantaneous forces and lower repetitive forces. Repetitive loading, especially when bone strain and/or strain rates are high, can create microdamage and result in stress fracture Aim—To measure in vivo strains and strain rates in human tibia during high impact and moderate impact exercises.

Methods—Three strain gauged bone staples were mounted percutaneously in a rosette pattern in the mid diaphysis of the medial tibia in six normal subjects, and in vivo tibial strains were measured during running at 17 km/h and drop jumping from heights of 26, 39, and 52 cm.

Results—Complete data for all three drop jumps were obtained for four of the six subjects. No statistically significant differences were found in compression, tension, or shear strains with increasing drop jump height, but, at the 52 cm height, shear strain rate was reduced by one third ($p = 0.03$). No relation was found between peak compression strain and calculated drop jump energy, indicating that subjects were able to dissipate part of the potential energy of successively higher drop jumps by increasing the range of motion of their knee and ankle joints and not transmitting the energy to their tibia. No statistically significant differences were found between the principal strains during running and drop jumping from 52 cm, but compression ($p = 0.01$) and tension ($p = 0.004$) strain rates were significantly higher during running.

Conclusions—High impact exercises, as represented by drop jumping in this experiment, do not cause higher tibial strains and strain rates than running and therefore are unlikely to place an athlete who is accustomed to fast running at higher risk for bone fatigue.

Key Words: bone; strain; biomechanics; stress fractures; impact

43. **Biomechanics and tennis**
    British Journal of Sports Medicine 2006;40:392-396
    B Elliott
    Correspondence to:
    Professor Elliott
    University of Western Australia, Perth, WA, Australia; bruce.elliott@uwa.edu.au

Success in tennis requires a mix of player talent, good coaching, appropriate equipment, and an understanding of those aspects of sport science pertinent to the game. This paper outlines the role that biomechanics plays in player development from sport science and sport medicine perspectives. Biomechanics is a key area in player development because all strokes have a fundamental mechanical structure and sports injuries primarily have a mechanical cause.

44. **Patellofemoral Stresses during Open and Closed Kinetic Chain Exercises**
    An Analysis Using Computer Simulation
    The American Journal of Sports Medicine, 29:480-487, 2001.

Zohara A. Cohen, MS, Hrvoje Roglic, MS, Ronald P. Grelsamer, MD, Jack H. Henry, MD, William N. Levine, MD, Van C. Mow, PhD and Gerard A. Ateshian, PhD*

Orthopaedic Research Laboratory, Departments of Mechanical Engineering and Orthopaedic Surgery, Columbia University, New York, New York

* Address correspondence and reprint requests to Gerard A. Ateshian, PhD, Orthopaedic Research Laboratory, Columbia University, 630 West 168th Street, Room BB 1412, New York, NY 10032.

Rehabilitation of the symptomatic patellofemoral joint aims to strengthen the quadriceps muscles while limiting stresses on the articular cartilage. Some investigators have advocated closed kinetic chain exercises, such as squats, because open kinetic chain exercises, such as leg extensions, have been suspected of placing supraphysiologic stresses on patellofemoral cartilage. We performed computer simulations on geometric data from five cadaveric knees to compare three types of open kinetic chain leg extension exercises (no external load on the ankle, 25-N ankle load, and 100-N ankle load) with closed kinetic chain knee-bend exercises in the range of 20° to 90° of flexion. The exercises were compared in terms of the quadriceps muscle forces, patellofemoral joint contact forces and stresses, and "benefit indices" (the ratio of the quadriceps muscle force to the contact stress). The study revealed that, throughout the entire flexion range, the open kinetic chain stresses were not supraphysiologic nor significantly higher than the closed kinetic chain exercise stresses. These findings are important for patients who have undergone an operation and may feel too unstable on their feet to do closed chain kinetic chain exercises. Open kinetic chain exercises at low flexion angles are also recommended for patients whose proximal patellar lesions preclude loading the patellofemoral joint in deeper flexion.

45. Occurrence of acute lower limb injuries in artistic gymnasts in relation to event and exercise phase

Br J Sports Med 2003;37:137-139.

P Kirialanis, P Malliou, A Beneka and K Giannakopoulos

Department of Physical Education and Sport Science, Democritus University of Thrace, Greece.

Correspondence to: Dr Malliou, Department of Physical Education and Sport Science, Democritus University of Thrace, 7th Km Komotini-Xanthi, 69100 Komotini, Greece;
malliou2002@yahoo.gr

Objectives: To record the incidence of lower limb injuries (acute and overuse syndromes) in Greek artistic gymnasts in relation to the event and exercise phase.

Methods: A total of 162 gymnasts (83 male and 79 female athletes) participating in the Greek artistic gymnastic championships were observed weekly for the 1999–2000 season.

Results: Ninety three (61.6 per cent) acute injuries and 58 (38.4 per cent) overuse syndromes were recorded. The most common anatomical location was the ankle (69 cases, 45.7 per cent), followed by the knee (40 cases, 26.5 per cent). The rate of mild injuries was 26.6 per cent (25 cases), that of moderate injuries was 44 per cent (41 cases), and that of major injuries was 29 per cent (27 cases). The incidence of injury to the ankle and knee was significantly higher in the floor exercise, especially during the landing phase, than in the other events.

Conclusions: By its nature, gymnastics predisposes to acute injuries, but up to 75 per cent are mild or moderate. Special attention should be paid to the floor exercise, especially the landing phase.

Key words: gymnastics; ankle; knee; injury.

46. Creatine supplementation and age influence muscle metabolism during exercise

J Appl Physiol, Vol. 85, Issue 4, 1349-1356, October 1998.

Sinclair A. Smith1, Scott J. Montain2, Ralph P. Matott2, Gary P. Zientara3, Ferenc A. Jolesz3, and Roger A. Fielding1

1 Department of Health Sciences, Sargent College of Health and Rehabilitation Sciences, Boston University, Boston, 02215; 2 United States Army Research Institute of Environmental Medicine, Natick, 01760; and 3 Brigham and Women's Hospital and Harvard Medical School, Department of Radiology, Boston, Massachusetts 02115.

Young [n = 5, 30 ± 5 (SD) yr] and middle-aged (n = 4, 58 ± 4 yr) men and women performed single-leg knee-extension exercise inside a whole body magnetic resonance system. Two trials were performed 7 days apart and consisted of two 2-min bouts and a third bout continued to exhaustion, all separated by 3 min of recovery. 31P spectra were used to determine pH and relative concentrations of Pi, phosphocreatine (PCr), and -ATP every 10 s. The subjects consumed 0.3 g · kg1 · day1 of a placebo (trial 1) or creatine (trial 2) for 5 days before each trial. During the placebo trial, the middle-aged group had a lower resting PCr compared with the young group (35.0 ± 5.2 vs. 39.5 ± 5.1 mmol/kg, $P < 0.05$) and a lower mean initial PCr resynthesis rate (18.1 ± 3.5 vs. 23.2 ± 6.0 mmol · kg1 · min1, $P < 0.05$). After creatine supplementation, resting PCr increased 15 per cent ($P < 0.05$) in the young group and 30 per cent (P < 0.05) in the middle-aged group to 45.7 ± 7.5 vs. 45.7 ± 5.5 mmol/kg, respectively. Mean initial PCr resynthesis rate also increased in the middle-aged group (P < 0.05) to a level not different from the young group (24.3 ± 3.8 vs. 24.2 ± 3.2 mmol · kg1 · min1). Time to exhaustion was increased in both groups combined after creatine supplementation (118 ± 34 vs. 154 ± 70 s, P < 0.05). In conclusion, creatine supplementation has a greater effect on PCr availability and resynthesis rate in middle-aged compared with younger persons.

Key Words: aging; creatine monohydrate; phosphocreatine; skeletal muscle; magnetic resonance spectroscopy.

47. **The Relationship between Genotype and Exercise Tolerance in Children with Cystic Fibrosis**

Am. J. Respir. Crit. Care Med., Volume 165, Number 6, March 2002, 762-765.

Hiran C. Selvadurai, Karen O. Mckay, Cameron J. Blimkie, Peter J. Cooper, Craig M. Mellis, and Peter P. Van asperen

Children's Chest Research Centre; Department of Respiratory Medicine, Children's Hospital Institute of Sports Medicine, The Children's Hospital at Westmead (Royal Alexandra Hospital for Children); Department of Paediatrics and Child Health, University of Sydney, New South Wales, Australia; and Department of Kinesiology, McMaster University, Hamilton, Ontario, Canada.

The relationship between fitness and genotype in children with cystic fibrosis (CF) and at least one copy of the F508 mutation was examined. Genotype was classified according to the second CF mutation. Fitness was measured by peak aerobic capacity (using a modified Bruce protocol during treadmill exercise) and anaerobic power (using the Wingate test on a cycle ergometer). The class of cystic fibrosis transmembrane regulator proteins (CFTR) mutation was statistically related with aerobic capacity, peak anaerobic power, body mass index, lung function (forced expiratory volume in one second), and disease severity as measured by the Shwachman score. Patients with mutations causing defective CFTR production (Class I) or processing (Class II) had a significantly lower peak aerobic capacity (28.6 ± 4.2 ml/kg/min and 31.7 ± 5.4 ml/kg/min, respectively) than those with a mutation conferring defective regulation of CFTR (Class III) (43.9 ± 6.4 ml/kg/min). The peak anaerobic power in subjects with mutations inducing decreased CFTR conduction (Class IV) or CFTR mRNA (Class V), were significantly higher (11.4 ± 1.7 and 11.6 ± 1.5 watts/kg, respectively) than children with Class I (9.7 ± 1.4 watts/kg), Class II (9.8 ± 1.4 watts/kg), or Class III (10.5 ± 1.8 watts/kg) mutations. There were no statistically significant differences in the lung function of patients with the different mutations. These results indicate a relationship between CF genotype and some measures of fitness, the mechanisms of which remain to be determined.

48. **The normal shoulder during freestyle swimming. An electromyographic and cinematographic analysis of twelve muscles**
     American Journal of Sports Medicine, Vol 19, Issue 6 569-576, 1991.

M Pink, J Perry, A Browne, ML Scovazzo and J Kerrigan
Biomechanics Laboratory, Centinela Hospital Medical Center, Inglewood, California 90301.

The shoulder in swimming is subjected to multiple factors that can lead to a high injury rate. To prevent injury, one must understand the biomechanics of swimming. This paper describes the electromyographic and cinematographic findings of 12 shoulder muscles in competitive swimmers without shoulder pain. The results show the three heads of the deltoid and the supraspinatus functioning in synchrony to place the arm at hand entry and exit, the rhomboids and upper trapezius to position the scapula for the arm, the pectoralis major and latissimus dorsi to propel the body, the subscapularis and serratus anterior as muscles with constant muscle activity, the teres minor functioning with the pectoralis major, and the infraspinatus active only to externally rotate the arm at midrecovery. This information is important to design optimal preventative and rehabilitative exercise programs.

49. **Type I collagen synthesis and degradation in peritendinous tissue after exercise determined by microdialysis in humans**
     The Journal of Physiology, 521.1, pp. 299-306, 1999.

Henning Langberg *[1], Dorthe Skovgaard *, Lars J. Petersen [1], Jens Bülow [1] and Michael Kjær *
* Sports Medicine Research Unit, Department of Rheumatology H and [1]Department of Clinical Physiology, Bispebjerg Hospital, Copenhagen, Denmark.

Physical activity is known to increase type I collagen synthesis measured as the concentration of biomarkers in plasma. By the use of microdialysis catheters with a very high molecular mass cut-off value (3000 kDa) we aimed to determine local type I collagen synthesis and degradation in the peritendinous region by measuring interstitial concentrations of a collagen propeptide (PICP; 100 kDa) and a collagen degradation product (ICTP; 9 kDa) as well as an inflammatory mediator (PGE2).

Seven trained human runners were studied before and after (2 and 72 h) 3 h of running (36 km). Two microdialysis catheters were placed in the peritendinous space ventral to the Achilles' tendon under ultrasound guidance and perfused with a Ringer-acetate solution containing 3H-labelled human type IV collagen and [15-3H(N)]PGE2 for in vivo recovery determination. Relative recovery was 37-59 per cent (range of the s.e.m. values) for both radioactively labelled substances.

PICP concentration decreased in both interstitial peritendinous tissue and arterial blood immediately after exercise, but rose 3-fold from basal 72 h after exercise in the peritendinous tissue (55 ± 10 µg l-1, mean ± s.e.m. (rest) to 165 ± 40 µg l-1 (72 h), $P < 0.05$) and by 25 per cent in circulating blood (160 ± 10 µg l-1 (rest) to 200 ± 12 µg l-1 (72 h), $P < 0.05$). ICTP concentration did not change in blood, but decreased transiently in tendon-related tissue during early recovery after exercise only. PGE2 concentration increased in blood during running, and returned to baseline in the recovery period, whereas interstitial PGE2 concentration was elevated in the early recovery phase.

The findings of the present study indicate that acute exercise induces increased formation of type I collagen in peritendinous tissue as determined with microdialysis and using dialysate fibre with a very high molecular mass cut-off. This suggests an adaptation to acute physical loading also in non-bone-related collagen in humans.

50.   Normal forces and myofibrillar disruption after repeated eccentric exercise

J Appl Physiol, Vol. 84, Issue 2, 492-498, February 1998.

Tibor Hortobágyi, Joseph Houmard, David Fraser, Ronald Dudek, Jean Lambert and James Tracy

Biomechanics and Human Performance Laboratories, School of Health and Human Performance, Department of Anatomy and Cell Biology, School of Medicine, and Department of Physical Therapy, School of Allied Health Sciences, East Carolina University, Greenville, North Carolina 27858.

To investigate the "rapid-adaptation" phenomenon, we examined force, neural, and morphological adaptations in 12 subjects who performed 100 eccentric contractions with the quadriceps muscle (bout 1) and repeated the same exercise after a 2-wk hiatus (bout 2). Two days after bout 1, quadriceps muscle strength and surface electromyographic (EMG) activity declined ~37 and 28 per cent, respectively, in the control group (n = 6). At day 2 after bout 1, significant increases occurred in patellar tendon reflex amplitude (~25 per cent), muscle soreness (fivefold), and serum creatine kinase (220 per cent), and 65 ± 12 per cent of the total number of pixels in the EMG indicated myofibrillar disruption. At day 7 after bout 1, all variables returned to normal. At day 2 after bout 2, no significant changes occurred in force, EMG, **creatine**

kinase, or soreness, but reflex amplitude increased, and 23 ± 4 per cent of the total number of pixels in the EMG still indicated myofibrillar disruption. The results suggest that the rapid force recovery following eccentric exercise is mediated at least in part by neural factors and that this recovery may occur independently of cell disruption.

Key Words: fatigue; electromyography; rapid adaptation; humans.

51.   Muscle Activity During Sit-Ups Using Abdominal Exercise Devices
The Journal of Strength and Conditioning Research: Vol. 13, No. 4, pp. 339–345.

William C. Whiting, A Stuart Rugg, B Andre Coleman, B and William J. Vincenta

a Department of Kinesiology, California State University, Northridge, California 91330-8287.

b Department of Kinesiology, Occidental College, Los Angeles, California 90041.

The purposes of this study were to assess the activity of selected muscles used during 4 sit-up exercises with and without the assistance of abdominal exercise devices and to determine what effect, if any, the devices have on muscle activity. Nineteen young, healthy subjects completed a series of unassisted abdominal exercises (basic crunch with arms up, basic crunch with arms down, oblique crunch, and reverse crunch). The same exercises also were performed using each of 4 exercise devices. Surface electromyography was recorded from the upper and lower rectus abdominis, external oblique, rectus femoris, and sternocleidomastoid during the concentric and eccentric phases of each repetition. Repeated-measures analysis of variance analyses were used to compare mean electromyographic activity across conditions. Results showed few significant differences in abdominal muscle activation among the conditions. Some differences were noted in rectus femoris and sternocleidomastoid activity when comparing unassisted exercise and exercise using the devices. The results suggest that abdominal devices such as those tested in this study do not elicit any greater or lesser involvement of the abdominal musculature than does performing similar exercises unassisted.

Keywords: electromyography, resistance exercise, biomechanics.

52.   Biomechanics and Neuroscience: A Failure to Communicate.
Exercise and Sport Sciences Reviews. 32(1):1-3, January 2004.
Enoka, Roger M.

This commentary is the third in a series commemorating the 50th anniversary of the American College of Sports Medicine. The charge to the commentators was to provide insight on the origins and directions in the fields of physical activity and disease prevention (Haskell), applied exercise physiology (Wilmore), biomechanics and neuroscience (Enoka), and the physiology of exercise (Holloszy). In contrast to the innovation and vitality that characterizes the activities of the College in most of these fields, the inclusion of biomechanics and neuroscience as essential elements in realizing the mission of the College has been much less impressive. What we have here, as the saying goes, is a failure to communicate.

53. Effect of a Prophylactic Brace on Wrist and Ulnocarpal Joint Biomechanics in a Cadaveric Model

The American Journal of Sports Medicine 31:736-743 (2003)

Marsha Grant-Ford, ATC, PhD*,,, Michael R. Sitler, EdD, ATC, Scott H. Kozin, MD, Mary F. Barbe, PhD and Ann E. Barr, PhD, PT
· Montclair State University, Montclair, New Jersey
· Temple University, Philadelphia, Pennsylvania
Shriner's Children's Hospital of Philadelphia, Philadelphia, Pennsylvania
Address correspondence and reprint requests to Marsha Grant-Ford, ATC, PhD, Montclair State University, 1 Normal Avenue, Upper Montclair, NJ 07043

Background: Wrist pain from repetitive dorsiflexion and compression during pommel horse exercises is common among male gymnasts.

Purpose: To determine the biomechanical effects of a prophylactic wrist brace on the wrist and ulnocarpal joints during mechanical loading in a cadaveric model.

Hypothesis: The lateral wedge of the palmar pad of the brace will compensate for positive ulnar variance, distributing contact forces more evenly across the radioulnar carpal joint.

Study Design: Controlled laboratory study.

Methods: Six male and six female fixed cadaveric forearm-wrist specimens were subjected to a 32.13-kg compressive load applied through the long axis of the pronated forearm with a dorsiflexed wrist in contact with a support surface. Wrist joint dorsiflexion angle and ulnocarpal joint intraarticular peak pressure were assessed under three brace conditions: Ezy ProBrace with and without palmar pad and a nonbraced control.

Results: Wrist joint dorsiflexion angle was significantly reduced by the Ezy ProBrace with and without the palmar pad. However, ulnocarpal joint intraarticular peak pressure was reduced only by the brace with pad.

Conclusion: Prevention of pathologic wrist changes requires intervention in pressure attenuation, which was achieved with the Ezy Pro Brace with palmar pad.

Clinical Relevance: This brace may decrease the cumulative effects of repetitive stress of pommel horse exercise training.

54. **Electromyographic Analysis of Four Popular Abdominal Exercises**
J Athl Train. 1993 Summer; 28(2): 120, 122, 124, 126.

Andrew W. Piering, BS
Alex P. Janowski, BS
William B. Wehrenberg, PhD
Martin T. Moore, MS, ATC
Ann C. Snyder, PhD
Member at Department of Human Kinetics, University of Wisconsin-Milwaukee, Milwaukee, WI 53211.

This study was designed to evaluate the effects of four specific sit-up exercises on muscular activity of the rectus abdominis. Pairs of surface electrodes were placed unilaterally on four quadrants of the rectus abdominis, delimited by tendinous inscriptions, in four male subjects. Electromyographic (EMG) recordings were taken while the subjects performed four different abdominal exercises. Each abdominal exercise was hypothesized to have a specific effect on one of the four quadrants of the rectus abdominis. The four exercises analyzed were: (1) long lying crunch, (2) bent knee crunch, (3) leg raise, and (4) vertical leg crunch. Analysis of the standardized EMG recordings demonstrated no significant differences in the mean muscle activity between the four different quadrants, in the mean muscle activity between the four different exercises, and in interactions between the exercises and the quadrants of the rectus abdominis. We conclude that none of the four abdominal exercises studied are specific for strengthening individual muscle quadrants of the rectus abdominis.

55. **Strain within the anterior cruciate ligament during hamstring and quadriceps activity**
American Journal of Sports Medicine, Vol 14, Issue 1 83-87.

P Renstrom, SW Arms, TS Stanwyck, RJ Johnson and MH Pope

The objectives of this study were to measure strain in the ACL during simulated: hamstring activity alone, quadriceps activity alone, and simultaneous quadriceps and hamstring activity. Seven knee specimens removed from cadavers were studied. Heavy sutures applied to load cells were attached to the hamstring and quadriceps tendons. Loads were then applied manually (hamstrings) and/or with an Instron testing machine (quadriceps) to simulate isometric contractions of the various muscle groups. Strain was measured using a Hall effect transducer. Acting alone, the isometric hamstring activity decreased ACL strain relative to the passive normal strain at all positions tested. Thus, hamstring exercises are not detrimental to ACL repairs or reconstruction and can be included early in the rehabilitation program after ACL surgery. Acting alone, at flexion angles of 0 degree to 45 degrees, the quadriceps significantly increased the strain within the ACL relative to the passive normal strain. Strain in the ACL during simultaneous hamstring and quadriceps activity was significantly higher than that during passive normal motion from full extension to 30 degrees of flexion. The hamstrings are not capable of masking the potentially harmful effects of simultaneous quadriceps contraction on freshly repaired or reconstructed ACLs unless the knee flexion angle exceeds 30 degrees.

56.   Isolation of the Vastus Medialis Oblique Muscle During Exercise
The American Journal of Sports Medicine 27:50-53 1999.

Edwin Mirzabeigi, MD*, Christopher Jordan, MD, JoAnne K. Gronley, DPT, Neal L. Rockowitz, MD and Jacquelin Perry, MD

Pathokinesiology Laboratory, Rancho Los Amigos Medical Center, Downey, California.

* Address correspondence and reprint requests to Edwin Mirzabeigi, MD, 1041 E. Yorba Linda Boulevard, Suite 8, Placentia, CA 92670.

The purpose of this study was to selectively challenge the vastus medialis oblique muscle in comparison with the vastus lateralis, the vastus intermedius, and the vastus medialis longus muscles by performing nine sets of strengthening exercises. These knee rehabilitation exercises included isometric knee extension with the hip at neutral, 30° external, and 30° internal rotation; isokinetic knee extension through full range; isokinetic knee extension in the terminal 30° arc; sidelying ipsilateral and contralateral full knee extension; and stand and jump from full squat. Electrical activity of the vastus medialis oblique, the vastus lateralis, the vastus intermedius, and the vastus medialis longus muscles was measured in eight uninjured subjects. Our study showed that isometric exercises in neutral and external rotation of the hip will challenge both the vastus medialis oblique and the vastus lateralis muscles. The results suggest that the electromyographic activity of the vastus medialis oblique muscle was not significantly greater than that of the vastus lateralis, the vastus intermedius, and the vastus medialis longus muscles during the nine sets of exercises. Results suggest that the vastus medialis oblique muscle cannot be significantly isolated during these exercises.

57. The effect of visual feedback exercises on balance in normal subject
Acta Otorrinolaringol Esp. 1994 May-Jun;45(3):161-5.

Barona R, Zapater E, Montalt J, Armengot M, Basterra J.

Servicio de ORL, Hospital General Universitario, Facultad de Medicina,
Valencia.

The effects of visual feedback exercises on balance was studied in
normal individuals, to evaluate the efficacy of visual feedback of postural
oscillation in improving stability. A DINAS-CAN dynamometric platform
designed by the Valencian Institute of Biomechanics (IBv) was used. Before
to commencing training sessions, we determined the following parameters in
each individual: (a) static stability, via posturography; and (b) individual ability
to displace and voluntarily maintain the center of gravity within the limits of
stability. All static measures were poorer after training, but the differences
were not significant (p > 0.01). In contrast, the exercises performed via visual
feedback of postural control improved significantly (p < 0.01). Training by
visual feedback facilitates integration of visual, somatosensory, and vestibular
information. In normal individuals, stability improves under excentric
conditions, but no improvement is seen in the central resting position.

58. Total power output generated during dynamic knee extensor exercise
at different contraction frequencies
J Appl Physiol 89: 1912-1918, 2000.

Richard A. Ferguson2, Per Aagaard3, Derek Ball2, Anthony J.
Sargeant2, and Jens Bangsbo1

1 Copenhagen Muscle Research Centre, Institute of Exercise and Sport
Sciences, August Krogh Institute, University of Copenhagen, DK
2100 Copenhagen, Denmark; 2 Neuromuscular Biology Group, Department of
Exercise and Sport Science, Manchester Metropolitan University, Alsager
ST7 2HL, United Kingdom; and 3 Department of Neurophysiology, Institute
of Medical Physiology, Panum Institute, University of Copenhagen, DK
2100 Copenhagen, Denmark

A novel approach has been developed for the quantification of total
mechanical power output produced by an isolated, well-defined muscle group
during dynamic exercise in humans at different contraction frequencies. The
calculation of total power output comprises the external power delivered to
the ergometer (i.e., the external power output setting of the ergometer) and the
"internal" power generated to overcome inertial and gravitational forces related
to movement of the lower limb. Total power output was determined at
contraction frequencies of 60 and 100 rpm. At 60 rpm, the internal power was
18 ± 1 W (range: 16-19 W) at external power outputs that ranged between

0 and 50 W. This was less (P < 0.05) than the internal power of 33 ± 2 W (27-38 W) at 100 rpm at 0-50 W. Moreover, at 100 rpm, internal power was lower (P < 0.05) at the higher external power outputs. Pulmonary oxygen uptake was observed to be greater (P < 0.05) at 100 than at 60 rpm at comparable total power outputs, suggesting that mechanical efficiency is lower at 100 rpm. Thus a method was developed that allowed accurate determination of the total power output during exercise generated by an isolated muscle group at different contraction frequencies.

Key Words: quadriceps; contraction velocity; muscle moment; internal power; internal work; mechanical efficiency.

59.   **Muscle GSH-Px activity after prolonged exercise, training, and selenium supplementation.**

Biol Trace Elem Res. 1995 Jan-Mar;47(1-3):279-85.

Tessier F, Hida H, Favier A, Marconnet P.

Laboratory of Biomechanics and Biology of Exercise, University of Nice, France.

A double-blind study of the effects of supplementing with selenium vs. placebo on the physiological responses to acute and chronic exercise was conducted in 24 healthy, nonsmoking males, mean age 22.9 +/- 2.1 yr, randomly divided into two groups of 12 (Pla/Sel). After a controlled period in the absence of training, all subjects were put on an individualized endurance training program with the same rules of progression and overload (3 sessions/wk x 10 wk). Supplementation, either real (240 micrograms of organic selenium/d in Sel group) or imaginary (Pla group) was administered during the same period. In each of the conditions Pre- and Post- (training +/- sel supplementation), muscle, plasma, and systemic parameters were determined before (BF) and after (AF) acute exercise, involving the repetition of muscle work cycles separated by 5-min recovery periods, combining 20 min at 65 per cent and a maximal duration of 100 per cent VO2 max of running on a treadmill, leading the subjects to exhaustion between 2 h 40 min and 3 h 30 min. Changes in parameters as a function of three independent variables: 1. Acute exercise (E); 2. Chronic exercise (T); and 3. Selenium supplementing (S) were tested with ANOVA and the Student's t-test on paired series. Among the variables examined, muscle glutathione peroxidase (GPx) presented a remarkable behavior.

60.   **Regulation of Plantar-Foot Kinetics During Exercises on Step Benches with Markedly Different Structural Properties**

The Journal of Strength and Conditioning Research: Vol. 14, No. 1, pp. 26–31.

George J. Salem, A Sam R. Ward, B and Thay Q. Leec

(a) Musculoskeletal Biomechanics Research Laboratory, Department of Biokinesiology and Physical Therapy, University of Southern California, Los Angeles, California 90033.

(b) Biomechanics Laboratory, Department of Kinesiology, California State University-Long Beach, Long Beach, California 90840.

(c) Orthopedic Biomechanics Laboratory, Department of Orthopaedic Surgery, University of California-Irvine, and the Department of Physical Medicine and Rehabilitation, Veterans Affairs Medical Center, Long Beach, California 90822.

The relationship between step-bench structural rigidity and plantar-foot kinetics during exercise was examined in experienced athletes. Using FSCAN insole sensors (Tekscan, Boston, MA), we recorded peak vertical plantar-foot forces, impulses, and loading rates of subjects as they stepped and bounded onto structurally different step benches. Structural rigidity for each step bench was calculated from load/deformation curves that were generated from 3-point loading of the step benches. The structural rigidity of step bench A was 272 per cent greater than that of step bench B and 325 per cent greater than that of step bench C ($p < 0.05$). Results of the stepping activities, however, indicated that the plantar-foot forces and impulses associated with step bench A were only 1.7 per cent and 3.0 per cent greater, respectively, than step bench B, and 3.0 per cent and 3.2 per cent greater, respectively, than step bench C ($p > 0.05$). Results of the bounding activities indicated that the plantar-foot forces and impulses associated with step bench A were only 9.4 per cent and 11.1 per cent greater, respectively, than step bench B, and 3.7 per cent and 11.1 per cent greater, respectively, than step bench C ($p > 0.05$). Loading rates during the bounding activities, however, were significantly greater in step bench A. Our findings suggest that despite step-bench structural rigidity differences as great as 3 orders of magnitude, plantar-foot reaction forces during exercise remain similar. These similarities suggest an in vivo mechanism regulating lower extremity stiffness and plantar-foot loading.

Key Words: bench-stepping, biomechanics, FSCAN.

61. Effects of Increasing Tibial Slope on the Biomechanics of the Knee
The American Journal of Sports Medicine 32:376-382 (2004)

J. Robert Giffin, MD, Tracy M. Vogrin, MS, Thore Zantop, Savio L-Y. Woo, PhD, DSc and Christopher D. Harner, MD*

From the Musculoskeletal Research Center, Department of Orthopaedic Surgery, University of Pittsburgh, Pittsburgh, Pennsylvania.

* Address correspondence to Christopher D. Harner, MD, Center for Sports Medicine, 3200 S. Water Street, Pittsburgh, PA 15219 (e-mail: harnercd@msx.upmc.edu).

Purpose: To determine the effects of increasing anterior-posterior (A-P) tibial slope on knee kinematics and in situ forces in the cruciate ligaments.

Methods: Ten cadaveric knees were studied using a robotic testing system using three loading conditions: (1) 200 N axial compression; (2) 134 N A-P tibial load; and (3) combined 200 N axial and 134 N A-P loads. Resulting knee kinematics were determined before and after a 5-mm anterior opening wedge osteotomy. Resulting in situ forces in each cruciate ligament were determined.

Results: Tibial slope was increased from $8.8 \pm 1.8°$ to $13.2 \pm 2.1°$, causing an anterior shift in the resting position of the tibia relative to the femur up to 3.6 ± 1.4 mm. Under axial compression, the osteotomy caused a significant anterior tibial translation up to 1.9 ± 2.5 mm (90°). Under A-P and combined loads, no differences were detected in A-P translation or in situ forces in the cruciates (intact versus osteotomy).

Conclusions: Results suggest that small increases in tibial slope do not affect A-P translations or in situ forces in the cruciate ligaments. However, increasing slope causes an anterior shift in tibial resting position that is accentuated under axial loads. This suggests that increasing tibial slope may be beneficial in reducing tibial sag in a PCL-deficient knee, whereas decreasing slope may be protective in an ACL-deficient knee.

Key Words: knee • ligament • PCL • osteotomy • kinematics

62. **Comparison of intersegmental tibiofemoral joint forces and muscle activity during various closed kinetic chain exercises**

American Journal of Sports Medicine, Vol 24, Issue 6 792-799 1996.

MJ Stuart, DA Meglan, GE Lutz, ES Growney and KN An

Biomechanics Laboratory, Mayo Clinic, Rochester, Minnesota, USA.

The purpose of this study was to analyze intersegmental forces at the tibiofemoral joint and muscle activity during three commonly prescribed closed kinetic chain exercises: the power squat, the front squat, and the lunge. Subjects with anterior cruciate ligament-intact knees performed repetitions of each of the three exercises using a 223-N (50-pound) barbell. The results showed that the mean tibiofemoral shear force was posterior (tibial force on femur) throughout the cycle of all three exercises. The magnitude of the posterior shear forces increased with knee flexion during the descent phase of each exercise. Joint compression forces remained constant throughout the descent and ascent phases of the power squat and the front squat. A net offset in extension for the moment about the knee was present for all three exercises. Increased quadriceps muscle activity and the decreased hamstring muscle activity are required to perform the lunge as compared with the power squat and the front squat. A posterior tibiofemoral shear force throughout the entire cycle of all three exercises in these subjects with anterior cruciate ligament-intact knees indicates that the potential loading on the injured or reconstructed anterior cruciate ligament is not significant. The magnitude of the posterior tibiofemoral shear force is not likely to be detrimental to the injured or reconstructed posterior cruciate ligament. These conclusions assume that the resultant anteroposterior shear force corresponds to the anterior and posterior cruciate ligament forces.

63. Closed-Chain Rehabilitation for Upper and Lower Extremities

J Am Acad Orthop Surg, Vol 9, No 6, November/December 2001.

W. Ben Kibler, MD and Beven Livingston, MS, PT

Dr. Kibler is Medical Director, Lexington Sports Medicine Center, Lexington, Ky. Mr. Livingston is Clinical Specialist, Lexington Sports Medicine Center.

Reprint requests: Dr. Kibler, Lexington Sports Medicine Center, 1221 South Broadway, Lexington, KY 40504.

Closed-chain exercise protocols are used extensively in rehabilitation of knee injuries and are increasingly used in rehabilitation of shoulder injuries. They are felt to be preferable to other exercise programs in that they simulate normal physiologic and biomechanical functions, create little shear stress across injured or healing joints, and reproduce proprioceptive stimuli. Because of these advantages, they may be used early in rehabilitation and have been integral parts of "accelerated" rehabilitation programs. The authors review the important components of a closed-chain rehabilitation program and provide examples of specific exercises that are used for rehabilitation of knee and shoulder injuries.

64. Low back loads over a variety of abdominal exercises: searching for the safest abdominal challenge.

Medicine and Science in Sports and Exercise. 29(6):804-811, June 1997.

Axler, Craig T.; Mcgill, Stuart M.

Abdominal exercises are prescribed for both the prevention and treatment of low back injury. However, these exercises sometimes appear to have hazardous effects on the lumbar spine. The purpose of this study was to identify quantitatively abdominal exercises that optimize the challenge to the abdominal muscles (rectus abdominis, external oblique, internal oblique) but impose minimal load penalty to the lumbar spine. Nine volunteers performed 12 different abdominal exercises. For a given task the maximum abdominal muscle EMG value was divided by the maximum compression value, resulting in an abdominal challenge versus spinal compression cost index. In general, the partial curl-ups generated the highest muscle challenge-to-spine cost indices. However, those exercises that generated the best challenge-to-cost indices did not necessarily record the lowest compression levels along with the highest EMG activations. No single exercise was found that optimally trained all of the abdominal muscles while at the same time incurring minimal intervertebral joint loads. It was concluded that a variety of selected abdominal exercises are required to sufficiently challenge all of the abdominal muscles and that these exercises will differ to best meet the different training objectives of individuals.

65.   In vivo dynamics of human medial gastrocnemius muscle-tendon complex during stretch-shortening cycle exercise.
Acta Physiologica Scandinavica, Volume 170 Page 127 - October 2000.
K. Kubo, H. Kanehisa, D. Takeshita, Y. Kawakami, S. Fukashiro & T. Fukunaga.

The purpose of this study was to investigate the dynamics of human muscle-tendon complex (MTC) during stretch-shortening cycle exercises through in vivo observation. A total of seven male subjects performed dorsi flexion followed by plantar flexion at two different frequencies, 0.3 Hz (slow) and 1.0 Hz (fast), in a toe-standing position. The fascicle length (LF) of the medial gastrocnemius muscle during the movements was determined using a real-time ultrasonography in vivo. The LF at the switching phase from dorsi to plantar flexion was significantly shorter in the fast exercise (54.4 ± 5.5 mm) than in the slow one (58.2 ± 5.4 mm), suggesting that the elongation of tendon structures at that time was significantly greater in the former than in the latter. Furthermore, at the initial stage of plantar flexion during the fast movement, the LF hardly changed with a rapid shortening of tendon structures at that time. The observed relation between MTC length and force showed that the behaviour of tendon structures contributed to 20.2 and 42.5 per cent of the total amount of work completed during plantar flexion phase in the slow and fast movements, respectively. Thus, the present results suggest that tendon structures make the dynamics of MTC more efficient during stretch-shortening cycle exercises by changing their lengths.

66. **Walking in simulated reduced gravity: mechanical energy fluctuations and exchange.**

J Appl Physiol 86: 383-390, 1999.

Timothy M. Griffin, Neil A. Tolani, and Rodger Kram.

Department of Integrative Biology, University of California, Berkeley, California 94720-3140.

Walking humans conserve mechanical and, presumably, metabolic energy with an inverted pendulum-like exchange of gravitational potential energy and horizontal kinetic energy. Walking in simulated reduced gravity involves a relatively high metabolic cost, suggesting that the inverted-pendulum mechanism is disrupted because of a mismatch of potential and kinetic energy. We tested this hypothesis by measuring the fluctuations and exchange of mechanical energy of the center of mass at different combinations of velocity and simulated reduced gravity. Subjects walked with smaller fluctuations in horizontal velocity in lower gravity, such that the ratio of horizontal kinetic to gravitational potential energy fluctuations remained constant over a fourfold change in gravity. The amount of exchange, or percent recovery, at 1.00 m/s was not significantly different at 1.00, 0.75, and 0.50 G (average 64.4 per cent), although it decreased to 48 per cent at 0.25 G. As a result, the amount of work performed on the center of mass does not explain the relatively high metabolic cost of walking in simulated reduced gravity.

Key Words: biomechanics; locomotion; human; mechanical work; energetics.

67. **Serratus Anterior Muscle Activity During Selected Rehabilitation Exercises**

The American Journal of Sports Medicine 27:784-791 (1999).

Michael J. Decker, MS, Robert A. Hintermeister, PhD, Kenneth J. Faber, MD and Richard J. Hawkins, MD.

Steadman Hawkins, Sports Medicine Foundation, Vail, Colorado.

Presented at the the American College of Sports Medicine annual conference, Denver, Colorado, May 1997.

Address correspondence and reprint requests to Michael J. Decker, MS, Steadman Hawkins Sports Medicine Foundation, 181 West Meadow Drive, Suite 1000, Vail, CO 81657.

The purpose of this study was to document the electromyographic activity and applied resistance associated with eight scapulohumeral exercises performed below shoulder height. We used this information to design a continuum of serratus anterior muscle exercises for progressive rehabilitation or training. Five muscles in 20 healthy subjects were studied with surface electrodes for the following exercises: shoulder extension, forward punch, serratus anterior punch, dynamic hug, scaption (with external rotation), press-up, push-up plus, and knee push-up plus. Electromyographic data were collected from the middle serratus anterior, upper and middle trapezius, and anterior and posterior deltoid muscles. Each exercise was partitioned into phases of increasing and decreasing force and analyzed for average and peak electromyographic amplitude. Resistance was provided by body weight, an elastic cord, or dumbbells. The serratus anterior punch, scaption, dynamic hug, knee push-up plus, and push-up plus exercises consistently elicited serratus anterior muscle activity greater than 20 per cent maximal voluntary contraction. The exercises that maintained an upwardly rotated scapula while accentuating scapular protraction, such as the push-up plus and the newly designed dynamic hug, elicited the greatest electromyographic activity from the serratus anterior muscle.

68. **Effects of long-term exercise on the biomechanical properties of the Achilles tendon of guinea fowl**

J Appl Physiol 90: 164-171, 2001.

Cindy I. Buchanan and Richard L. Marsh
Department of Biology, Northeastern University, Boston, Massachusetts 02115.

The purpose of this study was to determine the effect of long-term exercise on tendon compliance and to ascertain whether tendons adapt differently to downhill running vs. running on a level surface. We carried out this investigation on the gastrocnemius tendon of helmeted guinea fowl (Numida meleagris) that were trained for 8-12 wk before commencing experimental procedures. We used an in situ technique to measure tendon stiffness. The animals were deeply anesthetized with isofluorane during all in situ procedures. Our results indicate that long-term exercise increased tendon stiffness. This finding held true after normalization for the cross-sectional area of the free tendon, likely reflecting a change in the material properties of the exercised tendons. Whether training consisted of level or downhill running did not appear to influence response of the tendon to exercise. We hypothesize that the increased stiffness observed in tendons after a long-term running program may be a response to repeated stress and may function as a mechanism to resist tendon damage due to mechanical fatigue.

Key Words: endurance training; downhill running; tendon stiffness; Numida meleagris.

69. **High-impact exercise strengthens bone in osteopenic ovariectomized rats with the same outcome as Sham rats**

J Appl Physiol 95: 1032-1037, 2003. First published May 16, 2003.

Akiko Honda,1 Naota Sogo,1 Seigo Nagasawa,1 Takuya Shimizu,2 and Yoshihisa Umemura1

1Laboratory for Exercise Physiology and Biomechanics, School of Health and Sport Sciences, and 2Health Service Center, Chukyo University, Toyota 470-0393, Japan.

Submitted 26 August 2002 ; accepted in final form 6 May 2003.

The effect of jump exercise on middle-aged osteopenic rats was investigated. Forty-two 9-mo-old female rats were either sham-operated (Sham) or ovariectomized (OVX). Three months after surgery, the rats were divided into the following groups: Sham sedentary, Sham exercised, OVX sedentary, and OVX exercised. Rats in the exercise groups jumped 10 times/day, 5 days/wk, for 8 wk, with a jumping height of 40 cm. Less than 1 min was required for the jump training. After the experiment, the right tibia and femur were dissected, and blood was obtained from each rat. OVX rats were observed to have increased body weights and decreased bone mass in their tibiae and femurs. Jump-exercised rats, on the other hand, had significantly increased tibial bone mass, strength, and cortical areas. The bone mass and strength of OVX exercised rats increased to approximately the same extent as Sham exercised rats, despite estrogen deficiency or **osteopenia**. Our data suggest that jump exercise has beneficial effects on lower limb bone mass, strength, bone mineral density, and morphometry in middle-aged osteopenic rats, as well as in Sham rats.

Key Words: high-impact jump exercise; ovariectomy; osteopenic rats; bone mass; bone strength.

Address for reprint requests and other correspondence: A. Honda, School of Health and Sport Sciences, Chukyo Univ., 101 Tokodachi, Kaizu-cho, Toyota, Aichi 470-0393, Japan (E-mail: akiko@seiken. sass.chukyo-u.ac.jp).

70. **Right ventricular diastolic function in children with pulmonary regurgitation after repair of tetralogy of Fallot: volumetric evaluation by magnetic resonance velocity mapping**

The American College of Cardiology Foundation, 28:1827-1835,1996.

WA Helbing, RA Niezen, S Le Cessie, RJ van der Geest, J Ottenkamp, and A de Roos

Department of Pediatrics (Division of Pediatric Cardiology), Leiden University, The Netherlands.

Objectives: We sought to assess right ventricular diastolic function in young patients with corrected tetralogy of Fallot and pulmonary regurgitation.

Background: Pulmonary regurgitation is an important problem in repair of tetralogy of Fallot. Its effects on right ventricular diastolic function in children are unknown.

Methods: Nineteen children with repair of tetralogy of Fallot (mean age [+/- SD] 12 +/- 3 years, mean age at operation 1.5 +/- 1) and 12 healthy children were studied. Summation of magnetic resonance velocity mapping pulmonary and tricuspid volume flow curves provided right ventricular time-volume curves. Ventricular size was assessed with tomographic magnetic resonance imaging (MRI). Graded exercise testing was performed.

Results: Systematic and random differences (mean +/- SD) of velocity mapping and Doppler tricuspid time to peak velocities (peak E: 1 +/- 26 ms, r = 0.43; peak A: 2 +/- 11 ms, r = 0.76), E/A ratio (0.04 +/- 0.5, r = 0.63) and duration of pulmonary regurgitation (20 +/- 35 ms, r = 0.74) were satisfactory. In 6 patients (group I), late diastolic forward pulmonary artery flow was absent; in 13 patients (group II), this flow contributed 1 per cent to 14 per cent to right ventricular stroke volume. Significant differences were increased deceleration time (315 +/- 91 vs. 168 +/- 28 ms, p < 0.001), decreased filling fraction (44 +/- 11 vs. 55 +/- 16 per cent, p = 0.02) and increased peak early filling rate (378 +/- 124 vs. 286 +/- 112 ml/s, p = 0.018) between control subjects and group I, and increased deceleration time (230 +/- 40, p = 0.03) between control subjects and group II. Pulmonary regurgitation, ventricular size and ejection fraction did not differ significantly between patient groups. Exercise function was diminished with restrictive right ventricular physiology (p < 0.001, group II vs. control subjects).

Conclusions: Impaired relaxation and restriction to filling affect right ventricular function in children with repair of tetralogy of Fallot and pulmonary regurgitation. Restrictive right ventricular physiology is associated with decreased exercise function.

71.   **Patellofemoral pain syndrome. A critical review of the clinical trials on nonoperative therapy**
American Journal of Sports Medicine, Vol 25, Issue 2 207-212, 1997.
B Arroll, E Ellis-Pegler, A Edwards and G Sutcliffe
Royal New Zealand College of General Practitioners Research Unit, Department of General Practice, University of Auckland, New Zealand.

Many therapies have been advocated for treating patellofemoral pain, which suggests little consensus on optimal treatment. We reviewed the high-quality evidence for successful treatment of patellofemoral syndrome based on successful outcome information. To achieve this goal, we undertook a systematic search and critical appraisal of the literature on patellofemoral pain syndrome. Our definition of patellofemoral pain syndrome was broad and included patients with cartilage damage. We found five randomized controlled trials and some follow-up studies. The prognoses for most new cases of patellofemoral pain syndrome are good, although a proportion of patients with this syndrome will have persistent symptoms. Quadriceps muscle exercises were effective in treating this condition, and knee braces were not. Both prostheses and intramuscular glycosaminoglycan polysulfate had encouraging results for patients; however, these results need confirmation. There were many studies of biomechanics, which indicates that there is an assumption that an alteration of abnormal biomechanics would result in clinical benefit. Studies are needed that place more emphasis on the therapeutic benefit. There is limited evidence on which to base therapy, and there needs to be more high-quality research. Studies need to be longer, account for factors that predispose the patients, and have a more standardized means of assessing outcomes.

72. **Terrestrial Intermittent Exercise: Common Issues for Human Athletics and Comparative Animal Locomotion1**

American Zoologist 2001 41(2):219-228; 2001.

Randi B. Weinstein1

1 Department of Physiology, 1501 N. Campbell Avenue, University of Arizona, Tucson, Arizona 85724.

The earliest studies of intermittent exercise physiology noted that moving intermittently (i.e., alternating brief movements with brief pauses) could transform a heavy workload into a submaximal one that can be tolerated and sustained. The brief pauses that characterize intermittent locomotion permit at least partial recovery from prior activity. This research provided the foundation for the development of interval training and more recently for the re-evaluation of steady-state paradigms for comparative animal locomotion. In this paper I review key concepts underlying the performance of repeated activity. I provide examples from human athletics and training and comparative animal locomotion. To explore the limits of intermittent exercise performance, I examine the performance limits for continuous exercise and the rate and extent of the recovery of performance capacity following activity. While it is evident that altering locomotor behavior (i.e., moving intermittently) can alter the capacity of an animal to perform work, mathematical models of intermittent exercise could predict strategies (i.e., exercise intensity, exercise duration, and pause duration) that will increase performance limits for intermittent activity.

73.   Aged bone displays an increased responsiveness to low-intensity resistance exercise

J Appl Physiol 90: 1359-1364, 2001

Kathleen M. Buhl1, Christopher R. Jacobs1, Russell T. Turner2, Glenda L. Evans2, Peter A. Farrell3, and Henry J. Donahue1,4

Musculoskeletal Research Laboratory, Departments of 1 Orthopaedics and Rehabilitation, and 4 Cellular and Molecular Physiology, The Pennsylvania State University College of Medicine, Hershey, Pennsylvania 17033; 2 Department of Orthopaedic Surgery, Mayo Clinic, Rochester, Minnesota 55905; and 3 Department of Physiology, The Pennsylvania State University, University Park, Pennsylvania 16802.

The ability of bone to respond to increased loading as a function of age was tested by use of three-point bending and histomorphometry. The hindlimbs of male Fischer 344 rats of three age groups (young = 4 mo, adult = 12 mo, and old = 22 mo; n = 10 per age group) were progressively overloaded by training the rats to depress a lever high on the side of a cage while wearing a weighted backpack. This squatlike movement required full extension of the hindlimbs. Exercised (Exer) rats performed 50 repetitions three times per week for 9 wk. Pack weight was gradually increased to 65 per cent of body weight. Controls (n = 10 per age group) performed the same exercise without additional weight. Neither the mechanical properties of the femur nor histomorphometry in the proximal tibia was significantly affected in young or adult rats. However, old Exer rats were found to have significantly smaller medullary areas and a decreased trabecular spacing than their age-matched controls. These results suggest a greater sensitivity to increased loading in aged rats.

Key Words: bone mechanics; histomorphometry; exercise training; aging.

74.   The Human Gene Map for Performance and Health-Related Fitness Phenotypes

Medicine and Science in Sports and Exercise. 37(6):881-903, June 2005.

Wolfarth, Bernd 1; Bray, Molly S. 2; Hagberg, James M. 3; Perusse, Louis 4; Rauramaa, Rainer 5; Rivera, Miguel A. 6; Roth, Stephen M. 3; Rankinen, Tuomo 7; Bouchard, Claude 7

We began this series in 2000 with the aim of making available in an easily accessible format all the advances on the genetic basis of a large family of exercise-related traits. The current review presents the 2004 update of the human gene map for physical performance and health-related fitness phenotypes. It is based on peer-reviewed papers published by the end of 2004. The genes and markers with evidence of association or linkage with a performance or fitness phenotype in sedentary or active people, in adaptation to acute exercise, or for training-induced changes are positioned on the genetic map of all autosomes and the X chromosome. Negative studies are reviewed but a gene or locus must be supported by at least one positive study before being inserted on the map. One new feature is that we have incorporated the genes whose sequence variants have been associated with either the level of physical activity or indicators of sedentarism. By the end of 2000, in the early version of the gene map, 29 loci were depicted. In contrast, the 2004 human gene map for physical performance and health-related phenotypes includes 140 autosomal gene entries and quantitative trait loci, plus four on the X chromosome. Moreover, there are 16 mitochondrial genes in which sequence variants have been shown to influence relevant fitness and performance phenotypes. Thus, the map is growing in complexity and progress is being made. The number of laboratories and scientists concerned by the role of genes and sequence variations in exercise-related traits is rising. But exercise science and sports medicine is generally lagging behind in terms of utilizing the advances in genetic and genomic technologies.

75. Warm-up Stretches Reduce Sensations of Stiffness and Soreness after Eccentric Exercise.
Clinical Sciences
Medicine & Science in Sports & Exercise. 37(6):929-936, June 2005.
Reisman, Simone; Walsh, Lee D.; Proske, Uwe

Purpose: A commonly used method for warm-up before exercise is to stretch muscles. How this benefits performance remains uncertain. After a period of eccentric exercise, there is muscle damage accompanied by an increase in passive tension, perceived as a sensation of increased stiffness in the exercised muscles. We have tested the idea that warm-up stretches might reduce levels of passive tension to reduce sensations of stiffness and soreness after eccentric exercise.

Methods: Subjects eccentrically exercised elbow flexors of one arm on an isokinetic dynamometer. The other arm acted as a control. After the exercise, measurements were made of resting elbow angle, as an indication of passive tension levels, before and after one or five large, passive arm extensions. Additional measurements made at 24 h included soreness levels in response to muscle stretch or vibration.

Results: After the exercise, the relaxed elbow adopted a more flexed posture than normal, an effect that slowly subsided over the next 4 d. Five rapid arm extensions returned arm posture back to near control levels. The flexed posture then gradually redeveloped over the next hour. At 24 h postexercise, extending the arm produced some soreness as did muscle vibration. The pain from arm extension and vibration was reduced after a series of arm extensions.

Conclusions: The flexed posture at the elbow is due to an increase in passive tension in elbow flexors as a result of muscle damage from the eccentric exercise. Stretch reduces passive tension. Benefits from the lower tension are reduced sensations of stiffness and soreness. This represents a new proposal for the mechanism for passive stretches as a warm-up strategy.

76. **Muscle exercise after anterior cruciate ligament reconstruction of the knee—Part II: The development of the exercise method by simultaneous isometric contraction of the quadriceps and the hamstrings, and its biomechanics**
Nippon Seikeigeka Gakkai Zasshi. 1985 Dec;59(12):1051-8
Yasuda K, Sasaki T, Shirado O, Yagi T, Monji J.

An attempt was made to investigate the stress of the ACL in the simultaneous isometric contraction (IMC) of the quadriceps and the hamstrings by means of analysis of two-dimensional models, and to estimate electromyographically the forces of those muscles in that contraction. The anterior drawer force (ADF) in the simultaneous IMC decreased as the flexion angle of the knee increased. The average value of the angles, where the ADF became zero, was 7.4 degrees. The integrated EMGs of the quadriceps and the hamstrings in the simultaneous maximum IMC were equal to 30-60 per cent of those in separate maximum IMC. Clinical relevance: In the early stage of the rehabilitation after the ACL reconstruction, the simultaneous IMC of the quadriceps and the hamstrings is useful as one of the muscle exercise method, because that can be performed at the knee position near the full extension and can generate sufficient muscle force for exercise.

77. **A Comparison of Flexion and Extension Exercises in Workers at Risk for Developing Cumulative Trauma Disorder Randolph, Joann K.**
PhD, University of Cincinnati, Nursing : Doctoral Program in Nursing, 2000.
Linda S. Baas

Cumulative trauma disorders (CTDs) are soft tissue injuries of the muscles, nerves, and joints, such as carpal tunnel syndrome. CTDs are an accumulation of progressive pathological changes that ultimately culminate into an injury. The hallmark symptoms of clinical CTDs are discomfort, pain, and paresthesias. The severity of symptoms can vary between a transient aching, discomfort, and fatigue to significant pain and paresthesias that result in permanent disability. Upper extremity CTDs are common in industries that have jobs that include highly repetitive motion tasks. The prevalence of CTDs in these industries is significant, and has a considerable impact on both industry and the individual worker. This study was guided by theory from three separate disciplines, Biomechanics, Exercise Physiology, and Ergonomics. The purpose of this study was to test the effect of exercise on workers in an effort to reduce or delay discomfort, increase strength, and potentially reduce the progressive pathology of CTDs. Two exercise protocols at two intensities were performed by on workers doing occupational repetitive motion tasks. Flexion exercises were compared to extension exercises in a six-week exercise training program. Three industrial sites were used to conduct the study, all with a high incidence of upper extremity CTDs claims. A convenience sample of 85 subjects was initially entered into the study. Fifteen subjects dropped out of the study. The remaining 70 subjects were randomly assigned to one of four treatment exercise groups or a control group. The variables of interest were discomfort, as measured by a visual analog scale, and strength in six upper extremity muscle groups. A repeated measures ANOVA using a one-within, one-between design was used. The results of this study were as follows: iv Discomfort: Discomfort was significantly reduced in all subjects doing exercise training across the groups after six weeks [$F=43.85, (2, 62) p=. 000$]. Strength: An overall significant increase in strength was observed following six weeks of exercise training [$F=12.32, p=. 000$]. A significant difference in strength across all six muscles tested was also seen [$F=67.38, p=. 000$]. Finally, a significant interaction effect among the six muscle groups, the three time periods (baseline, three, and six weeks), and the five subject groups was observed [$F=1.53, p=. 035$]. However, the Mauchly's Test of Sphericity revealed that the sample had a high variance in strength across time. These data were interpreted cautiously due to the violation of this assumption. This study provides initial support for two exercise programs in workers doing repetitive motion tasks. Exercise training may be a factor in diminishing the individual workers' vulnerability to CTDs.

Key Words: cummulative trauma disease; discomfort; ctd; strength.

78. **The effect of either a pre or post exercise stretch on straight leg raise range of motion (SLR-ROM) in females.**
J Sci Med Sport. 2002 Dec;5(4):281-90.
Gill T, Wilkinson A, Edwards E, Grimmer K.

Centre for Population Studies in Epidemiology, Department of Human Services, South Australia.

This study examined the order effect of a hamstring muscle stretch and resisted hamstring exercises on straight leg raise range of movement (SLR-ROM), in a group of twenty females aged 20-34 years. The stretch was applied either immediately before or Immediately after a resisted hamstring exercise. Exercise significantly decreased SLR-ROM ($p < 0.05$) and stretching significantly increased SLR-ROM ($p < 0.05$). The overall change in SLR-ROM for the two groups showed that a significant increase in SLR-ROM was detected (at a low force level) in Group 1 subjects who performed exercise and then stretched. A non-significant increase in SLR-ROM was detected by the higher force level in Group 1 subjects. In contrast, Group 2 subjects (stretch then exercise) showed a non-significant reduction in SLR-ROM at both levels of force.

79.   **Trunk muscle activity during bridging exercises on and off a Swissball**
Chiropractic and Osteopathy 2005, 13:14 doi:10.1186/1746-1340-13-14
Gregory J Lehman, Wajid Hoda and Steven Oliver

Department of Graduate Studies, Canadian Memorial Chiropractic College, Toronto, ON, Canada.

Background

A Swiss ball is often incorporated into trunk strengthening programs for injury rehabilitation and performance conditioning. It is often assumed that the use of a Swiss ball increases trunk muscle activity. The aim of this study was to determine whether the addition of a Swiss ball to trunk bridging exercises influences trunk muscle activity.

Methods

Surface electrodes recorded the myoelectric activity of trunk muscles during bridging exercises. Bridging exercises were performed on the floor as well as on a labile surface (Swiss ball).

Results and Discussion

During the prone bridge the addition of an exercise ball resulted in increased myoelectric activity in the rectus abdominis and external oblique. The internal oblique and erector spinae were not influenced. The addition of a swiss ball during supine bridging did not influence trunk muscle activity for any muscles studied.

Conclusion

The addition of a Swiss ball is capable of influencing trunk muscle activity in the rectus abdominis and external oblique musculature during prone bridge exercises. Modifying common bridging exercises can influence the amount of trunk muscle activity, suggesting that exercise routines can be designed to maximize or minimize trunk muscle exertion depending on the needs of the exercise population.

80. Rehabilitation of the pitching shoulder

American Journal of Sports Medicine, Vol 13, Issue 4 223-235, 1985.

AM Pappas, RM Zawacki and CF McCarthy

Shoulder pain is a common complaint among baseball pitchers. Frequently, the nature of shoulder pathology can be traced to lack of flexibility and muscular imbalance. This paper describes: the normal biomechanics of a properly functioning shoulder during a baseball pitch, pathomechanics of shoulder problems, flexibility requirements of the throwing shoulder, and the muscular balance necessary for an effective throwing shoulder. Appropriate examination procedures are described along with remedial exercises which ensure normal glenohumeral motion and integrated muscle action.

81. Supine lower body negative pressure exercise simulates metabolic and kinetic features of upright exercise

J Appl Physiol, Vol. 89, Issue 2, 649-654, August 2000.

Wanda L. Boda1,2, Donald E. Watenpaugh2, Richard E. Ballard2, and Alan R. Hargens2

1 Department of Kinesiology, Sonoma State University, Rohnert Park 94928; and 2 Gravitational Research Branch, National Aeronautics and Space Administration Ames Research Center, Moffett Field, California 94035-1000.

Exercise within an artificial gravity environment may help prevent microgravity-induced deconditioning. We hypothesized that supine lower body negative pressure (LBNP) exercise simulates physiological and biomechanical features of upright exercise. Walking (4.5 ± 0.3 km/h) and running (8.0 ± 1.0 km/h) while supine within a LBNP exerciser were compared with walking and running while upright. Eight healthy subjects exercised for 5 min at each of the four posture/gait conditions. LBNP of 52 ± 4 mmHg generated one body weight of supine ground reaction force (GRF). Gait parameters and GRFs were measured during the third minute of exercise, and heart rate and oxygen consumption were measured during the fifth minute. Oxygen consumption during supine LBNP treadmill exercise [walking: 14.6 ± 0.9; running: 32.2 ± 1.6 (SE) ml · min1 · kg1] was similar to that during upright treadmill exercise (walking: 15.1 ± 0.9; running: 34.0 ± 1.9 ml · min1 · kg 1). Heart rate for supine LBNP exercise (grand mean: 133 ± 11 beats/min) was also similar to that for upright exercise (136 ± 11 beats/min). Footward forces integrated over each stride (330.5 ± 34.4 vs. 319.1 ± 29.6 N · s) and rate of force generation (26,483 ± 4,310 vs. 25,634 ± 4,434 N/s) were similar for upright and LBNP exercise, respectively. Our collective results indicate that supine exercise within LBNP can simulate the physiological stress and GRFs that are generated during upright gait.

Key Words: gait; ground reaction force; oxygen consumption; spaceflight; microgravity.

82. **Neuromuscular fatigue after maximal stretch-shortening cycle exercise**

J Appl Physiol, Vol. 84, Issue 1, 344-350, January 1998

V. Strojnik and P. V. Komi

Department of Biology of Physical Activity, University of Jyvskyl, 40100 Jyvskyl, Finland.

To examine some possible sites of fatigue during short-lasting maximally intensive stretch-shortening cycle exercise, drop jumps on an inclined sledge apparatus were analyzed. Twelve healthy volunteers performed jumps until they were unable to maintain jumping height >90 per cent of their maximum. After the workout, the increases in the blood lactate concentration and serum creatine kinase activation were statistically significant ($P < 0.001$ and $P < 0.05$, respectively) but rather small in physiological terms. The major changes after the workout were as follows: the single twitch was characterized by smaller peak torque ($P < 0.05$) and shorter time to peak ($P < 0.05$) and half-relaxation time ($P < 0.01$). The double-twitch torque remained at the same level ($P > 0.05$), but with a steeper maximal slope of torque rise ($P < 0.05$); during 20- and 100-Hz stimulation the torque declined (both $P < 0.01$) and the maximal voluntary torque changed nonsignificantly but with a smaller maximal slope of torque rise ($P < 0.01$) and a higher activation level ($P < 0.05$), accompanied by an increased electromyogram amplitude. These findings indicate that the muscle response after the short-lasting consecutive maximum jumps on the sledge apparatus may involve two distinct mechanisms acting in opposite directions: (1) The contractile mechanism seems to be potentiated through a shorter $Ca2+$ transient and faster cross-bridge cycling, as implied by twitch changes. (2) High-frequency action potential propagation shows an impairment, which is suggested as the possible dominant reason for fatigue in exercise of this type.

Key Words: fatigue sites; maximal intensity; short duration; electrical stimulation.

83. **High-impact exercise and growing bone: relation between high strain rates and enhanced bone formation**
J Appl Physiol, Vol. 88, Issue 6, 2183-2191, June 2000
Stefan Judex and Ronald F. Zernicke
McCaig Centre for Joint Injury and Arthritis Research, University of Calgary, Calgary, Alberta, Canada T2N 4N1.

We investigated whether high-impact drop jumps could increase bone formation in the middiaphyseal tarsometatarsus of growing rooster. Roosters were designated as sedentary controls (n = 10) or jumpers (n = 10). Jumpers performed 200 drop jumps per day for 3 wk. The mechanical milieu of the tarsometatarsus was quantified via in vivo strain gauges. Indexes of bone formation and mechanical parameters were determined in each of twelve 30° sectors subdividing the middiaphyseal cortex. Compared with baseline walking, drop jumping produced large peak strain rates (+740 per cent) in the presence of moderately increased peak strain magnitudes (+30 per cent) and unaltered strain distributions. Bone formation rates were significantly increased by jump training at periosteal (+40 per cent) and endocortical surfaces (+370 per cent). Strain rate was significantly correlated with the specific sites of increased formation rates at endocortical but not at periosteal surfaces. Previously, treadmill running did not enhance bone growth in this model. Comparing the mechanical milieus produced by running and drop jumps revealed that jumping significantly elevated only peak strain rates. This further emphasized the sensitivity of immature bone to high strain rates.

Key Words: bone adaptation; mechanical stimuli; cortical bone; modeling; rooster.

84. **An Analysis of Undergraduate Exercise Science Programs: An Exercise Science Curriculum Survey**
The Journal of Strength and Conditioning Research: Vol. 17, No. 3, pp. 536–540.
Craig L. Elder,a, b Thomas J. Pujol,a and Jeremy T. Barnesa
(a) Athletic Training Education, Southeast Missouri State University, Department of Health, Human Performance, and Recreation, Cape Girardeau, Missouri 63701.

(b) Address correspondence to Dr. Craig Elder, E-mail: celder@semo.edu
Undergraduate exercise science programs develop curricula by referring to standards set by professional organizations. A web-based survey was

administered to 235 institutions with exercise science undergraduate programs to evaluate their adherence to stated curricular guidelines. Results indicate that 29 per cent of institutions considered American College of Sports Medicine (ACSM) Knowledge, skills, and abilities (KSAs); 33 per cent both ACSM and National Association for Sport and Physical Education (NASPE) guidelines; 6 per cent ACSM, NASPE, and National Strength and Conditioning Association (NSCA); 8 per cent ACSM, NASPE, NSCA, and American Society of Exercise Physiologists, and 5 per cent NASPE. The two largest subgroups had good compliance with the areas of exercise physiology, biomechanics, and human anatomy and physiology. However, neither subgroup adhered to the areas of exercise prescription, testing, and implementation; exercise and aging; or exercise with special populations. Regardless of the implemented guideline(s), most institutions placed minimal emphasis on areas related to health promotion and many curricula did not require any field experience.

Reference Data:Elder, C.L., T.J. Pujol, and J.T. Barnes. An analysis of undergraduate exercise science programs: An exercise science curriculum survey.

Keywords: education, professional preparation, accreditation, certification.

85. **The relationship between physical fitness and clustered risk, and tracking of clustered risk from adolescence to young adulthood: eight years follow-up in the Danish Youth and Sport Study**

International Journal of Behavioral Nutrition and Physical Activity 2004, 1:6 doi:10.1186/1479-5868-1-6.

Lars Bo Andersen1, 2 , Henriette Hasselstrøm 1, Vivian Grønfeldt1 Stig Eiberg Hansen1 and Froberg Karsten3

1. Institute for Exercise and Sport Sciences, University of Copenhagen, Copenhagen, Denmark.

2. Department of Health, Norwegian University of Sport and Physical education, Oslo, Norway.

3. Institute of Sports Science and Clinical Biomechanics, SOU-Odence University, Odence.

Introduction

Cardiovascular disease (CVD) is usually caused by high levels of many risk factors simultaneously over many years. Therefore, it is of great interest to study if subjects stay within rank order over time in both the biological risk factors and the behaviour that influences these risk factors. Many studies have described stability (tracking) in single risk factors, especially in children where hard endpoints are lacking, but few have analysed tracking in clustered risk.

Methods

Two examinations were conducted 8 years apart. The first time, 133 males and 172 females were 16–19 years of age. Eight years later, 98 males and 137 females participated. They were each time ranked into quartiles by sex in four CVD risk factors all related to the metabolic syndrome. Risk factors were the ratio between total cholesterol and HDL, triglyceride, systolic BP and body fat. The upper quartile was defined as being at risk, and if a subject had two or more risk factors, he/she was defined as a case (15–20 per cent of the subjects). Odds ratios (OR) for being a case was calculated between quartiles of fitness in both cross-sectional studies. The stability of combined risk was calculated as the OR between cases and non-cases at the first examination to be a case at the second examination.

Results

ORs for having two or more risk factors between quartiles of fitness were 3.1, 3.8 and 4.9 for quartiles two to four, respectively. At the second examination, OR were 0.7, 3.5 and 4.9, respectively. The probability for "a case" at the first examination to be "a case" at the second was 6.0.

Conclusions

The relationship between an exposure like physical fitness and CVD risk factors is much stronger when clustering of risk factors are analysed compared to the relationship to single risk factors. The stability over time in multiple risk factors analysed together is strong. This relationship should be seen in the light of moderate or weak tracking of single risk factors, and is strong evidence for early intervention in children where risk factors cluster.

86. **Reduced arterial O2 saturation during supine exercise in highly trained cyclists**
    Acta Physiologica Scandinavica, Volume 158 Page 325 - December 1996.
    P. K. Pedersen, H. Mandøe, K. Jensen, C. Andersen & K. Madsen

Performance of intense dynamic exercise in highly trained athletes is associated with a reduced arterial haemoglobin saturation for O2 (SaO2) and lower arterial PO2 (PaO2). We hypothesized that compared with upright exercise, supine exercise would be accompanied by a smaller reduction in SaO_2 because of a lower maximal O_2 uptake (VPO_2max) and/or a more even ventilation–perfusion distribution. Eight elite bicyclists completed progressive cycle ergometry to exhaustion in both positions with concomitant determinations of ventilatory data, arterial blood gases and pH. During upright cycling VPO_2max averaged 75 ± 1.6 mL O_2 min-1 kg-1 ($\pm$SEM) and it was 10.6 ± 1.7 per cent lower during supine cycling ($P<0.001$). Also the maximal pulmonary and alveolar ventilation were lower during supine cycling (by 15 ± 2 per cent and 21 ± 3 per cent, respectively; $P<0.001$) which related to a 0.8 ± 0.1 L lower tidal volume ($P<0.001$). In all subjects and independent of work posture PaO_2 and SaO_2 decreased from rest to exhaustion (from 99 ± 3 to 82 ± 2 Torr and 98.1 ± 0.2 to 95.2 ± 0.4 per cent, respectively; $P<0.001$); alveolar–arterial PO_2 difference increased from 6 ± 2 to 37 ± 3 Torr in both body positions. At exhaustion arterial PCO_2 was lower in upright than in supine (33.4 ± 0.6 vs. 35.9 ± 0.9 Torr; $P<0.01$), suggesting a greater relative hyperventilation in upright. Arterial pH was similar in upright and supine at rest (both 7.41 ± 0.01) and at exhaustion (7.31 ± 0.01 vs. 7.32 ± 0.01, respectively). We conclude that despite a lower VPO_2max and supposedly an improved ventilation–perfusion distribution, altering body position from upright to supine does not influence arterial O_2 desaturation during intense exercise.

87.   The Effects of a Weight Belt on Trunk and Leg Muscle Activity and Joint Kinematics During the Squat Exercise

The Journal of Strength and Conditioning Research: Vol. 15, No. 2, pp. 235–240.

Attila J. Zink, A William C. Whiting, A William J. Vincent, A and Alice J. Mclainea

(a) Department of Kinesiology, California State University, Northridge, California 91330.

Fourteen healthy men participated in a study designed to examine the effects of weight-belt use on trunk- and leg-muscle myoelectric activity (EMG) and joint kinematics during the squat exercise. Each subject performed the parallel back squat exercise at a self-selected speed according to his own technique with 90 per cent of his 1RM both without a weight belt (NWB) and with a weight belt (WB). Myoelectric activity of the right vastus lateralis, biceps femoris, adductor magnus, gluteus maximus, and erector spinae was recorded using surface electrodes. Subjects were videotaped from a sagittal plane view while standing on a force plate. WB trials were completed significantly faster ($p < 0.05$) than NWB trials over the entire movement and in both the downward phase (DP) and upward phase (UP). No significant differences in EMG were detected between conditions for any of the muscle groups or for any joint angular kinematic variables during either phase of the lift. The total distance traveled by the barbell both anteriorly and vertically was significantly greater (p < 0.01) in the WB condition than the NWB condition. The velocity of the barbell was significantly greater (p < 0.01) both vertically and horizontally during both the DP and UP in the WB condition as compared with the NWB condition. These data suggest that the use of a weight belt during the squat exercise may affect the path of the barbell and speed of the lift without altering myoelectric activity. This suggests that the use of a weight belt may improve a lifter's explosive power by increasing the speed of the movement without compromising the joint range of motion or overall lifting technique.

Reference Data:Zink, A.J., W.C. Whiting, W.J. Vincent, and A.J. McLaine. The effects of a weight belt on trunk and leg muscle activity and joint kinematics during the squat exercise.

Keywords: biomechanics, EMG, powerlifting.

88. Upper Extremity Weight-Training Modifications for the Injured Athlete

The American Journal of Sports Medicine 26:732-742 (1998)

Martin Fees, MPT, ATC, CSCS*, Tony Decker, ATC, CSCS, Lynn Snyder-Mackler, ScD, PT, ATC and Michael J. Axe, MD,

* Joyner Sportsmedicine Institute, Inc., Gettysburg, Pennsylvania

Departments of Athletics, University of Delaware, Newark, Delaware

Departments of Physical Therapy, University of Delaware, Newark, Delaware.

Address correspondence and reprint requests to Michael J. Axe, MD, First State Orthopaedics, 4745 Ogletown-Stanton Road, Suite 225, Newark, DE 19713.

The ability of the health care professional to make correct decisions about the progression of weight-training is critical to the rehabilitation process. The purpose of this article is to describe our approach to modification of weight-lifting techniques using the injured shoulder as a model. Additionally, the impact of various upper extremity weight-training techniques on healthy athletes is discussed. The effects of grip, hand spacing, bar trajectory, and start and finishing positions on microtraumatic injury and return to weight-training activities after injury are considered. Several weight-training functional progressions for common multijoint exercises (such as bench press, shoulder press, power clean) are presented. Adaptations for periodization are also presented for implementation in the rehabilitation sequence. The weight-training modifications described in this paper will assist the health professional to safely return athletes to the weight room after shoulder injury.

89.   Electromyographic Activity and Applied Load During Shoulder Rehabilitation Exercises Using Elastic Resistance

The American Journal of Sports Medicine 26:210-220 (1998)

Robert A. Hintermeister, PhD, Gregory W. Lange, MS, Jeanne M. Schultheis, Michael J. Bey, MS and Richard J. Hawkins, MD

Steadman Hawkins Sports Medicine Foundation, Vail, Colorado

Presented at the American College of Sports Medicine Annual Conference, Cincinnati, Ohio, May 1996.

Address correspondence and reprint requests to Robert A. Hintermeister, PhD, Steadman Hawkins Sports Medicine Foundation, 181 W. Meadow Drive, Suite 1000, Vail, CO 81657.

Muscle activity (measured by electromyography) and applied load were measured during seven shoulder rehabilitation exercises done with an elastic resistance device. Nineteen men with no shoulder abnormalities performed seven exercises: external and internal rotation, forward punch, shoulder shrug, and seated rowing with a narrow, middle, and wide grip. Qualitative video (60 Hz) was synchronized with the electromyography data from eight muscles (2000 Hz). Fine-wire intramuscular electrodes were inserted into the supraspinatus and subscapularis muscles, and surface electrodes were placed over the anterior deltoid, infraspinatus, pectoralis major, latissimus dorsi, serratus anterior, and trapezius muscles. Ten trials per subject were analyzed for average and peak amplitude, and the results were expressed as a percentage of maximum voluntary contractions. The peak loads for all exercises ranged from 21 to 54 N. The muscle activity patterns suggest that these shoulder rehabilitation exercises incorporating elastic resistance, controlled movements, and low initial loading effectively target the rotator cuff and supporting musculature and are appropriate for postinjury and postoperative patients.

90.   Effect of Exercise-Induced Dehydration on Lactate Parameters During Incremental Exercise

Int J Sports Med 2005; 26: 854-858

R. Van Schuylenbergh[1], B. Vanden Eynde[1], P. Hespel[1]

1 Exercise Physiology and Biomechanics Laboratory, Department of Kinesiology, Faculty of Physical Education and Physiotherapy, K. U. Leuven, Leuven, Belgium.

Cyclists often use heart rate limits or power output zones, obtained from lactate parameters during incremental exercise testing, to control training intensity. However, the relationship between heart rate or power output, and blood lactate can be changed by several factors including dehydration. Therefore, in the current study we investigated the impact of exercise-induced dehydration on lactate parameters during graded exercise. Nine triathletes completed two test sessions in random order, with a 1-week interval. Each session consisted of 2 graded cycling tests to exhaustion (pretest, posttest), interspersed by a 2-h endurance exercise bout. In one session the cyclists received adequate fluid replacement (EH, 1350 ml · h-1) whilst in the other session dehydration was not prevented (DH, 225 ml · h-1). Subjects received equal amounts of carbohydrates (150 g) during either condition. The 4-mmol lactate threshold (OBLA) and the dmax lactate threshold (TH-Dm) were calculated from the power : lactate curves. Weight loss was 0.5 ± 0.3 kg in EH versus 2.5 ± 0.2 kg in DH ($p < 0.05$). Heart rate (HR) at TH-Dm remained unchanged in all test occasions. Conversely, HR at OBLA increased by <" 10 beats · min-1 from the pretest to the posttest ($p < 0.05$), in both EH and DH. Compared to the pretest, in the posttest power output at TH-Dm was reduced (minus <" 12 per cent, $p < 0.05$) in DH, but not in EH. Gross mechanical efficiency at TH-Dm was 20.7 ± 1 per cent in the pretest in EH and was not different from the pretest value in DH (21.4 ± 0.7 per cent, n.s.). Gross efficiency decreased in the posttest in DH (18.4 ± 0.6 per cent, $p < 0.05$), but not in EH (20.2 ± 0.8 per cent, n.s.). It is concluded that heart rate rather than power output should be used to monitor training load in cyclists exercising in environmental conditions predisposing to dehydration. Furthermore, in the latter condition, adequate rehydration is essential to preserve optimal mechanical efficiency.

Key words: Exercise testing - cycling - triathlon - fluid replacement.

91. Weight-bearing exercise and markers of bone turnover in female athletes

J Appl Physiol, Vol. 90, Issue 2, 565-570, February 2001

Dana L. Creighton1, Amy L. Morgan1, Debra Boardley1, and P. Gunnar Brolinson2

Departments of 1 Kinesiology and 2 Rehabilitative Services, College of Health and Human Services, University of Toledo, Toledo, Ohio 43606.

Weight-bearing activity provides an osteogenic stimulus, while effects of swimming on bone are unclear. We evaluated **bone mineral density** (BMD) and markers of bone turnover in female athletes (n = 41, age 20.7 yr) comparing three impact groups, high impact (High, basketball and volleyball, n = 14), medium impact (Med, soccer and track, n = 13), and nonimpact (Non, swimming, n = 7), with sedentary age-matched controls (Con, n = 7). BMD was assessed by dual-energy X-ray absorptiometry at the lumbar spine, femoral neck (FN), Ward's triangle, and trochanter (TR); bone resorption estimated from urinary cross-linked N-telopeptides (NTx); and bone formation determined from serum osteocalcin. Adjusted BMD (g/cm; covariates: body mass index, weight, and

calcium and calorie intake) was greater at the FN and TR in the High group
(1.27 ± 0.03 and 1.05 ± 0.03) than in the Non (1.05 ± 0.04 and 0.86 ± 0.04) and
Con (1.03 ± 0.05 and 0.85 ± 0.05) groups and greater at the TR in the Med
group (1.01 ± 0.03) than in the Non (0.86 ± 0.04) and Con (0.85 ± 0.05) groups.
Total body BMD was higher in the High group (4.9 ± 0.12) than in the Med
(4.5 ± 0.12), Non (4.2 ± 0.14), and Con (4.1 ± 0.17) groups and greater in the
Med group than in the Non and Con groups. Bone formation was lower in the
Non group (19.8 ± 2.6) than in the High (30.6 ± 3.0) and Med (32.9 ± 1.9, P 0.05)
groups. No differences in a marker of bone resorption (NTx) were noted. This
indicates that women who participate in impact sports such as volleyball and
basketball had higher BMDs and bone formation values than female swimmers.

Key Words: osteocalcin; physical activity; mechanical loading.

92.   **Sagittal Plane Knee Translation and Electromyographic Activity
During Closed and Open Kinetic Chain Exercises in Anterior Cruciate
Ligament-Deficient Patients and Control Subjects**

The American Journal of Sports Medicine 29:72-82 (2001)

Joanna Kvist, RPT, PhD*,, and Jan Gillquist, MD, PhD*

Divisions of Sports Medicine, Faculty of Health Science, Linköping
University, Linköping, Sweden.

Physical Therapy, Department of Neuroscience and Locomotion, Faculty
of Health Science, Linköping University, Linköping, Sweden.

Address correspondence and reprint requests to Joanna Kvist, RPT,
PhD, Sports Medicine and Physical Therapy, Department of Neuroscience
and Locomotion, Faculty of Health Sciences, Linköping University, SE-581 85
Linköping, Sweden.

Using electrogoniometry and electromyography, we measured tibial
translation and muscle activation in 12 patients with unilateral anterior cruciate
ligament injury and in 12 control subjects. Measurements were made during
an active extension exercise with 0-, 4-, and 8-kg weights and during squats on
two legs and on one leg where the projection of the center of gravity was
placed over, behind, and in front the feet. In the uninjured subjects, tibial
translation increased with increasing load except during the squat with the
center of gravity behind the feet, which produced the smallest translation. For
the active extension exercises, translation was greater during eccentric activity.
In the anterior cruciate ligament-injured knees, all squats resulted in similar
translation, which was smaller than that during the active extension exercise.
The highest muscle activation was seen during squats. Hamstring muscle
activity was low. Increased static laxity in the anterior cruciate ligament-deficient
knee can be controlled during closed but not during open kinetic chain

exercises. Coactivation of the quadriceps and gastrocnemius muscles seems to be important for knee stability, whereas hamstring muscle coactivation was insignificant. To minimize sagittal translation during nonoperative management of anterior cruciate ligament-deficient knees, closed kinetic chain exercises are preferable to open kinetic chain exercises, and importance should be attached to the spontaneous coactivation of the quadriceps and gastrocnemius muscles.

93. Subscapularis Muscle Activity during Selected Rehabilitation Exercises

The American Journal of Sports Medicine 31:126-134 (2003)

Michael J. Decker, MS, John M. Tokish, MD, Henry B. Ellis, Michael R. Torry, PhD and Richard J. Hawkins, MD

From the Steadman-Hawkins Sports Medicine Foundation, Vail, Colorado

Presented in part at the Fourth World Congress of Biomechanics, Calgary, Canada, August 2002.

Address correspondence to Michael J. Decker, MS, mike.decker@mail.utexas.edu.

Address reprint requests to Michael R. Torry, PhD, Biomechanics Research Laboratory, Steadman-Hawkins Sports Medicine Foundation, 181 West Meadow Drive, Suite 1000, Vail, CO 81657.

Background: The upper and lower portions of the subscapularis muscle are independently innervated and activated.

Hypothesis: Upper and lower portions of the subscapularis muscle demonstrate different activation levels and require different exercises for rehabilitation.

Study Design: Controlled laboratory study.

Methods: Fifteen healthy subjects performed seven shoulder-strengthening exercises. Electromyographic data were collected from the latissimus dorsi, teres major, pectoralis major, infraspinatus, supraspinatus, and upper and lower subscapularis muscles.

Results: Upper subscapularis muscle activity was greater than lower subscapularis muscle activity for all exercises except for internal rotation with $0°$ of humeral abduction. The push-up plus and diagonal exercises consistently stressed the upper and lower subscapularis muscles to the greatest extent.

Conclusions: Humeral abduction was found to have a strong influence on the selective activation of the upper versus the lower subscapularis muscle and thus supported the design of different exercise continuums. In addition, the push-up plus and diagonal exercises were found to be superior to traditional internal rotation exercises for activating both functional portions of the subscapularis muscle.

Clinical Relevance: Our results showing that the upper and lower portions of the subscapularis muscle are functionally independent may affect training or rehabilitation protocols for the rotator cuff muscles.

94.   A Home Exercise Program for Tibial Bone Strengthening Based on in Vivo Strain Measurements.
American Journal of Physical Medicine and Rehabilitation. 80(6):433-438, June 2001.

Milgrom, Charles MD; Miligram, Michael MD; Simkin, Ariel PhD; Burr, David PhD; Ekenman, Ingrid MD; Finestone, Aharon MD

Objective: To compare the strain and strain rates generated during lower limb calisthenics with walking, an exercise that has been found to have only minimal effect on bone mass. Strengthening of bone, while it still has adaptive ability, can be achieved by exercise. Mechanical loading during physical activity produces strains and strain rates within the bones. It is thought that strain and strain rates higher than the usual provide the stimulus for the bones' adaptation.

Design: Three strain-gauged bone staples were inserted percutaneously in a 30[degrees] rosette pattern in the medial aspect of the midtibial diaphysis of two volunteers. The principal compression, tension, shear strains, and strain rates were measured during various lower limb calisthenics and compared with those of jogging and walking.

Results: Zig-zag hopping was in the grouping of exercises with the highest principal compression, tension, and shear strains and compression strain rates, whereas walking was in the lowest or next-to-the-lowest grouping for all principal strain or strain rates.

Conclusion: Zig-zag hopping, based on the high strain and strain rates that it produces, may be an optimal tibial bone-strengthening exercise.

95.   Effects of exercise on physiological and psychological variables in cancer survivors.
Medicine and Science in Sports and Exercise. 34 (12):1863-1867, December 2002.

Burnham, Timothy R.; Wilcox, Anthony

Purpose: The primary purpose of this study was to examine the effect of aerobic exercise on physiological and psychological function in patients rehabilitating from cancer treatment. A second purpose was to evaluate the differential effects of low- and moderate-intensity exercise on these variables.

Methods: Eighteen survivors of breast or colon cancer (15 female and 3 male, 40-65 yr of age) served as subjects. The subjects were matched by aerobic capacity and scores on a Quality of Life questionnaire, and then randomly assigned to a control, low- (25-35 per cent heart rate reserve (HRR)), or a moderate- (40-50 per cent HRR) intensity exercise group. The exercise groups performed lower-body aerobic exercise three times a week for 10 wk. After the exercise training, there were no statistically significant differences between the two exercise groups on any of the physiological variables. Therefore, the exercise groups were combined into one group for the final analysis.

Results: The results revealed statistically significant increases in aerobic capacity ($P < 0.001$) and lower-body flexibility ($P = 0.027$), a significant decrease in body fat ($P < 0.001$), and a significant increase in quality of life ($P < 0.001$) and a measure of energy ($P = 0.038$) in the exercise group when compared with the control group.

Conclusion: Low- and moderate-intensity aerobic-exercise programs were equally effective in improving physiological and psychological function in this population of cancer survivors. Aerobic exercise appears to be a valuable and well-tolerated component of the cancer-rehabilitation process.

96. **Increased Workload Enhances Force Output During Pedaling Exercise in Persons With Poststroke Hemiplegia**
Stroke. 1998;29:598-606.
D. A. Brown, PhD, PT; S. A. Kautz, PhD
From the Rehabilitation Research and Development Center, VA Palo Alto Health Care System (Calif).

Correspondence to David A. Brown, PhD, PT, Rehabilitation Research and Development Center (153), VA Palo Alto Health Care System, 3801 Miranda Ave, Palo Alto, CA 94306. E-mail brown@roses.stanford.edu

Background and Purpose : A principle of poststroke rehabilitation is that effort should be avoided since it leads to increased spasticity and produces widespread associated abnormal reactions. Although weakness also contributes to movement dysfunction after a stroke, it has been feared that heightened activity levels during strength training will further exacerbate the abnormal tone imbalance present in spastic hemiplegia. The purpose of this study was to test this hypothesis by quantifying the effects of increased workload on motor performance during different speeds of pedaling exercise in persons with poststroke hemiplegia.

Methods : Twelve healthy elderly subjects and 15 subjects with poststroke hemiplegia of greater than 6 months since onset were tested. The experimental protocol consisted of having subjects pedal at 12 randomly ordered workload and cadence combinations (45-J, 90-J, 135-J, and 180-J workloads at 25, 40, and 55 rpm). Pedal reaction forces were measured and used to calculate work done by each leg, including net positive and negative components. An electromyogram was recorded from seven leg muscles.

Results—The main finding was that net mechanical work done by the plegic leg increased as workload increased in 75 of 81 instances without increasing the percentage of inappropriate muscle activity.

Conclusions—This study provides evidence that persons with hemiplegia increase force output by their plegic limb when pedaling against higher workloads without exacerbation of impaired motor control. Therefore, exertional pedaling exercise is a beneficial intervention for achieving gains in muscular force output without worsening motor control impairments.

Key Words: exercise • hemiplegia • motor activity • muscle spasticity.

97.   **Effects of voluntary exercise and genetic selection for high activity levels on HSP72 expression in house mice**

J Appl Physiol 96: 1270-1276, 2004.

Jason G. Belter,1 Hannah V. Carey,2 and Theodore Garland, Jr.1

Departments of 1Zoology and 2Comparative Biosciences, University of Wisconsin-Madison, Madison, Wisconsin 53706.

We studied expression of heat shock protein 72 (HSP72) in female mice from four replicate lines that had been selectively bred for high voluntary wheel running (S) and from four random-bred control lines (C). Mice from generation 23 were sampled after 6 days of wheel access, and those from generation 14 were sampled after 8 wk of access to wheels either free to rotate or locked. Mice from S lines ran 2.6 times as many revolutions per day as did those from C lines. Western blotting of tissues from generation 23 mice indicated that S mice had elevated HSP72 expression in triceps surae muscle, but levels in spleen, kidney, heart, and lung were similar in S and C mice. HSP72 expression in triceps surae from generation 14 mice was measured by ELISA and analyzed with a two-way analysis of covariance. The interaction between wheel type and line type (S vs. C) was statistically significant, and subsequent analyses indicated that S mice had significantly elevated HSP72 expression only when housed with free wheels. Mice with the previously described mini-muscle phenotype (Houle-Leroy P, Guderley H, Swallow JG, and Garland T Jr. Am J Physiol Regul Integr Comp Physiol 284: R433-R443, 2003) occurred in both generations and had elevated HSP72 expression in triceps surae. For the generation 23 sample, wheel running as a covariate had a significant negative association with HSP72 expression, and the effect of line type was still statistically significant. Therefore, the increased HSP72 expression of S mice is not a simple proximate effect of their increased wheel running.

Key Words: adaptation; artificial selection; exercise physiology; stress proteins; wheel-running behavior; heat shock protein 72

Address for reprint requests and other correspondence: H. V. Carey, Dept. of Comparative Biosciences, School of Veterinary Medicine, Univ. of Wisconsin-Madison, Madison, WI 53706 (E-mail: careyh @ svm. vetmed. wisc. edu).

98. **Pharyngeal dysphagia in postesophagectomy patients: correlation with deglutitive biomechanics**

Ann Thorac Surg 2000;69:989-992

Caryn S. Easterling, MSa, Michael Bousamra, II, MDb, Ivan M. Lang, DVM, PhDa, Mark K. Kern, MSa, Terilynn Nitschke, MSa, Eytan Bardan, MDa, Reza Shaker, MDa

(a) Dysphagia Institute, Division of Gastroenterology and Hepatology, Milwaukee, Wisconsin, USA.

(b) Division of Cardiothoracic Surgery, Medical College of Wisconsin, Zablocki Veterans Affairs Medical Center, Milwaukee, Wisconsin, USA.

Address reprint requests to Dr Shaker, Division of Gastroenterology and Hepatology, Froedtert Memorial Lutheran Hospital, 9200 W Wisconsin Ave, Milwaukee, WI 53226.

Background : Because of the transient nature of pharyngeal phase dysphagia, posttranshiatal esophagectomy patients provide a model for studying the correlation of dysphagic symptoms and aspiration with deglutitive biomechanics.

Methods : We studied 8 transhiatal esophagectomy patients (age range, 51 to 78 years) and 8 normal age-matched controls in upright position using lateral and anteroposterior (AP) projection videofluoroscopy during three 5 mL barium swallows.

Results : The maximum upper esophageal sphincter (UES) AP diameter and maximum anterior excursion of the hyoid bone in patients with transhiatal esophagectomy who experienced aspiration (6.2 ± 0.6 and 9.0 ± 2.0 mm, respectively) were significantly smaller than those of age-matched normal controls (9.4 ± 0.7 and 17.0 ± 1.0 mm, respectively). Resolution of aspiration was associated with a significant increase in AP diameter of the UES as well as anterior and superior excursion of the hyoid bone ($p < 0.05$).

Conclusions : Dysphagic symptoms and aspiration in posttranshiatal esophagectomy patients are associated with significant abnormalities of deglutitive biomechanics. Improvement in deglutitive biomechanics is associated with resolution of dysphagic symptoms as well as postdeglutitive aspiration in these patients.

3

Endurance Variables

1.   **Elite athletes and the gene for angiotensin-converting enzyme**
      J Appl Physiol, Vol. 87, Issue 3, 1035-1037, September 1999

      **Roger R. Taylor1, Cyril D. S. Mamotte2, Kieran Fallon3, and Frank
M. van Bockxmeer2,4**
      1 Departments of Cardiology and Medicine, Royal Perth Hospital and
The University of Western Australia, Perth, Western Australia 6001;
2 Department of Biochemistry, Royal Perth Hospital, Perth, Western Australia
6001; 3 Australian Institute of Sport, Belconnen, Australian Capital Territory
2616; and 4 Department of Pathology, The University of Western Australia,
Nedlands, Western Australia 6009, Australia.

      The deletion (D) allele of the gene for **angiotensin-converting enzyme**
(ACE) is associated with higher plasma and tissue levels of the enzyme and
has also been related to a variety of cardiovascular complications, particularly
myocardial infarction. On the basis of indirect evidence, we hypothesized that
inheritance of the D allele would contribute to elite athletic ability. Over a
period of 4 yr, 120 Caucasian athletes who were national (Australian)
representatives in sports demanding a high level of aerobic fitness were
recruited. Their ACE genotypes were compared with those of a community
control group recruited randomly from the electoral roll. There was no difference
in ACE genotype frequencies between the two groups. The DD genotype
frequency was 30 per cent in athletes and 29 per cent in the control group, and
the II genotype frequency was 22.5 and 22 per cent, respectively. The results
do not exclude the possibility that ACE genotype could be related to some
attribute relating to a specific type of elite athletic ability or that there may be
a difference between genders. Larger studies are desirable.

Key Words: deletion allele; insertion allele; inheritance; physical performance

2. **Effects of Aerobic Exercise on the Physical Performance and Incidence of Treatment-Related Complications After High-Dose Chemotherapy**
Blood, Vol. 90 No. 9 (November 1), 1997: pp. 3390-3394

Fernando Dimeo, Sebastian Fetscher, Winand Lange, Roland Mertelsmann, and Joseph Keul

From the Department of Rehabilitation, Prevention and Sports Medicine, the Department of Hematology and Oncology, Freiburg University Medical Center, Freiburg in Breisgau, Germany.

Loss of physical performance is a universal problem of cancer patients undergoing chemotherapy. We postulated that this impairment can be partially prevented by aerobic exercise. In a randomized study, 33 cancer patients receiving high-dose chemotherapy followed by autologous peripheral blood **stem cell transplantation** (training group, T) performed an exercise program consisting of biking on an **ergometer** in the supine position after an interval-training pattern for 30 minutes daily during hospitalization. Patients in the control group (C, n = 37) did not train. Maximal physical performance was assessed with a treadmill test by admission and discharge. Physical performance of the two groups was not different on admission. The decrement in performance during hospitalization was 27 per cent greater in the control group than in the training group (P = .05); this resulted in a significantly higher maximal physical performance at discharge in the trained patients (P = .04). Duration of neutropenia (P = .01) and thrombopenia (P = .06), severity of diarrhea (P = .04), severity of pain (P = .01), and duration of hospitalization (P = .03) were reduced in the training group. We conclude that aerobic exercise can be safely carried out immediately after high-dose chemotherapy and can partially prevent loss of physical performance. Based on the potential significance of the observed outcomes, further studies are warranted to confirm our results.

3. **Relationship between activity levels, aerobic fitness, and body fat in 8-to 10-yr-old children**
J Appl Physiol, Vol. 86, Issue 4, 1428-1435, April 1999

Ann V. Rowlands, Roger G. Eston, and David K. Ingledew

School of Sport, Health, and Physical Education Sciences, University of Wales, Bangor LL57 2EN, Wales, United Kingdom.

The relationships between children's activity, aerobic fitness, and fatness are unclear. Indirect estimates of activity, e.g., heart rate (HR) and recall, may mask any associations. The purpose of this study was to assess these relationships by using the Tritrac-R3D, a pedometer, and heart rate. Thirty-four children, ages 8-10 yr, participated in the study. The Tritrac and **pedometer** were worn for up to 6 days. HR was measured for 1 day. Activity measured by Tritrac or pedometer correlated positively to fitness in the whole group (Tritrac, $r = 0.66$; pedometer, $r = 0.59$; $P < 0.01$) and in boys and girls separately ($P < 0.05$) and correlated negatively to fatness in the whole group ($r = 0.42$, $P < 0.05$). In contrast, HR did not correlate significantly to fitness, and HR of >139 beats/min correlated positively to fatness in girls ($r = 0.64$, $P < 0.05$). This suggests that HR is misleading as a measure of activity. This study supports a positive relationship between activity and fitness and suggests a negative relationship between fatness and activity.

Key words: physical activity; accelerometry; pedometry; heart rate.

4. **Intrinsic risk factors for exercise-related injuries among male and female army trainees**
   American Journal of Sports Medicine, Vol 21, Issue 5 705-710, 1993.
   BH Jones, MW Bovee, JM Harris 3rd and DN Cowan
   Occupational Medicine Division, U.S. Army Research Institute of Environmental Medicine, Natick, MA 01760.

   Physical training-related injuries are common among army recruits and other vigorously active populations, but little is known about their causation. To identify intrinsic risk factors, we prospectively measured 391 army trainees. For 8 weeks of basic training, 124 men and 186 women (79.3 per cent) were studied. They answered questionnaires on past activities and sports participation, and were measured for height, weight, and body fat percentage; 71 per cent of the subjects took an initial army physical training test. Women had a significantly higher incidence of time-loss injuries than men, 44.6 per cent compared with 29.0 per cent. During training, more time-loss injuries occurred among the 50 per cent of the men who were slower on the mile run, 29.0 per cent versus 0.0 per cent. Slower women were likewise at greater risk than faster ones, 38.2 per cent versus 18.5 per cent. Men with histories of inactivity and with higher body mass index were at greater injury risk than other men, as were the shortest women. We conclude that female gender and low aerobic fitness measured by run times are risk factors for training injuries in army trainees, and that other factors such as prior activity levels and stature may affect men and women differently.

5. **Effects of erythropoietin administration in training athletes and possible indirect detection in doping control.**
   Medicine & Science in Sports & Exercise. 31(5):639-645, May 1999.
   Audran, Michel; Gareau, Raynald; Matecki, Stephane; Durand, Fabienne; Chenard, Claire; Sicart, Marie-therese; Marion, Benedicte; Bressolle, Francoise

This study investigated the effects of repeated subcutaneous injection of rHuEpo (50 IU[middle dot]kg-1) in athletes and proposes a method based on the measurement in blood samples of the sTfR/serum protein ratio to determine if the observed values of this marker are related to rHuEpo abuse.

Methods: Serum erythropoietin concentrations, and hematological and biochemical parameters were evaluated, during treatment and for 25 d post-treatment in nine training athletes. Moreover, the effect of rHuEpo administrations on the maximum oxygen uptake (O2max) and **ventilatory threshold** (VT) of these athletes was also studied. Threshold values for sTfr and the sTfr/serum protein ratio were determined from 233 subjects (185 athletes, 15 athletes training at moderately high altitude, and 33 subjects living at >3000 m).

Results: Significant changes in **reticulocytes, hemoglobin** (Hb) concentration, **hematocrit** (Hct), sTfr, and sTfr /serum proteins were observed during and after rHuEpo treatment. The maximal heart rate of 177 beats [middle dot] min-1 at the beginning of the study was significantly higher than the value of 168 beats[middle dot]min-1 after 26 d of rHuEpo administration. Compared with the values measured at baseline, the VT measured after rHuEpo administration occurred at a statistically significant high level of oxygen uptake.

Conclusions: When oxygen uptake measured at the VT was expressed as a percentage of O2 max, the values obtained were also significantly higher. The increased values of Tfr and sTfr/serum proteins, respectively, above 10 [mu]g[middle dot]mL-1 and 153, indicated the probable intake of rHuEpo.

6.   **Physical activity patterns associated with cardiorespiratory fitness and reduced mortality: the Aerobics Center Longitudinal Study.**
      Am J Public Health. 1998 December; 88(12): 1807–1813.
      J R Stofan, L DiPietro, D Davis, H W Kohl, 3rd, and S N Blair
      John B. Pierce Laboratory, New Haven, CT 06519, USA.

Objectives: This study examined cross sectionally the physical activity patterns associated with low, moderate, and high levels of cardiorespiratory fitness.

Methods: Physical activity was assessed by questionnaire in a clinic population of 13,444 men and 3972 women 20 to 87 years of age. Estimated **energy expenditure** (kcal.wk-1) and volume (min.wk-1) of reported activities were calculated among individuals at low, moderate, and high fitness levels (assessed by maximal exercise tests).

Results: Average leisure time energy expenditures of 525 to 1650 kcal.wk-1 for men and 420 to 1260 kcal.wk-1 for women were associated with moderate to high levels of fitness. These levels of energy expenditure can be achieved with a brisk walk of approximately 30 minutes on most days of the week. In fact, men in the moderate and high fitness categories walked between 130 and 138 min.wk-1, and women in these categories walked between 148 and 167 min.wk-1.

Conclusions: Most individuals should be able to achieve these physical activity goals and thus attain a cardiorespiratory fitness level sufficient to result in substantial health benefits.

7. **Aerobic endurance training improves soccer performance**
Medicine and Science in Sports and Exercise. 33(11):1925-1931, November 2001.
HELGERUD, JAN; ENGEN, LARS CHRISTIAN; WISLOFF, ULRIK; HOFF, JAN

Purpose: The aim of the present study was to study the effects of aerobic training on performance during soccer match and soccer specific tests.

Methods: Nineteen male elite junior soccer players, age 18.1 +/- 0.8 yr, randomly assigned to the training group (N = 9) and the control group (N = 10) participated in the study. The specific aerobic training consisted of interval training, four times 4 min at 90-95 per cent of maximal heart rate, with a 3-min jog in between, twice per week for 8 wk. Players were monitored by video during two matches, one before and one after training.

Results: In the training group: a) maximal oxygen uptake (VO2max) increased from 58.1 +/- 4.5 mL[middle dot]kg-1[middle dot]min-1 to 64.3 +/- 3.9 mL[middle dot]kg-1[middle dot]min-1 (P < 0.01); b) lactate threshold improved from 47.8 +/- 5.3 mL[middle dot]kg-1[middle dot]min-1 to 55.4 +/- 4.1 mL[middle dot]kg-1[middle dot]min-1 (P < 0.01); c) **running economy** was also improved by 6.7 per cent (P < 0.05); d) distance covered during a match increased by 20 per cent in the training group (P < 0.01); e) number of sprints increased by 100 per cent (P < 0.01); f) number of involvements with the ball increased by 24 per cent (P < 0.05); g) the average work intensity during a soccer match, measured as percent of maximal heart rate, was enhanced from 82.7 +/- 3.4 per cent to 85.6 +/- 3.1 per cent (P < 0.05); and h) no changes were found in maximal vertical jumping height, strength, speed, kicking velocity, kicking precision, or quality of passes after the training period. The control group showed no changes in any of the tested parameters.

Conclusion: Enhanced aerobic endurance in soccer players improved soccer performance by increasing the distance covered, enhancing work intensity, and increasing the number of sprints and involvements with the ball during a match.

8.   Determination of maximal lactate steady state response in selected sports events

Medicine and Science in Sports and Exercise. 28(2):241-246, February 1996.

Beneke, Ralph; Von Duvillard, Serge Petelin

Maximal lactate steady state (MLSS) refers to the upper limit of blood lactate concentration indicating an equilibrium between lactate production and lactate elimination during constant workload. The aim of the present study was to investigate whether different levels of MLSS may explain different blood lactate concentration (BLC) levels at submaximal workload in the sports events of rowing, cycling, and speed skating. Eleven rowers (mean +/- SD, age 20.1 +/- 1.5 yr, height 188.7 +/- 6.2 cm, weight 82.7 +/- 8.0 kg), 16 cyclists and triathletes (age 23.6 +/- 3.0 yr, height 181.4+/- 5.6 cm, weight 72.5 +/- 6.2 kg), and 6 speed skaters (age 23.3+/- 6.6 yr, height 179.5 +/- 7.5 cm, weight 73.2 +/- 5.6 kg) performed an incremental load test to determine maximal workload and several submaximal 30-min constant workloads for MLSS measurement on a rowing **ergometer**, a cycle ergometer, and on a speed-skating track. Maximal workload was higher (P <= 0.05) in rowing (416.8 +/- 46.2 W) than in cling (358.6 +/- 34.4 W) and speed skating (383.5 +/- 40.9 W). The level of MLSS differed (P <= 0.001) in rowing (3.1 +/- 0.5 mmol[middle dot]l-1), cycling (5.4 +/- 1.0 mmol[middle dot]l-1), and in speed skating (6.6 +/- 0.9 mmol.l-1). MLSS workload was higher (P <= 0.05) in rowing (316.2 +/- 29.9 W) and speed skating (300.5 +/- 43.8 W) than in cycling (257.8 +/- 34.6 W). No differences (P > 0.05) in MLSS workload were found between speed skating and rowing. MLSS workload intensity as related to maximal workload was independent (P > 0.05) of the sports event: 76.2 per cent +/- 5.7 per cent in rowing, 71.8 per cent +/- 4.1 per cent in cycling, and 78.1 per cent +/- 4.4 per cent in speed skating. Changes in MLSS do not respond with MLSS workload, the MLSS workload intensity, or with the metabolic profile of the sports event. The observed differences in MLSS and MLSS workload may correspond to the sport-specific mass of working muscle.

9.   Interval training at V[spacing dot above]O2max: effects on aerobic performance and overtraining markers

Medicine and Science in Sports and Exercise. 31(1):156-163, January 1999.

Billat, Veronique l.; Flechet, Bruno; Petit, Bernard; Muriaux, Gerard; Koralsztein, Jean-pierre

Interval training at V[spacing dot above]O2max: effects on aerobic performance and overtraining markers. Med. Sci. Sports Exerc., Vol. 31, No. 1, pp. 156-163, 1999.

Purpose: Between inefficient training and overtraining, an appropriate training stimulus (in terms of intensity and duration) has to be determined in accordance with individual capacities. Interval training at the minimal velocity associated with V[spacing dot above]O2max (vV[spacing dot above]O2max) allows an athlete to run for as long as possible at V[spacing dot above]O2max. Nevertheless, we don't know the influence of a defined increase in training volume at vV[spacing dot above]O2max on aerobic performance, **noradrenaline**, and heart rate.

Methods: Eight subjects performed 4 wk of normal training (NT) with one session per week at vV[spacing dot above]O2max, i.e., five repetitions run at 50 per cent of the time limit at vV[spacing dot above]O2max, with recovery of the same duration at 60 per cent vV[spacing dot above]O2max. They then performed 4 wk of overload training (OT) with three interval training sessions at vV[spacing dot above]O2max.

Results: Normal training significantly improved their velocity associated with V[spacing dot above]O2max (20.5 +/- 0.7 vs 21.1 +/- 0.8 km[middle dot]h-1, P = 0.02). As a result of improved running economy (50.6 +/- 3.5 vs 47.5 +/- 2.4 mL[middle dot]min-1[middle dot]kg-1, P = 0.02), V[spacing dot above]O2max was not significantly different (71.6 +/- 4.8 vs 72.7 +/- 4.8 mL[middle dot]min-1[middle dot]kg-1). Time to exhaustion at vV[spacing dot above]O2max was not significantly different (301 +/- 56 vs 283 +/- 41 s) as was performance (i.e., distance limit run at vV[spacing dot above]O2max: 2052.2 +/- 331 vs 1986.2 +/- 252.9 m). Heart rate at 14 km[middle dot]h-1 decreased significantly after NT (162 +/- 16 vs 155 +/- 18 bpm, P < 0.01). Lactate threshold remained the same after normal training (84.1 +/- 4.8 per cent vV[spacing dot above]O2max). Overload training changed neither the performance nor the factors concerning performance. However, the submaximal heart rate measured at 14 km[middle dot]h-1 decreased after overload training (155 +/- 18 vs 150 +/- 15 bpm). The maximal heart rate was not significantly different after NT and OT (199 +/- 9.5, 198 +/- 11, 194 +/- 10.4, P = 0.1). Resting plasma norepinephrine (veinous blood sample measured by high pressure liquid chromatography), was unchanged (2.6 vs 2.4 nm[middle dot]L-1, P = 0.8). However, plasma norepinephrine measured at the end of the vV[spacing dot above]O2max test increased significantly (11.1 vs 26.0 nm[middle dot]L-1, P = 0.002).

Conclusion: Performance and aerobic factors associated with the performance were not altered by the 4 wk of intensive training at vV[spacing dot above]O2max despite the increase of plasma noradrenaline.

10. Ginseng Supplementation Does Not Enhance Healthy Young Adults' Peak Aerobic Exercise Performance

Journal of the American College of Nutrition, Vol. 17, No. 5, 462-466 (1998)

Jason D. Allen, MEd,, Jeff McLung, PhD, Arnold G. Nelson, PhD and Michael Welsch, PhD

Department of Health and Human Performance (J.D.A., J.M.) Louisiana State University.

Baton Rouge, Louisiana

Western Carolina University and Department of Kinesiology (J.D.A., A.G.N., M.W.) Louisiana State University, Baton Rouge, Louisiana.

Address reprint requests to: Jason D. Allen, Department of Kinesiology, H. P. Long Field House, Louisiana State University, Baton Rouge, LA 70803-7101

Objective: To determine the short term effects (21 days) of 200 mg (7 per cent standardized) Panax ginseng supplementation vs. placebo on peak aerobic exercise performance in healthy young adults, with unrestricted diets.

Methods: Twenty men and eight women (age=23.2±3.2 years, height=175.8±8.6 cm; weight=75.2±15.3 kg) were randomly assigned to either a Panax ginseng or placebo group for a period of 3 weeks in a double blind design. Prior to and following treatment the subjects performed a symptom limited graded exercise test on a Schwinn Airdyne ergometer. The data were analyzed using an analysis of variance.

Results: No significant treatment effect was observed for the dependent variables of VO2, exercise time, workload, **plasma lactate** and hematocrit at peak levels, or for heart rate and rate of perceived exertion at 150 watts, 200 watts and peak.

Conclusions: The results of this study do not support an ergogenic effect on peak aerobic exercise performance following a 3-week supplementation period of 200 mg 7 per cent Panax ginseng in healthy young adults with moderate exercise capacities and unrestricted diets.

Key Words: ginseng, VO2max, aerobic, performance, supplement, ergogenic aid.

11.   **Intermittent hypobaric hypoxia stimulates erythropoiesis and improves aerobic capacity.**

Medicine and Science in Sports and Exercise. 31(2):264-268, February 1999.

Rodriguez, Ferran A.; Casas, Hector; Casas, Mireia; Pages, Teresa; Rama, Ramon; Ricart, Antoni; Ventura, Josep L.; Ib ez, Jordi; Viscor, Gines

Purpose: The purpose of the study was to examine the effect of a very short intermittent exposure to moderate hypoxia in a hypobaric chamber on aerobic performance capacity at sea level and the erythropoietic response.

The effects of **hypobaric hypoxia** alone and combined with low-intensity exercise were also compared.

Methods: Seventeen members of three high-altitude expeditions were exposed to intermittent hypoxia in a hypobaric chamber over 9 d at simulated altitude, which was progressively increased from 4000 to 5500 m in sessions ranging from 3 to 5 h[middle dot]d-1. One group (N = 7; HE group) combined passive exposure to hypoxia with low-intensity exercise on a cycle **ergometer**. Another group (N = 10; H group) was only exposed to passive hypoxia. Before and after the exposure to hypoxia, medical status, performance capacity, and complete hematological and hemorheological profile of subjects were evaluated.

Results: No significant differences were observed between the two groups (HE vs H) in any of the parameters studied, indicating that hypoxia alone was responsible for the changes. After the acclimation period, a significant increase in exercise time (mean difference: +3.9 per cent; $P < 0.01$), and maximal pulmonary ventilation (+5.5 per cent; $P < 0.05$) was observed during the maximal incremental test at sea level. Individual lactate-velocity curves significantly shifted to the right ($P < 0.05$), thus revealing an improvement of aerobic endurance. A significant increase was found in PCV (42.1-45.1 per cent; $P < 0.0001$), RBC count (5.16 to 5.79 [middle dot]106[middle dot]mm-3; $P < 0.0001$), **reticulocytes** (0.5 to 1.1 per cent; $P < 0.0001$) and hemoglobin (Hb) concentration (14.2 to 16.7 g[middle dot]dL-1; $P < 0.002$).

Conclusions: It was concluded that short-term hypobaric hypoxia can activate the erythropoietic response and improve the aerobic performance capacity in healthy subjects.

12. Soccer specific aerobic endurance training

Br J Sports Med 2002;**36**:218-221

J Hoff, U Wisløff, L C Engen, O J Kemi and J Helgerud

Department of Physiology and Biomedical Engineering, Norwegian University of Science and Technology, N-7489 Trondheim, Norway

Correspondence to:

Dr Hoff, Department of Physiology and Biomedical Engineering, Norwegian University of Science and Technology, N-7489 Trondheim, Norway; Jan.Hoff@medisin.ntnu.no

Background: In professional soccer, a significant amount of training time is used to improve players' aerobic capacity. However, it is not known whether soccer specific training fulfils the criterion of effective endurance training to improve maximal oxygen uptake, namely an exercise intensity of 90–95 per cent of maximal heart rate in periods of three to eight minutes.

Objective: To determine whether ball dribbling and small group play are appropriate activities for interval training, and whether heart rate in soccer specific training is a valid measure of actual work intensity.

Methods: Six well trained first division soccer players took part in the study. To test whether soccer specific training was effective interval training, players ran in a specially designed dribbling track, as well as participating in small group play (five a side). Laboratory tests were carried out to establish the relation between heart rate and oxygen uptake while running on a treadmill. Corresponding measurements were made on the soccer field using a portable system for measuring oxygen uptake.

Results: Exercise intensity during small group play was 91.3 per cent of maximal heart rate or 84.5 per cent of maximal oxygen uptake. Corresponding values using a dribbling track were 93.5 per cent and 91.7 per cent. No higher heart rate was observed during soccer training.

Conclusions: Soccer specific exercise using ball dribbling or small group play may be performed as aerobic interval training. Heart rate monitoring during soccer specific exercise is a valid indicator of actual exercise intensity.

Key Words: football; anaerobic threshold; work economy; soccer performance.

13.   Maximal aerobic capacity in African-American and Caucasian prepubertal children

Am J Physiol Endocrinol Metab, Vol. 273, Issue 4, E809-E814, October 1997

Christina A. Trowbridge, Barbara A. Gower, Tim R. Nagy, Gary R. Hunter, Margarita S. Treuth, and Michael I. Goran

Division of Physiology and Metabolism, Department of Nutrition Sciences, University of Alabama at Birmingham, Birmingham, Alabama 35294-3360.

The purpose of this study was to examine differences in resting, submaximal, and maximal (O2 max) oxygen consumption (O2) in African-American (n = 44) and Caucasian (n = 31) prepubertal children aged 5-10 yr. Resting O2 was measured via indirect calorimetry in the fasted state. Submaximal O2 and O2 max were determined during an all out, progressive treadmill exercise test appropriate for children. Dual-energy X-ray absorptiometry was used to determine total fat mass (FM), soft lean tissue mass (LTM), and leg soft LTM. Doubly labeled water was used to determine total energy expenditure (TEE) and activity energy expenditure (AEE). A significant effect of ethnicity ($P < 0.01$) was found for O2 max but not resting or submaximal O2, with African-American children having absolute O2 max

~15 per cent lower than Caucasian children (1.21 ± 0.032 vs. 1.43 ± 0.031 l/min, respectively). The lower O2 max persisted in African-American children after adjustment for soft LTM (1.23 ± 0.025 vs. 1.39 ± 0.031 l/min; $P < 0.01$), leg soft LTM (1.20 ± 0.031 vs. 1.43 ± 0.042 l/min; $P < 0.01$), and soft LTM and FM (1.23 ± 0.025 vs. 1.39 ± 0.031 l/min; $P < 0.01$). The lower **O2 max** persisted also after adjustment for TEE (1.20 ± 0.02 vs. 1.38 ± 0.0028 l/min $P < 0.001$) and AEE (1.20 ± 0.024 vs. 1.38 ± 0.028 l/min; $P < 0.001$). In conclusion, our data indicate that African-American and Caucasian children have similar rates of O2 at rest and during submaximal exercise, but O2 max is ~15 per cent lower in African-American children, independent of soft LTM, FM, leg LTM, TEE, and AEE.

Key Words: oxygen consumption; fitness; energy expenditure; ethnicity

14. Meta-analysis of the age-associated decline in maximal aerobic capacity in men: relation to training status

Am J Physiol Heart Circ Physiol, Vol. 278, Issue 3, H829-H834, March 2000

Teresa M. Wilson and Hirofumi Tanaka

Human Cardiovascular Research Laboratory, Center for Physical Activity, Disease Prevention, and Aging, Department of Kinesiology and Applied Physiology, University of Colorado at Boulder, Boulder, Colorado 80309.

Based on cross-sectional data, we recently reported that, in contrast to the prevailing view, the rate of decline in maximal oxygen consumption (O2 max) with age is greater in physically active compared with sedentary healthy women. We tested this hypothesis in men using a meta-analytic study of **O2 max** values in the published literature. A total of 242 studies (538 subject groups and 13,828 subjects) met the inclusion criteria and were arbitrarily separated into sedentary (214 groups, 6,231 subjects), active (159 groups, 5,621 subjects), and endurance-trained (165 groups, 1,976 subjects) populations. Body fat percent increased with age in sedentary and active men ($P < 0.001$), whereas no change was observed in endurance-trained men. O2 max was inversely and strongly related to age within each population ($r = 0.80$ to 0.88, all $P < 0.001$) and was highest in endurance-trained and lowest in sedentary populations at any age. Absolute rates of decline in O2 max with age were not different ($P > 0.05$) in sedentary (4.0 ml · kg1 · min1 · decade1), active (4.0), and endurance-trained (4.6) populations. Similarly, there were no group differences ($P > 0.05$) in the relative (per cent) rates of decline in O2 max with advancing age (8.7, 7.3, and 6.8 per cent/decade, respectively). Maximal heart rate was inversely related to age within each population ($r = 0.88$ to 0.93, all $P < 0.001$), but the rate of age-related reduction was not different among the populations. There was a significant decline in running mileage and speed with advancing age in the endurance-trained men. The present cross-sectional meta-analytic findings do not support the hypothesis that the rate of decline in O2 max with age is related to habitual aerobic exercise status in men.

Key Words: aging; exercise.

15.   **Stress fractures. Identifiable risk factors**
American Journal of Sports Medicine, Vol. 19, Issue 6 647-652, 1991.
M Giladi, C Milgrom, A Simkin and Y Danon
Tel Aviv Medical Center, Ichilov Hospital, Israel.

To answer the question why such large differences in stress fracture morbidity rates (2 per cent to 64 per cent) exist in different countries, we prospectively evaluated 312 recruits for possible risk factors for stress fractures. Prior to training, each recruit underwent an evaluation including the following: orthopaedic examination, foot and tibial **radiograph**s, measurements of tibial bone width, bone mineral content, **bone density**, aerobic physical fitness and leg power, assessments of **somatotype** and smoking habits, and evaluation of sociological and psychological factors. Using a multivariate analysis, two risk factors were identified: recruits with stress fractures had significantly narrower tibiae (P less than 0.001), and a higher degree of external rotation of the hip (P = 0.016). These two variables were independent and cumulative. Stress fracture morbidity was 17 per cent, 29 per cent, and 45 per cent when neither, one, or both risk factors were present, respectively (P less than 0.001). Identification of these risk factors might explain the susceptibility of some people to stress fractures.

16.   **Injury rates from walking, gardening, weightlifting, outdoor bicycling, and aerobics**
Medicine and Science in Sports and Exercise. 30(8):1246-1249, August 1998.

Powell, Kenneth E.; Heath, Gregory W.; Kresnow, Marcie-jo; Sacks, Jeffrey J.; Branche, Christine M.

Purpose: The objective of this survey was to estimate the frequency of injuries associated with five commonly performed moderately intense activities: walking for exercise, gardening and yard work, weightlifting, aerobic dance, and outdoor bicycling.

Methods: National estimates were derived from weighted responses of over 5,000 individuals contacted between April 28 and September 18, 1994, via random-digit dialing of U.S. residential telephone numbers. Self-reported participation in these five activities in the late spring and summer of 1994 was common, ranging from an estimated 14.5 +/- 1.2 per cent of the population for aerobics (nearly 30 million people) to 73.0 +/- 1.5 per cent for walking (about 138 million people).

Results: Among participants, the activity-specific 30-d prevalence of injury ranged from 0.9 +/- 0.5 per cent for outdoor bicycle riding to 2.4 +/- 1.3 per cent for weightlifting. The estimated number of people injured in the 30 d before their interview ranged from 330,000 for outdoor bicycle riding to 2.1 million for gardening or yard work. Incidence rates for injuries causing reduced participation in activity were 1.1 +/- 0.5[middle dot]100 participants[middle dot]30 d for walking, 1.1 +/- 0.4 for gardening, and 3.3 +/- 1.9 for weightlifting. During walking and gardening, men and women were equally likely to be injured, but younger people (18-44 yr) were more likely to be injured than older people (45+ yr). Injury rates were low, yet large numbers of people were injured because participation rates were high. Most injuries were minor, but injuries may reduce participation in these otherwise beneficial activities.

Conclusions: Additional studies to confirm the magnitude of the problem, to identify modifiable risk factors, and to recommend methods to reduce the frequency of such injuries are needed.

17.   Aerobic capacity and cognitive performance in a cross-sectional aging study.
Medicine and Science in Sports and Exercise. 29(10):1357-1365, October 1997.

Van Boxtel, Martin P. J.; Paas, Fred G. W. C.; Houx, Peter J.; Adam, Jos J.; Teeken, Joep C.; Jolles, Jellemer

In a population unselected for aerobic fitness status, aerobic fitness([spacing dot above]VO2max) and its interaction with age were used to predict performance on several cognitive measures known to be affected by chronological age. It was hypothesized that, in particular, cognitively demanding tasks would be sensitive to aerobic capacity. Healthy subjects between 24 and 76 yr of age (N = 132) were recruited from a larger study into determinants of cognitive aging (Maastricht Aging Study-MAAS). All participants took part in a submaximal bicycle **ergometer** protocol and an extensive neurocognitive examination, including tests of intelligence, verbal memory, and simple and complex cognitive speed. Participants engaged more hours a week in aerobic sports and felt healthier than the nonparticipants of the same age did. No group differences were found in the basic anthropometric characteristics height, weight, and BMI. Two of four subtasks that reflect complex cognitive speed (Stroop color/word interference and Concept Shifting Test) showed main and interaction effects with age of aerobic capacity in a hierarchical regression analysis, accounting for up to 5 per cent of variance in parameter score after correction for age, sex, and intelligence main effects. These findings fit well within a moderator model of aerobic fitness in cognitive aging. They add to the notion that aerobic fitness may selectively and age-dependently act on cognitive processes, in particular those that require relatively large attentional resources.

18.   **Twenty-year follow-up of aerobic power and body composition of older track athletes**
Journal of Applied Physiology, Vol. 82, No. 5, pp. 1508-1516, May 1997
Michael L. Pollock, Larry J. Mengelkoch, James E. Graves, David T. Lowenthal, Marian C. Limacher, Carl Foster, and Jack H. Wilmore
Departments of Medicine and Exercise and Sport Sciences, Center for Exercise Science, University of Florida, and Geriatric Research, Education and Clinical Center, Veterans Affairs Medical Center, Gainesville, Florida 32610.

The purpose was to determine the aerobic power (maximal oxygen uptake) and body composition of older track athletes after a 20-yr follow-up (T3). At 20 yr, 21 subjects [mean ages: 50.5 ± 8.5 yr at initial evaluation (T1), 60.2 ± 8.8 yr at 10-yr follow-up (T2), and 70.4 ± 8.8 yr at 20-yr follow-up (T3)] were divided into three intensity groups: high (H; remained elite; n = 9); moderate (M; continued frequent moderate-to-rigorous endurance training; n = 10); and low (L; greatly reduced training; n = 2). All groups decreased in maximal oxygen uptake at each testing point (H, 8 and 15 per cent; M, 13 and 14 per cent; and L, 18 and 34 per cent from T1 to T2 and T2 to T3, respectively). Maximal heart rate showed a linear decrease of ~5-7 beats · min1 · decade1 and was independent of training status. Body weight remained stable for the H and M groups and percent fat increased ~2-2.5 per cent/decade. Although fat-free weight decreased at each testing point, there was a trend for those who began weight-training exercise to better maintain it. Cross-sectional analysis at T3 showed that leg strength and bone mineral density were generally maintained from age 60 to 89 yr. Those who performed weight training had a greater arm region bone mineral density than those who did not. These longitudinal data show that the physiological capacities of older athletes are reduced despite continued vigorous endurance exercise over a 20-yr period (~8-15 per cent/decade). Changes in body composition appeared to be less than those shown for the healthy sedentary population and were related to changes in training habits.

Key Words: aging; maximal oxygen uptake; weight training; bone mineral density.

19.   **Benefits from aerobic exercise in patients with major depression: a pilot study**
Br J Sports Med 2001; *35*:114-117, 2001.
F Dimeo1, M Bauer2, I Varahram1, G Proest2 and U Halter2

1. Department of Sports Medicine, Freie Universitaet, Berlin, Germany.
2. Department of Psychiatry.

Correspondence to: Dr Dimeo, Freie Universitaet Berlin, Benjamin Franklin Medical Center, Department of Sports Medicine, Clayallee 229, 14195 Berlin, Germany ferdimeo@zedat.fu-berlin.de

Background: Several reports indicate that physical activity can reduce the severity of symptoms in depressed patients. Some data suggest that even a single exercise bout may result in a substantial mood improvement.

Objective: To evaluate the short term effects of a training programme on patients with moderate to severe major depression.

Methods: Twelve patients (mean (SD) age 49 (10) years; five men, seven women) with a major depressive episode according to the Diagnostic and Statistical Manual of the American Society of Psychiatry (DSM IV) criteria participated. The mean (SD) duration of the depressive episode was 35 (21) weeks (range 12–96). Training consisted of walking on a treadmill following an interval training pattern and was carried out for 30 minutes a day for 10 days.

Results: At the end of the training programme, there was a clinically relevant and statistically significant reduction in **depression** scores (Hamilton Rating Scale for Depression: before, 19.5 (3.3); after, 13 (5.5); p = 0.002. Self assessed intensity of symptoms: before, 23.2 (7); after, 17.7 (8.1); p = 0.006. Values are mean (SD)). Subjective and objective changes in depression scores correlated strongly (r = 0.66, p = 0.01).

Conclusions: Aerobic exercise can produce substantial improvement in mood in patients with major depressive disorders in a short time.

Key Words: affective disorders; depression; major depression; refractory depression; exercise.

20. Effects of Lifestyle Activity vs Structured Aerobic Exercise in Obese Women

JAMA. 1999;281:335-340.

Ross E. Andersen, PhD; Thomas A. Wadden, PhD; Susan J. Bartlett, PhD; Babette Zemel, PhD; Tony J. Verde, PhD; Shawn C. Franckowiak

Objective : To examine short- and long-term changes in weight, body composition, and cardiovascular risk profiles produced by diet combined with either structured aerobic exercise or moderate-intensity lifestyle activity.

Design : Sixteen-week randomized controlled trial with 1-year follow-up, conducted from August 1995 to December 1996.

Participants and Setting : Forty obese women (mean body mass index [weight in kilograms divided by the square of height in meters], 32.9 kg/m2;

mean weight, 89.2 kg) with a mean age of 42.9 years (range, 21-60 years) seen in a university-based weight management program.

Interventions Structured aerobic exercise or moderate lifestyle activity; low-fat diet of about 1200 kcal/d.

Main Outcome : Measures Changes in body weight, body composition, cardiovascular risk profiles, and physical fitness at 16 weeks and at 1 year.

Results : Mean (SD) weight losses during the 16-week treatment program were 8.3 (3.8) kg for the aerobic group and 7.9 (4.2) kg for the lifestyle group (within groups, P<.001; between groups, P = .08). The aerobic group lost significantly less **fat-free mass** (0.5 [1.3] kg) than the lifestyle group (1.4 [1.3] kg; P = .03). During the 1-year follow-up, the aerobic group regained 1.6 [5.5] kg, while the lifestyle group regained 0.08 (4.6) kg. At week 16, serum triglyceride levels and total cholesterol levels were reduced significantly (P<.001) from baseline (16.3 per cent and 10.1 per cent reductions, respectively) but did not differ significantly between groups and were not different from baseline or between groups at week 68.

Conclusions : A program of diet plus lifestyle activity may offer similar health benefits and be a suitable alternative to diet plus structured aerobic activity for obese women.

Author Affiliations: Division of Geriatric Medicine and Gerontology (Dr Andersen and Mr Franckowiak) and Department of Medicine (Dr Bartlett), Johns Hopkins University School of Medicine, Baltimore, Md; Department of Psychiatry, University of Pennsylvania School of Medicine, Philadelphia (Dr Wadden); Children's Hospital of Philadelphia (Dr Zemel); and Department of Sports Science, Cabrini College, Radnor, Pa (Dr Verde).

21.   The epidemiology of aerobic dance injuries
American Journal of Sports Medicine, Vol 14, Issue 1 67-72, 1986.
JG Garrick, DM Gillien and P Whiteside

Aerobic dance is currently the largest organized fitness activity primarily for women in the United States. In an attempt to identify and characterize the health problems associated with it, 351 students and 60 instructors from six facilities were followed for 16 weeks with weekly telephone calls. Of the 327 medical complaints reported during 29,924 hours of documented activity, only 84 (0.28 per hundred hours) resulted in any disability and only 2.1 per cent required medical care. The shin/leg, foot and ankle accounted for nearly two-thirds of the injuries. Instructors were twice as likely to be injured as students. Both a history of prior orthopaedic problems and a lack of involvement in other fitness activities resulted in higher injury rates. Injury rates were influenced by the design and conduct of the aerobic program but not by brand of shoe or type of flooring. Aerobic dance appears to offer students the potential for fitness enhancement with a minimal risk of injury.

22.   Type of activity: resistance, aerobic and leisure versus occupational physical activity.
Medicine and Science in Sports and Exercise. 33(6) Supplement:S364-S369, June 2001.
Howley, Edward T.
Purpose: To define and describe the essential terminology associated with dose-response issues in physical activity and health.
Methods: Recent consensus documents, position stands, and reports were used to provide reference definitions and methods of classifying physical activity and exercise.
Results: The two principal categories of physical activity are occupational physical activity (OPA) and **leisure-time physical activity** (LTPA). OPA is usually referenced to an 8-h d, whereas the duration of LTPA is quite variable. LTPA includes all forms of aerobic activities, structured endurance exercise programs, resistance-training programs, and sports. Energy expenditure associated with aerobic activity can be expressed in absolute terms (kJ[middle dot]min-1), referenced to body mass (METs), or relative to some maximal physiological response (i.e., maximal heart rate (HR) or aerobic power (O2max)). The net cost of physical activity should be used to express energy expenditure relative to dose-response issues. The intensity of resistance training is presented in terms relative to the greatest weight that can be lifted one time in good form (1RM). The intensity of OPA followed the guidance of a previous consensus conference. The intensity of most LTPA can be categorized using the standard aerobic exercise classifications; however, for long-duration (2+ hours) LTPA, the classifications for OPA may be more appropriate.
Conclusion: Physical activities should be classified in a consistent and standardized manner in terms of both energy expenditure and the relative effort required.

23.   Aerobic Fitness, Not Energy Expenditure, Influences Subsequent Increase in Adiposity in Black and White Children
PEDIATRICS Vol. 106 No. 4 October 2000, p. e50
Maria S. Johnson*, Reinaldo Figueroa-Colon, Sara L. Herd, David A. Fields, Min Sun, Gary R. Hunter, and Michael I. Goran*
From the * Department of Preventive Medicine, Institute for Prevention Research, University of Southern California, Los Angeles, California; and

Department of Nutrition Sciences, University of Alabama at Birmingham, Birmingham, Alabama.

Background: Low levels of energy expenditure and aerobic fitness have been hypothesized to be risk factors for obesity. Longitudinal studies to determine whether energy expenditure influences weight gain in whites have provided conflicting results. To date, no studies have examined this relationship in blacks or whether aerobic fitness influences weight gain in white or black children.

Methods: One hundred fifteen children, 72 white (55 girls and 17 boys) and 43 black (24 girls and 19 boys) were recruited for this study. Aerobic fitness, resting, total, and activity-related **energy expenditure** and **body composition** were measured at baseline. The children returned annually for 3 to 5 repeated measures of body composition. The influence of the initial measures of energy expenditure and fitness on the subsequent rate of increase in adiposity was examined, adjusting for initial body composition, age, ethnicity, gender, and Tanner stage. Because 20 children did not attain maximum oxygen consumption, the sample size for the combined analysis was 95.

Results: Initial fat mass was the main predictor of increasing adiposity in this cohort of children, with greater initial fat predicting a higher rate of increase of adiposity. There was also a significant negative relationship between aerobic fitness and the rate of increasing adiposity ($F1,82 = 3.92$). With every increase of .1 L/minute of fitness, there was a decrease of .081 kg fat per kg of lean mass gained. None of the measures of energy expenditure significantly predicted increasing adiposity in white or black children.

Conclusions: Initial fat mass was the dominant factor influencing increasing adiposity; however, aerobic fitness was also a significant independent predictor of increasing adiposity in this cohort of children. Resting, total, or activity-related energy expenditure did not predict increasing adiposity. It seems that aerobic fitness may be more important than absolute energy expenditure in the development of obesity in white or black children.

Key words: energy expenditure, fitness, longitudinal, obesity.

24.   The development of aerobic power in young athletes
Journal of Applied Physiology, Vol 75, Issue 3 1160-1167, 1993.
A. Baxter-Jones, H. Goldstein and P. Helms
Portex Anaesthesia, Intensive Therapy, and Respiratory Medicine Unit, University of London, United Kingdom.

Previous studies investigating the effects of training in children have been hampered in their interpretation by the confounding effects of growth and development. We followed the development of maximal aerobic power

(VO2max) in 453 athletes drawn from soccer, swimming, gymnastics, and tennis. Study design was of a mixed longitudinal type with five age cohorts (8, 10, 12, 14 and 16 yr) followed for 3 consecutive years. A multilevel regression modeling procedure was used to identify the independent effects of predictor variables while accounting for the effects of growth, such as changes in body size. When age, height, and weight were controlled for, VO2max in males significantly increased with pubertal status, indicated by the coefficient value of 0.15 l/min being greater than its associated SE of 0.07 l/min. Females showed a similar pattern, with a coefficient value of 0.13 +/- 0.07 l/min, although the significant increase in VO2max (P < 0.05) found in males in the latter stages of puberty was not shown in females. Swimmers had the highest VO2max values (P < 0.001) at all ages.

25. Adult Female Hip Bone Density Reflects Teenage Sports-Exercise Patterns But Not Teenage Calcium Intake

PEDIATRICS Vol. 106 No. 1 July 2000, pp. 40-44

Tom Lloyd*, Vernon M. Chinchilli*, Nan Johnson-Rollings*, Kessey Kieselhorst, Douglas F. Eggli§, and Robert Marcus

From the Departments of * Health Evaluation Sciences, Clinical Nutrition, and § Radiology, Pennsylvania State University, College of Medicine, Hershey, Pennsylvania; and Department of Medicine, Stanford University and Veterans Affairs Medical Center, Palo Alto, California.

Objective : To examine how cumulative teenage **sports** histories and time-averaged teenage calcium intake are related to total body bone mineral gain between ages 12 and 18 years and to proximal femur **bone mineral density** (BMD) at age 18 years.

Design : Longitudinal.

Setting : University Hospital and local suburban community in Central Pennsylvania.

Study Participants : Eighty-one white females in the ongoing Penn State Young Women's Health Study.

Outcome Measures : Total body and proximal femur (hip) bone measurements by dual energy radiograph absorptiometry; nutrient intakes, including calcium, from 33 days of prospective food records collected at regular intervals between ages 12 and 18 years; and self-reported **sports**-exercise scores between ages 12 and 18 years.

Results : Cumulative **sports**-exercise scores between ages 12 and 18 years were associated with hip BMD at age 18 years (r = .42) but were not related to total body bone mineral gain. Time-averaged daily calcium intake, which ranged from 500 to 1500 mg/day in this cohort was not associated with hip BMD at age 18 years, or with total body bone mineral gain at age 12 through 18 years.

Conclusions. The amount of physical activity that distinguishes a primarily sedentary teenager from one who engages in some form of exercise on a nearly daily basis is related to a significant increase in peak hip BMD. Key words: peak hip bone density, teenage sport histories, osteoporosis prevention.

26.   The effects of strength training on endurance performance and muscle characteristics.
Medicine and Science in Sports and Exercise. 31(6):886-891, June 1999.
Bishop, David; Jenkins, David G.; Mackinnon, Laurel T.; Mceniery, Michael; Carey, Michael F.

Purpose: The purpose of this study was to determine the effects of resistance training on endurance performance and selected muscle characteristics of female cyclists.

Methods: Twenty-one endurance-trained, female cyclists, aged 18-42 yr, were randomly assigned to either a resistance training (RT; N = 14) or a control group (CON; N = 7). Resistance training (2x[middle dot]wk-1) consisted of five sets to failure (2-8 RM) of parallel squats for 12 wk. Before and immediately after the resistance-training period, all subjects completed an incremental cycle test to allow determination of both their **lactate threshold** (LT) and **peak oxygen consumption** O2). In addition, endurance performance was assessed by average power output during a 1-h cycle test (OHT), and leg strength was measured by recording the subject's one repetition maximum (1 RM) concentric squat. Before and after the 12-wk training program, resting muscle was sampled by needle biopsy from m. vastus lateralis and analyzed for fiber type diameter, fiber type percentage, and the activities of 2-oxoglutarate dehydrogenase and phosphofructokinase.

Results: After the resistance training program, there was a significant increase in 1 RM concentric squat strength for RT (35.9 per cent) but not for CON (3.7 per cent) ($P < 0.05$). However, there were no significant changes in OHT performance, LT, O2, muscle fiber characteristics, or enzyme activities in either group ($P > 0.05$).

Conclusion: The present data suggest that increased leg strength does not improve cycle endurance performance in endurance-trained, female cyclists.

27.   Generation of reactive oxygen species after exhaustive aerobic and isometric exercise.
Medicine and Science in Sports and Exercise. 32(9):1576-1581, September 2000.
Alessio, Helaine M.; Hagerman, ann E.; Fulkerson, Bethany K.; Ambrose, Jessica; Rice, Robyn E.; Wiley, Ronald L.

Many studies have implicated elevated oxygen consumption (O2) associated with aerobic exercise as contributing to oxidative stress. Only a few studies have investigated nonaerobic exercise and its relation to pro-oxidant and antioxidant activities.

Purpose: The purpose of this study was to compare biomarkers of oxidative stress: lipid peroxidation, protein oxidation, and total antioxidants in blood after exhaustive aerobic (AE) and nonaerobic isometric exercise (IE).

Methods: Blood samples were collected from 12 subjects who performed a maximum AE and IE test and were analyzed for **thiobarbituric acid** (TBARS), **carbonyls, lipid hydroperoxides** (LH), and **oxygen radical absorbance capacity** (ORAC).

Results: O2 increased 14-fold with AE compared with 2-fold with IE. Protein carbonyls increased 67 per cent ($P < 0.05$) pre- to immediately and 1 h post-AE, and 12 per cent pre- to immediately post-IE and returned to baseline 1 h post-IE. TBARS did not increase significantly with either treatment. LH increased 36 per cent above rest during IE compared with 24 per cent during AE ($P < 0.05$). ORAC increased 25 per cent ($P < 0.05$) pre- to post-AE, compared with 9 per cent ($P < 0.05$) pre- to post-IE.

Conclusion: There was evidence of oxidative stress after both exhaustive aerobic and isometric exercise. Lipid hydroperoxides, protein carbonyls, and total antioxidants increased after both IE and AE. Due to the different metabolic demands of aerobic and isometric exercise, we can rule out a mass action effect of O2 as the sole mechanism for exercise-induced oxidative stress.

28. Measures of Submaximal Aerobic Performance Evaluate and Predict Functional Response to Growth Hormone (GH) Treatment in GH-Deficient Adults1

The Journal of Clinical Endocrinology and Metabolism Vol. 84, No. 12 4570-4577, 1999.

Linda J. Woodhouse, Sylvia L. Asa, Scott G. Thomas and Shereen Ezzat

Departments of Physical Therapy, Laboratory Medicine and Pathobiology, and Medicine, The University of Toronto, Toronto, Ontario M5G 1X5, Canada.

Address correspondence and requests for reprints to: Dr. Shereen Ezzat, Mount Sinai Hospital, University of Toronto, 600 University Avenue, Toronto, Ontario M5G 1X5, Canada. E-mail: sezzat@mtsinai.on.ca.

The impact of GH on functional performance in GH-deficient adults is not well understood. To investigate the effects of GH on skeletal muscle, physical, and functional capacity, we randomized 28 GH-deficient adults to receive 3 months of recombinant human GH [rhGH: somatotropin, 6.25 μg/kg lean body mass (LBM) for 1 month, 12.5 μg/kg LBM thereafter] in a double-blind placebo-controlled cross-over trial. We measured muscle fiber type, size, and insulin-like growth factor I messenger RNA, aerobic capacity [maximal oxygen uptake (**VO2max**), **ventilation threshold** (VeT)], isokinetic strength, oxygen-cost-of-walking at normal and fast speeds, and fatigue determined by the profile of mood states questionnaire. As expected, GH treatment decreased body fat, increased LBM, increased muscle fiber size, and increased muscle insulin-like growth factor-I messenger RNA 5-fold; however, muscle strength remained unchanged. At baseline, VeT occurred at a high percentage of maximal VO2max (73.3 per cent ± 2.6) because of low VO2max (1.74 ± 0.1 L/min or 20.7 ± 1.3 mL/kg·min). Walking required high oxygen consumptions representing from 83 ± 4 per cent of VeT at normal speeds to 120 ± 5 per cent of VeT at fast speeds. After rhGH, there was a significant (P = 0.03) increase in VeT (18 per cent), compared with placebo. This was paralleled by a nonsignificant rise in VO2max. Functionally, rhGH treatment decreased the oxygen cost of walking, relative to VeT, at normal (14 per cent decrease, P = 0.019) and fast (21 per cent decrease, P = 0.004) SPW speeds. A 3-variable model (baseline fast SPW speed, VeT/VO2max, and VeT) accounted for 39 per cent of the variance of change in self-reported fatigue. These data indicate that GH-deficient adults require a high fraction of VeT for daily activities, explaining the perception of increased fatigue and impaired physical performance. The actions of rhGH on muscle fiber size translate into physiological improvement in submaximal aerobic capacity and result in functional improvement in walking ability but do not necessarily alter strength. Thus, measures of effort-independent submaximal aerobic performance provide novel objective determinants of functional impairment and fatigue and can be used to evaluate and predict response to GH treatment.

29. Aerobic and anaerobic arm-cranking power outputs of males with lower limb impairments: Relationship with sport participation intensity, age, impairment and functional classification
March 1998, Volume 36, Number 3, Pages 205-212
Yeshayahu Hutzler1,a, Shai Ochana1, Ron Bolotin2 and Eliezer Kalina2
1.   The Zinman College for Physical Education and Sports Sciences, Wingate Institute, Israel 42902.
2.   Israeli Defence Force Veteran Sports and Rehabilitation Center, Netania, Israel 42902.

Fifty individuals with lower limb impairments including spinal cord injury, polio and amputations underwent aerobic and anaerobic arm-cranking tests in a standardized laboratory setting. Based on linear regression models applied with age as dependent variable aerobic performance variable including HRmax (R=0.395, P=0.004), and POaer (R=0.31, P=0.021) were subjected to ANCOVA adjusting for age in order to determine the significance of participation intensity (competitive vs leisure) and type of physical impairment. Anaerobic performance variables were not influenced by age and thereby subjected to 1-Way ANOVA with the same independent variables. Participation intensity and type of impairment significantly discriminated (P<0.001) between athletes in all power variables. Linear regression models have shown moderate but significant (P<0.001) relationship with functional ability (bases on International Wheelchair Basketball Federation classification system). In anaerobic mean power (MP) classification accounted for 42 per cent of the variance, while in anaerobic peak power (PP) and aerobic Power (POaer) for 38 per cent and 30 per cent respectively. By means of a post hoc Tukey analysis significant differences were observed between athletes with a high level paraplegia (class 1) and those with one leg affected by polio or amputations (classes 4, 4.5). Athletes with low level **paraplegia** and two legs affected by **polio** (classes 2?3.5) had values in-between. Based on the descriptive evaluation, a three group scheme was conceptualized and resubjected to ANOVA. Significant intergroup differences were thus obtained only for PP. Descriptive PP data for each group were transformed into a five category table in order to provide reference values for fitness estimation in males with lower limb impairments of various etiologies.

Key Words: physical fitness; arm-cranking ergometry; lower limb impairments; spinal cord injury; physical activity; classification.

30. Hematological indices of erythropoietin administration in athletes.

Int J Sports Med. 1993 Aug;14(6):307-11.

Casoni I, Ricci G, Ballarin E, Borsetto C, Grazzi G, Guglielmini C, Manfredini F, Mazzoni G, Patracchini M, De Paoli Vitali E, et al.

Centro Studi Biomedici Applicati allo Sport, Istituto di Chimica Biologica, Universita degli Studi, Ferrara, Italia.

Recombinant human erythropoietin (EPO), commercially available since 1988, is thought to be used by athletes in aerobic sports for the purpose of increasing oxygen transport and aerobic power. In an attempt to identify EPO administration, we have studied the peripheral blood of 20 subjects practising sports at an amateur level. Automated **cytometry** was performed on the blood samples before and during 45 days of EPO treatment. The same hematological indices were determined for a control population that consisted of 240 elite athletes from various sports. As expected following EPO treatment, RBC, [Hb] and Hct increased significantly (increments of 8 per cent, 6.3 per cent and 11 per cent, respectively). A significant increase in reticulocyte count was also observed. In addition, automated erythrocyte analysis showed a significant increase in cells with a volume > 120 fl and hemoglobin content (HC) < 28 pg (hypochromic macrocytes, or MacroHypo): 0.06 +/- 0.09 per cent before EPO, 0.48 +/- 0.63 per cent after EPO. The EPO-treated subjects differed from the control population having higher values for Hct, mean corpuscular volume (MCV), Macro and MacroHypo. To investigate the possibility of using such variations in blood parameters to identify EPO treatment, individual values for Hct, MCV, Macro and MacroHypo for treated subjects and controls were plotted. Using the percentages of MacroHypo, a cut-off value surpassed in approximately 50 per cent of the treated subjects and in none of the controls was established.

31.   An epidemiologic study of sports and weight lifting as possible risk factors for herniated lumbar and cervical discs. The Northeast Collaborative Group on Low Back Pain
American Journal of Sports Medicine, Vol 21, Issue 6 854-860, 1993.
       DJ Mundt, JL Kelsey, AL Golden, MM Panjabi, H Pastides, AT Berg, J Sklar and T Hosea
       Columbia University, New York, New York.
       The associations between participation in several specific sports, use of free weights, and use of weight lifting equipment and herniated lumbar or cervical intervertebral discs were examined in a case-control epidemiologic study. Specific sports considered were baseball or softball, golf, bowling, swimming, diving, jogging, aerobics, and racquet sports. Included in the final analysis were 287 patients with **lumbar disc herniation** and 63 patients with **cervical disc herniation**, each matched by sex, source of care, and decade of age to 1 control who was free of disc herniation and other conditions of the back or neck. Results indicated that most sports are not associated with an increased risk of herniation, and may be protective. Relative risk estimates for the association between individual sports and lumbar or cervical herniation were generally less than or close to 1.0. There was, however, a weak positive association between bowling and herniation at both the lumbar and cervical regions of the spine. Use of weight lifting equipment was not associated with herniated lumbar or cervical disc, but a possible association was indicated between use of free weights and risk of cervical herniation (relative risk, 1.87; 95 per cent confidence interval, 0.74 to 4.74).

32.   Modeling developmental changes in strength and aerobic power in children
J Appl Physiol 84: 963-970, 1998.
       Alan M. Nevill1, Roger L. Holder2, Adam Baxter-Jones3, Joan M. Round4, and David A. Jones4

1 School of Human Sciences, Liverpool John Moores University, Liverpool L3 3AK; 2 School of Mathematics and Statistics and 4 School of Sport and Exercise Sciences, University of Birmingham, Birmingham B15 2TT; and 3 Department of Child Health, University of Aberdeen, Aberdeen AB9 2ZD, United Kingdom.

The present study examined two contrasting multilevel model structures to describe the developmental (longitudinal) changes in strength and aerobic power in children: 1) an additive polynomial structure and 2) a multiplicative structure with allometric body size components. On the basis of the maximum log-likelihood criterion, the multiplicative "allometric" model was shown to be superior to the additive polynomial model when fitted to the data from two published longitudinal studies and to provide more plausible solutions within and beyond the range of observations. The multilevel regression analysis of study 1 confirmed that aerobic power develops approximately in proportion to body mass, m1/3. The analyses from study 2 identified a significant increase in quadriceps and biceps strength, in proportion to body size, plus an additional contribution from age, centered at about peak height velocity (PHV). The positive "age" term for boys suggested that at PHV the boys were becoming stronger in the quadriceps and biceps in relation to their body size. In contrast, the girls' age term was either negligible (quadriceps) or negative (biceps), indicating that at PHV the girls' strength was developing in proportion to or, in the case of the biceps, was becoming weaker in relation to their body size.

Key Words: multilevel regression; longitudinal growth; multiplicative models; allometric body size components.

33. Energy specificity of rock climbing and aerobic capacity in competitive sport rock climbers.

J Sports Med Phys Fitness. 1995 Mar;35(1):20-4.

Billat V, Palleja P, Charlaix T, Rizzardo P, Janel N.

Department in Physical Activity Science, University Paris 12, Creteil, France.

Over the past few years, competitive rock climbing has experienced increased popularity world wide. In 1989, the first six-event World Cup competition was held with all events contested on artificial modular walls. The aim of this study was to determine the extent to which oxidative metabolism is utilized in competitive rock climbing with regard to the climber's maximal O2 consumption (VO2max). VO2max—was measured with two direct triangular protocols: the first from running ("running" VO2max) and the second from pull offs performed with arms and before arms ("pulling" VO2). Moreover, VO2 was also before measured during two competitive climbing routes difficulty quantified 7b on the European numerical scale ranging from 5 to 9. However these routes had different profiles: route 1 was more complex from the informational aspect, holds being smaller and more difficult to see even though the second route was presumed harder from the physical point of view, the holds being bigger but the profile being steeper. The first and the second route involved only 45.6 per cent and 37.7 per cent of the "running" VO2max but 111.6 per cent and 92.3 per cent of the "pulling" VO2max. Heart rates (HR) were equal to 176 bpm and 159 bpm i.e. 85.5 per cent and 77 per cent of maximal HR respectively. Blood lactate collected three minutes after the end of the two ascents were 5.7 mmol.1(-1) and 4.3 mmol.1(-1). The paired "t" test indicated no significant differences in heart rates for the two exercises condition i.e. climbing route. These results suggest that the competitive rock climbing elicit particularly arms since heart rate is high for a relatively low value of VO2.

34.   **The efficacy of accumulated short bouts versus single daily bouts of brisk walking in improving aerobic fitness and blood lipid profiles**
Health Education Research, Vol. 14, No. 6, 803-815, December 1999
K. Woolf-May, E. M. Kearney1, A. Owen3, D. W. Jones2, R. C. R. Davison and S. R. Bird

Department of Sport and Exercise Science, Canterbury Christ Church University College, Canterbury CT1 1QU,
1.   Department of Pathology, Queen Elizabeth the Queen Mother Hospital, Margate CT9 4AN, and
2.   Haemophilia Centre and
3.   Department of Cardiology, Kent and Canterbury Hospital, Canterbury CT1 3NG, UK.

Fifty-six subjects (19 men and 37 woman) aged between 40 and 66 completed the study. They were allocated into three walking groups and a control group (C). The three walking groups performed the same total amount of walking for 18 weeks, but completed it in bouts of differing durations and frequencies. These were Long Walkers (LW; 20–40 min/bout), Intermediate Walkers (IW; 10–15 min/bout) and Short Walkers (SW; 5–10 min/bout); with the IW and SW performing more than one bout of walking a day. Following the 18 week walking programme, compared to the C group all walking groups showed similar improvements in fitness as determined by a reduction in blood lactate during a graded **treadmill** walking test (LW 1.0 mmol/l; IW 0.8 mmol/l; SW 1.2 mmol/l; C 0.2 mmol/l; P = 0.003) and reduction in final heart rate (LW 8 beats/min; IW 6 beats/min; SW 10 beats/min; C 0 beats/min; P = 0.056). Also compared to the C group, the LW and IW groups recorded statistically significant decreases in low-density lipoprotein cholesterol (LW 0.29 mmol/l;

IW 0.41 mmol/l; P = 0.024), whereas the control group showed a mean increase of 0.22 mmol/l. The LW and IW groups also showed significant reductions in apolipoprotein (apo) A-II (LW 0.05 g/l; IW 0.02 g/l; SW 0.01 g/l; C 0.00 g/l; P = 0.012) with the LW recording a statistically significant increase in the ratio of apo A-I/A-II (LW, 0.19, P = 0.044). In conclusion, some health benefits were achieved from all walking programmes. However, whilst the changes in aerobic fitness were similar, the effects upon blood lipid profiles were not. The findings from this study suggest that the LW regimen was most effective in benefiting blood lipid profile, followed by the IW regimen, with the SW being least potent. Nevertheless, for the sedentary/low-active members of society, any improvement in health may be considered as important. Therefore accumulated bouts of moderate intensity exercise, which according to theories of exercise behaviour may be more easily incorporated into an individual's lifestyle than single prolonged bouts, may be advocated for health promotion but may not be as effective as the traditionally prescribed 20–40 min bouts.

35. **Aerobic responses of prepubertal boys to two modes of training**
Br J Sports Med 2000; *34*:168-173.

Craig A Williams, Neil Armstrong and Julian Powell
Children's Health and Exercise Research Centre, University of Exeter, Heavitree, Exeter EX1 2LU, United Kingdom
Correspondence to: Dr C A Williams.

Objective : To investigate the effects of two contrasting eight week training programmes on the aerobic performance of 39 prepubescent boys (mean age 10.1 years).

Methods : All boys were volunteer subjects from three city schools and the schools were matched by a health related behaviour questionnaire. All of the boys were assessed as Tanner stage one for genitalia and pubic hair development. Criterion laboratory tests included peak O2 as assessed by an incremental discontinuous treadmill test to voluntary exhaustion. Submaximal measurements of heart rate, minute ventilation (E) and O2 were also recorded during the **treadmill** test. One of the schools provided the control group (n = 14), and boys from the other schools followed two contrasting training programmes. The first was a sprint interval running programme (n = 12) comprising 10 second and 30 second sprints, and the second a continuous cycle **ergometer** programme (n = 13) maintaining a heart rate in the range 80–85 per cent of maximum for 20 minutes on a Monark cycle ergometer. After eight weeks training three times a week, the three groups were retested.

Results : There were no significant differences in peak O2 (p>0.05) with training in either of the groups. Neither were there significant changes in any of the submaximal variables O2, E, or heart rate (p>0.05).

Conclusion—The findings of this study indicate that neither eight week sprint interval running nor continuous cycle ergometer training programmes significantly improve maximal or submaximal indicators of the aerobic performance of prepubertal boys.

Key Words: oxygen uptake; aerobic performance; training; prepubescent; boys.

36. The Effect of Endurance Training on Parameters of Aerobic Fitness
Sports Medicine, Volume 29, Number 6, 1 June 2000, pp. 373-386(14)

Endurance exercise training results in profound adaptations of the cardiorespiratory and neuromuscular systems that enhance the delivery of oxygen from the atmosphere to the mitochondria and enable a tighter regulation of muscle metabolism. These adaptations effect an improvement in endurance performance that is manifest as a rightward shift in the 'velocity-time curve'. This shift enables athletes to exercise for longer at a given absolute exercise intensity, or to exercise at a higher exercise intensity for a given duration. There are 4 key parameters of aerobic fitness that affect the nature of the velocity-time curve that can be measured in the human athlete. These are the maximal oxygen uptake (O), exercise economy, the lactate/ventilatory threshold and oxygen uptake kinetics. Other parameters that may help determine endurance performance, and that are related to the other 4 parameters, are the velocity at O (V-O) and the maximal lactate steady state or critical power. This review considers the effect of endurance training on the key parameters of aerobic (endurance) fitness and attempts to relate these changes to the adaptations seen in the body's physiological systems with training. The importance of improvements in the aerobic fitness parameters to the enhancement of endurance performance is highlighted, as are the training methods that may be considered optimal for facilitating such improvements.

Keywords: Aerobic exercise; Endurance training; Exercise performance.

37. Training High - Living Low: Changes of Aerobic Performance and Muscle Structure with Training at Simulated Altitude
Int J Sports Med 2001, 22: 579-585

J. Geiser1, M. Vogt2, R. Billeter2, C. Zuleger1, F. Belforti1, H. Hoppeler2

1.   Institut de Physiologie, Université de Fribourg, Fribourg, Switzerland
2.   Anatomisches Institut, Universität Bern, Bern, Switzerland

This study was undertaken to test the hypothesis that endurance training in hypoxia is superior to training of the same intensity in normoxia. To avoid adaptation to hypoxia, the subjects lived under normoxic conditions when not training. A secondary objective of this study was to compare the effect of high- vs. moderate-intensity training on aerobic performance variables. Thirty-three men without prior endurance training underwent a cycle ergometer training of 6 weeks, 5 d/week, 30 minutes/d. The subjects were assigned to 4 groups, N-high, N-low, H-high and H-low based on the training criteria normoxia (N; corresponding to a training altitude of 600 m), vs. hypoxia (H; training altitude 3850 m) and intensity (high; corresponding to 80 per cent and low: corresponding to 67 per cent of VÿO2max). VÿO2max measured in normoxia increased between 8.5 to 11.1 per cent, independent of training altitude or intensity. VÿO2max measured in hypoxia increased between 2.9 and 7.2 per cent. Hypoxia training resulted in significantly larger increases than normoxia training. Maximal power that subjects could maintain over a thirty-minute period (measured in normoxia or hypoxia) increased from 12.3 - 26.8 per cent independent of training altitude. However, subjects training at high intensity increased performance more than subjects training at a low intensity. Muscle volume of the knee-extensors as measured by magnetic resonance imaging increased significantly in the H-high group only (+ 5.0 per cent). Mitochondrial volume density measured by EM-morphometry in biopsy samples of m. vastus lat. increased significantly in all groups with the highest increase seen in the H-high group (+ 59 per cent). Capillary length density increased significantly in the H-high group only (+ 17.2 per cent). The main finding of this study is that in previously untrained people, training in hypoxia while living at low altitude increases performance in normoxia to the same extent as training in normoxia, but leads to larger increases of aerobic performance variables when measured under hypoxic conditions. Training intensity had no effect on the gain of VÿO2max. On the level of skeletal muscle tissue, the combination of hypoxia with high training intensity constitutes the most effective stimulus for increasing muscle oxidative capacity.

Key Words: Hypoxia, training intensity, endurance, VÿO2max, biopsy, human, mitochondrial density, capillary length density.

38. Aerobic exercise as therapy for cancer fatigue.
Medicine and Science in Sports and Exercise. 30(4):475-478, April 1998.
Dimeo, Fernando; Rumberger, Brigitta G; Keul, Joseph

Purpose: Fatigue and impairment of physical performance are common and severe problems of cancer patients. We describe the effect of an aerobic exercise program designed for cancer patients suffering from these symptoms.

Methods: Five cancer patients (4 female, 1 male, age 18 to 55), participated in the training program. Fatigue had been present for a time ranging between 5 wk and 18 months and hindered the patients from carrying out normal daily activities. The training program consisted of walking daily on a treadmill with an intensity corresponding to a lactate concentration of 3 +/- 0.5 mmol[middle dot]L-1 and was carried out for 6 wk.

Results: By the end of the exercise program we observed an improvement in maximal physical performance (from 6.4 +/- 0.4 km[middle dot]h-1 to 7.5+/- 0.9 km[middle dot]h-1, P < 0.05) and maximal walked distance (from 1640 +/- 724 m to 3300 +/- 953 m, P < 0.05). Heart rate and lactate concentration by an equivalent submaximal workload (5 km[middle dot]h-1) were significant reduced (from 138 +/- 21 beats[middle dot]min-1 to 113 +/- 20 beats[middle dot]min-1, P < 0.05, and from 2.6 +/- 1.4 mmol[middle dot]L-1 to 1.3+/- 0.6 mmol[middle dot]L-1, P < 0.05); all patients experienced a clear reduction of fatigue and could carry out normal daily activities again without substantial limitations.

Conclusion: We conclude that an aerobic exercise program of precisely defined intensity, duration, and frequency can be prescribed as therapy for primary fatigue in cancer patients.

39.   **Age-related declines in maximal aerobic capacity in regularly exercising vs. sedentary women: a meta-analysis**
Journal of Applied Physiology, Vol. 83, No. 1, pp. 160-165, July 1997.
Margaret D. Fitzgerald1, Hirofumi Tanaka1, Zung V. Tran2, and Douglas R. Seals1, 3

1. Human Cardiovascular Research Laboratory, Center for Physical Activity, Disease Prevention, and Aging, Department of Kinesiology, University of Colorado, Boulder 80309; 2. Center for Research in Ambulatory Health Care Administration, Medical Group Management Association, Englewood 80112; and 3. Divisions of Cardiology and Geriatric Medicine, Department of Medicine, University of Colorado Health Sciences Center, Denver, Colorado 80262.

Our purpose was to determine the relationship between habitual aerobic exercise status and the rate of decline in maximal aerobic capacity across the adult age range in women. A meta-analytic approach was used in which mean maximal oxygen consumption (**O2 max**) values from female subject groups (ages 18-89 yr) were obtained from the published literature. A total of 239 subject groups from 109 studies involving 4,884 subjects met the inclusion criteria and were arbitrarily separated into sedentary (groups = 107; subjects = 2,256), active (groups = 69; subjects = 1,717), and endurance-trained (groups = 63; subjects = 911) populations. O2 max averaged 29.7 ± 7.8, 38.7 ± 9.2, and 52.0 ± 10.5 ml · kg1 · min1, respectively, and was inversely related to age within each population (r = 0.82 to 0.87, all P < 0.0001). The rate of decline in O2 max with increasing subject group age was lowest in sedentary women (3.5 ml · kg1 · min1 · decade1), greater in active women (4.4 ml · kg1 · min1 · decade1), and greatest in endurance-trained women (6.2 ml · kg1 · min1 · decade1) (all P < 0.001 vs. each other). When expressed as percent decrease from mean levels at age ~25 yr, the rates of decline in O2 max were similar in the three populations (10.0 to 10.9 per cent/decade). There was no obvious relationship between aerobic exercise status and the rate of decline in maximal heart rate with age. The results of this cross-sectional study support the hypothesis that, in contrast to the prevailing view, the rate of decline in maximal aerobic capacity with age is greater, not smaller, in endurance-trained vs. sedentary women. The greater rate of decline in O2 max in endurance-trained populations may be related to their higher values as young adults (baseline effect) and/or to greater age-related reductions in exercise volume; however, it does not appear to be related to a greater rate of decline in maximal heart rate with age.

Key Words: Aging; exercise; maximal oxygen consumption.

40. **Randomised, controlled walking trials in postmenopausal women: the minimum dose to improve aerobic fitness?**
Br J Sports Med 2002;**36**:189-194.

T-M Asikainen, S Miilunpalo, P Oja, M Rinne, M Pasanen, K Uusi-Rasi and I Vuori

Urho Kaleva Kekkonen Institute for Health Promotion Research, Tampere, Finland.

Correspondence to:

Dr Asikainen, The UKK Institute for Health Promotion Research, PO Box 30, FIN-33501, Tampere, Finland;

tm.asikainen@sci.fi

Background: The American College of Sports Medicine recommends 20–60 minutes of aerobic exercise three to five days a week at an intensity of 40/50–85 per cent of maximal aerobic power (**VO2MAX**) reserve, expending a total of 700–2000 kcal (2.93–8.36 MJ) a week to improve aerobic power and body composition.

Objective: To ascertain the minimum effective dose of exercise.

Methods: Voluntary, healthy, non-obese, sedentary, postmenopausal women (n = 121), 48–63 years of age, were randomised to four low dose walking groups or a control group; 116 subjects completed the study. The exercise groups walked five days a week for 24 weeks with the following intensity (per cent of VO2MAX) and energy expenditure (kcal/week): group W1, 55 per cent/1500 kcal; group W2, 45 per cent/1500 kcal; group W3, 55 per cent/1000 kcal; group W4, 45 per cent/1000 kcal. VO2MAX was measured in a direct maximal treadmill test. Submaximal aerobic fitness was estimated as heart rates at submaximal work levels corresponding to 65 per cent and 75 per cent of the baseline VO2MAX. The body mass index (BMI) was calculated and percentage of body fat (F per cent) estimated from skinfolds.

Results: The net change (the differences between changes in each exercise group and the control group) in VO2MAX was 2.9 ml/min/kg (95 per cent confidence interval (CI) 1.5 to 4.2) in group W1, 2.6 ml/min/kg (95 per cent CI 1.3 to 4.0) in group W2, 2.4 ml/min/kg (95 per cent CI 0.9 to 3.8) in group W3, and 2.2 ml/min/kg (95 per cent CI 0.8 to 3.5) in group W4. The heart rates in standard submaximal work decreased 4 to 8 beats/min in all the groups. There was no change in BMI, but the F per cent decreased by about 1 per cent unit in all the groups.

Conclusions: Walking (for 24 weeks) at moderate intensity 45 per cent to 55 per cent of VO2MAX, with a total weekly energy expenditure of 1000–1500 kcal, improves VO2MAX and body composition of previously sedentary, non-obese, postmenopausal women. This dose of exercise apparently approaches the minimum effective dose.

Keywords: walking; dose-response; postmenopausal women; randomised controlled trial; aerobic fitness

Abbreviations: VO2MAX, Maximal aerobic power; BMI, body mass index; HRT, hormone replacement therapy; F per cent, percentage of body fat

41.   A history of physical activity, cardiovascular health and longevity
International Journal of Epidemiology 2001;30:1184-1192.
Jeremy N Morris, DSc, DPH, FRCP
Ralph S Paffenbarger, Jra,b, Steven N Blairc and I-Min Leeb,d

(a)   Division of Epidemiology, Stanford University School of Medicine, Stanford, CA 94305–5405, USA.

(b)   Department of Epidemiology, Harvard School of Public Health, Boston, MA 02115, USA.

(c)   The Cooper Institute for Aerobics Research, Dallas, TX 75230, USA.

        d Division of Preventive Medicine, Department of Medicine, Brighamand Women's Hospital and Harvard Medical School, Boston, MA 02215, USA.

        Ralph S Paffenbarger Jr, Stanford University School of Medicine, HRP Redwood Building T213B, Stanford, CA 94305–5405, USA. E-mail: paff@stanford.edu

Since Hippocrates first advised us more than 2000 years ago that exercise—though not too much of it—was good for health, the epidemiology of physical activity has developed apace with the epidemiological method itself. It was only in the mid-20th century that Professor Jeremy N Morris and his associates used quantitative analyses, which dealt with possible selection and confounding biases, to show that vigorous exercise protects against **coronary heart disease** (CHD). They began by demonstrating an apparent protection against CHD enjoyed by active conductors compared with sedentary drivers of London double-decker buses. In addition, postmen seemed to be protected against CHD like conductors, as opposed to less active government workers.

The Morris group pursued the matter further, adapting classical infectious disease epidemiology to the new problems of chronic, non-communicable diseases. Realizing that if physical exercise were to be shown to contribute to the prevention of CHD, it would have to be accomplished through study of leisure-time activities, presumably because of a lack of variability in intensities of physical work. Accordingly, they chose typical sedentary middle-management grade men for study, obtained 5-minute logs of their activities over a 2-day period, and followed them for non-fatal and fatal diseases. In a subsequent study, Morris et al. queried such executive-grade civil servants by detailed mail-back questionnaires on their health habits and health status. They then followed these men for chronic disease occurrence, as in the earlier survey. By 1973 they had distinguished between 'moderately vigorous' and 'vigorous' exercise. In both of these civil service surveys, they demonstrated strong associations between moderately vigorous or vigorous exercise and CHD occurrence, independent of other associations, in age classes 35–64 years.

In the last 30 years, with modern-day computers, a large number of epidemiological studies have been conducted in both sexes, in different ethnic groups, in broad age classes, in a variety of social groups, and on most continents of the world. These studies have extended and amplified those of the Morris group, thereby helping to solidify the cause-and-effect evidence that exercise protects against heart disease and averts premature mortality.

Key Words : Physical activity, coronary heart disease, cardiovascular health, social medicine, exercise science, prospective cohort studies, incidence rates, all-cause mortality, longevity, medical history.

Accepted : 14 March 2001.

42. **Adipose tissue lipolysis is increased during a repeated bout of aerobic exercise**

J Appl Physiol, Vol. 88, Issue 4, 1277-1283, April 2000

V. Stich1, I. de Glisezinski2, M. Berlan3, J. Bulow4, J. Galitzky3, I. Harant2, H. Suljkovicova1, M. Lafontan3, D. Rivière2, and F. Crampes2

1. Department of Sport Medicine, Charles University, 100 00 Prague 10, Czech Republic; 2. Laboratoire des Adaptations de l'Organisme à l'Exercice

Musculaire, Centre Hospitalier Universitaire Purpan, 31059 Toulouse; 3. Institut National de la Santé et de la Recherche Médicale, Unité 317, Laboratoire de Pharmacologie Médicale et Clinique, Faculté de Médecine, 31043 Toulouse, France; and 4. Department of Clinical Physiology and Nuclear Medicine, Bispebjerg Hospital, 2400 Copenhagen, Denmark.

The goal of the study was to examine whether lipid mobilization from adipose tissue undergoes changes during repeated bouts of prolonged aerobic exercise. Microdialysis of the subcutaneous adipose tissue was used for the assessment of lipolysis; glycerol concentration was measured in the dialysate leaving the adipose tissue. Seven male subjects performed two repeated bouts of 60-min exercise at 50 per cent of their maximal aerobic power, separated by a 60-min recovery period. The exercise-induced increases in extracellular glycerol concentrations in adipose tissue and in plasma glycerol concentrations were significantly higher during the second exercise bout compared with the first ($P < 0.05$). The responses of plasma **nonesterified fatty acids** and plasma **epinephrine** were higher during the second exercise bout, whereas the response of norepinephrine was unchanged and that of growth hormone lower. Plasma insulin levels were lower during the second exercise bout. The results suggest that adipose tissue lipolysis during aerobic exercise of moderate intensity is enhanced when an exercise bout is preceded by exercise of the same intensity and duration performed 1 h before. This response pattern is associated with an increase in the exercise-induced rise of epinephrine and with lower plasma insulin values during the repeated exercise bout.

Key Words: microdialysis; norepinephrine; epinephrine; growth hormone.

43. **Association among Physical Activity Level, Cardiorespiratory Fitness, and Risk of Musculoskeletal Injury**
American Journal of Epidemiology Vol. 154, No. 3 : 251-258.

Jennifer M. Hootman1, Carol A. Macera2, Barbara E. Ainsworth3, Malissa Martin4, Cheryl L. Addy3 and Steven N. Blair4

1. Division of Adult and Community Health, National Center for Chronic Disease Prevention and Health Promotion, Centers for Disease Control and Prevention, Atlanta, GA.
2. Division of Nutrition and Physical Activity, National Center for Chronic Disease Prevention and Health Promotion, Centers for Disease Control and Prevention, Atlanta, GA.
3. Department of Epidemiology and Biostatistics, School of Public Health, University of South Carolina, Columbia, SC.

4.	Department of Health, Physical Education, Recreation, and Safety, Middle Tennessee State University, Murfreesboro, TN.

5.	Cooper Institute for Aerobics Research, Dallas, TX.

To help public health practitioners promote physical activities with a low risk of injury, this study determined the relation among type and duration of physical activity, cardiorespiratory fitness, and musculoskeletal injury in a sample of adults enrolled in the Aerobics Center Longitudinal Study. Subjects included 4,034 men and 967 women who underwent a baseline physical examination between 1970 and 1985 and who returned a mailed follow-up survey in 1986. At baseline, a **treadmill** graded exercise test was used to measure cardiorespiratory fitness. At follow-up, subjects reported injuries and type and duration of physical activity in the preceding 12 months. Polytomous logistic regression was used to estimate the association among physical activity type and duration, cardiorespiratory fitness, and injury. The risk of sustaining an activity-related injury increased with higher duration of physical activity per week and cardiorespiratory fitness levels. Results suggest that cardiorespiratory fitness may be a surrogate for unmeasured components of physical activity, such as exercise intensity. Among walkers, increasing duration of activity per week was not associated with an increased risk of injury. Results suggest that, for most adults, walking is a safe form of physical activity associated with a lower risk of injury than running or sport participation.

Key Words: exercise; logistic models; musculoskeletal system; physical fitness; wounds and injuries.

## 44.	Carotid baroreflex responsiveness to head-up tilt-induced central hypovolaemia: effect of aerobic fitness

J Physiol (2003), 551.2, pp. 601-608.

Shigehiko Ogoh*, Stefanos Volianitis†, Peter Nissen†, D. Walter Wray*, Niels H. Sechert† and Peter B. Raven*

*Department of Integrative Physiology, University of North Texas Health Science Center at Fort Worth, TX, USA and †The Copenhagen Muscle Research Centre and Department of Anaesthesia, Rigshospitalet, University of Copenhagen, Copenhagen, Denmark.

This investigation examined the interaction between carotid baroreflex (CBR) responsiveness during head-up tilt (HUT)-induced central hypovolaemia and aerobic fitness. Seven average fit (AF) individuals, with a mean maximal oxygen uptake (**O2max**) of 49 ± 1 (ml O2) kg-1min-1, and seven high fit (HF) individuals, with a O2max of 61 ± 1 (ml O2) kg-1 min-1, voluntarily participated in the investigation. After 10-15 min supine, each subject was exposed to nine levels of progressively increasing HUT by 10 deg increments from -20 deg to +60 deg. During the final 3 min of each stage of HUT, the CBR responsiveness was measured using a rapid pulse (500 ms) train of neck pressure (NP) and neck suction (NS) ranging from +40 to -80 Torr. The maximal gain of the carotid-HR (Gmax-HR) and carotid-MAP (Gmax-MAP) baroreflex function curves was identified as measures of CBR responsiveness. During HUT-induced decreases in thoracic admittance, an index of central blood volume (CBV), the Gmax-HR and Gmax-MAP of the AF subjects increased more than the Gmax-HR and Gmax-MAP of the HF subjects (P < 0.05). The data demonstrate that the increase in the CBR responsiveness during a tilt-induced progressive unloading of the cardiopulmonary baroreceptors was attenuated in endurance-trained subjects. These findings provide an explanation for the predisposition to orthostatic hypotension and intolerance in well-trained athletes.

45.　Edema of Pregnancy: A Comparison of Water Aerobics and Static Immersion

Obstetrics and Gynecology 1999;94:726-729.

TAMI KENT, MSPT, JENNIFER GREGOR, MSPT, LAILA DEARDORFF, MSPT and VERN KATZ, MD

From the Sacred Heart Medical Center, Eugene, Oregon, and Providence Medical Center, Portland, Oregon.

Address reprint requests to: Vern L. Katz, MD, Center for Genetics and Maternal-Fetal Medicine, 677 East 12th Avenue, Suite N-520, Eugene, OR 97401.

Objective: To compare the edema-relieving effects of static immersion with water aerobics.

Methods: Eighteen healthy women between 20 and 33 weeks' gestation were studied standing on land, immersed to the axilla, and participating in a water aerobics class, each for 30 minutes.

Results: Water aerobics and the static immersion led to a similar diuresis, 187 and 180 mL, respectively. Both were significantly greater than standing 30 minutes on land, 65 mL (P < .01). The dilutional effect as measured by a decline in urine specific gravity was also similar between static immersion and water aerobics and greater than standing on land (P < .01). Standing on land led to a small increase in leg volume compared with water aerobics or static immersion (P <.01).

Conclusion: Water aerobics had diuretic and edema-relieving effects similar to static immersion. When women develop edema of pregnancy, water aerobics classes may be used as a potential treatment.

46. "Leg spring" characteristics and the aerobic demand of running.
Medicine and Science in Sports and Exercise. 30(5):750-754, May 1998.
Heise, Gary D.; Martin, Philip E.

Purpose: By applying a simple, linear mass-spring model to running, the normalized leg spring stiffness (Kleg), the normalized effective vertical stiffness (Kvert), and the mass-specific mechanical power output of the spring (Psp) were determined and correlated with aerobic demand. The purpose of the study was to determine whether leg spring characteristics explain any of the interindividual variability observed in aerobic demand at a given submaximal running speed.

Methods: Recreational runners (N = 16) ran on a treadmill at 3.35 m[middle dot]s-1 for physiological measures and overground for biomechanical measures. The latter included a sagittal plane video record of the running motion and ground reaction data.

Results: We found no relationship between the aerobic demand of running and Kleg (r = -0.18), an inverse relationship between aerobic demand and Kvert (r = -0.48), and a positive correlation between aerobic demand and Psp (r = 0.45).

Conclusions: The inverse relationship between Kvert and **aerobic demand** indicates that less economical runners possess a more compliant running style during ground contact. This running style may place greater force demands on extensor musculature.

47. Energy cost of sport rock climbing in elite performers
British Journal of Sports Medicine, Vol 33, Issue 1 14-18, 1999.
J Booth, F Marino, C Hill and T Gwinn
Department of Biomedical Science, University of Wollongong, NSW.

Objectives: To assess oxygen uptake (VO2), blood lactate concentration ([La(b)]), and heart rate (HR) response during indoor and outdoor sport climbing.

Methods: Seven climbers aged 25 (SE 1) years, with a personal best ascent without preview or fall (on sight) ranging from 6b to 7a were assessed using an indoor vertical **treadmill** with artificial rock hand/foot holds and a discontinuous protocol with climbing velocity incremented until voluntary fatigue. On a separate occasion the subjects performed a 23.4 m outdoor rock climb graded 5c and taking 7 min 36 s (SE 33 s) to complete. Cardiorespiratory parameters were measured using a telemetry system and [La(b)] collected at rest and after climbing.

Results: Indoor climbing elicited a peak oxygen uptake (VO2climb-peak) and peak HR (HRpeak) of 43.8 (SE 2.2) ml/kg/min and 190 (SE 4) bpm, respectively and increased blood lactate concentration [La(b)] from 1.4 (0.1) to 10.2 (0.6) mmol/l (p < 0.05). During outdoor climbing VO2 and HR increased to about 75 per cent and 83 per cent of VO2climb-peak and HRpeak, respectively. [La(b)] increased from 1.3 (0.1) at rest to 4.5 mmol/l (p < 0.05) at 2 min 32 s (8 s) after completion of the climb. CONCLUSIONS: The results suggest that for elite climbers outdoor sport rock climbs of five to 10 minutes' duration and moderate difficulty require a significant portion of the VO2climb-peak. The higher HR and VO2 for outdoor climbing and the increased [La(b)] could be the result of repeated isometric contractions, particularly from the arm and forearm muscles.

48.   **Aerobic Conditioning in Mild Asthma Decreases the Hyperpnea of Exercise and Improves Exercise and Ventilatory Capacity***
       Chest. 2000;118:1460-1469.

Teal S. Hallstrand, MD; Peter W. Bates, MD, FCCP and Robert B. Schoene, MD

* From the Division of Pulmonary and Critical Care Medicine (Drs. Hallstrand and Schoene), University of Washington, Seattle, WA; and the Department of Medicine (Dr. Bates), Maine Medical Center, Portland, ME.

Correspondence to: Teal S. Hallstrand, MD, Division of Pulmonary and Critical Care Medicine, Department of Medicine, University of Washington, 1959 NE Pacific St, BB-1253 Health Sciences Center, Box 356522, Seattle, WA 98195-8673;e-mail: tealh@u.washington.edu

Study objective: To determine the effect of an aerobic conditioning program on fitness, respiratory physiology, and resting lung function in patients with mild asthma.

Design: Prospective cohort study.

Setting: Outpatient rehabilitation facility.

Methods: Five patients with mild intermittent asthma and five normal control subjects completed a 10-week aerobic conditioning program. Pulmonary function studies and noninvasive cardiopulmonary exercise tests were performed before and after the conditioning program.

Results: After aerobic conditioning, there were significant gains in maximum oxygen consumption (**O2max**; 22.73 mL/kg/min vs 25.29 mL/kg/min, p = 0.01, **asthma**; 22.94 mL/kg/min vs 27.85 mL/kg/min, p = 0.03, control) and anaerobic threshold (0.99 L/min vs 1.09 L/min, p = 0.03, asthma; 0.89 L/min vs 1.13 L/min, p = 0.01, control) in both groups. Although FEV1 was unchanged, the maximum voluntary ventilation (MVV) improved in the asthma group (96.0 L/min vs 108.2 L/min, p = 0.08, asthma; 134.0 L/min vs 131.2 L/min, p = 0.35, control). During exercise, **minute ventilation** (E) for each level of work was decreased in the asthma group after conditioning, while little change occurred in the control group (68.48 L/min vs 51.70 L/min at initial O2max, p = 0.02, asthma; 65.82 L/min vs 63.12 L/min at initial O2max, p = 0.60, control). A significant decrease in the ventilatory equivalent (E/oxygen consumption, 40.8 vs 30.4 at O2max, p = 0.02, asthma; 37.2 vs 35.8 4 at O2max, p = 0.02, control) and the dyspnea index (E/MVV) at submaximal (0.44 vs 0.38, p = 0.05, asthma; 0.32 vs 0.38, p < 0.01, control) and maximal exercise (0.72 vs 0.63, p = 0.03, asthma; 0.49 vs 0.62, p = 0.02, control) occurred in the asthma group.

Conclusions: Exercise rehabilitation improves aerobic fitness in both asthmatic and nonasthmatic participants of a 10-week aerobic fitness program. Additional benefits of improved ventilatory capacity and decreased hyperpnea of exercise occurred in patients with mild asthma.

Key Words: asthma • exercise-induced bronchospasm • rehabilitation.

49. **Greater rate of decline in maximal aerobic capacity with age in physically active vs. sedentary healthy women**

J Appl Physiol, Vol. 83, Issue 6, 1947-1953, December 1997

Hirofumi Tanaka1, Christopher A. Desouza1, Pamela P. Jones1, Edith T. Stevenson1, Kevin P. Davy1, and Douglas R. Seals1,2

1. Human Cardiovascular Research Laboratory, Center for Physical Activity, Disease Prevention, and Aging, Department of Kinesiology, University of Colorado, Boulder 80309; and 2. Divisions of Cardiology and Geriatric Medicine, Department of Medicine, Center on Aging, University of Colorado Health Sciences Center, Denver, Colorado 80262.

Using a meta-analytic approach, we recently reported that the rate of decline in maximal oxygen uptake (O2 max) with age in healthy women is greatest in the most physically active and smallest in the least active when expressed in milliliters per kilogram per minute per decade. We tested this hypothesis prospectively under well-controlled laboratory conditions by studying 156 healthy, nonobese women (age 20-75 yr): 84 endurance-trained runners (ET) and 72 sedentary subjects (S). ET were matched across the age range for age-adjusted 10-km running performance. Body mass was positively related with age in S but not in ET. Fat-free mass was not different with age in ET or S. Maximal respiratory exchange ratio and rating of perceived exertion were similar across age in ET and S, suggesting equivalent voluntary maximal efforts. There was a significant but modest decline in running mileage, frequency, and speed with advancing age in ET. O2 max (ml · kg1 · min1) was inversely related to age (P < 0.001) in ET (r = 0.82) and S (r = 0.71) and was higher at any age in ET. Consistent with our meta-analysic findings, the absolute rate of decline in O2 max was greater in ET (5.7 ml · kg1 · min1 · decade1) compared with S (3.2 ml · kg1 · min1 · decade1; P < 0.01), but the relative (per cent) rate of decline was similar (9.7 vs 9.1 per cent/decade; not significant). The greater absolute rate of decline in **O2 max** in ET compared with S was not associated with a greater rate of decline in maximal heart rate (5.6 vs. 6.2 beats · min1 · decade1), nor was it related to training factors. The present cross-sectional findings provide additional evidence that the absolute, but not the relative, rate of decline in maximal aerobic capacity with age may be greater in highly physically active women compared with their sedentary healthy peers. This difference does not appear to be related to age-associated changes in maximal heart rate, body composition, or training factors.

Key Words: aging; maximal oxygen uptake; maximal heart rate; endurance exercise training.

50.   **Analysis of the aerobic-anaerobic transition in elite cyclists during incremental exercise with the use of electromyography**
British Journal of Sports Medicine, Vol 33, Issue 3 178-185, 1999.

A Lucia, O Sanchez, A Carvajal and JL Chicharro
Departamento de Ciencias Morfologicas y Fisiologia, Universidad Europea de Madrid, Spain.

Objectives: To investigate the validity and reliability of surface **electromyography** (EMG) as a new non-invasive determinant of the metabolic response to incremental exercise in elite cyclists. The relation between EMG activity and other more conventional methods for analysing the aerobic-anaerobic transition such as blood lactate measurements (lactate threshold (LT) and onset of blood lactate accumulation (OBLA)) and ventilatory parameters (ventilatory thresholds 1 and 2 (VT1 and VT2)) was studied.

Methods: Twenty eight elite road cyclists (age 24 (4) years; **VO2MAX** 69.9 (6.4) ml/kg/min; values mean (SD)) were selected as subjects. Each of them performed a ramp protocol (starting at 0 W, with increases of 5 W every 12 seconds) on a cycle **ergometer** (validity study). In addition, 15 of them performed the same test twice (reliability study). During the tests, data on gas exchange and blood lactate levels were collected to determine VT1, VT2, LT, and OBLA. The root mean squares of EMG signals (rms-EMG) were recorded from both the vastus lateralis and the rectus femoris at each intensity using surface electrodes.

Results: A two threshold response was detected in the rms-EMG recordings from both muscles in 90 per cent of subjects, with two breakpoints, EMGT1 and EMGT2, at around 60-70 per cent and 80-90 per cent of VO2MAX respectively. The results of the reliability study showed no significant differences ($p > 0.05$) between mean values of EMGT1 and EMGT2 obtained in both tests. Furthermore, no significant differences ($p > 0.05$) existed between mean values of EMGT1, in the vastus lateralis and rectus femoris, and VT1 and LT (62.8 (14.5) and 69.0 (6.2) and 64.6 (6.4) and 68.7 (8.2) per cent of VO2MAX respectively), or between mean values of EMGT2, in the vastus lateralis and rectus femoris, and VT2 and OBLA (86.9 (9.0) and 88.0 (6.2) and 84.6 (6.5) and 87.7 (6.4) per cent of VO2MAX respectively).

Conclusion: rms-EMG may be a useful complementary non-invasive method for analysing the aerobic- anaerobic transition (ventilatory and lactate thresholds) in elite cyclists.

51.   Use of Ergogenic Aids by Athletes
J Am Acad Orthop Surg, Vol. 9, No 1, January/February 2001.
Marc D. Silver, MD
Dr. Silver is Assistant Clinical Professor of Orthopaedics and Rehabilitation, Yale University School of Medicine, New Haven, Conn.

Reprint requests: Dr. Silver, Department of Orthopaedics and Rehabilitation, Yale University School of Medicine, One Long Wharf Drive, New Haven, CT 06511.

"Ergogenic aid" is defined as any means of enhancing energy utilization, including energy production, control, and efficiency. Athletes frequently use ergogenic aids to improve their performance and increase their chances of winning in competition. It is estimated that between 1 and 3 million male and female athletes in the United States alone have used anabolic steroids. In response to the problem of drug use, many athletic organizations have established policies prohibiting the use of certain pharmacologic, physiologic, and nutritional aids by athletes and have implemented drug testing programs to monitor compliance. Therefore, it is important for physicians to be knowledgeable about the available ergogenic aids so they can appropriately treat and counsel the athletic patient.

52.   Influence of cholesterol status on blood lipid and lipoprotein enzyme responses to aerobic exercise
J Appl Physiol, Vol. 89, Issue 2, 472-480, August 2000
Peter W. Grandjean1, Stephen F. Crouse2, and J. James Rohack3
1 Department of Health and Human Performance, Auburn University, Auburn University, Alabama 36849-5323; and 2 Applied Exercise Science Laboratory and 3 College of Medicine, Texas A&M University, College Station, Texas 77843

To compare postexercise changes in plasma lipids and lipoprotein enzymes in 13 hypercholesterolemic (HC) and 12 normocholesterolemic men [total cholesterol (TC) 252 ± 5 vs. 179 ± 5 mg/dl], fasting blood samples were obtained 24 h before, immediately, 24, and 48 h after a single bout of treadmill walking (70 per cent peak O2 consumption, 500 kcal expenditure). Significant findings ($P < 0.05$ for all) for plasma volume-adjusted lipid and enzyme variables were that TC, low-density-lipoprotein cholesterol, and cholesterol ester transfer protein activity were higher in the HC group but did not influence the lipid responses to exercise. Across groups, TC was transiently reduced immediately after exercise but returned to baseline levels by 24 h postexercise. Decreases in triglyceride and increases in high-density-lipoprotein cholesterol (HDL-C) and HDL3-C were observed 24 h after exercise and lasted through 48 h. Lipoprotein lipase activity was elevated by 24 h and remained elevated 48 h after exercise. HDL2-C, cholesterol ester transfer protein activity, hepatic triglyceride lipase, and lecithin: cholesterol acyltransferase activities did not change after exercise. These data indicate that the exercise-induced changes in HDL-C and triglyceride are similar in HC and normocholesterolemic men and may be mediated, at least in part, by an increase in lipoprotein lipase activity.

Key Words: hypercholesterolemia; lipoproteins; lipoprotein lipase activity; lecithin: cholesterol acyltransferase activity; cholesterol ester transfer protein activity.

53.   **Dance-based aerobic exercise may improve indices of falling risk in older women**

Age and Ageing 2002; 31: 261-266

Ryosuke Shigematsu, Milan Chang1, Noriko Yabushita2, Tomoaki Sakai2, Masaki Nakagaichi3, Hosung Nho4 and Kiyoji Tanaka5

Japan Foundation for Aging and Health, Higashiura, Chita, Aichi, Japan

1.   Laboratory of Epidemiology, Demography, and Biometry, National Institute on Aging, Bethesda, MD, USA

2.   Doctoral Program of Health and Sport Sciences, University of Tsukuba, Tsukuba, Ibaraki, Japan

3.   Foundation for Advancement of International Science, Tsukuba, Ibaraki, Japan

4.   College of Physical Education, University of Kyung Hee, Kyungki-do, Korea

5.   Institute of Health and Sport Sciences and Center for Tsukuba Advanced Research Alliance, University of Tsukuba, Tsukuba, Ibaraki, Japan

Objective: to determine the effect of dance-based aerobic exercise on indices of falling in older women.

Design: an exercise intervention trial with participants assigned either to an exercise group or to a control group.

Setting: an exercise hall at a community centre for senior citizens.

Participants: thirty-eight healthy women aged 72–87 years, living independently in the community.

Intervention: twenty women performed dance-based aerobic exercise for 60 minutes, 3 days a week, for 12 weeks. The exercise included **single-leg standing**, squatting, marching, and **heel touching**; and **targeted balance**, strength, locomotion/agility, and motor processing.

Main outcome measures: single-leg balance with eyes open/closed and functional reach as balance, hand-grip strength and keeping a half-squat position as strength, walking time around two cones and 3-minute walking distance as locomotion/agility, and hand-reaction time and foot tapping as motor processing.

Results: at the pre-test, both exercise and control groups performed similarly in all tests. At the end of the intervention, the exercise group showed significantly greater single-leg balance with eyes closed, functional reach, and walking time around two cones. In contrast, there were no significant improvements in any of the test measures in the control group.

Conclusions: dance-based aerobic exercise specifically designed for older women may improve selected components of balance and locomotion/agility, thereby attenuating risks of falling.

Key Words: balance • locomotion • agility.

54. **Spectrum of aerobic endurance running performance in eleven inbred strains of rats**

J Appl Physiol, Vol. 85, Issue 2, 530-536, August 1998

John C. Barbato, Lauren Gerard Koch, Ahmad Darvish, George T. Cicila, Patricia J. Metting, and Steven L. Britton

Department of Physiology and Molecular Medicine, Medical College of Ohio, Toledo, Ohio 43614-5804

The goal of this study was to identify inbred rat strains that could serve as useful models for exploration of the genetic basis of aerobic endurance performance. Six rats of each gender from 11 different inbred strains were tested for 1) maximal running capacity on a treadmill and 2) **isolated cardiac performance**. Running performance was estimated from 1) duration of the run, 2) distance run, and 3) vertical work performed. Cardiac output, during constant preload and afterload, was taken as a measure of cardiac performance from an isolated working heart preparation. The COP rats were the lowest performers and the DA rats were the best performers by all estimates of running performance. Across the 11 strains, the distance run correlated positively with isolated cardiac performance ($r = 0.87$). Estimates of performance were as follows (COP vs. DA strain, respectively): duration of run, 19.9 ± 1.8 vs. 41.5

± 2.2 min; distance run, 298 ± 30 vs. 840 ± 64 m; vertical work, 15 ± 1.7 vs. 40 ± 4.4 kg/m. These ~2.5-fold differences in running performance between the COP and DA suggest that these strains could serve as models for evaluation of the genetic basis of variance in aerobic performance.

Key Words: treadmill; selective breeding; fitness; exercise; cardiac; functional genomics; working heart; cardiac performance.

55.   The effect of exercise training on aerobic fitness, immune indices, and quality of life in HIV+ patients
Medicine and Science in Sports and Exercise. 30(1):11-16, January 1998.
Stringer, William W.; Berezovskaya, Marina; O'brien, William A.; Beck, C. Keith; Casaburi, Richard

Purpose: Thirty four HIV+ patients participated in a 6-wk aerobic exercise training program to determine whether exercise improved aerobic fitness, immune indices, and quality of life.

Methods: Subjects were assigned to three groups: control (no regular aerobic exercise), moderate exercise, and heavy exercise training. At study entry and exit (in each subject) we evaluated aerobic function with a symptom limited cardiopulmonary exercise test, immune indices with CD4 counts and Candida skin tests, viral replication with plasma HIV RNA measurements, and quality of life with a HIV+ population validated questionnaire.

Results: Aerobic fitness increased significantly in both exercise groups relative to the control group; immune indices changed very little among all three groups; however, the **Candida skin tests** (mm2) increased significantly in the moderate group; viral replication was essentially unchanged in all three groups; quality of life (QOL) markers improved in both exercising groups but not the control group. There were no opportunistic infections during the study.

Conclusions: Exercise training resulted in a substantial improvement in aerobic function while immune indices were essentially unchanged. Quality of life markers improved significantly with exercise. Exercise training is safe and effective in this patient group and should be promoted for HIV+ patients.

56.   Effect of cycling experience, aerobic power, and power output on preferred and most economical cycling cadences.
Medicine and Science in Sports and Exercise. 29(9):1225-1232, September 1997.
Marsh, Anthony P.; Martin, Philip E.

To determine the effects of cycling experience, fitness level, and power output on preferred and most economical cycling cadences: (1) the preferred cadence (PC) of 12 male cyclists, 10 male runners, and 10 less-trained male noncyclists was determined at 75, 100, 150, 200, and 250 W for cyclists and runners and 75, 100, 125, 150, and 175 W for the less-trained group; and 2) steady-state aerobic demand was determined at six cadences (50, 65, 80, 95, 110 rpm and PC) at 100, 150, and 200 W for cyclists and runners and 75, 100, and 150 W for less-trained subjects. Cyclists and runners ([spacing dot above]VO2max: 70.7 +/- 4.1 and 72.5 +/- 2.2 mL[middle dot]kg-1[middle dot]min-1, respectively) maintained PC between 90 and 100 rpm at all power outputs and both groups selected similar cadences at each power output. In contrast, the less-trained group ([spacing dot above]VO2max= 44.2 +/- 2.8 mL[middle dot]kg-1[middle dot]min-1) selected lower cadences at all common power outputs and reduced cadence from approximately 80 rpm at 75 W to 65 rpm at 175 W. The preferred cadences of all groups were significantly higher than their respective most economical cadences at all power outputs. Changes in power output had little effect on the most economical cadence, which was between 53.3 and 59.9 rpm, in all groups. It was concluded that cycling experience and minimization of aerobic demand are not critical determinants of PC in well-trained individuals. It was speculated that less-trained noncyclists, who cycled at a higher percentage of[spacing dot above]VO2max, may have selected lower PC to reduce aerobic demand.

57. **Blood pressure lowering effect of low intensity aerobic training in elderly hypertensive patients.**

Medicine and Science in Sports and Exercise. 30(6):818-823, June 1998.

Motoyama, Mitsugi; Sunami, Yoshiyuki; Kinoshita, Fujihisa; Kiyonaga, Akira; Tanaka, Hiroaki; Shindo, Munehiro; Irie, Takashi; Urata, Hidenori; Sasaki, Jun; Arakawa, Kikuo

Purpose: The purpose of this investigation was to determine the effect of 9 months of low intensity aerobic training on blood pressure in elderly hypertensive patients who were receiving antihypertensive medication.

Methods: The training group (N = 13; mean age 75.4 +/- 5.4 yr) agreed to take part in physical training using a **treadmill** with an exercise intensity at the blood lactate threshold (LT) for 30 min three to six times a week for 9 months. The rest (N = 13; mean age 73.1 +/- 4.2 yr) served as controls.

Results: The resting systolic (-15 +/- 8 mm Hg), mean (-11 +/- 6 mm Hg), and diastolic **blood pressures** (-9 +/- 9 mm Hg) decreased significantly after 3 months of training and the blood pressure of all participants stabilized at a significantly lower level by the end of the study (9 months) in the training group, whereas no significant changes in blood pressure were found in the control group. Both the pretraining systolic and diastolic blood pressure of those recruited patients negatively correlated with those changes after the training (SBP: P < 0.01; DBP: P < 0.05, respectively). After 1 month of detraining in five patients, the blood pressure levels were similar to those in the pretraining state. The LT increased significantly in the training group (P < 0.01).

Conclusion: In conclusion, an additional antihypertensive effect of mild aerobic training at the LT was confirmed in elderly patients receiving antihypertensive medication. The cessation of such training in five patients, however, resulted in a relatively rapid return to pretraining levels within a month.

58.   A Self-Paced Step Test to Predict Aerobic Fitness in Older Adults in the Primary Care Clinic
Journal of the American Geriatrics Society, Volume 49 Page 632 - MAY 2001.

Robert J. Petrella, MD, PhD,*¶ John J. Koval, PhD, David A. Cunningham, PhD,§¶ and Donald H. Paterson, PhD¶

Objectives: To study the potential usefulness of a submaximal self-paced step test as a prediction of maximal aerobic capacity (VO2max) in older adults in the primary care setting.

Design: Data were collected during a prospective randomized study of an exercise program.

Setting: Four university family medical clinics in London, Ontario, Canada.

Participants: A random sample of 240 healthy older (e"65) men (n = 118) and women (n = 122) from four family medical clinics underwent self-paced step testing in the clinic with a family physician (n = 16), and step testing and a maximal exercise **treadmill** test with measurement of respired gases in an exercise laboratory. Testing was done in random order (clinic/laboratory) separated by 2 weeks and then repeated at 52 weeks, following introduction of an exercise program. Relationships between outcome variables were examined by Pearson correlation coefficients while prediction of VO2max was examined using multivariate regression analysis. Cross-validation with 30 age-matched hypertensive and 40 age-matched post-hip arthroplasty patients was used to test the accuracy of the predictive models.

Measurements: Measured **VO2max**, predicted VO2max, step test time, step test heart rate, body mass index (BMI), and O2 pulse.

Results: Two hundred women (n = 108) and men (n = 92) completed both the initial and 52-week assessments. Stepping time, heart rate, age, BMI, and O2 pulse were strongly associated with VO2max for both a normal and a fast step pace and were chosen to develop the predictive model. Normal step-pace correlation with VO2max (ml/kg/min) was no different (female 0.93: male 0.91) from fast pace (0.95:0.90) with no difference between clinic and laboratory measurement at baseline or 52 weeks. Cross-validation showed no significant difference from the main group using the predictive model.

Conclusions: The self-paced step test is a safe and simple clinical instrument that strongly and reliably predicts VO2max, is sensitive to change, and is generalizable in the family practice setting among community-dwelling older adults differing in fitness and health status.

59. **Prevalence and types of injuries in aerobic dancers**
American Journal of Sports Medicine, Vol 16, Issue 4 403-407, 1988.
LA Rothenberger, JI Chang and TA Cable
Moses H. Cone Hospital, Greensboro, North Carolina 27401-1007.

A sample of 726 aerobic dancers was surveyed by questionnaire to document the prevalence, types, and severity of injuries experienced. Data were gathered on demographics, exercise behavior, and environmental conditions during a 1 week period. Most of the subjects (66 per cent) engaged in **aerobic dance** classes at least every other day, with a mean exercise time of 195 minutes per week. Twenty-eight percent of the subjects had been exercising 1 to 2 years, and 26 per cent had been exercising 2 years or longer. Forty-nine percent of the subjects reported a history of at least one injury related to aerobic dancing. Most of the injuries were to the shin (24.5 per cent), lower back (12.9 per cent), and ankle (12.2 per cent). Among those subjects injured, 23 per cent reportedly saw a physician because of their injury. The frequency with which subjects exercised was associated with a history of injury. Subjects who exercised fewer than four times per week reported fewer injuries (43 per cent) than those who exercised four times per week (60 per cent) or more (66 per cent). This study is a first step toward providing data to help physicians counsel aerobic dancers regarding injury prevention.

60. **Specific Genetic Markers of Endurance Performance and o2max.**
Exercise and Sport Sciences Reviews. 29(1):15-19, January 2001.
Hagberg, James M. 1; Moore, Geoffrey E. 2; Ferrell, Robert E. 3
Recent advances have revolutionized genetic studies of quantitative traits. Mitochondrial DNA and creatine kinase variations may influence o2max. Other data strongly suggest that angiotensin-converting enzyme genotype affects o2max and endurance performance capacity, but the mechanisms are unclear. A recent genome-wide scan study also has provided candidate loci requiring further study.

61.   **Resistance and aerobic training in older men: effects on O2 peak and the capillary supply to skeletal muscle**

Journal of Applied Physiology, Vol. 82, No. 4, pp. 1305-1310, April 1997.

R. T. Hepple, S. L. M. Mackinnon, J. M. Goodman, S. G. Thomas, and M. J. Plyley

Department of Physiology, Graduate Department of Community Health, and Department of Physical Therapy, University of Toronto, Toronto, Ontario, Canada M5S 3J7

Both aerobic training (AT) and resistance training (RT) may increase aerobic power (O2 peak) in the older population; however, the role of changes in the capillary supply in this response has not been evaluated. Twenty healthy men (age 65-74 yr) engaged in either 9 wk of lower body RT followed by 9 wk of AT on a cycle ergometer (RTAT group) or 18 wk of AT on a cycle ergometer (ATAT group). RT was performed three times per week and consisted of three sets of four exercises at 6-12 repetitions maximum. AT was performed three times per week for 30 min at 60-70 per cent heart rate reserve. O2 peak was increased after both RT and AT ($P < 0.05$). Biopsies (vastus lateralis) revealed that the number of capillaries per fiber perimeter length was increased after both AT and RT ($P < 0.05$), paralleling the changes in O2 peak, whereas capillary density was increased only after AT ($P < 0.01$). These results, and the finding of a significant correlation between the change in capillary supply and O2 peak ($r = 0.52$), suggest the possibility that similar mechanisms may be involved in the increase of O2 peak after high-intensity RT and AT in the older population.

Key Words: capillaries; aerobic power; aging; oxygen flux.

62.   **Aerobic and anaerobic power responses to the practice of taekwon-do**

Br J Sports Med, 35:231-234, 2001.

A F Melhim

Department of Exercise Science, Faculty of Physical Education, Yarmouk University, PO Box 5040, Irbid 21163, Jordan

Correspondence to: Dr Melhim ayedm@hotmail.com

Background : Practising the martial art of taekwon-do (TKD) has been proposed to have beneficial effects on cardiovascular fitness as well as general physical ability. Furthermore, TKD masters and participants have promoted TKD as a total fitness programme. Research studies substantiating this, however, seem to be lacking, perhaps because TKD is recognised more as a method of self defence than a fitness programme.

Methods : Nineteen TKD practitioners with an average age of 13.8 years and 10.4 months of TKD training experience were recruited to participate. Measurements included resting heart rate, aerobic power, anaerobic power, and anaerobic capacity.

Results : Paired test analysis showed no significant differences in either resting heart rate or aerobic power after training. However, significant differences were observed in anaerobic power and anaerobic capacity (p = 0.05). The increases in anaerobic power and anaerobic capacity were 28 per cent and 61.5 per cent respectively.

Conclusion : The practice of TKD promotes anaerobic power and anaerobic capacity, but not aerobic power, in male adolescents.

Key Words: taekwon-do; poomses; VO2MAX; anaerobic power; anaerobic capacity.

63. Physiological determinants of cross-country ski racing performance.

Medicine and Science in Sports and Exercise. 33(8):1379-1384, August 2001.

Mahood, Nicholas V.; Kenefick, Robert W.; Kertzer, Robert; Quinn, Timothy J.

Purpose: Previous laboratory testing has identified the importance of upper-body aerobic and anaerobic power to cross-country skiing performance. The purpose of this investigation was to extend laboratory research into a field setting to identify predictors of performance through ski-specific testing.

Methods: Thirteen male collegiate skiers performed three field-testing sessions on roller skis to establish lactate threshold (LT) and ski economy (ECON) and maximal oxygen uptake (SK O2max) and a 1-km double-pole time trial (UBTT) to determine peak upper-body oxygen uptake (UB O2). As a measure of skiing performance, the subjects performed a 10-km skating time trial (TT) and were ranked according to competitive season performance (RANK).

Results: Significant correlations (P < 0.05) were found between SK O2max, LT O2, UB O2, and RANK (r = -0.66 to -0.84) and TT time (r = -0.74 to -0.79), as well as ECON to RANK (r = 0.57) and TT time (r = 0.68). Time to complete the UBTT (UB time) exhibited the strongest correlation to both RANK (r = 0.95) and TT time (r = 0.92). Multiple regression analyses revealed that UB time was the best predictor of RANK and TT time, as demonstrated by the significant [beta] values (0.77, P < 0.001, and 0.79, P < 0.001, respectively). The importance of the UB component was further seen in that UB time was still the best predictor of performance when the subjects were divided into two distinct groups of greater and lesser competitive ability.

Conclusions: These findings identify the importance of the upper body component to cross-country skiing performance, suggesting a need to focus on upper-body conditioning within a well-rounded endurance training program. Additionally, the UBTT exhibits potential as a simple field test to predict cross-country skiing performance over more sophisticated and costly laboratory and field testing.

64.   Ambulatory estimates of maximal aerobic power from foot -ground contact times and heart rates in running humans

Appl Physiol, Vol. 91, Issue 1, 451-458, July 2001

Peter G. Weyand1,3, Maureen Kelly1,3, Thomas Blackadar2, Jesse C. Darley2, Steven R. Oliver2, Norbert E. Ohlenbusch2, Sam W. Joffe2, and Reed W. Hoyt1

(1) United States Army Research Institute for Environmental Medicine, Natick 01760; (2) FitSense Technology Incorporated, Wellesley 02481; and (3) Concord Field Station, Museum of Comparative Zoology, Harvard University, Bedford, Massachusetts 01730.

Seeking to develop a simple ambulatory test of maximal aerobic power (**O2 max**), we hypothesized that the ratio of inverse foot-ground contact time (1/tc) to heart rate (HR) during steady-speed running would accurately predict O2 max. Given the direct relationship between 1/tc and mass-specific O2 uptake during running, the ratio 1/tc · HR should reflect mass-specific O2 pulse and, in turn, aerobic power. We divided 36 volunteers into matched experimental and validation groups. O2 max was determined by a **treadmill** test to volitional fatigue. Ambulatory monitors on the shoe and chest recorded foot-ground contact time (tc) and steady-state HR, respectively, at a series of submaximal running speeds. In the experimental group, aerobic fitness index (1/tc · HR) was nearly constant across running speed and correlated with O2 max ($r = 0.90$). The regression equation derived from data from the experimental group predicted O2 max from the 1/tc · HR values in the validation group within 8.3 per cent and 4.7 ml O2 · kg1 · min1 ($r = 0.84$) of measured values. We conclude that simultaneous measurements of foot-ground constant times and heart rates during level running at a freely chosen constant speed can provide accurate estimates of maximal aerobic power.

Key Words: aerobic fitness index; oxygen pulse; cost coefficient; locomotion; running mechanics.

65.   Influence of water run training on the maintenance of aerobic performance

Medicine and Science in Sports and Exercise. 28(8):1056-1062, August 1996.

Wilber, Randall L.; Moffatt, Robert J.; Scott, Bradley E.; Lee, Dae T.; Cucuzzo, Nicholas A.

The purpose of this study was to examine the effect of a 6-wk deep water running program on the maintenance of cardio-respiratory performance ([spacing dot above]VO2max, ventilatory threshold, running economy); metabolic measurements of blood glucose, blood lactate, and plasma norepinephrine; and body composition. Sixteen trained male runners ([spacing dot above]VO2max = 58.6+/- 3.6 ml[middle dot]kg-1 [middle dot]min-1) were assigned to one of two groups matched by [spacing dot above]**VO2max, treadmill** run (R) or water run (WR). Subjects participated in their respective training programs, which consisted of workouts of a) 30 min at 90-100 per cent [spacing dot above]VO2max and b) 60 min at 70-75 per cent [spacing dot above]VO2max alternated daily for 5 d[middle dot]wk-1. Following 6 wk of workouts, no significant intra- or intergroup differences were observed for treadmill [spacing dot above]VO2max for R (pre = 58.4 +/- 2.3, post = 60.1 +/- 3.6 ml[middle dot]kg-1[middle dot]min-1) and WR(pre = 58.7 +/- 4.7, post = 59.6 +/- 5.4 ml[middle dot]kg-1[middle dot]min-1). Similarly, ventilatory threshold was unaltered in R (pre = 47.5 +/- 1.8, post = 48.2 +/- 3.3 ml[middle dot]kg-1[middle dot]min-1) and WR (pre = 46.5 +/- 6.4, post = 47.4 +/- 6.7 ml[middle dot]kg-1[middle dot]min-1), nor were there any changes in running economy in R (pre = 48.4 +/- 2.3, post = 48.9 +/- 2.0 ml[middle dot]kg-1[middle dot]min-1 at 255 m[middle dot]min-1) and WR (pre = 51.8 +/- 2.0, post = 48.9 +/- 2.2 ml[middle dot]kg-1[middle dot]min-1 at 255 m[middle dot]min-1). No significant differences were observed within or between groups for maximal blood glucose, blood lactate, and plasma norepinephrine concentration as well as for body composition indices. It was concluded that deep water running may serve as an effective training alternative to land-based running for the maintenance of aerobic performance for up to 6 wk in trained endurance athletes.

66. **Physiological Outcomes of Aerobic Exercise Training in Hemiparetic Stroke Patients**
Stroke. 1995;26:101-105.
Kathleen Potempa, DNSc; Martita Lopez, PhD; Lynne T. Braun, PhD; J. Peter Szidon, MD; Louis Fogg, PhD Tyler Tincknell, MS
From The Stroke Rehabilitation Research Program, University of Illinois at Chicago (K.P., L.F., T.T.), and the Departments of Medicine (L.T.B., J.P.S.) and Psychology and Social Sciences (M.L.), Rush Presbyterian St Luke's Medical Center, Chicago, Ill.
Correspondence to Dr K. Potempa, The Stroke Rehabilitation Research Program, University of Illinois at Chicago (m/c 802), 845 S Damen Ave, Chicago, IL 60612-7350.

Background and Purpose : In hemiparetic individuals, low endurance to exercise may compound the increased energy cost of movement and contribute to poor rehabilitation outcomes. The purpose of this investigation was to describe how hemiparetic stroke patients responded to intense exercise and aerobic training.

Methods : Forty-two subjects were randomly assigned to an exercise training group or to a control group. Treatments were given three times per week for 10 weeks in similar laboratory settings. Baseline and posttest measurements were made of maximal oxygen consumption, heart rate, workload, exercise time, resting and submaximal blood pressures, and sensorimotor function.

Results : Only experimental subjects showed significant improvement in maximal oxygen consumption, workload, and exercise time. Improvement in sensorimotor function was significantly related to the improvement in aerobic capacity. After treatment, experimental subjects showed significantly lower systolic blood pressure at submaximal workloads during the graded exercise test.

Conclusions : We conclude that hemiparetic stroke patients may improve their aerobic capacity and submaximal exercise systolic blood pressure response with training. Sensorimotor improvement is related to the improvement in aerobic capacity.

Key Words: blood pressure • exercise • rehabilitation

67.   **Is physical activity or aerobic power more influential on reducing cardiovascular disease risk factors?**

Medicine & Science in Sports & Exercise. 30(10):1521-1529, October 1998.

Mcmurray, Robert G.; Ainsworth, Barbara E.; Harrell, Joanne S.; Griggs, Thomas R.; Williams, O. Dale

Purpose: This study determined the relationship between aerobic power $V\dot{O}_2max$), physical activity (PA), and cardiovascular disease (CVD) risk factors. The study also determined how increased $V\dot{O}_2max$ and increased PA levels influence CVD risk factors of 576 low-fit adults ($V\dot{O}_2max < 30$ mL·kg-1·min-1).

Methods: PA (Baeke questionnaire) and $V\dot{O}_2max$ (submaximal cycle test) of 1664 law enforcement trainees were evaluated with respect to the CVD risk factors of total **cholesterol**, blood pressure (BP) [BP], **smoking,** and **obesity** using separate logistic regression, adjusting for age, gender, and the other major CVD risk factors.

Results: Compared with the lowest tertile of $V\dot{O}_2max$, the highest tertile had a reduced relative risk (RR) for elevated cholesterol (RR, 0.56; CI, 0.36-0.43), BP (RR, 0.32; CI, 0.15-0.62) and obesity (RR, 0.09; CI,

0.06-0.12). The middle tertile of V[spacing dot above]O2max compared with the lowest had reduced RR for elevated diastolic BP (RR, 0.44; CI, 0.23-0.66) and obesity (RR: 0.38; CI 0.28-0.50). High PA tertile, compared with low PA tertile, only had lower RR for high systolic BP (RR, 0.48; CI, 0.23-0.95). Compared with the low PA tertile, moderate or high PA had no reduction in any of the RR (P > 0.05). Participation in a 9-wk exercise program by low-fit individuals resulted in a 9 per cent increase in PA levels (P < 0.02); however, only those subjects who increased V[spacing dot above]O2max (>3 mL[middle dot]kg-1[middle dot]min-1; N = 345) had a reduction in RR for high cholesterol (RR: 0.62; CI 0.42-0.92) and systolic BP (RR: 0.57; CI 0.40-0.80). No reduction in RR were noted for diastolic BP or obesity.

Conclusions: Aerobic power appears to have more of an influence on CVD risk factors than PA levels. Further, in low-fit persons, it appears that PA resulting in an increased aerobic power is associated with a reduction in CVD risk factors of cholesterol and BP in as little as 9 wk.

68. **Treadmill Aerobic Exercise Training Reduces the Energy Expenditure and Cardiovascular Demands of Hemiparetic Gait in Chronic Stroke Patients**
Stroke, 1997;28:326-330.

R.F. Macko, MD; C.A. DeSouza, PhD; L.D. Tretter, BS; K.H. Silver, MD; G.V. Smith, PhD; P.A. Anderson, PhD; Naomi Tomoyasu, PhD; P. Gorman, MD D.R. Dengel, PhD

The Neurology and Geriatrics Services and the Geriatrics Research, Education, and Clinical Center, Baltimore (Md) Department of Veterans Affairs Medical Center (R.F.M., L.D.T., K.H.S., N.T.); Departments of Neurology (R.F.M., K.H.S., P.G.), Physical Therapy (G.V.S., P.A.A.), and Medicine, Division of Gerontology (R.F.M., K.H.S.), University of Maryland School of Medicine, Baltimore; Department of Kinesiology, University of Colorado at Boulder (C.A.D.); and Division of Geriatrics and the Geriatrics Research, Education, and Clinical Center, Ann Arbor (Mich) Department of Veterans Affairs Medical Center (D.R.D.).

Correspondence to Richard Macko, MD, Department of Neurology, University of Maryland School of Medicine, 22 N Greene St, Baltimore, MD 21201-1595.

Background and Purpose : Elevated energy costs of hemiparetic gait contribute to functional disability after stroke, particularly in physically deconditioned older patients. We investigated the effects of 6 months of treadmill aerobic exercise training on the energy expenditure and cardiovascular demands of submaximal effort ambulation in stroke patients with chronic hemiparetic gait.

Methods: Nine older stroke patients with chronic hemiparetic gait were enrolled in a 6-month program of low-intensity aerobic exercise using a graded treadmill. Repeated measures of energy expenditure based on steady state oxygen consumption during a standardized 1-mph submaximal effort **treadmill** walking task were performed before and after training.

Results : Six months of exercise training produced significant reductions in energy expenditure (n=9; 3.40±0.27 versus 2.72±0.25 kcal/min [mean±SEM]; P<.005) during a given submaximal effort treadmill walking task. Repeated measures analysis in the subset of patients (n=8) tested at baseline and after 3 and 6 months revealed that reductions in energy expenditure were progressive (F=11.1; P<.02) and that exercise-mediated declines in both oxygen consumption (F=9.7; P<.02) and respiratory exchange ratio (F=13.4; P<.01) occurred in a strong linear pattern. These stroke patients could perform the same standardized submaximal exercise task at progressively lower heart rates after 3 months (96±4 versus 87±4 beats per minute) and 6 months of training (82±4 beats per minute; F=35.4; P<.002).

Conclusions : Six months of low-intensity treadmill endurance training produces substantial and progressive reductions in the energy expenditure and cardiovascular demands of walking in older patients with chronic hemiparetic stroke. This suggests that task-oriented aerobic exercise may improve functional mobility and the cardiovascular fitness profile in this population.

Key Words: cerebrovascular disorders • energy metabolism • exercise • hemiplegia • rehabilitation.

69.   **Effect of weight reduction, obesity predisposition, and aerobic fitness on skeletal muscle mitochondrial function**

Am J Physiol Endocrinol Metab, Vol. 278, Issue 1, E153-E161, January 2000.

D. Enette Larson-Meyer1, Bradley R. Newcomer2, Gary R. Hunter3, James E. McLean3, Hoby P. Hetherington4, and Roland L. Weinsier1

1 Division of Physiology and Metabolism, Department of Nutrition Sciences, 2 Department of Critical and Diagnostic Care, and 3 Department of Human Studies, The University of Alabama at Birmingham, Birmingham, Alabama 35294; and 4 Medical Department, Brookhaven National Laboratory, Upton, New York 11973.

We used 31P magnetic resonance spectroscopy to measure maximal mitochondrial function in 12 obesity-prone women before and after diet-induced weight reduction and in 12 matched, never-obese, and 7 endurance-trained controls. Mitochondrial function was modeled after maximum-effort plantar flexion from the phosphocreatine recovery time constant (TCPCr), the ADP recovery time constant (TCADP), and the rate of change in PCr during the first 14 s of recovery (OxPhos). Weight reduction was not associated with a significant change in mitochondrial function by TCPCr, TCADP, or OxPhos. Mitochondrial function was not different between postobese and never-obese controls by TCPCr [35.1 ± 2.5 (SE) vs. 34.6 ± 2.5 s], TCADP (22.9 ± 1.8 vs. 21.2 ± 1.8 s), or OxPhos (0.26 ± 0.03 vs. 0.25 ± 0.03 mM ATP/s), postobese vs. never-obese, respectively. However, TCADP was significantly faster (14.5 ± 2.3 s), and OxPhos was significantly higher (0.38 ± 0.04 mM ATP/s) in the endurance-trained group. These results suggest that maximal mitochondrial function is not impaired in normal-weight obesity-prone women relative to their never-obese counterparts but is increased in endurance-trained women.

Key Words: nuclear magnetic resonance; skeletal muscle; oxidative phosphorylation; endurance training.

70.   **Left ventricular function in response to the transition from aerobic to anaerobic metabolism.**
      Medicine & Science in Sports & Exercise. 29(8):1040-1047, August 1997.

      Pokan, Rochus; Hofmann, Peter; Von Duvillard, Serge P.; Beaufort, Friedrich; Schumacher, Martin; Fruhwald, Fritz M.; Zweiker, Robert; Eber, Bernd; Gasser, Robert; Brandt, Dieter; Smekal, Gerhard; Klein, Werner; Schmid, Peter

      The purpose of this investigation was to study myocardial function at rest, during three phases of energy supply, and during recovery. Radionuclide angiography was performed during the aerobic phase (phase I, rest-first lactate increase), the aerobic-anaerobic transition phase (phase II, first lactate increase-second lactate increase), the anaerobic phase (phase III, second lactate increase-maximal work performance (Pmax)), and during recovery. Thirty-eight male patients (59 +/- 7 d after myocardial infarction) were compared with 19 healthy control subjects and 21 sports students of comparable age. Left ventricular ejection fraction (LVEF) increased from rest to phase I and from phase I to phase II in sports students and control subjects. During phase III, LVEF did not change significantly in sports students, but it decreased significantly in control subjects. This is in contrast to the patients, who showed an increase of LVEF from resting values (47 +/- 3 per cent) to phase I (50 +/- 1 per cent), no change during phase II(51 +/- 2 per cent), and a decrease to resting values (45 +/- 2) during phase III. All subjects showed an increase in stroke volume (SV) during phase I and II, reaching a maximum at phase II. This was evidenced by an improvement of the systolic function with a constant **left ventricular end-diastolic volume** (EDV) in control subjects and sports students. In contrast, an improved SV in patients was achieved through an increase in EDV and a less distinct increase in the left ventricular end-systolic volume (ESV). Maximal LVEF values were measured during the first 90 s of recovery in all subjects. Values during recovery are not representative of load dependent myocardial function. This increase in LVEF does not cause an increase in cardiac output but is a consequence of changes in the EDV and ESV, which decrease again immediately after the end of exercise performance.

71.   **National physical education curriculum: motor and cardiovascular health related fitness in Greek adolescents**
Br J Sports Med 2003;**37**:311-314
Y Koutedakis1 and C Bouziotas2
1.   Department of Sports and Exercise Science, Thessaly University, Trikala, Greece
2.   School of Sport, Performing Arts and Leisure, University of Wolverhampton, UK
Correspondence to:
Professor Koutedakis, Department of Sport and Exercise Science, University of Thessaly, Karies, 42100 Trikala, Greece;
y.koutedakis@uth.gr

Background: State school physical education (PE) programmes are common throughout Greece. However, it is not known if the main objectives of the Greek PE curriculum are achieved.

Objective: To assess the current national PE curriculum in relation to selected motor and cardiovascular health related fitness parameters.

Methods: A sample of 84 Greek schoolboys (mean (SD) age 13.6 (0.3) years, height 160.7 (8.6) cm, weight 50 (10.8) kg) volunteered. Forty three indicated participation only in school PE classes and habitual free play (PE group). The remaining 41 were involved in extracurricular organised physical activities in addition to school PE and habitual free play (PE+ group). The subjects underwent anthropometric, motor (flexibility, balance, standing broad jump, hand grip, sit ups, and plate tapping), and cardiovascular health related (percentage body fat, aerobic fitness, and physical activity) fitness assessments.

Results: Children in the PE group had inferior motor and cardiovascular health related fitness profiles compared with those in the PE+ group. Body fat (20.3 (8.8) v 13.9 (3.5); $p < 0.001$), aerobic fitness (34.7 (3.7) v 43.9 (4.2); $p < 0.001$), and time spent in intensive physical activity (0.2 (0.2) v 0.7 (0.3); p<0.001) showed the greatest differences between the two groups. In the pupils in the PE group, these were lower than the levels proposed to be necessary to combat future health risks. Adjustments for confounding variables showed a decrease in the significance of motor fitness, but not in cardiovascular health related parameters.

Conclusions: The national PE curriculum for Greek secondary schools does not achieve the required levels of motor and cardiovascular health related fitness and should be reconsidered.

Key Words: aerobic fitness; body fat; coronary heart disease; physical activity; adolescents.

Abbreviations: PE, physical education; MET, metabolic equivalent.

72. **Relationships Between Aerobic Energy Cost, Performance and Kinematic Parameters in Roller Ski Skating**
Int J Sports Med 2002; 23: 191-195.
G. Y. Millet[1], S. Perrey[2], R. Candau[3], J. D. Rouillon[2]

1. Groupe Analyse du Mouvement - Faculté des Sciences du Sport, Dijon Cedex, France
2. Laboratoire des Sciences du Sport - UFR STAPS, Besançon, France
3. Laboratoire Sport, Performance, Santé - Faculté des Sciences du Sport, Montpellier, France

The aims of this study were to test the hypotheses that 1) the aerobic energy cost of roller ski skating (CS) is significantly related to level of performance and 2) a significant part of inter-individual differences of CS can be explained by kinematic parameters of skating locomotion. Oxygen uptake, kinematics of the knee and ankle joint, EMG of the *vastus lateralis* (VL) and *gastrocnemius lateralis* (GL) muscles, and roller ski velocity were recorded in 13 skiers who roller skied at 19.0 ± 0.1 km × h-1. CS was found to be 2.51 ± 0.35 J × kg-1 × m-1 and significantly correlated with the skiers' level of performance ($r = 0.61$; $p < 0.05$). Significant relationships were found between CS and 1) knee angular amplitude ($r = 0.75$; $p < 0.01$) during the concentric phase, 2) VL average EMG during the concentric phase ($r = 0.72$; $p < 0.01$) and 3) VL and GL average EMG during the eccentric phase ($p < 0.05$). The results of this study showed that a significant part of performance could be explained by the aerobic energy cost of locomotion in skating. It can also be suggested that differences in upper/lower body utilization and/or in mechanical efficiency may explain the differences in CS.

Key Words: EMG - joint kinematics - stretch-shortening cycle.

73.   Metabolic demands of intense aerobic interval training in competitive cyclists.

Medicine and Science in Sports and Exercise. 33(2):303-310, February 2001.

Stepto, Nigel K.; Martin, David T.; Fallon, Keiran E.; Hawley, John. A.

Purpose: To investigate the metabolic demands of a single session of intense aerobic interval training in highly trained competitive endurance cyclists.

Methods : Seven cyclists (peak O2 uptake [O2peak] 5.14 +/- 0.23 L.min-1, mean +/-SD) performed 8 x 5 min work bouts at 86 +/- 2 per cent of O2peak with 60-s recovery. Muscle biopsies were taken from the vastus lateralis immediately before and after the training session, whereas pulmonary gas exchange and venous blood were sampled at regular intervals throughout exercise.

Results : Muscle glycogen concentration decreased from 501 +/- 91 to 243 +/- 51 mmol[middle dot]kg-1 dry mass (P < 0.01). High rates of total carbohydrate oxidation were maintained throughout exercise (340 [mu]mol[middle dot]kg-1[middle dot]min-1), whereas fat oxidation increased from 16 +/- 8 during the first to 25 +/- 13 [mu]mol[middle dot]kg-1[middle dot]min-1 during the seventh work bout (P < 0.05). **Blood lactate** concentration remained between 5 and 6 mM throughout exercise, whereas muscle lactate increased from 6 +/- 1 at rest to 32 +/- 12 mmol[middle dot]kg-1 d.m. immediately after the training session (P < 0.01). Although muscle pH decreased from 7.09 +/- 0.06 at rest to 7.01 +/- 0.03 at the end of the session (P < 0.01), blood pH was similar after the first and seventh work bouts (7.34). Arterial oxygen saturation (per centSPO2) fell to 95.6 +/- 1 per cent during the first work bout and remained at 94 per cent throughout exercise: the 60-s rest intervals were adequate to restore per centSPO2 to 97 per cent.

Conclusion : Highly trained cyclists are able to sustain high steady state aerobic power outputs that are associated with high rates of glycogenolysis and total energy expenditure similar to those experienced during a 60-min competitive ride.

74.   An overview of the issues: physiological effects of bed rest and restricted physical activity

Medicine & Science in Sports & Exercise. 29(2):187-190, February 1997.

Convertino, Victor A.; Bloomfield, Susan A.; Greenleaf, John E.

Reduction of exercise capacity with confinement to bed rest is well recognized. Underlying physiological mechanisms include dramatic reductions in maximal stroke volume, cardiac output, and oxygen uptake. However, bed rest by itself does not appear to contribute to cardiac dysfunction. Increased muscle fatigue is associated with reduced **muscle blood flow, red cell volume, capillarization**, and oxidative enzymes. Loss of muscle mass and bone density may be reflected by reduced muscle strength and higher risk for injury to bones and joints. The resultant deconditioning caused by bed rest can be independent of the primary disease and physically debilitating in patients who attempt to reambulate to normal active living and working. A challenge to clinicians and health care specialists has been the identification of appropriate and effective methods to restore physical capacity of patients during or after restricted physical activity associated with prolonged bed rest. The examination of physiological responses to bed rest deconditioning and exercise training in healthy subjects has provided significant information to develop effective rehabilitation treatments. The successful application of acute exercise to enhance orthostatic stability, daily endurance exercise to maintain aerobic capacity, or specific resistance exercises to maintain musculoskeletal integrity rather than the use of surgical, pharmacological, and other medical treatments for clinical conditions has been enhanced by investigation and understanding of underlying mechanisms that distinguish physical deconditioning from the disease. This symposium presents an overview of cardiovascular and musculoskeletal deconditioning associated with reduced physical work capacity following prolonged bed rest and exercise training regimens that have proven successful in ameliorating or reversing these adverse effects.

75. Sports and recreation related injury episodes in the US population, 1997–99

Inj Prev 2003;9:117-123

J M Conn, J L Annest and J Gilchrist

National Center for Injury Prevention and Control, Centers for Disease Control and Prevention, Atlanta, Georgia.

Correspondence to:

Judith M Conn, Office of Statistics and Programming, National Center for Injury Prevention and Control, Centers for Disease Control and Prevention, 4770 Buford Hwy (MS-K59), Atlanta, GA 30341–3724, USA;

jconn@cdc.gov

Objective: To characterize sports and recreation related (SR) injury episodes in the US population. SR activities are growing in popularity suggesting the need for increased awareness of SR injuries as a public health concern for physically active persons of all ages in the US population.

Setting: The National Health Interview Survey (NHIS) is a face-to-face household survey conducted yearly by the National Center for Health Statistics, part of the Centers for Disease Control and Prevention. Demographic and health data are collected from a nationally representative sample of the civilian, non-institutionalized population residing in the US.

Methods: Medically attended injury events reported in the 1997–99 Injury Section of the NHIS were categorized according to the associated sport or recreational activity using a classification scheme based on the International Classification of External Causes of Injury system. Episodes where the injured person received any type of medical attention (that is, medical advice or treatment) from any health care provider were used to report the incidence, severity, and nature of SR injuries sustained by US citizens.

Results: Annually, an estimated seven million Americans received medical attention for SR injuries (25.9 injury episodes per 1000 population). For 5–24 year olds, this national estimate was about 42 per cent higher than estimates based on SR injuries seen only in emergency departments over a similar time frame. The highest average annual SR injury episode rates were for children ages 5–14 years (59.3 per 1000 persons) and persons aged 15–24 years (56.4 per 1000 persons). The SR injury episode rate for males was more than twice the rate for females. The age adjusted injury rate for whites was 1.5 times higher than for blacks (28.8 v 19.0 per 1000 population). Basketball was the most frequently mentioned SR activity when the injury episode occurred, with a rate of about four injury events per 1000 population. Strains and sprains accounted for 31 per cent of injury episodes. An estimated 1.1 million SR episode related injuries involve the head or neck region, of which 17 per cent were internal head injuries. The most common mechanisms of injury were struck by/against (34 per cent), fall (28 per cent), and overexertion (13 per cent).

Conclusion: As physical activity continues to be promoted as part of a healthy lifestyle, SR injuries are becoming an important public health concern for both children and adults. Prevention efforts aimed at reducing SR injuries through targeting high risk activities, places of occurrence, activity, risk behaviors, and use of protective devices need to go beyond focusing on children and also consider physically active adults.

Key Words: sports injuries; recreation injuries.

76.   **Predicting Athletic Performance with Self- Confidence and Somatic and Cognitive Anxiety as a Function of Motor and Physiological Requirements in Six Sports**
      Journal of Personality, Volume 55 Page 139 - March 1987.
      Jim Taylor[1]

The purpose of the present study is to examine the ability of certain psychological attributes to predict performance in six National Collegiate Athletic Association Division I collegiate sports Eighty-four athletes from the varsity sports teams of cross country running, alpine and nordic skiing tennis, basketball, and track and field at the University of Colorado completed a questionnaire adapted from Martens (1977, Martens et al 1983) that measured their trait levels of self-confidence (Bandura, 1977), somatic anxiety and cognitive anxiety (Martens, 1977 Martens et al, 1983) In addition, at three to six competitions during the season, the members of the cross country running and tennis teams filled out a state measure (Martens et al 1983) of the three attributes from one to two hours prior to the competition Following each competition, subjective and objective ratings of performance were obtained, and for all sports coaches' ratings of performance and an overall seasonal team ranking were determined as seasonal performance measures The sports were dichotomized along motor and physiological dimensions Results indicate that all three psychological attributes were significant predictors of performance in both fine motor anaerobic sports and gross motor, aerobic sports Further, clear differences in these relationships emerged as a function of the dichotomization In addition, unexpected sex differences emerged The findings are discussed relative to prior research and their implications for future research.

77. The Effects of Supraphysiologic Doses of Testosterone on Muscle Size and Strength in Normal Men

Shalender Bhasin, M.D., Thomas W. Storer, Ph.D., Nancy Berman, Ph.D., Carlos Callegari, M.D., Brenda Clevenger, B.A., Jeffrey Phillips, M.D., Thomas J. Bunnell, B.A., Ray Tricker, Ph.D., Aida Shirazi, R.Ph., and Richard Casaburi, Ph.D., M.D.

Background : Athletes often take androgenic steroids in an attempt to increase their strength. The efficacy of these substances for this purpose is unsubstantiated, however.

Methods : We randomly assigned 43 normal men to one of four groups: placebo with no exercise, testosterone with no exercise, placebo plus exercise, and testosterone plus exercise. The men received injections of 600 mg of **testosterone** enanthate or **placebo** weekly for 10 weeks. The men in the exercise groups performed standardized weight-lifting exercises three times weekly. Before and after the treatment period, fat-free mass was determined by underwater weighing, muscle size was measured by magnetic resonance imaging, and the strength of the arms and legs was assessed by bench-press and squatting exercises, respectively.

Results : Among the men in the no-exercise groups, those given testosterone had greater increases than those given placebo in muscle size in their arms (mean [±SE] change in triceps area, 424±104 vs. -81±109 mm2; P<0.05) and legs (change in quadriceps area, 607±123 vs. -131±111 mm2; P<0.05) and greater increases in strength in the bench-press (9±4 vs. -1±1 kg, P<0.05) and squatting exercises (16±4 vs. 3±1 kg, P<0.05). The men assigned to testosterone and exercise had greater increases in fat-free mass (6.1±0.6 kg) and muscle size (triceps area, 501±104 mm2; quadriceps area, 1174±91 mm2) than those assigned to either no-exercise group, and greater increases in muscle strength (bench-press strength, 22±2 kg; squatting-exercise capacity, 38±4 kg) than either no-exercise group. Neither mood nor behavior was altered in any group.

Conclusions : Supraphysiologic doses of testosterone, especially when combined with strength training, increase fat-free mass and muscle size and strength in normal men.

From the Department of Medicine, Charles R. Drew University of Medicine and Science, Los Angeles (S.B., C.C., B.C.); the Exercise Science Laboratory, El Camino College, Torrance, Calif. (T.W.S., T.J.B.); the Department of Medicine, Harbor–UCLA Medical Center, Torrance, Calif. (N.B., J.P., R.C.); and the Department of Public Health, Oregon State University, Corvallis (R.T., A.S.).

Address reprint requests to Dr. Bhasin at the Division of Endocrinology, Metabolism and Molecular Medicine, Charles R. Drew University of Medicine and Science, 1621 E. 120th St., MP #2, Los Angeles, CA 90059.

78.   **Comparison of Aerobic Exercise, Clomipramine, and Placebo in the Treatment of Panic Disorder**

Am J Psychiatry 155:603-609, May 1998

Andreas Broocks, M.D., Borwin Bandelow, M.D., Gunda Pekrun, M.A., Annette George, M.D., Tim Meyer, M.D., Uwe Bartmann, M.A., Ursula Hillmer-Vogel, M.D. and Eckart Rüther, M.D.

Objective: The purpose of this study was to compare the therapeutic effect of exercise for patients with panic disorder to a drug treatment of proven efficacy and to placebo.

Method: Forty-six outpatients suffering from moderate to severe panic disorder with or without agoraphobia (DSM-III-R criteria) were randomly assigned to a 10-week treatment protocol of regular aerobic exercise (running), clomipramine (112.5 mg/day), or **placebo** pills.

Results: The dropout rate was 31 per cent for the exercise group, 27 per cent for the placebo group, and 0 per cent for the clomipramine group. In comparison with placebo, both exercise and clomipramine led to a significant decrease in symptoms according to all main efficacy measures (analysis of variance, last-observation-carried-forward method and completer analysis). A direct comparison of exercise and clomipramine revealed that the drug treatment improved anxiety symptoms significantly earlier and more effectively. Depressive symptoms were also significantly improved by exercise and clomipramine treatment.

Conclusions: These results suggest that regular aerobic exercise alone, in comparison with placebo, is associated with significant clinical improvement in patients suffering from panic disorder, but that it is less effective than treatment with clomipramine.

79.   Creatine supplementation in endurance sports.
Medicine and Science in Sports and Exercise. 30(7):1123-1129, July 1998.

Engelhardt, Martin; Neumann, Georg; Berbalk, Anneliese; Reuter, Iris

Purpose: Creatine is a physiologically active substance indispensable to muscle contraction. The increase in **creatine phosphate** obtained by supplementation is greater than the increase in total creatine achieved by specific sports training. Less well-trained people can produce an immediate energy store when supplementing creatine such as is otherwise achieved by top athletes on normal nutrition by means of speed and power training. The publications so far available indicate that creatine accumulation in muscle was accomplished using relatively high doses (20 g daily over 5 d). The objective of our study was to investigate the alterations in creatine and creatinine concentrations following lower dosages.

Methods: As intermediate and finishing spurts under anaerobic conditions are gaining in importance in endurance sports, we created a special exercise test for triathletes combining endurance and interval performance. After a pretreatment exercise test was performed, the athletes ingested 6 g of creatine daily, divided into two portions for 5 d. On day 6, another exercise test was performed.

Results: Creatine supplementation was found to have no influence on the cardiovascular system, oxygen uptake, and blood lactate concentration. The fall in blood glucose during the exercise test was significantly reduced after consumption of creatine. Although interval power performance was significantly increased by 18 per cent, endurance performance was not influenced.

Conclusions: We conclude that creatine supplementation at doses of 6 g daily has positive effects on short-term exercise included into aerobic endurance exercise.

80. **Cardiovascular autonomic function correlates with the response to aerobic training in healthy sedentary subjects**

Am J Physiol Heart Circ Physiol 285: H1747-H1752, 2003.

Arto J. Hautala,1,2 Timo H. Mäkikallio,1,2 Antti Kiviniemi,1 Raija T. Laukkanen,3 Seppo Nissilä,3 Heikki V. Huikuri,2 and Mikko P. Tulppo1,2

1Merikoski Rehabilitation and Research Center, Oulu; 2Division of Cardiology, Department of Medicine, University of Oulu, Oulu; and 3Polar Electro, Kempele, Finland.

Individual responses to aerobic training vary from almost none to a 40 per cent increase in aerobic fitness in sedentary subjects. The reasons for these differences in the training response are not well known. We hypothesized that baseline cardiovascular autonomic function may influence the training response. The study population included sedentary male subjects (n = 39, 35 ± 9 yr). The training period was 8 wk, including 6 sessions/wk at an intensity of 70–80 per cent of the maximum heart rate for 30–60 min/session. Cardiovascular autonomic function was assessed by measuring the power spectral indexes of heart rate variability from 24-h R-R interval recordings before the training period. Mean peak O2 uptake increased by 11 ± 5 per cent during the training period (range 2–19 per cent). The training response correlated with age (r = –0.39, P = 0.007) and with the values of the high-frequency (HF) spectral component of R-R intervals (HF power) analyzed over the 24-h recording (r = 0.46, P = 0.002) or separately during the daytime hours (r = 0.35, P = 0.028) and most strongly during the nighttime hours (r = 0.52, P = 0.001). After adjustment for age, HF power was still associated with the training response (e.g., P = 0.001 analyzed during nighttime hours). These data show that cardiovascular autonomic function is an important determinant of the response to aerobic training among sedentary men. High vagal activity at baseline is associated with the improvement in aerobic power caused by aerobic exercise training in healthy sedentary subjects.

Cardiovascular autonomic function; vagal activity; aerobic training response.

81. **Heat acclimation, aerobic fitness, and hydration effects on tolerance during uncompensable heat stress**

J Appl Physiol, Vol. 84, Issue 5, 1731-1739, May 1998.

Stephen S. Cheung and Tom M. McLellan

Defence and Civil Institute of Environmental Medicine, Human Protection and Performance Section, North York M3M 3B9; Graduate Department of Community Health, University of Toronto, Toronto, Ontario, Canada M5S 1A8.

The purpose of the present study was to determine the separate and combined effects of aerobic fitness, short-term **heat acclimation**, and **hypohydration** on tolerance during light exercise while wearing nuclear, biological, and chemical protective clothing in the heat (40°C, 30 per cent relative humidity). Men who were moderately fit [(MF); <50 ml · kg1 · min1 maximal O2 consumption; n = 7] and highly fit [(HF); >55 ml · kg1 · min1 maximal O2 consumption; n = 8] were tested while they were euhydrated or hypohydrated by ~2.5 per cent of body mass through exercise and fluid restriction the day preceding the trials. Tests were conducted before and after 2 wk of daily heat acclimation (1-h treadmill exercise at 40°C, 30 per cent relative humidity, while wearing the nuclear, biological, and chemical protective clothing). Heat acclimation increased sweat rate and decreased skin temperature and rectal temperature (Tre) in HF subjects but had no effect on tolerance time (TT). MF subjects increased sweat rate but did not alter heart rate, Tre, or TT. In both MF and HF groups, hypohydration significantly increased Tre and heart rate and decreased the respiratory exchange ratio and the TT regardless of acclimation state. Overall, the rate of rise of skin temperature was less, while Tre, the rate of rise of Tre, and the TT were greater in HF than in MF subjects. It was concluded that exercise-heat tolerance in this uncompensable heat-stress environment is not influenced by short-term heat acclimation but is significantly improved by long-term aerobic fitness.

Key Words: heat exhaustion; temperature regulation; hypohydration .

82. A Randomized Study of the Effects of Aerobic Exercise by Lactating Women on Breast-Milk Volume and Composition

The New England Journal of Medicine, Number 7, Volume 330:449-453, February 17, 1994.

Kathryn G. Dewey, Cheryl A. Lovelady, Laurie A. Nommsen-Rivers, Megan A. McCrory, and Bo Lonnerdal

Background : The potential risks and benefits of regular exercise during lactation have not been adequately evaluated. We investigated whether regular aerobic exercise had any effects on the volume or composition of breast milk.

Methods : Six to eight weeks post partum, 33 sedentary women whose infants were being exclusively breast-fed were randomly assigned to an exercise group (18 women) or a control group (15 women). The exercise program consisted of supervised aerobic exercise (at a level of 60 to 70 percent of the heart-rate reserve) for 45 minutes per day, 5 days per week, for 12 weeks. Energy expenditure, dietary intake, body composition, and the volume and composition of breast milk were assessed at 6 to 8, 12 to 14, and 18 to 20 weeks post partum. Maximal oxygen uptake and the plasma prolactin response to nursing were assessed at 6 to 8 and 18 to 20 weeks.

Results : The women in the exercise group expended about 400 kcal per day during the exercise sessions but compensated for this energy expenditure with a higher energy intake than that recorded by the control women (mean [±SD] intake, 2497 ±436 vs. 2168 ±328 kcal per day at 18 to 20 weeks; P<0.05). Maximal oxygen uptake increased by 25 percent in the exercising women but by only 5 percent in the control women (P<0.001). There were no significant differences between the two groups in maternal body weight or fat loss, the volume or composition of the breast milk, the infant's weight gain, or maternal prolactin levels during the 12-week study.

Conclusions : In this study, aerobic exercise performed four or five times per week beginning six to eight weeks post partum had no adverse effect on lactation and significantly improved the cardiovascular fitness of the mothers.

From the Department of Nutrition, University of California, Davis (K.G.D., L.A.N., M.A.M., B.L.), and the Department of Food, Nutrition and Food Service Management, University of North Carolina, Greensboro (C.A.L.).

Address reprint requests to Dr. Dewey at the Department of Nutrition, University of California, Davis, CA 95616-8669.

83.   **Physical activity, sports participation, and risk factors in adolescents.**
Medicine & Science in Sports & Exercise. 29(6):788-793, June 1997.
      Boreham, Colin A.; Twisk, Jos; Savage, Maurice J.; Cran, Gordon W.; Strain, John J.

The purpose of this study was to analyze the relationships between physical activity (ACT), including **sports participation** (SP) and antecedent risk factors for coronary heart disease (CHD), in a representative sample of adolescents from Northern Ireland, a region of high coronary mortality. Biological and behavioral risk factors were measured in a random sample of 1015 school children aged 12 and 15 yr. ACT and SP were assessed by self-report questionnaire, and relationships with biological risk factors were analyzed with stepwise multiple linear regression after controlling for potential confounders. Results showed that in 15-yr-old males ACT was beneficially associated with systolic blood pressure (P < 0.05), lipid profile, and cardiorespiratory fitness (both P < 0.01). In 15-yr-old females, SP was associated beneficially with fatness and cardiorespiratory fitness. Odds ratios calculated from logistic regression revealed that for the older children, a relatively small drop (-20 per cent) in ACT(boys) or SP (girls) was significantly related to the probability of exposure to multiple risk factors. Overall, relationships were stronger for males rather than females and for older rather than younger children. This study provides further evidence for beneficial associations between ACT, SP, and CHD risk status in adolescents.

84. Opioid Receptor Blockade Eliminates Mood Effects of Aerobic Gymnastics

*Int J Sports Med,*23: 155-157 2002.

A.Järvekülg1, A. Viru1
1 Institute of Exercise Biology, University of Tartu, Tartu, Estonia

The contribution of opioid receptors to the mood effects of aerobic gymnastics was tested by oral administration of **naltrexone** (25 or 50 mg) in 12 healthy women (aged 22 - 30 years). The opioid receptor blockade eliminated decreased **anxiety**, negative affect level and depressiveness as well as increased positive affect level, as found in a placebo trial after a 50 min session of aerobic gymnastics. 50 mg of naltrexone was more effective than 25 mg. Administration of 50 mg of naltrexone without exercise did not cause any significant changes in anxiety, positive and negative affect levels or depressiveness.

Key Words: Anxiety · depressiveness · naltrexone · positive and negative affect levels.

85. Changes in aerobic power of women, ages 20-64 yr.

Medicine and Science in Sports and Exercise. 28(7):884-891, July 1996.

Jackson, Andrew S.; Wier, Larry T.; Ayers, Greta W.; Beard, Earl F.; Stuteville, Joseph E.; Blair, Steven N.

This study quantified and compared the cross-sectional and longitudinal influence of age, self-report physical activity (SR-PA), and **body composition** (per cent fat) on the decline of maximal aerobic power ([spacing dot above]VO2peak) of women. The cross-sectional sample consisted of 409 healthy women, ages 20-64 yr. The 43 women of the longitudinal sample were from the same population and examined twice, the mean time between tests was 3.7 (+/-2.2) yr. Peak oxygen uptake was determined by indirect calorimetry during a maximal **treadmill** test. The zero-order correlation of -0.742 between [spacing dot above]VO2peak and per centfat was significantly (P < 0.05) higher then the SR-PA (r = 0.626) and age correlations (r = -0.633). Linear regression defined the cross-sectional age-related decline in [spacing dot above]VO2peak at 0.537 ml[middle dot]kg-1[middle dot]min-1[middle dot]yr-1. Multiple regression analysis (R = 0.851) showed that adding per centfat and SR-PA and their interaction to the regression model reduced the age regression weight of-0.537, to -0.265 ml[middle dot]kg-1[middle dot]min-1[middle dot]yr-1. Statistically controlling for time differences between tests, general linear models analysis showed that longitudinal changes in aerobic power were due to independent changes in per centfat and SR-PA, confirming the cross-sectional results. These findings are consistent with men's data from the same lab showing that about 50 per cent of the cross-sectional age-related decline in [spacing dot above]VO2peak was due to per cent fat and SR-PA.

86.   Effects of Resistance vs. Aerobic Training Combined With an 800 Calorie Liquid Diet on Lean Body Mass and Resting Metabolic Rate
Journal of the American College of Nutrition, Vol. 18, No. 2, 115-121, 1999.

Randy W. Bryner, EdD, Irma H. Ullrich, MD FACN, Janine Sauers, MS, David Donley, MS, Guyton Hornsby, PhD, Maria Kolar, MD and Rachel Yeater, PhD

Department of Human Performance and Applied Exercise Science (R.W.B., J.S., D.D., G.H., R.Y.), West Virginia University, Morgantown, West Virginia.

Department of Medicine, School of Medicine (I.H.U., M.K.), West Virginia University, Morgantown, West Virginia.

Address reprint requests to: Randy W. Bryner, EdD, Department of Human Performance and Applied Exercise Science, PO Box 9227, 8317 HSC, Morgantown, WV 26506.

Objective: Utilization of very-low-calorie diets (VLCD) for weight loss results in loss of lean body weight (LBW) and a decrease in **resting metabolic rate** (RMR). The addition of aerobic exercise does not prevent this. The purpose of this study was to examine the effect of intensive, high volume resistance training combined with a VLCD on these parameters.

Methods: Twenty subjects (17 women, three men), mean age 38 years, were randomly assigned to either standard treatment control plus diet (C+D), n=10, or resistance exercise plus diet (R+D), n=10. Both groups consumed 800 kcal/day liquid formula diets for 12 weeks. The C+D group exercised 1 hour four times/week by walking, biking or stair climbing. The R+D group performed resistance training 3 days/week at 10 stations increasing from two sets of 8 to 15 repetitions to four sets of 8 to 15 repetitions by 12 weeks. Groups were similar at baseline with respect to weight, body composition, aerobic capacity, and resting metabolic rate.

Results: Maximum oxygen consumption (Max VO2) increased significantly ($p<0.05$) but equally in both groups. Body weight decreased significantly more ($p<0.01$) in C+D than R+D. The C+D group lost a significant ($p<0.05$) amount of LBW (51 to 47 kg). No decrease in LBW was observed in R+D. In addition, R+D had an increase ($p<0.05$) in RMR O2 ml/kg/min (2.6 to 3.1). The 24 hour RMR decreased ($p<0.05$) in the C+D group.

Conclusion: The addition of an intensive, high volume resistance training program resulted in preservation of LBW and RMR during weight loss with a VLCD.

Key words: resistance training, weight loss, resting metabolic rate, very-low-calorie diet, diet.

87. **Sport activity in adolescence: associations with health perceptions and experimental behaviours**
   Health Education Research, Vol. 14, No. 2, 225-233, April 1999.

C. Ferron, F. Narring, M. Cauderay and P.-A. Michaud
Institut Universitaire de Médecine Sociale et Préventive, Bugnon 17, 1005 Lausanne, Switzerland.

Despite the relevance of this research topic from a public health perspective, there is currently a lack of objective data on European adolescents' sport activity, notably the associations between their sport habits and their health attitudes and behaviours, which may have important consequences both in terms of **somatic** (cardiovascular) **health** and **mental health**. The objective of the present study was to determine the direction and strength of the associations between the frequency of sport and health variables; in particular, perceptions of health, self image, substance use and experimental behaviours. Data were collected as part of the 1993 Swiss Multicentric Adolescent Survey on Health. In this survey, anonymous self-administered questionnaires were distributed to a national representative sample of 10 000 in-school adolescents (15–20 years of age). **Univariate analyses** explored the relationships between the level of sport activity and health variables; then logistic regression analyses examined the strength of these relationships. According to the results, half of the sample do sports more than twice a week, boys more often as part of a sports club. Differences between non-athletic and athletic adolescents describe the latter as having less somatic complaints, more confidence in their future health, a better body image, a lesser tendency to attempt suicide, a higher frequency of use of the car seat belt, and a lower use of tobacco, wine and marijuana. Links between the frequency of sport activity and the locus of control related to health, general satisfaction with life or sexual behaviours are less strong. It must be noticed that the cross-sectional data collection precludes the establishment of a causal relationship between exercise and health behaviours. However, the existing links underline the coexistence of positive health characteristics and sport activity, suggesting that an incitement to get involved in physical activity may be a necessary component of a comprehensive prevention approach among adolescents.

88. **Evaluation of quality of life in elderly healthy subjects after aerobic and/or mental training**
   Archives of Gerontology and Geriatrics, Volume 28, Issue 1 , Pages 9-22 ,January 1999. **C. Fabrea, *, J. Massé-Birona, K. Chamaria, A. Varrayb, P. Muccia and Ch Préfauta**

(a)   Laboratoire de Physiologie des Interactions, Hôpital A. de Villeneuve, Service EFR, 34295 Montpellier Cedex 05 France

(b)   Laboratoire Sport Santé Développement, EAD 2040, UFR STAPS, Université Montpellier I, 700 Avenue du Pic Saint Loup, 34090 Montpellier, France

This study proposed different techniques of **mental rehabilitation** to healthy elderly subjects in order to assess the results in terms of subjectively perceived changes in quality of life. Thirty-two elderly subjects (60–76 years) were assigned to one of the four groups: aerobic training, **mental training**, combined aerobic and mental training and a control group. Before and after 2 months of training, all subjects took two memory tests. After training, a French validated questionnaire of quality of life was administered individually. Memory parameters such as logical memory (P<0.05), paired associated learning (P=0.05) and memory quotient (P=0.01) were enhanced in all groups except the control group, but in terms of quality of life all the elderly subjects were dissatisfied. and ventilatory threshold were significantly improved in the two groups who were engaged in a physical training program (AT and AMT) and these improvements were associated with a better quality of life in the domain of functional life. Association of the two techniques did not enhance the results for cognitive function. In conclusion, despite objective improvement in cognitive function, all subjects reported dissatisfaction in terms of improvement in quality of life, whatever their assigned group. Nevertheless, an improvement in quality of life was acknowledged after aerobic training for the physical component of functional life.

Key Words: Quality of life; Healthy elderly subjects; Mental training; Aerobic training.

Index Terms: quality of life; aged; exercise; cognition; mental test; training.

89.   Effect of training on lactate/ventilatory thresholds: a meta-analysis.
Medicine and Science in Sports and Exercise. 29(6):837-843, June 1997.
Londeree, Ben R.

The purpose of the investigation was to determine the effect of exercise training intensity on the lactate and ventilatory thresholds in sedentary and in active subjects using meta-analysis procedures. The original analyses included 85 study groups from 34 studies. The dependent variable was oxygen consumption at the specified threshold, and the independent variables were training intensity (control and four intensities ranging from below threshold to near maximum) and fitness level (sedentary and conditioned). Data were analyzed statistically using methods described by Hedges and Olkin (13). The results showed that sedentary subjects (effect size (ES) = 2.32) improved significantly over controls (ES = 0.15), while conditioned subjects (ES = 0.63) showed nonsignificant gains. There were no significant differences among training intensities within the fitness categories (Sed ES = 1.6-3.1; Cond ES = 0.3-1.1) although the conditioned subjects tended to respond better to high intensity training (ES of 1.1 vs 0.4). It was concluded that training at an intensity near the lactate or ventilatory threshold is an adequate training stimulus for improving the thresholds for sedentary subjects, but a higher intensity may be necessary for conditioned subjects. Detraining will reduce lactate and ventilatory thresholds.

90. **The reproducibility of the Bruce protocol exercise test for the determination of aerobic capacity in older women.**

Medicine and Science in Sports and Exercise. 29(8):1109-1113, August 1997.

Fielding, Roger A.; Frontera, Walter R.; Hughes, Wirginia A.; Fisher, Elizabeth C.; Evans, W. J.

The reproducibility of the Bruce exercise test protocol for the determination of maximal aerobic capacity was evaluated in sedentary older women. Seventeen women between the ages of 51 and 68 yr performed five maximal graded exercise tests to volitional fatigue on a treadmill. [spacing dot above]VO2max(mL[middle dot]kg-1[middle dot]min-1) values averaged 27.5 +/- 1.1; 28.3 +/- 1.3; 28.4 +/- 1.3; 29.6 +/- 1.5; and 28.2 +/- 1.4 for trials 1-5, respectively, and were not significantly different. Criteria for a plateau in [spacing dot above]VO2 at the point of exhaustion were met in 21 out of 85 tests (25 per cent). The mean coefficient of variation in [spacing dot above] VO2max for the subjects for the 5 tests was 6.5 per cent (range, 2.0-14 per cent). Pearson's correlation coefficients for the study variables were significant, indicating good agreement between repeated tests (r2: between 0.70 to 0.89). Although there were no significant differences among the mean [spacing dot above]VO2max values in the 5 trials, 11 subjects had a 1.0 mL[middle dot]kg-1[middle dot]min-1 or greater increase in the[spacing dot above]VO2max from test 1 to test 2, and only 6 subjects had no change or a decrease in [spacing dot above]VO2max. The mean difference between T2 and T3 was lower (T1 vs T2: 0.8 mL[middle dot]kg-1[middle dot]min-1, T2 vs T3: 0.1 mL[middle dot]kg-1[middle dot]min- (1) indicating slightly better agreement between the second and third test. Estimates of the between and within subject variance revealed a low within subject variance (4.2(mL[middle dot]kg-1[middle dot]min-1) (2) compared to the between subject variance (22.1(mL[middle dot]kg-1[middle dot]min-1)2). This study demonstrates that a commonly used exercise testing protocol generates highly reproducible measurements of [spacing dot above]VO2max in women between 51 and 68 yr. The mean differences between tests and the high level of agreement between repeated tests suggests that a single measurement of [spacing dot above]VO2max can be performed to assess functional aerobic capacity in this population.

91. **Pyruvate ingestion for 7 days does not improve aerobic performance in well-trained individuals**

    J Appl Physiol, Vol. 89, Issue 2, 549-556, August 2000.

    Michael A. Morrison, Lawrence L. Spriet, and David J. Dyck

    Department of Human Biology and Nutritional Sciences, University of Guelph, Guelph, Ontario, Canada N1G 2W1

    The purposes of the present studies were to test the hypotheses that lower dosages of oral pyruvate ingestion would increase blood **pyruvate** concentration and that the ingestion of a commonly recommended dosage of pyruvate (7 g) for 7 days would enhance performance during intense aerobic exercise in well-trained individuals. Nine recreationally active subjects (8 women, 1 man) consumed 7, 15, and 25 g of pyruvate and were monitored for a 4-h period to determine whether blood metabolites were altered. Pyruvate consumption failed to significantly elevate blood pyruvate, and it had no effect on indexes of carbohydrate (blood **glucose**, lactate) or lipid metabolism (blood glycerol, plasma free fatty acids). As a follow-up, we administered 7 g/ day of either placebo or pyruvate, for a 1-wk period to seven, well-trained male cyclists (maximal oxygen consumption, 62.3 ± 3.0 ml · kg1 · min1) in a randomized, double-blind, crossover trial. Subjects cycled at 74-80 per cent of their maximal oxygen consumption until exhaustion. There was no difference in performance times between the two trials (placebo, 91 ± 9 min; pyruvate, 88 ± 8 min). Measured blood parameters (insulin, peptide C, glucose, lactate, **glycerol**, free fatty acids) were also unaffected. Our results indicate that oral pyruvate supplementation does not increase blood pyruvate content and does not enhance performance during intense exercise in well-trained cyclists.

    Key Words: ergogenic aid; cycling; blood metabolites.

92. **Randomized trial of the short-term effects of dieting compared with dieting plus aerobic exercise on lactation performance1, 2, 3**

    American Journal of Clinical Nutrition, Vol. 69, No. 5, 959-967, May 1999.

    Megan A McCrory, Laurie A Nommsen-Rivers, Paul A Molé, Bo Lönnerdal and Kathryn G Dewey

Background: Limiting postpartum weight retention is important for preventing adult obesity, but the effect of weight loss on lactation has not been studied adequately.

Objective: We evaluated whether weight loss by dieting, with or without aerobic exercise, adversely affects lactation performance.

Design: At 12 ± 4 wk postpartum, exclusively breast-feeding women were randomly assigned for 11 d to a diet group (35 per cent energy deficit; n = 22), a diet plus exercise group (35 per cent net energy deficit; n = 22), or a control group (n = 23). Milk volume, composition, and energy output; maternal weight, body composition, and plasma prolactin concentration; and infant weight were measured before and after the intervention.

Results: Weight loss averaged 1.9, 1.6, and 0.2 kg in the diet, diet + exercise, and control groups, respectively (P < 0.0001) and was composed of 67 per cent fat in the diet group and nearly 100 per cent fat in the diet + exercise group. Change in **milk volume**, composition, and energy output and infant weight did not differ significantly among groups. However, there was a significant interaction between group and baseline percentage body fat: in the diet group only, milk energy output increased in fatter women and decreased in leaner women. The plasma prolactin concentration was higher in the diet and diet + exercise groups than in the control group.

Conclusions: Short-term weight loss (1 kg/wk) through a combination of dieting and aerobic exercise appears safe for breast-feeding mothers and is preferable to weight loss achieved primarily by dieting because the latter reduces maternal lean body mass. Longer-term studies are needed to confirm these findings.

Key Words: Adipose tissue mobilization • body composition • breast milk • energy expenditure • energy intake • aerobic exercise • lactation • prolactin • obesity • weight loss • women.

93. **Eighteen days of "living high, training low" stimulate erythropoiesis and enhance aerobic performance in elite middle-distance runners**
J Appl Physiol 100: 203-211, 2006.

Julien V. Brugniaux,1 Laurent Schmitt,1,2 Paul Robach,1,3 Gérard Nicolet,2 Jean-Pierre Fouillot,1 Stéphane Moutereau,4 Françoise Lasne,5 Vincent Pialoux,6 Philippe Saas,7 Marie-Claude Chorvot,7 Jérémy Cornolo,1 Niels V. Olsen,8 and Jean-Paul Richalet1

1Université Paris 13, Laboratoire "Réponses cellulaires et fonctionnelles à l'hypoxie," Bobigny; 2Centre National de Ski Nordique, Prémanon; 3Ecole Nationale de Ski et d'Alpinisme, Chamonix; 4Laboratoire de Biochimie, Hôpital Henri-Mondor, Créteil; 5Laboratoire National de Dépistage du Dopage,

Chatenay-Malabry; 6Laboratoire de Physiologie-Biologie du Sport, Faculté de Médecine, Clermont-Ferrand; 7Plateforme de BioMonitoring, Inserm U645/ Unité Propre de Recherche et d'Enseignement Supérieur EA2284, Establissement Français du Sang Bourgogne Franche-Comté, Besançon, France; and 8University of Copenhagen, Department of Pharmacology, The Panum Institute, Copenhagen, Denmark.

The efficiency of "living high, training low" (LHTL) remains controversial, despite its wide utilization. This study aimed to verify whether maximal and/or submaximal aerobic performance were modified by LHTL and whether these effects persist for 15 days after returning to normoxia. Last, we tried to elucidate whether the mechanisms involved were only related to changes in oxygen-carrying capacity. Eleven elite middle-distance runners were tested before (Pre), at the end (Post1), and 15 days after the end (Post2) of an 18-day LHTL session. Hypoxic group (LHTL, n = 5) spent 14 h/day in hypoxia (6 nights at 2,500 m and 12 nights at 3,000 m), whereas the control group (CON, n = 6) slept in normoxia (1,200 m). Both LHTL and CON trained at 1,200 m. Maximal oxygen uptake and maximal aerobic power were improved at Post1 and Post2 for LHTL only (+7.1 and +3.4 per cent for maximal oxygen uptake, +8.4 and +4.7 per cent for maximal aerobic power, respectively). Similarly oxygen uptake and ventilation at ventilatory threshold increased in LHTL only (+18.1 and +12.2 per cent at Post1, +15.9 and +15.4 per cent at Post2, respectively). Heart rate during a 10-min run at 19.5 km/h decreased for LHTL at Post2 (−4.4 per cent). Despite the stimulation of erythropoiesis in LHTL shown by the 27.4 per cent increase in serum transferrin receptor and the 10.1 per cent increase in total hemoglobin mass, red cell volume was not significantly increased at Post1 (+9.2 per cent, not significant). Therefore, both maximal and submaximal aerobic performance in elite runners were increased by LHTL mainly linked to an improvement in oxygen transport in early return to normoxia and probably to other process at Post2. intermittent hypoxia; maximal oxygen uptake; carbon monoxide rebreathing technique; soluble transferrin receptor; erythroid burst-forming unit.

Address for reprint requests and other correspondence: J. V. Brugniaux, UFR SMBH, 74 rue Marcel Cachin, 93017 Bobigny cedex, France (e-mail: jbrugniaux@free.fr)

94.   Heritability of aerobic power and anaerobic energy generation during exercise
Journal of Applied Physiology, Vol 70, Issue 1 357-362, 1991.
R. Fagard, E. Bielen and A. Amery
Department of Pathophysiology, University of Leuven, Belgium.

Twenty-nine pairs of monozygotic twins and 19 pairs of dizygotic twins, all male, ages 18-31 yr, performed a graded uninterrupted exercise test on the

bicycle ergometer to exhaustion. By use of path analysis, the genetic variance of measured peak O2 uptake was estimated at 77 per cent (P less than 0.001), at 71 per cent (P less than 0.001) after adjustment for weight and skinfold thickness, and at 66 per cent (P less than 0.001) after additional adjustment for weekly hours of sports participation. O2 uptake at a heart rate of 150 beats/ min, a submaximal estimate of exercise capacity, showed less genetic variance, i.e., 61 per cent (P less than 0.001) before and 50 per cent (P less than 0.001) after weight adjustment and only 16 per cent (NS) after correction for life-style factors. Similarly, the heritability of peak O2 uptake, when estimated from submaximal data, was 68 per cent (P less than 0.001), 40 per cent (P = 0.05), and 26 per cent (NS), respectively. Mechanical efficiency had no significant genetic component. O2 uptake at the respiratory exchange ratio of 0.95 and the slope of the curvilinear relationship between CO2 output and O2 uptake, used to assess the anaerobic energy generation during progressive exercise, showed significant (P less than 0.001) genetic variance before (72 and 74 per cent) and after adjustment for weight (67 and 69 per cent) and sports participation (63 and 57 per cent). The heritability of peak aerobic power remained significant (58 per cent; P less than 0.001) after adjustment for these expressions of anaerobic energy generation. In conclusion, the genetic variance of measured peak O2 uptake is significant and persists after adjustment for anthropometric characteristics, life-style factors, anaerobic energy generation, and mechanical efficiency.

95.   High-speed running performance is largely unaffected by hypoxic reductions in aerobic power
J Appl Physiol, Vol. 86, Issue 6, 2059-2064, June 1999.
    Peter G. Weyand, Cherie S. Lee, Ricardo Martinez-Ruiz, Matthew W. Bundle, Matthew J. Bellizzi, and Seth Wright
    Museum of Comparative Zoology, Concord Field Station, Harvard University, Bedford, Massachusetts 01730.
    We tested the importance of aerobic metabolism to human running speed directly by altering inspired oxygen concentrations and comparing the maximal speeds attained at different rates of oxygen uptake. Under both normoxic (20.93 per cent O2) and hypoxic (13.00 per cent O2) conditions, four fit adult men completed 15 all-out sprints lasting from 15 to 180 s as well as progressive, discontinuous treadmill tests to determine maximal oxygen uptake and the metabolic cost of steady-state running. Maximal aerobic power was lower by 30 per cent (1.00 ± 0.15 vs. 0.77 ± 0.12 ml O2 · kg1 · s1) and sprinting rates of oxygen uptake by 12-25 per cent under **hypoxic** vs. normoxic conditions while the metabolic cost of submaximal running was the same. Despite reductions in the aerobic energy available for sprinting under hypoxic conditions, our subjects were able to run just as fast for sprints of up to 60 s

and nearly as fast for sprints of up to 120 s. This was possible because rates of anaerobic energy release, estimated from oxygen deficits, increased by as much as 18 per cent, and thus compensated for the reductions in aerobic power. We conclude that maximal metabolic power outputs during sprinting are not limited by rates of anaerobic metabolism and that human speed is largely independent of aerobic power during all-out runs of 60 s or less.

Key Words: sprinting; locomotion; oxygen deficit; anaerobic metabolism.

96.   **Summary and agreement statement of the first International Conference on Concussion in Sport, Vienna 2001***
       *Br J Sports Med,*36:6-7, 2002.

   M Aubry, Chief Medical Officer1, R Cantu, Chief, Neurosurgery Service and Director, Sports Medicine Service2, J Dvorak, Chairman3, T Graf-Baumann4, K Johnston, Chair5, J Kelly, Associate Professor of Clinical Neurology6, M Lovell, Director7, P McCrory8, W Meeuwisse9 and P Schamasch, Director10,11

1.   International Ice Hockey Federation
2.   Emerson Hospital, Concord, MA, USA. Medical Director, National Center for Catastrophic Sports Injury Research, Chapel Hill, NC, USA
3.   FIFA Medical Research and Assessment Center (F-MARC), Wilhelm Neurologist and Director of Schulthess Clinic, Zurich, Switzerland
4.   FIFA Medical Research and Assessment Center (F-Marc), Tenningen, Germany
5.   Concussion in Sport Group, FIFA, IIHF, IOC; Neurosurgeon and Director of Neurotrauma, McGill University Health Centre (MUHC), McGill University and McGill Sport Medicine Centre, Montreal, Canada
6.   Northwestern University Medical School, Chicago Neurological Institute, Chicago, IL, USA
7.   Sports Medicine Concussion Program, University of Pittsburgh. Co-director, National Hockey League Neuropsychology Program, Pittsburgh, PA, USA
8.   Brain Research Institute and Center for Sports Medicine Research and Education, University of Melbourne, Melbourne, Australia
9.   University of Calgary Sport Medicine Center, Sport Injury Consultant, National Hockey League, Calgary, Alberta, Canada
10.   International Olympic Committee Medical Commission, Lausanne, Switzerland
11.   the Concussion in Sport (CIS) Group
       Correspondence to:
       Dr Johnston, Division of Neurosurgery, Montreal General Hospital, 1650 Cedar Ave, Room L7-524, Montreal, Quebec, Canada H3G 1A4

97. Physiological and anthropometric characteristics of amateur rugby league players

The British Journal of Sports Medicine 34:303-307, 2000.

Tim J Gabbett

School of Physiotherapy and Exercise Science, Faculty of Health Sciences, Griffith University Gold Coast, Queensland, Australia

Correspondence to: T J Gabbett, School of Physiotherapy and Exercise Science, Faculty of Health Sciences, Griffith University Gold Coast, PMB50 Gold Coast Mail Centre, Queensland, Australia 9726 email: t.gabbett@mailbox.gu.edu.au

Objectives: To investigate the physiological and anthropometric characteristics of amateur rugby league players.

Methods : Thirty five amateur rugby league players (19 forwards and 16 backs) were measured for height, body mass, percentage body fat (sum of four skinfolds), muscular power (vertical jump), speed (10 m and 40 m sprint), and maximal aerobic power (multistage fitness test). Data were also collected on match frequency, training status, playing experience, and employment related physical activity levels.

Results : The 10 m and 40 m **sprint, vertical jump**, percentage body fat, and multistage fitness test results were 20–42 per cent poorer than previously reported for professional rugby league players. Compared with forwards, backs had significantly ($p<0.01$) lower body mass (79.7 (74.7–84.7) kg v 90.8 (86.2–95.4) kg) and significantly ($p<0.01$) greater speed during the 40 m sprint (6.45 (6.35–6.55) v 6.79 (6.69–6.89) seconds). Values for percentage body fat, vertical jump, 10 m sprint, and maximal aerobic power were not significantly different ($p>0.05$) between forwards and backs. When compared with professional rugby league players, the training status of amateur rugby league players was 30–53 per cent lower, with players devoting less than three hours a week to team training sessions and about 30 minutes a week to individual training sessions. The training time devoted to the development of muscular power (about 13 minutes a week), speed (about eight minutes a week), and aerobic fitness (about 34 minutes a week) did not differ significantly ($p>0.05$) between forwards and backs. At the time of the field testing, players had participated, on average, in one 60 minute match every eight days.

Conclusions : The physiological and anthropometric characteristics of amateur rugby league players are poorly developed. These findings suggest that position specific training does not occur in amateur rugby league. The

poor fitness of non-elite players may be due to a low playing intensity, infrequent matches of short duration, and/or an inappropriate training stimulus.
Key Words: conditioning; fitness; non-elite; training; rugby.

98.   Wingate test performance in children with asthma: aerobic or anaerobic limitation?
Medicine and Science in Sports and Exercise. 29(4):430-435, April 1997.

Counil, Francois-pierre; Varray, Alain; Karila, Chantal; Hayot, Maurice; Voisin, Michel; Prefaut, Christian

To investigate the anaerobic capacity in children with bronchial asthma, eight male children with atopic asthma (age: 12 +/- 1.7 yr) and seven healthy control subjects (age: 12 +/- 1 yr) performed a 30-s all-out exercise test: the Wingate anaerobic test (WanT). Post-exercise plasma **epinephrine** (E), **norepinephrine** (NE), venous epinephrine (La), and **blood pH** levels were determined. Peak power (Ppeak), mean power (Pm), and total energy expenditure (Wtot) during the WanT were assessed. The relative importance of aerobic (WO2) and anaerobic (Wana) energy release during the WanT was also evaluated. In comparison with control subjects, the children with asthma exhibited lower Ppeak (W[middle dot]kg-1): 6 +/- 1.14 vs 7.3 +/- 0.5, P < 0.05; lower Pm (W[middle dot]kg-1): 4.7 +/- 0.8 vs 5.9 +/- 0.5, P < 0.05; and lower Wtot (Jg-1): 140.3 +/- 25 vs 176.9 +/- 19, P < 0.05. The relative contribution of WO2 (26 per cent) and Wana (74 per cent) to the Wtot was identical in both groups. Blood lactate and pH kinetics revealed significantly lower La values and less acidosis in the asthmatic group (P < 0.001). Lastly, E (pg[middle dot]ml-1) concentrations were lower in the asthmatic group: 274.96 +/- 84.58 vs 901.28 +/- 604.76, P < 0.05. These results suggest a reduced anaerobic capacity in children with asthma. A diminished adrenergic response to exhausting exercise, leading to a decreased anaerobic glycolysis, could partly account for this phenomenon.

99.   Influence of Aerobic Fitness Level on Measured and Estimated Perceived Exertion During Exhausting Runs
Int J Sports Me, 25: 270-277, 2004.

M. Garcin1, L. Mille-Hamard1, V. Billat2
1.   Laboratoire d'Etudes de la Motricité Humaine, Faculté des Sciences du Sport et de l'Education Physique, Université de Lille, France
2.   Centre de Médecine du Sport C.C.A.S., Paris, France

The purpose of the present investigation was 1) to study the effects of fitness level on perceived exertion (RPE) and estimated time limit (ETL) scales during exhausting runs, and 2) to predict time to exhaustion from RPE or ETL values collected during a constant run exercise. Eight high-fitness level and twelve moderate-fitness level endurance trained males performed two exhausting exercises on a 400-m running track. The first test was a graded exercise using a portable metabolic system to determine maximal oxygen uptake (V·O2max), the velocity associated with V·O2max (vV·O2max), the velocity at the lactate threshold (vLT) and the velocity at delta 50 (vÄ50 : the velocity halfway between vV·O2max and vLT). The second test was a constant run exercise at vÄ50 to determine the time to exhaustion at this intensity (tlimvÄ50). Moderate-fitness level athletes perceived exercise to be relatively more strenuous and felt that they could continue for less time than high-fitness level athletes at similar relative velocities. There was no effect of fitness level on perceived exertion for a given relative exercise duration. RPE corresponding to vLT was not statistically significantly different between the two levels groups. For the two groups, measured and predicted exhaustion time values, which were calculated from linear extrapolation of RPE and ETL values collected during the first 4 minutes of a submaximal constant run exercise, were not statistically significantly correlated. These results indicate that the aerobic fitness level seems to influence perceived exertion only during graded exercise. Consequently, if RPE is used to prescribe an exercise intensity, the prescription must be individualised regarding the aerobic fitness level of the athlete except for exercise intensities corresponding to vLT. Moreover, the perceived exertion pattern at the beginning of a submaximal constant run exercise could not be considered as a sensitive predictor of the point of self-imposed exhaustion whatever the fitness level of the athletes.

Key Words: Perceived exertion - exhaustion time - fitness level – running.

100. **Improvements in Cardiorespiratory Fitness Attenuate Age-related Weight Gain in Healthy Men and Women: The Aerobics Center Longitudinal Study**
International Journal of Obesity, Volume 22, Number 1, Pages 55-62, January 1998.
L DiPietro1,a, H W Kohl III2, C E Barlow3 and S N Blair3
1. The John B Pierce Laboratory and Department of Epidemiology and Public Health, Yale University School of Medicine, New Haven, CT
2. Baylor Sports Medicine Institute, Baylor College of Medicine, Houston, TX
3. Division of Epidemiology and Clinical Applications, Institute for Aerobics Research, Dallas, TX, USA
(a) Correspondence: Loretta DiPietro, PhD, MPH, The John B. Pierce Laboratory, 290 Congress Avenue, New Haven, CT 06519, USA.

Objective: To determine the longitudinal relation of change in cardiopulmonary fitness to subsequent change in body weight in a cohort of healthy middle-aged adults.

Design: Prospective cohort study.

Subjects: Participants were 4599 men and 724 women receiving at least three medical examinations between 1970 and 1994. Examinations included assessment of cardiorespiratory fitness by maximal exercise tests and measurement of body weight.

Measurements: Change in fitness was calculated as the difference in maximal treadmill time between the first and second examination (mean interval, 1.8 y). Weight change was calculated as the difference in body weight between the first and last examination (mean follow-up, 7.5 y).

Results: There was a small, yet statistically significant weight gain over the follow-up (0.61?5.29 kg for men and 1.51?4.67 kg for women; P<0.001). Estimates from the multiple linear regression modeling show that each 1 min improvement in treadmill time, significantly attenuated weight gain in both men (b=-0.60; P<0.001) and women (b=-0.60; P<0.001), respectively. Moreover, each 1 min improvement in treadmill time, reduced the odds of a 5 kg gain by 14 per cent in men (odds ratios (OR))=0.86; 95 per cent confidence interval (CI): 0.83-0.89) and by 9 per cent in women (OR=0.91; 95 per centCI:0.83-1.00) and the odds of a 10 kg gain by 21 per cent in both men (OR=0.79;95 per cent CI:0.75-0.84) and women (OR=0.79;95 per centCI:0.67-0.93)

Conclusions: Improvements in fitness, appear important in attenuating age-related weight gain in healthy middle-aged adults. Thus, an active lifestyle should be promoted early and maintained through adulthood to prevent substantial weight gain and obesity with age.

Key Words: exercise; obesity; overweight; physical activity; physical fitness.

101.   **Improved athletic performance in highly trained cyclists after interval training.**

Medicine and Science in Sports and- Exercise. 28(11):1427-1434, November 1996.

Lindsay, Fiona H.; Hawley, John A.; Myburgh, Kathryn H.; Schomer, Helgo H.; Noakes, Timothy D.; Dennis, Steven C.

This study determined whether a 4-wk high-intensity interval training program (HIT) would improve the 40-km time trial performances (TT40) of 8 competitive cyclists (peak O2 uptake 5.2 +/- 0.4 I[middle dot]min-1) with a background of moderate-intensity endurance training (BASE). Before intervention, all cyclists were tested on at least three separate occasions to ensure that their baseline performances were stable. In these tests, peak sustained power output (PPO) was measured during a progressive exercise test, muscular resistance to fatigue was determined during a timed ride to exhaustion at 150 per cent of PPO (TF150), and a TT40 was performed on a cycle-simulator. The coefficient of variation for all baseline tests was <1.7 +/- 1.3 per cent (mean +/- SD). Cyclists then replaced 15 +/- 2 per cent of their [almost equal to]300 km[middle dot]wk-1 BASE training with HIT, which took place on 6 d and consisted of six to eight 5-min repetitions at 80 per cent of PPO, with 60-s recovery between work bouts. HIT significantly improved TT40 (56.4 +/- 3.6 vs 54.4 +/- 3.2 min; P < 0.001), PPO (416 +/- 32 vs 434 +/- 34 W;P < 0.01) and TF150 (60.5 +/- 9.3 vs 72.5 +/- 7.6 s; P < 0.01). The faster TT40 was due to a significant increase in both the cyclists' absolute (301 +/- 42 vs 326 +/- 43 W;P < 0.0001) and relative (72.1 +/- 5.6 vs 75.0 +/- 6.8 per cent of PPO; P < 0.05) power output after HIT. These results indicate that a 4-wk program of HIT increased the PPO and fatigue resistance of competitive cyclists and improved their 40-km time trial performances.

102. Effects of exercise training on aerobic and functional capacity of end-stage renal disease patients

Clinical Physiology, Volume 22 Page 115 - March 2002

Pelagia Koufaki[1], Thomas H. Mercer[1] & Patrick F. Naish[2]

The aim was to assess the effects of exercise training on aerobic and functional capacity of patients with end-stage renal disease (ESRD). Patients completed an incremental exercise test on a cycle ergometer to determine VO2 peak and VO2 at ventilatory threshold (VT; V-slope). On a separate day they performed two constant load exercise tests on a cycle ergometer at 90 per cent of VT and at a workload of 33 W, to determine VO2 kinetics. Functional capacity was assessed using measurements of sit-to-stands (STS-5, STS-60) and a walk test. Dialysis patients were randomly allocated to an exercise (ET: n=18, age=57·3 years) or control (C: n=15, age=50·5 years) group. The ET group participated in an exercise training programme involving cycling for 3 months. Repeated measures ANOVA revealed significant time by group interactions (P < 0·05) following training for VO2 peak (ET: 17 ± 6·1 versus 19·9 ± 6·3, C: 19·5 ± 4·7 versus 18·8 ± 4·9 ml kg min1) and VO2–VT (ET: 10·7 ± 3·5 versus 11·8 ± 3·3, C:12·9 ± 3·2 versus 11·9 ± 3·5 ml kg min1). VO2 kinetics remained unchanged in both groups at 90 per cent -VT, but a trend (P=0·059) towards faster kinetics at the 33 W was observed (ET: 49·6 ± 19·5 versus 37·8 ± 12·7, C: 42·8 ± 13 versus 49·4 ± 20·2 s). Significant time by group interactions (P < 0·05) were also observed for STS-5 (ET: 14·7 ± 6·2 versus 11·0 ± 3·3, C: 12·8 ± 4·4 versus 12·7 ± 4·8 s) and STS-60 measurements (ET: 21·2 ± 7·2 versus 26·9 ± 6·2, C: 23·7 ± 6·8 versus 24·1 ± 7·2). Three months of exercise rehabilitation significantly improves peak exercise capacity of patients with ESRD. Measurements of VO2 kinetics and functional capacity suggest that longer time might be needed to induce peripheral adaptations.

103.   The multistage 20 metre shuttle run test for aerobic fitness
*J Sports Sc*i. 1988 Summer;6(2):93-101.
Leger LA, Mercier D, Gadoury C, Lambert J.
Departement d'education physique, Universite de Montreal, Quebec, Canada.

A maximal multistage 20 m shuttle run test was designed to determine the maximal aerobic power of schoolchildren, healthy adults attending fitness class and athletes performing in sports with frequent stops and starts (e.g. basketball, fencing and so on). Subjects run back and forth on a 20 m course and must touch the 20 m line; at the same time a sound signal is emitted from a prerecorded tape. Frequency of the sound signals is increased 0.5 km h-1 each minute from a starting speed of 8.5 km h-1. When the subject can no longer follow the pace, the last stage number announced is used to predict maximal oxygen uptake (VO2max) (Y, ml kg-1 min-1) from the speed (X, km h-1) corresponding to that stage (speed = 8 + 0.5 stage no.) and age (A, year): Y = 31.025 + 3.238 X - 3.248A + 0.1536AX, r = 0.71 with 188 boys and girls aged 8-19 years. To obtain this regression, the test was performed individually. Right upon termination VO2 was measured with four 20 s samples and VO2max was estimated by retroextrapolating the O2 recovery curve at time zero of recovery. For adults, similar measurements indicated that the same equation could be used keeping age constant at 18 (r = 0.90, n = 77 men and women 18-50 years old). Test-retest reliability coefficients were 0.89 for children (139 boys and girls 6-16 years old) and 0.95 for adults (81 men and women, 20-45 years old).

104.   Influences of cardiorespiratory fitness levels and other predictors on cardiovascular disease mortality in men.
Medicine and Science in Sports and Exercise. 30(6):899-905, June 1998.
Farrell, Stephen W.; Kampert, James B.; Kohl, Harold W. Lii; Barlow, Carolyn E.; Macera, Caroline A.; Paffenbarger, Ralph S. Jr.; Gibbons, Larry W.; Blair, Steven N.

Purpose: This investigation quantifies the relation between cardiorespiratory fitness levels and cardiovascular disease (CVD) mortality within strata of other CVD predictors.

Methods: Participants included 25,341 male Cooper Clinic patients who underwent a maximal graded exercise test. CVD death rates were determined for low (least fit one-fifth), moderate (next two-fifths), and high (top two-fifths) cardiorespiratory fitness categories by strata of smoking habit, blood cholesterol level, resting blood pressure, and health status. There were 226 cardiovascular deaths during 211,996 man-years of follow-up.

Results: For individuals with none of the major CVD predictors (smoking, elevated resting systolic blood pressure, elevated blood cholesterol), there was a strong inverse relation ($P = 0.001$) between fitness level and CVD mortality. An inverse relation between CVD mortality and fitness level was seen within strata of cholesterol levels and health status. No evidence of a trend ($P = 0.60$) for decreased mortality was seen across fitness levels for individuals with elevated systolic blood pressure; however, a strong inverse gradient ($P < 0.001$) was seen across fitness levels for individuals with normal systolic blood pressure. There was a tendency for association between high levels of fitness and decreased CVD mortality in smokers compared with low and moderately fit smokers ($P < 0.076$). There was no significant association between level of fitness and CVD mortality for individuals with multiple (two or more) predictors ($P = 0.325$). Approximately 20 per cent of the 226 CVD deaths in the population studied were attributed to low fitness level.

Conclusions: Moderate and high levels of cardiorespiratory fitness seem to provide some protection from CVD mortality, even in the presence of well established CVD predictors.

105. State anxiety responses to 60 minutes of cross training

British Journal of Sports Medicine, **36**:105-107, 2002.

B S Hale, K R Koch and J S Raglin

Human Performance Laboratories, Indiana University, Bloomington, Indiana, USA

Correspondence to:

Mr Hale, Department of Kinesiology, Indiana University, HPER 112, Bloomington, Indiana 47405, USA;

brehale@indiana.edu

Objectives: Significant reductions in **state anxiety** following bouts of aerobic exercise have been consistently noted, whereas changes are generally absent after acute resistance training. However, the influence of a single exercise session involving both modes on state anxiety has not been examined.

Methods: To address this, state anxiety responses to 60 minutes of cross training were examined in 16 collegiate athletes (12 women, four men). Each subject completed two cross training exercise sessions (30 minutes of resistance training, 30 minutes of bicycle ergometry) in which the order of the exercises was reversed, with a minimum of one week between sessions. Each exercise mode was completed at about 70 per cent of maximum. State anxiety (SAI-Y1) was assessed five minutes before, and 0, 10, and 60 minutes after exercise.

Results: Repeated measures analysis of variance showed a significant ($p < 0.05$) main effect for time. However, the main effect for order and the order by time interaction were not significant. Post hoc analysis showed that state anxiety was reduced ($p < 0.05$) from baseline (mean (SD) = 34.8 (7.9)) at 10 minutes (32.1 (7.5)) and 60 minutes (30.4 (5.9)) after exercise, but not at 0 minutes (33.8 (6.9)).

Conclusions: The results indicate that combined sessions of aerobic and resistance exercise are associated with reductions in state anxiety, and that the order in which the exercise is completed does not influence this response.

Key Words: cross training; resistance exercise; aerobic exercise; state anxiety.

106. Reliability and validity of measures taken during the Chester step test to predict aerobic power and to prescribe aerobic exercise

Br J Sports Med, 2004;**38**:197-205

J P Buckley1, J Sim1, R G Eston2, R Hession1 and R Fox1
1. Keele University, Stoke, UK
2. University of Wales, Bangor, UK
Correspondence to:
Dr J P Buckley
Department of Physiotherapy Studies, MacKay Building, Keele University, Stoke ST5 5BG, UK; j.p.buckley@keele.ac.uk

Objectives: To evaluate the reliability and validity of measures taken during the **Chester step test** (CST) used to predict VO2max and prescribe subsequent exercise.

Methods: The CST was performed twice on separate days by 7 males and 6 females aged 22.4 (SD 4.6) years. Heart rate (HR), ratings of perceived exertion (RPE), and oxygen uptake (VO2) were measured at each stage of the CST.

Results: RPE, HR, and actual VO2 were the same at each stage for both trials but each of these measures was significantly different between CST stages ($p < 0.0005$). Intertrial bias ±95 per cent limits of agreement (95 per cent LoA) of HR reached acceptable limits at CST stage IV (-2±10 beats/min) and for RPE at stages III (0.2±1.4) and IV (0.5±1.9). Age estimated HRmax significantly overestimated actual HRmax of 5 beats/min (p = 0.016) and the 95 per cent LoA showed that this error could range from an underestimation of 17 beats/min to an overestimation of 7 beats/min. Estimated versus actual VO2 at each CST stage during both trials showed errors ranging between 11 per cent and 19 per cent. Trial 1 underestimated actual VO2max by 2.8 ml/kg/min (p = 0.006) and trial 2 by 1.6 ml/kg/min (not significant). The intertrial agreement in predicted VO2max was relatively narrow with a bias ±95 per cent LoA of - 0.8±3.7 ml/kg/min. The RPE and per centHRmax (actual) correlation improved with a second trial. At all CST stages in trial 2 RPE: per centHRmax coefficients were significant with the highest correlations at CST stages III (r = 0.78) and IV (r = 0.84).

Conclusion: CST VO2max prediction validity is questioned but the CST is reliable on a test-retest basis. VO2max prediction error is due more to VO2 estimation error at each CST stage compared with error in age estimated HRmax. The HR/RPE relation at >50 per cent VO2max reliably represents the recommended intensity for developing cardiorespiratory fitness, but only when a practice trial of the CST is first performed.

Key Words: ratings of perceived exertion; heart rate; oxygen uptake; analysis of agreement.

Abbreviations: CST, Chester step test; RPE, ratings of perceived exertion.

107. **Aerobic exercise training reduces plasma endothelin-1 concentration in older women**

J Appl Physiol 95: 336-341, 2003.

Seiji Maeda, 1, 2 Takumi Tanabe,2 Takashi Miyauchi,1,3 Takeshi Otsuki,2 Jun Sugawara,1 Motoyuki Iemitsu,3 Shinya Kuno,2 Ryuichi Ajisaka,2 Iwao Yamaguchi,3 and Mitsuo Matsuda2

1Center for Tsukuba Advanced Research Alliance, 2Institute of Health and Sport Sciences, and 3Institute of Clinical Medicine, University of Tsukuba, Tsukuba, Ibaraki 305-0006, Japan

Endothelial function deteriorates with aging. On the other hand, exercise training improves the function of vascular endothelial cells. Endothelin-1 (ET-1), which is produced by vascular endothelial cells, has potent constrictor and proliferative activity in vascular smooth muscle cells and, therefore, has been implicated in regulation of vascular tonus and progression of atherosclerosis. We previously reported significantly higher plasma ET-1 concentration in middle-aged than in young humans, and recently we showed that plasma ET-1 concentration was significantly decreased by aerobic exercise training in healthy young humans. We hypothesized that plasma ET-1 concentration increases with age, even in healthy adults, and that lifestyle modification (i.e., exercise) can reduce plasma ET-1 concentration in previously sedentary older adults. We measured plasma ET-1 concentration in healthy young women (21–28 yr old), healthy middle-aged women (31–47 yr old), and healthy older women (61–69 yr old). The plasma level of ET-1 significantly increased with aging (1.02 ± 0.08, 1.33 ± 0.11, and 2.90 ± 0.20 pg/ml in young, middle-aged, and older women, respectively). Thus plasma ET-1 concentration was markedly higher in healthy older women than in healthy young or middle-aged women (by 3- and 2-fold, respectively). In healthy older women, we also measured plasma ET-1 concentration after 3 mo of aerobic exercise (cycling on a leg **ergometer** at 80 per cent of ventilatory threshold for 30 min, 5 days/wk). Regular exercise significantly decreased plasma ET-1 concentration in the healthy older women (2.22 ± 0.16 pg/ml, $P < 0.01$) and also significantly reduced their blood pressure. The present study suggests that regular aerobic-endurance exercise reduces plasma ET-1 concentration in older humans, and this reduction in plasma ET-1 concentration may have beneficial effects on the cardiovascular system (i.e., prevention of progression of hypertension and/or atherosclerosis by endogenous ET-1).

Key Words: regular exercise; vascular endothelium; endothelial function

Address for reprint requests and other correspondence: M. Matsuda, Institute of Health and Sport Sciences, University of Tsukuba, Tsukuba, Ibaraki 305-8574, Japan (E-mail: m-matsuda@taiiku.tsukuba.ac.jp).

108. **Aerobic exercise training reduces plasma endothelin-1 concentration in older women**

*Br J Sports Med,*2002;**36**:282-289.

Seiji Maeda,1,2 Takumi Tanabe,2 Takashi Miyauchi, 1, 3 Takeshi Otsuki, 2 Jun Sugawara, 1 Motoyuki Iemitsu, 3 Shinya Kuno, 2 Ryuichi Ajisaka, 2 Iwao Yamaguchi, 3 and Mitsuo Matsuda 2

1Center for Tsukuba Advanced Research Alliance, 2Institute of Health and Sport Sciences, and 3Institute of Clinical Medicine, University of Tsukuba, Tsukuba, Ibaraki 305-0006, Japan.

Endothelial function deteriorates with aging. On the other hand, exercise training improves the function of vascular endothelial cells. Endothelin-1 (ET-1), which is produced by vascular endothelial cells, has potent constrictor and proliferative activity in vascular smooth muscle cells and, therefore, has been implicated in regulation of vascular tonus and progression of atherosclerosis. We previously reported significantly higher plasma ET-1 concentration in middle-aged than in young humans, and recently we showed that plasma ET-1 concentration was significantly decreased by aerobic exercise training in healthy young humans. We hypothesized that plasma ET-1 concentration increases with age, even in healthy adults, and that lifestyle modification (i.e., exercise) can reduce plasma ET-1 concentration in previously sedentary older adults. We measured plasma ET-1 concentration in healthy young women (21–28 yr old), healthy middle-aged women (31–47 yr old), and healthy older women (61–69 yr old). The plasma level of ET-1 significantly increased with aging (1.02 ± 0.08, 1.33 ± 0.11, and 2.90 ± 0.20 pg/ml in young, middle-aged, and older women, respectively). Thus plasma ET-1 concentration was markedly higher in healthy older women than in healthy young or middle-aged women (by 3- and 2-fold, respectively). In healthy older women, we also measured plasma ET-1 concentration after 3 mo of aerobic exercise (cycling on a leg ergometer at 80 per cent of ventilatory threshold for 30 min, 5 days/wk). Regular exercise significantly decreased plasma ET-1 concentration in the healthy older women (2.22 ± 0.16 pg/ml, $P < 0.01$) and also significantly reduced their blood pressure. The present study suggests that regular aerobic-endurance exercise reduces plasma ET-1 concentration in older humans, and this reduction in plasma ET-1 concentration may have beneficial effects on the cardiovascular system (i.e., prevention of progression of hypertension and/or atherosclerosis by endogenous ET-1).

Key Words: regular exercise; vascular endothelium; endothelial function

Address for reprint requests and other correspondence: M. Matsuda, Institute of Health and Sport Sciences, University of Tsukuba, Tsukuba, Ibaraki 305-8574, Japan (E-mail: m-matsuda@taiiku.tsukuba.ac.jp).

4

Flexibility Variables

1. **Balance control, flexibility, and cardiorespiratory fitness among older Tai Chi practitioners**

   Br J Sports Med 2000; *34*:29-34

   Youlian Hong1, Jing Xian Li1 and P D Robinson2

   1. Department of Sports Science and Physical Education, The Chinese University of Hong Kong, Hong Kong
   2. University College Worcester, United Kingdom

   Correspondence to: Professor Y Hong, Department of Sports Science and Physical Education, The Chinese University of Hong Kong, Shatin, NT, Hong Kong.

   Background : Tai Chi Chuan (TTC) exercise has beneficial effects on the components of physical condition and can produce a substantial reduction in the risk of multiple falls. Previous studies have shown that short term TCC exercise did not improve the scores in the single leg stance test with eyes closed and the sit and reach test. There has apparently been no research into the effects of TCC on total body rotation flexibility and heart rate responses at rest and after a three minute step test.

   Methods : In this cross sectional study, 28 male TCC practitioners with an average age of 67.5 years old and 13.2 years of TCC exercise experience were recruited to form the TCC group. Another 30 sedentary men aged 66.2 were selected to serve as the control group. Measurements included resting heart rate, left and right single leg stance with eyes closed, modified sit and reach test, total body rotation test (left and right), and a three minute step test.

   Results : Compared with the sedentary group, the TCC group had significantly better scores in resting heart rate, three minute step test heart rate, modified sit and reach, total body rotation test on both right and left side (p<0.01), and both right and left leg standing with eyes closed (p<0.05). According to the American Fitness Standards, the TCC group attained the 90th percentile rank for sit and reach and total body rotation test, right and left.

Conclusion : Long term regular TCC exercise has favourable effects on the promotion of balance control, flexibility, and cardiovascular fitness in older adults.

Key Words: Tai Chi; balance; falls; flexibility; cardiovascular fitness; aged.

2. **A controlled study of the effects of a supervised cardiovascular fitness training program on the manifestations of primary fibromyalgia.**
Arthritis Rheum. 1988 Sep;31(9):1135-41.
McCain GA, Bell DA, Mai FM, Halliday PD.
Division of Rheumatology, University of Western Ontario, London, Canada.

Forty-two patients with primary **fibromyalgia** were randomized into a 20-week program consisting of either cardiovascular fitness (CVR) training or simple flexibility exercises (FLEX) that did not lead to enhanced cardiovascular fitness. Patients were supervised by the same medical fitness instructors. Patients in neither group had contact with members of the other group, and were blinded as to the exercise taught to the alternative group. Groups met for 60 minutes 3 times each week. The compliance rate was 90%. Thirty-eight patients completed the study (18 with CVR training and 20 with FLEX). Blind assessments (standardized in preliminary trials to achieve acceptable inter-rater agreement) were performed by the same 2 examiners. After 20 weeks, patients receiving CVR training showed significantly improved cardiovascular fitness scores compared with those receiving FLEX training (t[35] = -4.22, P less than 0.003). Logistic regression analysis showed clinically and statistically significant improvements in pain threshold scores, which were measured directly over fibrositic tender points, in patients undergoing CVR (t[35] = 2.21, P less than 0.04). There was also a trend toward improvement in pain scores (visual analog scale) in the CVR group, but this did not reach statistical significance. There was no improvement in the percentage of body area affected by fibrositic symptoms or the number of nights per week or hours per night of disturbed sleep (self-report inventories). However, compared with the FLEX group, the CVR-trained patients improved significantly in both patient and physician global assessment scores.

3.   **Effects of Exercise Training on Frailty in Community-Dwelling Older Adults: Results of a Randomized, Controlled Trial**
*Journal of the American Geriatrics Society,*Volume 50 Page 1921 - December 2002

Ellen F. Binder, MD,* Kenneth B. Schechtman, PhD,† Ali A. Ehsani, MD,* Karen Steger-May, MA, Marybeth Brown, PhD, David R. Sinacore, PhD, Kevin E. Yarasheski, PhD,* and John O. Holloszy, MD*

Objectives: Although deficits in skeletal muscle strength, gait, balance, and oxygen uptake are potentially reversible causes of frailty, the efficacy of exercise in reversing frailty in community-dwelling older adults has not been proven. The aim of this study was to determine the effects of intensive exercise training (ET) on measures of physical frailty in older community-dwelling men and women.

Design : Randomized controlled trial.

Setting : Medical school research center.

Participants : One hundred fifteen sedentary men and women (mean age ± standard deviation = 83 ± 4) with mild to moderate physical frailty, as defined by two of the following three criteria: **Modified Physical Performance Test** (modified PPT) score between 18 and 32, **peak oxygen uptake** (.VO2 peak) between 10 and 18 mL/kg/min, and self-report of difficulty or assistance with one basic **activity of daily living** (ADL), or two instrumental ADLs.

Intervention : Participants were randomly assigned to a control group that performed a 9-month low-intensity home exercise program (control) or an exercise-training program (ET). The control intervention primarily consisted of flexibility exercises. ET began with 3 months of flexibility, light-resistance, and balance training. During the next 3 months, resistance training was added, and, during the next 3 months, endurance training was added.

Measurements : Modified PPT score, .VO2 peak, performance of ADLs as measured by the Older Americans Resources and Services instrument, and the **Functional Status Questionnaire** (FSQ).

Results : ET resulted in significantly greater improvements than home exercise in three of the four primary outcome measures. Adjusted 95% confidence bounds on the magnitude of improvement in the ET group compared with the control group were 1.0 to 5.2 points for the modified PPT score, 0.9 to 3.6 mL/kg/min for .VO2 peak, and 1.6 to 4.9 points for the FSQ score.

Conclusions : Our results show that intensive ET can improve measures of physical function and preclinical disability in older adults who have impairments in physical performance and oxygen uptake and are not taking hormone replacement therapy better than a low-intensity home exercise program.

4. **A randomized controlled study of the Arthritis Self-Management Programme in the UK**

Health Education Research, Vol. 15, No. 6, 665-680, December 2000

Julie H. Barlow, Andy P. Turner and Chris C. Wright

Psychosocial Rheumatology Research Centre, School of Health and Social Sciences, Coventry University, Priory Street, Coventry CV1 5FB, UK

The objective of this study was to determine whether the **Arthritis Self-Management Programme** (ASMP) improves perceptions of control, health behaviours and health status, and changes use of health care resources. The design was a pragmatic randomized controlled study; participants were allocated to ASMP (Intervention Group) or a 4-month waiting-list Control Group. The Intervention Group completed a 12-month follow-up. In total, 544 people with arthritis were recruited from the community—311 in the Intervention Group and 233 in the Control Group. **Main outcome measures included**: arthritis self-efficacy, health behaviours (exercise, cognitive symptom management, diet and relaxation) and health status (pain, fatigue, anxiety, depression and positive affect). At 4 months follow-up, the ASMP had a significant effect on arthritis self-efficacy for other symptoms and pain subscales. Performance of a range of health behaviours (cognitive symptom management, communication with physicians, dietary habit, exercise and relaxation) was significantly greater among the Intervention Group. The Intervention Group were significantly less depressed and had greater positive mood. In addition, trends towards decreases on fatigue and anxiety were noted. Physical functioning, pain and GP visits remained stable at 4 months. A similar pattern of findings was found at 12 months follow-up for the Intervention Group. Furthermore, a significant improvement was found on pain and visits to GPs had decreased. Apart from a small improvement on physical functioning among the Intervention Group participants with osteoarthritis 12 months, all effects were independent of the type of arthritis. The findings suggest that the ASMP is effective in promoting improvements in perception of control, health behaviours and health status, when delivered in UK settings.

5. **Impingement syndrome in athletes**

American Journal of Sports Medicine, Vol 8, Issue 3 151-158, 1980.

RJ Hawkins and JC Kennedy

Athletes, particularly those who are involved in sporting activities requiring repetitive overhead use of the arm (for example, tennis players, swimmers, baseball pitchers, and quarterbacks), may develop a painful shoulder. This is often due to impingement in the vulnerable avascular region of the supraspinatus and biceps tendons. With the passage of time, degeneration and tears of the rotator cuff may result. Pathologically the syndrome has been classified into Stage I (**edema** and **hemorrhage**), Stage II (**fibrosis** and **tendonitis**), and Stage III (**tendon degeneration, bony changes, and tendon ruptures**). The impingement syndrome may be a problem for the young, active, and competitive athlete as well as the casual weekend athlete. The "impingement sign" which reproduces pain and resulting facial expression when the arm is forceably forward flexed (jamming the greater tuberosity against the anteroinferior surface of the acromion) is the most reliable physical sign in establishing the diagnosis. Flexibility exercises, strengthening programs, and special training techniques are a preventive and treatment requirement. Rest and local modalities such as ice, ultrasound, and antiinflammatory agents are usually effective to lessen the inflammatory reaction. Surgical decompression by resecting the coracoacromial ligament or a more definitive anterior acromioplasty may rarely be indicated.

6.   **Preseason strength and flexibility imbalances associated with athletic injuries in female collegiate athletes**
      American Journal of Sports Medicine, Vol 19, Issue 1 76-81, 1991.
      JJ Knapik, CL Bauman, BH Jones, JM Harris and L Vaughan
      U.S. Army Research Institute of Environmental Medicine, Natick, Massachusetts 01760-5007.

      One hundred thirty-eight female collegiate athletes, participating in eight weightbearing varsity sports, were administered preseason strength and flexibility tests and followed for injuries during their sports seasons. Strength was measured as the maximal **isokinetic torque** of the right and left knee flexors and knee extensors at 30 and 180 deg/sec. Flexibility was measured as the active range of motion of several lower body joints. An athletic trainer evaluated and recorded injuries occurring to the athletes in practice or competition. Forty percent of the women suffered one or more injuries. Athletes experienced more lower extremity injuries if they had: 1) a right knee flexor 15% stronger than the left knee flexor at 180 deg/sec; 2) a right hip extensor 15% more flexible than the left hip extensor; 3) a knee flexor/knee extensor ratio of less than 0.75 at 180 deg/sec. There was a trend for higher injury rates to be associated with knee flexor or hip extensor imbalances of 15% or more on either side of the body. These data demonstrate that specific strength and flexibility imbalances are associated with lower extremity injuries in female collegiate athletes.

7.   **Intrinsic risk factors for exercise-related injuries among male and female army trainees**
      American Journal of Sports Medicine, Vol 21, Issue 5 705-710, 1993.
      BH Jones, MW Bovee, JM Harris 3rd and DN Cowan

Occupational Medicine Division, U.S. Army Research Institute of Environmental Medicine, Natick, MA 01760.

Physical training-related injuries are common among army recruits and other vigorously active populations, but little is known about their causation. To identify intrinsic risk factors, we prospectively measured 391 army trainees. For 8 weeks of basic training, 124 men and 186 women (79.3%) were studied. They answered questionnaires on past activities and sports participation, and were measured for height, weight, and body fat percentage; 71% of the subjects took an initial army physical training test. Women had a significantly higher incidence of time-loss injuries than men, 44.6% compared with 29.0%. During training, more time-loss injuries occurred among the 50% of the men who were slower on the mile run, 29.0% versus 0.0%. Slower women were likewise at greater risk than faster ones, 38.2% versus 18.5%. Men with histories of inactivity and with higher body mass index were at greater injury risk than other men, as were the shortest women. We conclude that female gender and low aerobic fitness measured by run times are risk factors for training injuries in army trainees, and that other factors such as prior activity levels and stature may affect men and women differently.

8. **The effect of exercise on patellar tracking in lateral patellar compression syndrome**
American Journal of Sports Medicine, Vol 20, Issue 4 434-440, 1992.
SA Doucette and EM Goble
Mountain West Physical Therapy, Western Surgical Center, Logan, UT 84321.

The influence of a physical therapy program on pain and patellar tracking was investigated clinically and radiologically with tangential views in 51 knees with lateral patellar compression syndrome. A pre test-post test design was used to evaluate physical measurements of patellar alignment in subjects who had had patellofemoral pain for a minimum of 6 weeks. Eighty-four percent of the subjects were pain-free after an average of 8 weeks of rehabilitation or 11 physical therapy visits, with a mean quadriceps strength to total body weight ratio of 61% in women and 86% in men. The pretest-posttest difference in Merchant's congruence angle was significant at a probability of 0.0066 in the patients who were pain-free after exercise, demonstrating less lateral patellar tracking. The pretest-posttest difference in **iliotibial band flexibility** was significant at a probability of 0.0017, with the patients who were pain-free after exercise becoming more flexible. No significant differences were observed from before to after exercise in the **patellofemoral index, Q angle**, hamstring flexibility, thigh measurement, sclerotic subchondral bone, or **sulcus angle**. We were unable to predict which subjects would become pain-free with exercise by patellar position because the group that improved began more laterally tilted. The results of this study indicate that patellar tracking is improved with vastus medialis oblique strengthening, iliotibial band stretching, and joint mobility exercise in the majority of subjects with lateral patellar compression syndrome.

9.   **Exercise training improves left ventricular systolic function in older men**
Circulation, Vol 83, 96-103, 1991
AA Ehsani, T Ogawa, TR Miller, RJ Spina and SM Jilka
Department of Medicine, Mallinckrodt Institute of Radiology, St. Louis, MO.

To determine whether endurance exercise training can improve left ventricular systolic function in older men, 10 healthy sedentary men (64 +/- 3 years old; mean +/- SD) were studied. Training consisted of endurance exercise 4 +/- 0.3 days per week for 11.8 +/- 2.5 months at a progressively increasing intensity of 60-80% of maximal O2 uptake (Vo2max) with additional brief bouts of exercise equal to 93 +/- 13% of Vo2max. Vo2max increased from 29.6 +/- 4.1 to 37.2 +/- 5.7 ml/kg/min (p less than 0.001). Percent body fat was decreased (17.8 +/- 3.6% versus 15.6 +/- 3.6%; p less than 0.001). Before training, left ventricular ejection fraction, determined by electrocardiographic-gated equilibrium blood pool imaging, increased only modestly during exercise (from 66.3 +/- 6.7% at rest to 70.6 +/- 6.9% at peak exercise). After training, the increase in ejection fraction during exercise was significantly greater (from 67 +/- 4.8% at rest to 77.6 +/- 7.5% at peak exercise) than that observed before training and was similar to that in young sedentary men (64 +/- 7% at rest versus 74 +/- 9% at peak exercise). Although the changes in systolic pressure from rest to exercise were similar, end-systolic volume decreased significantly at peak exercise after (51 +/- 12 versus 38 +/- 13 ml; p less than 0.005) but not before (46 +/- 8 versus 43 +/- 13 ml; p = NS) training with a shift in the end- systolic volume-systolic blood pressure relation to the left compatible with enhanced inotropic state.

10.   **Resistance exercise training increases mixed muscle protein synthesis rate in frail women and men 76 yr old**
Am J Physiol Endocrinol Metab, Vol. 277, Issue 1, E118-E125, July 1999
Kevin E. Yarasheski, Jina Pak-Loduca, Debbie L. Hasten, Kathleen A. Obert, Mary Beth Brown, and David R. Sinacore
Claude D. Pepper Older American's Independence Center, Divisions of Geriatrics and Gerontology and Metabolism, Endocrinology, and Diabetes, Washington University Medical Center, St. Louis, Missouri 63110.

Muscle atrophy (sarcopenia) in the elderly is associated with a reduced rate of muscle protein synthesis. The purpose of this study was to determine if weight-lifting exercise increases the rate of muscle protein synthesis in physically frail 76- to 92-yr-old women and men. Eight women and 4 men with mild to moderate physical frailty were enrolled in a 3-mo physical therapy program that was followed by 3 mo of supervised weight-lifting exercise. Supervised weight-lifting exercise was performed 3 days/wk at 65-100% of initial 1-repetition maximum on five upper and three lower body exercises. Compared with before resistance training, the in vivo incorporation rate of [13C] leucine into vastus lateralis muscle protein was increased after resistance training in women and men ($P < 0.01$), although it was unchanged in five 82 ± 2-yr-old control subjects studied two times in 3 mo. Maximum voluntary knee extensor muscle torque production increased in the supervised resistance exercise group. These findings suggest that muscle contractile protein synthetic pathways in physically frail 76- to 92-yr-old women and men respond and adapt to the increased contractile activity associated with progressive resistance exercise training.

Key Words: sarcopenia; stable isotopes; mass spectrometry; physical activity.

11.   ACSM Position Stand: The Recommended Quantity and Quality of Exercise for Developing and Maintaining Cardiorespiratory and Muscular Fitness, and Flexibility in Healthy Adults.

Medicine & Science in Sports & Exercise. 30(6):975-991, June 1998.

Pollock, Michael L. Ph.D., FACSM (Chairperson); Gaesser, Glenn A. Ph.D., FACSM (Co-chairperson); Butcher, Janus D. M.D., FACSM; Despres, Jean-Pierre Ph.D.; Dishman, Rod K. Ph.D., FACSM; Franklin, Barry A. Ph.D., FACSM; Garber, Carol Ewing Ph.D., FACSM

Abstract:

Summary: ACSM Position Stand on The Recommended Quantity and Quality of Exercise for Developing and Maintaining Cardiorespiratory and Muscular Fitness, and Flexibility in Adults. Med. Sci. Sports Exerc., Vol. 30, No. 6, pp. 975-991, 1998. The combination of frequency, intensity, and duration of chronic exercise has been found to be effective for producing a training effect. The interaction of these factors provide the overload stimulus. In general, the lower the stimulus the lower the training effect, and the greater the stimulus the greater the effect. As a result of specificity of training and the need for maintaining muscular strength and endurance, and flexibility of the major muscle groups, a well-rounded training program including aerobic and resistance training, and flexibility exercises is recommended. Although age in itself is not a limiting factor to exercise training, a more gradual approach in applying the prescription at older ages seems prudent. It has also been shown that aerobic endurance training of fewer than 2 d[middle dot]wk-1, at less than 40-50% of V[spacing dot above]O2R, and for less than 10 min-1 is generally not a sufficient stimulus for developing and maintaining fitness in healthy adults. Even so, many health benefits from physical activity can be achieved at lower intensities of exercise if frequency and duration of training are increased appropriately. In this regard, physical activity can be accumulated through the day in shorter bouts of 10-min durations.

In the interpretation of this position stand, it must be recognized that the recommendations should be used in the context of participant's needs, goals, and initial abilities. In this regard, a sliding scale as to the amount of time allotted and intensity of effort should be carefully gauged for the cardiorespiratory, muscular strength and endurance, and flexibility components of the program. An appropriate **warm-up** and **cool-down** period, which would include flexibility exercises, is also recommended. The important factor is to design a program for the individual to provide the proper amount of physical activity to attain maximal benefit at the lowest risk. Emphasis should be placed on factors that result in permanent lifestyle change and encourage a lifetime of physical activity.

12.   12-month Tai Chi training in the elderly: its effect on health fitness.
Medicine & Science in Sports & Exercise. 30(3):345-351, March 1998.
Lan, Ching; Lai, Jin-shin; Chen, Ssu-yuan; Wong, May-kuen

Purpose: The objective of this study was to evaluate the effect of Tai Chi Chuan(TCC) on health fitness in older individuals.

Methods: Thirty-eight community-dwelling persons aged 58 to 70 yr completed this study. The TCC group included 9 men and 11 women; the control group included 9 men and 9 women. The TCC group practiced TCC for 11.2 +/- 1.4 months, with the attendance of 4.6 +/- 1.3 times[middle dot]wk-1. Each session included 20 min of warm-up, 24 min of TCC practice, and 10 min of cooldown. The exercise intensity was 52-63% of the heart rate range. Cardiorespiratory function, strength, flexibility, and percent of **body fat** were evaluated before and at the end of this study.

Results: The male TCC group showed 16.1% increase in [spacing dot above]VO2max (P< 0.01), 11[degrees] increase in thoracic/lumbar flexibility (P < 0.05), 18.1% increase in muscle strength of knee extensor (P < 0.01), and 15.4% increase of knee flexor (P < 0.05). The female TCC group showed 21.3%

increase in [spacing dot above]VO2max (P < 0.01), 8.8[degrees] increase in flexibility (P < 0.05), 20.3% increase in muscle strength of knee extensor (P < 0.05), and 15.9% increase of knee flexor (P < 0.05). The control group showed no significant change in these variables.

Conclusions: The results indicate that a 12-month **Tai Chi Chuan** program is effective for improving health fitness of the elderly.

13. Exercise dose-response effects on quality of life and independent living in older adults.

Article

Medicine & Science in Sports & Exercise. 33(6) Supplement:S598-S608, June 2001.

Spirduso, Waneen W.; Cronin, D. Leilani

Purpose: The purpose of this study was to determine if exercise operates in a dose-response fashion to influence well-being and to postpone dependency.

Methods: A computer-assisted search was made by using the following key words resistance training, strength training, function, exercise, elderly, quality of life, frailty, physical activity, independence, performance, aerobic training, mobility, well-being, and disability. Review articles and personal files were also used, and a critical review of research studies meeting the criteria described in the methods section of the article was conducted.

Results: In large sample correlational studies and prospective longitudinal studies, researchers consistently report that measures of physical function in old adults are related to feelings of well-being, and that old adults who are physically active also report higher levels of well-being and physical function, but the results of randomized intervention studies of aerobic and/or resistive strength training do not always support this relationship. Even if changes in well-being and physical function were reported, no evidence was found that levels of intensity operated in a dose-response fashion to influence these changes. Research design problems included ineffective aerobic or strength training treatments, widely varying participation and effort of the research participants, and both treatment and physical function tests that were not appropriate for the physical status of the participants.

Conclusion: The most consistent results were that long-term physical activity is related to postponed disability and independent living in the oldest-old subjects. Even in individuals with chronic disease, systematic participation in physical activities enhances physical function.

14. **Increasing Hamstring Flexibility Decreases Lower Extremity Overuse Injuries in Military Basic Trainees**

The American Journal of Sports Medicine, 27:173-176 (1999).

Donald E. Hartig, MD and John M. Henderson, DO*

Hughston Clinic, P.C., Columbus, Georgia

* Address correspondence and reprint requests to John M. Henderson, DO, The Hughston Clinic, P.C., POB 9517, Columbus, Georgia 31908-9517

The purpose of this intervention study was to prove that increasing flexibility of the hamstring musculotendinous unit would decrease the number of lower extremity overuse injuries that occur in military infantry basic trainees. Two different companies going through basic training at the same time were used. Hamstring flexibility was checked at the beginning and at the end of the 13-week infantry basic training course. The control company (N = 148) proceeded through normal basic training. The intervention company (N = 150) followed the same program but added three hamstring stretching sessions to their already scheduled fitness program. All subsequent lower extremity **overuse injuries** were recorded through the troop medical clinic. Hamstring flexibility increased significantly in the intervention group compared with the control group. The number of injuries was also significantly lower in the intervention group. Forty-three injuries occurred in the control group for an incidence rate of 29.1%, compared with 25 injuries in the intervention group for an incidence rate of 16.7%. Thus, in this study, the number of lower extremity overuse injuries was significantly lower in infantry basic trainees with increased hamstring flexibility.

15. **A Controlled Trial of Exercise Rehabilitation after Heart Transplantation**

The New England Journal oj Medicine, Volume 340:272-277, Number 4, January 28, 1999.

Jon A. Kobashigawa, M.D., David A. Leaf, M.D., Nancy Lee, P.T., Michael P. Gleeson, B.S., HongHu Liu, Ph.D., Michele A. Hamilton, M.D., Jaime D. Moriguchi, M.D., Nobuyuki Kawata, M.D., Kim Einhorn, B.S., Elise Herlihy, R.N., and Hillel Laks, M.D.

Background : In patients who have received a cardiac transplant, the denervated donor heart responds abnormally to exercise and **exercise tolerance** is reduced. The role of physical exercise in the treatment of patients who have undergone cardiac transplantation has not been determined. We assessed the effects of training on the capacity for exercise early after cardiac transplantation.

Methods : Twenty-seven patients who were discharged within two weeks after receiving a heart transplant were randomly assigned to participate in a six-month structured cardiac-rehabilitation program (exercise group, 14 patients) or to undergo unstructured therapy at home (control group, 13 patients). Each patient in the exercise group underwent an individualized program of muscular-strength and aerobic training under the guidance of a physical therapist, whereas control patients received no formal exercise training. Cardiopulmonary stress testing was performed at base line (within one month after heart transplantation) and six months later.

Results : As compared with the control group, the exercise group had significantly greater increases in peak oxygen consumption (mean increase, 4.4 ml per kilogram of body weight per minute [49 percent] vs. 1.9 ml per kilogram per minute [18 percent]; P=0.01) and workload (mean increase, 35 W [59 percent] vs. 12 W [18 percent]; P=0.01) and a greater reduction in the **ventilatory equivalent** for carbon dioxide (mean decrease, 13 [20 percent] vs. 6 [11 percent]; P=0.02). The mean dose of prednisone, the number of patients taking antihypertensive medications, the average number of episodes of rejection and of infection during the study period, and weight gain did not differ significantly between the groups.

Conclusions : When initiated early after cardiac transplantation, exercise training increases the capacity for physical work.

Source Information : From the Divisions of Cardiology and Cardiothoracic Surgery, University of California at Los Angeles School of Medicine (J.A.K., M.P.G., H. Liu, M.A.H., J.D.M., N.K., K.E., H. Laks); the West Los Angeles Veterans Affairs Medical Center (D.A.L.); and the Department of Rehabilitation Services, University of California at Los Angeles Medical Center (N.L., E.H.) — all in Los Angeles.

Address reprint requests to Dr. Kobashigawa at the Division of Cardiology, Center for Health Sciences 47-123, UCLA Medical Center, 10833 LeConte Ave., Los Angeles, CA 90095, or at jonk@mednet.ucla.edu .

16. **Effects of Exercise Involving Predominantly Either Joint-Reaction or Ground-Reaction Forces on Bone Mineral Density in Older Women**
Wendy M. Kohrt, 1   Ali A. Ehsani, 1   Stanley J. Birge Jr.1
Journal of Bone and Mineral Research, August 1997:12:1253-1261
1 Washington University School of Medicine, Division of Geriatrics and Gerontology, Department of Internal Medicine, St. Louis, Missouri, U.S.A.

Address reprint requests to: Wendy M. Kohrt, Ph.D. Washington University School of Medicine 660 S. Euclid, Box 8113 St. Louis, MO 63110 U.S.A.

This study compared the effects of two exercise training programs, 11 months in duration, on **bone mineral density** (BMD) in older, sedentary women. Thirty-nine women, aged 60–74 years, were assigned to the following groups: (a) a group that performed exercises that introduced stress to the skeleton through ground-reaction forces (GRF) (i.e., walking, jogging, stairs); (b) a group that performed exercises that introduced stress to the skeleton through **joint-reaction forces** (JRF) (i.e., weight lifting, rowing); or (c) a no-exercise control group. BMD of the whole body, lumbar spine, proximal femur, and distal forearm was assessed five times at 3-month intervals. The GRF and JRF exercise programs resulted in significant and similar increases in BMD of the whole body ($2.0 \pm 0.8\%$ and $1.6 \pm 0.4\%$, respectively), lumbar spine ($1.8 \pm 0.7\%$ and $1.5 \pm 0.5\%$, respectively), and Ward's triangle region of the proximal femur ($6.1 \pm 1.5\%$ and $5.1 \pm 2.1\%$, respectively). There was a significant increase in BMD of the femoral neck only in response to the GRF exercise program (GRF, $3.5 \pm 0.8\%$; JRF, "$0.2 \pm 0.7\%$"). There were no significant changes in BMD in control subjects. Among all exercisers, there was a significant inverse ($r =$ "0.52, $p < 0.01$) relationship between increases in whole body BMD and reductions in fat mass, suggesting a dose response effect of exercise on bone mass. Although femoral neck BMD was responsive only to the GRF exercise program, some adaptations (i.e., increase in lean body mass and strength) that were specific to the JRF exercise program may be important in preventing osteoporotic fractures by reducing the risk for falls. It remains to be determined whether all of these benefits can be gained through a training program that combines the different types of exercises employed in this study.

17.   Have We Oversold the Benefit of Late-Life Exercise?

The Journals of Gerontology Series A: Biological Sciences and Medical Sciences, 56:M412-M423 (2001)

Julie J. Keysora and Alan M. Jettea

a Sargent College of Health and Rehabilitation Sciences, Boston University, Massachusetts

Alan M. Jette, Boston University, Sargent College of Health and Rehabilitation Sciences, 635 Commonwealth Avenue, Boston, MA 02215.

Decision Editor: John E. Morley, MB, BCh

Background : Increasing exercise among older adults to improve function and prevent or decrease disability is widely promoted in developed countries. This review seeks to critically evaluate the degree to which existing scientific evidence supports these claims.

Methods : A literature review was performed in Medline and Best Evidence databases for the years 1985 to 2000. Experimental and quasi-experimental aerobic and resistance exercise interventions were reviewed for impairment, function, and disability outcomes. The impact of exercise on specific impairments, functions, and disabilities was examined by summarizing the findings reported across all studies.

Results. Thirty-one studies were identified. Impairment and functional outcomes were reported in 97% and 81% of the studies, respectively; half of the studies examined disability outcomes. The most consistent positive effects of late-life exercise were observed in strength, aerobic capacity, flexibility, walking, and standing balance, with over half of the studies that examined these outcomes finding positive effects. Of the studies that examined physical, social, emotional, or overall disability outcomes, most found no improvements. In the five studies that reported reduced physical disability, the effect sizes ranged from .23 to .88.

Conclusions. Late-life exercise clearly improves strength, aerobic capacity, flexibility, and physical function. Existing scientific evidence, however, does not support a strong argument for late-life exercise as an effective means of reducing disability. This may be due, in part, to methodological limitations in studies that have examined disability outcomes. On the other hand, the theoretical basis of interventions aimed at reducing disability may need to extend beyond exercise and address behavioral and social factors.

18. Exercise training in a predominantly African-American group of stroke survivors.

*Medicine and Science in Sports and Exercise,*32(12):1990-1996, December 2000.

Rimmer, James H.; Riley, Barth; Creviston, Todd; Nicola, and Terry

Purpose: The purpose of this study was to determine the effects of a 12-wk exercise training program in a predominantly African-American group of stroke survivors with multiple comorbidities.

Methods: A lag-control group design was employed to provide training to all participants (N = 35). Two 12-wk training iterations were arranged. Participants trained 3 d[middle dot]wk-1 for 60 min[middle dot]d-1 (cardiovascular, 30 min; strength, 20 min; flexibility, 10 min). Outcome measures included peak O2 (mL[middle dot]min-1, mL[middle dot]kg-1[middle dot]min-1), **maximal workload** (MW), time to exhaustion (TTE), 10 RM on two **Life Fitness strength machines**, grip strength (GS), body weight (BW), total skinfolds (TS), **waist to hip ratio** (WHR), hamstring/low back flexibility (HLBF), and shoulder flexibility (SF).

Results: Compared with controls, the exercise group showed significant gains in peak O2 (P < 0.01), strength (P < 0.01), HLBF (P < 0.01), and body composition (BW and BMI, P < 0.05; TS, P < 0.01). There was no significant difference between exercise and controls on WHR, SF, and GS.

Discussion: A supervised exercise training program for stroke survivors with multiple comorbidities was highly effective in improving overall fitness, potentially reducing the risk of further disease and disability. Greater effort must be made on the part of the public health community to increase access to community-based physical activity programs for persons with stroke.

19.   Review Article: Exercise, Aging, and Muscle Protein Metabolism

The Journals of Gerontology Series A: Biological Sciences and Medical Sciences ,58:M918-M922 (2003).

Kevin E. Yarasheski

Washington University School of Medicine, St. Louis, Missouri.

Age-associated alterations in muscle protein quantity and quality that adversely affect muscle structure, composition, and function have been referred to as sarcopenia. Muscle protein is metabolically active, and the age-associated loss of muscle protein mass is related to a loss of physical function and an inability to perform activities of daily living (physical frailty). It is important to maintain adequate reserves of muscle protein and amino acids as we age. As in all cachectic conditions, sarcopenia can be explained by an imbalance between the rates of muscle protein synthesis and muscle proteolysis, in which net muscle protein balance is negative. This review summarizes evidence that supports the notion that: (a) advancing age and physical frailty are associated with a reduction in the fasting rate of mixed and myosin heavy chain protein synthesis, which contributes to muscle protein wasting in advancing age; (b) this impairment can be corrected because resistance exercise acutely and dramatically increases the rate of muscle protein synthesis in men and women aged 76 years and older; and (c) resistance exercise training maintains a modest increment in the rate of muscle protein synthesis and contributes to muscle hypertrophy and improved muscle strength in frail elderly men and women. The cellular mechanisms responsible for these adaptations, as well as the role of nutrition and hormone replacement in reversing sarcopenia, require further investigation.

20.   Is there a role for exercise in the prevention of osteoporotic fractures?

British Journal of Sports Medicine, Vol 33, Issue 6 378-386, 1999.

OM Rutherford

CIB, Biomedical Sciences, Imperial College School of Medicine, South Kensington, London, United Kingdom.

Objectives: To examine whether there is a role for exercise in improving **bone mineral density** (BMD), particularly in postmenopausal women. The effects of different types of exercise are examined together with their effects at selected skeletal sites. The role of activity in reducing falls and hip fractures will also be considered as well as the potentially negative effects of excessive exercise.

Methods: A literature search over the past 20 years was conducted and landmark papers selected.

Results: Certain types of exercise have been found to exert moderate benefits on BMD of the wrist, spine, and hip. Most studies do not detect a difference between the effects of endurance activities and strength training for BMD of the spine. It has been more difficult to isolate the optimal type of activity for effecting an osteogenic response at the hip, but recent evidence suggests that high impact work such as stepping and jumping may be effective at this site. The combination of hormone replacement therapy and exercise would appear to be more effective than either intervention on its own. Certain types of exercises have additional benefits, such as muscle strengthening, which could reduce the incidence of falls. Excessive exercise can lead to menstrual disturbances in female athletes and this in turn can cause bone loss, particularly from the spine.

Conclusions: Exercise across the life span should be encouraged in order to maximise peak bone mass, reduce age related bone loss, and maintain muscle strength and balance. Although the effects of exercise on BMD later in life are small, epidemiological evidence suggests that being active can nearly halve the incidence of hip fractures in the older population. This effect is most probably multifactorial through the positive effects on bone, muscle strength, balance, and joint flexibility. Younger women should be aware of the dangers to the skeleton of menstrual disorders.

21. **The effect of strength and flexibility training on skeletal muscle electromyographic activity, stiffness, and viscoelastic stress relaxation response**
American Journal of Sports Medicine, Vol 25, Issue 5 710-716, 1997.
K Klinge, SP Magnusson, EB Simonsen, P Aagaard, K Klausen and M Kjaer
August Krogh Institute, Copenhagen, Denmark.

The present study examined whether isometric strength training alone or isometric strength training combined with flexibility training of the hamstring muscles altered the viscoelastic response during stretch. Twelve male subjects performed isometric training (strength) on one side and isometric and flexibility training (strength and flexibility) on the other side for 13 weeks; 10 other subjects served as controls. Passive torque offered by the hamstring muscle group was measure during passive knee extension using a dynamometer. The knee was passively extended to a predetermined final position at 0.0875 rad/sec (dynamic phase), where it remained stationary for 90 seconds (static phase). The slope of the line (stiffness) and the area under the curve (energy) in the dynamic phase, and the decline in passive torque (viscoelastic stress relaxation) in the static phase were analyzed. Isometric strength was determined with a dynamometer. A strength test and a stretch maneuver were administered before and after the training period. All variables were unchanged in the control group. Isometric strength increased similarly on both training sides by 43%. The stretch maneuver showed that energy, stiffness, and passive torque increased on both training sides while low-level electromyographic recordings remained constant. Furthermore, the viscoelastic stress relaxation response (31% to 33%) was unaffected by the training. The addition of flexibility exercise had no significant effect on these strength training responses. These data suggest that an increase in isometric strength is accompanied by changes in the material properties of the muscle that are unaffected by flexibility exercises.

22. **A Randomized, Controlled Pilot Study of a Home-Based Exercise Program for Individuals With Mild and Moderate Stroke**
Stroke, 1998;29:2055-2060.

Pamela Duncan, PhD, PT; Lorie Richards, PhD, OT; Dennis Wallace, PhD; Joni Stoker-Yates, PT; Patricia Pohl, PhD, PT; Carl Luchies, PhD; Abna Ogle, MD; Stephanie Studenski, MD, MPH

From the Center on Aging, University of Kansas Medical Center (P.D., L.R., D.W., J.S-Y., P.P., C.L., S.S.); Department of Veterans Affairs Medical Center, Kansas City (P.D., S.S.); and Departments of Health Services Administration (P.D.), Physical (P.P.) and Occupational Therapy (L.R.), Internal Medicine (S.S.), Preventive Medicine (D.W.), and Physical Medicine and Rehabilitation (A.O.), School of Engineering, University of Kansas (C.L.), Kansas City, Kan.

Correspondence to Pamela Duncan, PhD, PT, University of Kansas Medical Center, Center on Aging, 3901 Rainbow Blvd, Kansas City, KS 66160-7117. E-mail pduncan@kumc.edu

Background and Purpose—Many stroke survivors have minimal to moderate neurological deficits but are physically deconditioned and have a high prevalence of cardiovascular problems; all of these are potentially modifiable with exercise. The purposes of this randomized, controlled pilot study were (1) to develop a home-based balance, strength, and endurance program; (2) to evaluate the ability to recruit and retain stroke subjects; and (3) to assess the effects of the interventions used.

Methods : Twenty minimally and moderately impaired stroke patients who had completed inpatient rehabilitation and who were 30 to 90 days after stroke onset were randomized to a control group or to an experimental group that received a therapist-supervised, 8-week, 3-times-per-week, home-based exercise program. The control group received usual care as prescribed by the patients' physicians. Baseline and postintervention assessments included the **Fugl-Meyer Motor Assessment**, the **Barthel Index of Activities of Daily Living** (ADL), the **Lawton Scale of Instrumental** ADL, and the Medical Outcomes Study–36 Health Status Measurement. Functional assessments of balance and gait included a 10-m walk, 6-Minute Walk, and the Berg Balance Scale. Upper extremity function was evaluated by the Jebsen Test of Hand Function.

Results : Of 22 patients who met study criteria, 20 completed the study and 2 refused to participate. The experimental group tended to improve more than control group in motor function (Fugl-Meyer Upper Extremity: mean change in score, 8.4 versus 2.2; Fugl-Meyer Lower Extremity: 4.7 versus -0.9; gait velocity: median change, 0.25 versus .09 m/s; 6-Minute Walk: 195 versus 114 ft; Berg Balance Score: 7.8 versus 5; and Medical Outcomes Study–36 Health Status Measurement of Physical Function: 15.5 versus 9). There were no trends in differences in change scores by the Jebsen Test of Hand Function, Barthel Index, and Lawton Instrumental ADL Scale.

Conclusions : This study demonstrated that a randomized, controlled clinical trial of a poststroke exercise program is feasible. Measures of neurological impairments and lower extremity function showed the most benefit. Effects of the intervention on upper extremity dexterity and functional health status were equivocal. The lasting effects of the intervention were not assessed.

Key Words: exercise • rehabilitation • stroke management.

23. **Exercise in preventing falls and fall related injuries in older people: a review of randomised controlled trials**
Br J Sports Med 2000; *34*:7-17.
Melinda M Gardner, M Clare Robertson and A John Campbell
Department of Medical and Surgical Sciences, University of Otago Medical School, Dunedin, New Zealand

Correspondence to: M M Gardner, Department of Medical and Surgical Sciences, Dunedin School of Medicine, PO Box 913, Dunedin, New Zealand.

Objective—To assess the effectiveness of exercise programmes in preventing falls (and/or lowering the risk of falls and fall related injuries) in older people.

Design : A review of controlled clinical trials designed with the aim of lowering the risk of falling and/or fall injuries through an exercise only intervention or an intervention that included an exercise component

Main outcome measures : Falls, fall related injuries, time between falls, costs, cost effectiveness.

Subjects : A total of 4933 men and women aged 60 years and older.

Results : Eleven trials meeting the criteria for inclusion were reviewed. Eight of these trials had separate exercise interventions, and three used interventions with an exercise programme component. Five trials showed a significant reduction in the rate of falls or the risk of falling in the intervention group.

Conclusions : Exercise is effective in lowering falls risk in selected groups and should form part of falls prevention programmes. Lowering fall related injuries will reduce health care costs but there is little available information on the costs associated with programme replication or the cost effectiveness of exercise programmes aimed at preventing falls in older people.

Key Words: exercise; elderly; falls; cost effectiveness.

24.   Improved Exercise Tolerance and Quality of Life With Cardiac Rehabilitation of Older Patients After Myocardial Infarction

Circulation. 2003;107:2201.

Results of a Randomized, Controlled Trial

Niccolò Marchionni, MD; Francesco Fattirolli, MD; Stefano Fumagalli, MD; Neil Oldridge, PhD; Francesco Del Lungo, MD; Linda Morosi, MD; Costanza Burgisser, MD; Giulio Masotti, MD

From the Department of Critical Care Medicine and Surgery (N.M., F.F., S.F., F.D.L., L.M., C.B., G.M.), Unit of Gerontology and Geriatric Medicine, University of Florence and Azienda Ospedaliera Careggi, Florence, Italy, and the Center for Aging Research (N.O.), Schools of Allied Health Sciences and Medicine, Indiana University, Regenstrief Institute for Health Care, Indianapolis, Ind, and the Center for Urban Population Health, University of Wisconsin-Milwaukee, Wis.

Correspondence to Niccolò Marchionni, MD, Department of Critical Care Medicine and Surgery, University of Florence, Via delle Oblate, 4. 50141 Florence, Italy. E-mail nmarchionni@unifi.it

Background : Whether **cardiac rehabilitation** (CR) is effective in patients older than 75 years, who have been excluded from most trials, remains unclear. We enrolled patients 46 to 86 years old in a randomized trial and assessed the effects of 2 months of **post-myocardial infarction** (MI) CR on total work capacity (TWC, in kilograms per meter) and health-related quality of life (HRQL).

Methods and Results : Of 773 screened patients, 270 without cardiac failure, dementia, disability, or contraindications to exercise were randomized to outpatient, hospital-based CR (Hosp-CR), home-based CR (Home-CR), or no CR within 3 predefined age groups (middle-aged, 45 to 65 years; old, 66 to 75 years; and very old, >75 years) of 90 patients each. TWC and HRQL were determined with cycle **ergometry** and **Sickness Impact Profile at baseline**, after CR, and 6 and 12 months later. Within each age group, TWC improved with Hosp-CR and Home-CR and was unchanged with no CR. The improvement was similar in middle-aged and old persons but smaller, although still significant, in very old patients. TWC reverted toward baseline by 12 months with Hosp-CR but not with Home-CR. HRQL improved in middle-aged and old CR and control patients but only with CR in very old patients. Complications were similar across treatment and age groups. Costs were lower for Home-CR than for Hosp-CR.

Conclusions : Post-MI Hosp-CR and Home-CR are similarly effective in the short term and improve TWC and HRQL in each age group. However, with lower costs and more prolonged positive effects, Home-CR may be the treatment of choice in low-risk older patients.

Key Words: aging • coronary disease • exercise • myocardial infarction • quality of life.

25. **Effects of HRT and exercise training on insulin action, glucose tolerance, and body composition in older women**

J Appl Physiol ,Vol. 90, Issue 6, 2033-2040, June 2001

Ellen M. Evans1, Rachael E. Van Pelt2, Ellen F. Binder1, Daniel B. Williams3, Ali A. Ehsani1, and Wendy M. Kohrt2

1 Department of Internal Medicine, Division of Geriatrics and Gerontology, and 3 Department of Obstetrics and Gynecology, Washington University School of Medicine, St. Louis, Missouri 63110; and 2 Department of Medicine, Division of Geriatric Medicine, University of Colorado Health Sciences Center, Denver, Colorado 80262.

The independent and combined effects of exercise training and hormone replacement therapy (HRT) on body composition, fat distribution, glucose tolerance, and insulin action were studied in postmenopausal women, aged 68 ± 5 yr, assigned to control (n = 19), exercise (n = 18), HRT (n = 15), and exercise + HRT (n = 16) groups. The exercise consisted of 2 mo of flexibility exercises followed by 9 mo of endurance exercise. HRT was conjugated estrogens 0.625 mg/day and trimonthly medroxyprogesterone acetate 5 mg/day for 13 days. Total and regional body composition were measured by dual-energy X-ray absorptiometry. Serum glucose and insulin responses were measured during a 2-h oral glucose tolerance test. There were significant main effects of exercise on reductions in total and regional (trunk, arms, legs) fat mass, increase in leg fat-free mass, and improvements in glucose tolerance and insulin action. There were significant main effects of HRT on the reduction of total fat mass (HRT, 3.0 ± 4.0 kg; no HRT, 1.3 ± 2.6 kg), with a strong trend for reductions in trunk and leg fat mass (both P = 0.07). There was also a significant improvement in insulin action in response to HRT. These results suggest that there are independent and additive effects of exercise training and HRT on the reduction in fat mass and improvement in insulin action in postmenopausal women; the effect of HRT on insulin action may be mediated, in part, through changes in central adiposity.

Key Words: hormone replacement therapy; insulin resistance; abdominal obesity; estrogens.

26. **Randomised, controlled walking trials in postmenopausal women: the minimum dose to improve aerobic fitness?**
Br J Sports Med, 2002; **36**: 189-194, 2002.

T-M Asikainen, S Miilunpalo, P Oja, M Rinne, M Pasanen, K Uusi-Rasi and I Vuori

Urho Kaleva Kekkonen Institute for Health Promotion Research, Tampere, Finland

Correspondence to:

Dr Asikainen, The UKK Institute for Health Promotion Research, PO Box 30, FIN-33501, Tampere, Finland;

tm.asikainen@sci.fi

Background: The American College of Sports Medicine recommends 20–60 minutes of aerobic exercise three to five days a week at an intensity of 40/50–85% of maximal aerobic power (VO2MAX) reserve, expending a total of 700–2000 kcal (2.93–8.36 MJ) a week to improve aerobic power and body composition.

Objective: To ascertain the minimum effective dose of exercise.

Methods: Voluntary, healthy, non-obese, sedentary, postmenopausal women (n = 121), 48–63 years of age, were randomised to four low dose walking groups or a control group; 116 subjects completed the study. The exercise groups walked five days a week for 24 weeks with the following intensity (% of VO2MAX) and energy expenditure (kcal/week): group W1, 55%/1500 kcal; group W2, 45%/1500 kcal; group W3, 55%/1000 kcal; group W4, 45%/1000 kcal. VO2MAX was measured in a direct maximal treadmill test. Submaximal aerobic fitness was estimated as heart rates at submaximal work levels corresponding to 65% and 75% of the baseline VO2MAX. The body mass index (BMI) was calculated and percentage of body fat (F%) estimated from skinfolds.

Results: The net change (the differences between changes in each exercise group and the control group) in VO2MAX was 2.9 ml/min/kg (95% confidence interval (CI) 1.5 to 4.2) in group W1, 2.6 ml/min/kg (95% CI 1.3 to 4.0) in group W2, 2.4 ml/min/kg (95% CI 0.9 to 3.8) in group W3, and 2.2 ml/min/kg (95% CI 0.8 to 3.5) in group W4. The heart rates in standard submaximal work decreased 4 to 8 beats/min in all the groups. There was no change in BMI, but the F% decreased by about 1% unit in all the groups.

Conclusions: Walking (for 24 weeks) at moderate intensity 45% to 55% of VO2MAX, with a total weekly energy expenditure of 1000–1500 kcal, improves VO2MAX and body composition of previously sedentary, non-obese, postmenopausal women. This dose of exercise apparently approaches the minimum effective dose.

Key Words: walking; dose-response; postmenopausal women; randomised controlled trial; aerobic fitness.

Abbreviations: VO2MAX, Maximal aerobic power; BMI, body mass index; HRT, hormone replacement therapy; F%, percentage of body fat.

27. Age and aerobic exercise training effects on whole body and muscle protein metabolism

Am J Physiol Endocrinol Metab 286: E92-E101, 2004.

Kevin R. Short,1 Janet L. Vittone,2 Maureen L. Bigelow,1 David N. Proctor,3 and K. Sreekumaran Nair1

Divisions of 1Endocrinology and 2General Internal Medicine, Department of Internal Medicine, and 3Department of Anesthesiology, Mayo Clinic, Rochester, Minnesota 55905.

Aging in humans is associated with loss of lean body mass, but the causes are incompletely defined. Lean tissue mass and function depend on continuous rebuilding of proteins. We tested the hypotheses that whole body and mixed muscle protein metabolism declines with age in men and women and that aerobic exercise training would partly reverse this decline. Seventy-eight healthy, previously untrained men and women aged 19-87 yr were studied before and after 4 mo of bicycle training (up to 45 min at 80% peak heart rate, 3-4 days/wk) or control (flexibility) activity. At the whole body level, protein breakdown (measured as [13C]leucine and [15N]phenylalanine flux), Leu oxidation, and protein synthesis (nonoxidative Leu disposal) declined with age at a rate of 4-5% per decade (P < 0.001). Fat-free mass was closely correlated with protein turnover and declined 3% per decade (P < 0.001), but even after covariate adjustment for fat-free mass, the decline in protein turnover with age remained significant. There were no differences between men and women after adjustment for fat-free mass. Mixed muscle protein synthesis also declined with age 3.5% per decade (P < 0.05). Exercise training improved aerobic capacity 9% overall (P < 0.01), and mixed muscle protein synthesis increased 22% (P < 0.05), with no effect of age on the training response for either variable. **Fat-free mass**, whole body protein turnover, and resting metabolic rate were unchanged by training. We conclude that rates of whole body and muscle protein metabolism decline with age in men and women, thus indicating that there is a progressive decline in the body's remodeling processes with aging. This study also demonstrates that aerobic exercise can enhance muscle protein synthesis irrespective of age.

Key Words: leucine; phenylalanine; amino acid kinetics; resting metabolic rate; fractional synthesis rate; aging.

Address for reprint requests and other correspondence: K. S. Nair, Endocrinology Research Unit, Mayo Clinic, 200 First St. SW, Rochester, MN 55905 (E-mail: nair.sree@mayo.edu).

28. **Current Concepts in the Rehabilitation of the Overhead Throwing Athlete**
     The American Journal of Sports Medicine, 30:136-151 (2002).
     Kevin E. Wilk, PT*,, Keith Meister, MD and James R. Andrews, MD,¶
·   HealthSouth Rehabilitation Corporation and American Sports Medicine Institute, Birmingham, Alabama.
· || Tampa Bay Devil Rays Baseball Team, Tampa Bay, Florida
·   Department of Orthopaedics, Division of Sports Medicine, University of Florida, Gainesville, Florida.
     Alabama Sports Medicine and Orthopaedic Center, Birmingham, Alabama.

Address correspondence and reprint requests to Kevin E. Wilk, PT, HealthSouth Rehabilitation Corporation, 1201 11th Avenue South, Suite 100, Birmingham, AL 35202.

The overhead throwing motion is an extremely skillful and intricate movement that is very stressful on the shoulder joint complex. The overhead throwing athlete places extraordinary demands on this complex. Excessively high stresses are applied to the shoulder joint because of the tremendous forces generated by the thrower. The thrower's shoulder must be lax enough to allow excessive external rotation, but stable enough to prevent symptomatic humeral head subluxations, thus requiring a delicate balance between mobility and functional stability. We refer to this as the **"thrower's paradox."** This balance is frequently compromised, which leads to injury. Numerous types of injuries may occur to the surrounding tissues during overhead throwing. Frequently, injuries can be successfully treated with a well-structured and carefully implemented nonoperative rehabilitation program. The key to successful nonoperative treatment is a thorough clinical examination and accurate diagnosis. Athletes often exhibit numerous adaptive changes that develop from the repetitive microtraumatic stresses observed during overhead throwing. Treatment should focus on the restoration of these adaptations during the rehabilitation program. In this article, the typical musculoskeletal profile of the overhead thrower and various rehabilitation programs for specific injuries are discussed. Rehabilitation follows a structured, multiphase approach with emphasis on controlling inflammation, restoring muscle balance, improving soft tissue flexibility, enhancing proprioception and neuromuscular control, and efficiently returning the athlete to competitive throwing.

29. Comparative effects of two physical activity programs on measured and perceived physical functioning and other health-related quality of life outcomes in older adults

Journals of Gerontology Series A: Biological Sciences and Medical Sciences, Vol 55, Issue 2 M74-M83, 2000.

AC King, LA Pruitt, W Phillips, R Oka, A Rodenburg and WL Haskell
Stanford Center for Research in Disease Prevention, Stanford University School of Medicine, Palo Alto, California 94304-1583, USA. king@scrdp.stanford.edu

Background: Although inactivity is an important contributor to impaired functioning and disability with age, little is known concerning how improvements in physical functioning and well-being in older adults vary with the type of physical activity undertaken.

Methods: One hundred three adults age 65 years and older, recruited via population- based methods, were randomized to 12 months of community-based, moderate-intensity endurance and strengthening exercises (Fit & Firm) or stretching and flexibility exercises (Stretch & Flex). A combination of class- and home-based exercise formats was used. Measured and self- rated physical performance along with perceived functioning and well- being were assessed pre- and postintervention.

Results: Fit & Firm subjects showed greater 12-month improvements in both measured and self- rated endurance and strength compared to Stretch & Flex subjects. Stretch & Flex subjects reported greater improvements in bodily pain, and Stretch & Flex men evidenced greater improvements in flexibility relative to Fit & Firm subjects. Although overall exercise adherence was high in both exercise conditions (approximately 80%), subjects in both conditions showed better adherence to the home- versus class-based portions of their exercise prescriptions.

Conclusions: Community-based programs focusing on moderate-intensity endurance and strengthening exercises or flexibility exercises can be delivered through a combination of formats that result in improvement in important functional and well-being outcomes. This represents one of the first studies to report significant improvements in an important quality of life outcome-bodily pain-with a regular regimen of stretching and flexibility exercises in a community-based sample of older adults.

30.   **Improvement of muscle flexibility. A comparison between two techniques**
      American Journal of Sports Medicine, Vol 13, Issue 4 263-268, 1985.
      D Wallin, B Ekblom, R Grahn and T Nordenborg
      Forty-seven male subjects were randomly assigned to 4 different groups. Three groups of 10 subjects trained three times a week with a modified contract-relax (CR) method for improving muscle flexibility. Seventeen subjects trained during the same time with a traditional **ballistic stretch** (BS) method. After 30 days (14 training sessions) the latter group switched over to the CR method. The results showed that the CR method was significantly better than the BS method for improving muscle flexibility in the four different, bilateral muscle groups studied. After the initial 30 days the three groups of 10 subjects trained one, three, and five times a week, respectively, for another 30 days. The results showed that once a week was enough to maintain improved flexibility, while three and five times a week increased it further. The former BS group improved muscle flexibility between the 30th and 60th day, as expected from the results of the initial 30 days with the three CR groups, when training with the CR method three times a week.

31.   **The Effects of Strength Training, Cardiovascular Training and Their Combination on Flexibility of Inactive Older Adults**
      Int J Sports Med 2002; 23: 112-119.
      I.G. Fatouros1, K. Taxildaris1, S. P. Tokmakidis1, V. Kalapotharakos1, N. Aggelousis1, S. Athanasopoulos1, I. Zeeris1, I. Katrabasas1

1 Democritus University of Thrace, Dept. of Physical Education & Sport Science, Komotini, Greece

The purpose of this study was to investigate the effects of aerobic training, strength training and their combination on joint range of motion of inactive older individuals. Thirty-two inactive older men (65 - 78 yr) were assigned to one of four groups (n = 8 per group): control (C), strength training (ST), cardiovascular training (CT), and combination of strength and aerobic training (SA). Subjects in the S, A, and SA trained three times a week for 16 weeks. ST included 10 resistance exercises for the major muscle groups at an intensity of 55 - 80 % of 1-RM and CT included walking/ jogging at 50 - 80 % of maximal heart rate. Body weight and height, physical activity level and maximal oxygen uptake (VOÿ2max) were measured before the training period. Isokinetic (60 and 180 deg × sec-1) and concentric strength (1-RM in bench and leg press) were assessed prior to and at the end of the training period. Hip flexion, extension, abduction, and adduction, shoulder extension, flexion, and adduction, knee flexion, elbow flexion and sit-and-reach score were determined before and at 8 and 16 weeks of training. There were no differences between groups in VÿO2max, body weight, and height (p < 0.05). ST and SA but not CT and C increased isokinetic and concentric strength at the end of the training period (p < 0.05). ST and SA increased significantly (p < 0.05) sit-and-reach performance, elbow flexion, knee flexion, shoulder flexion and extension and hip flexion and extension both at mid- and post-training. CT increased (p < 0.05) only hip flexion and extension at post training. Results indicate that resistance training may be able to increase range of motion of a number of joints of inactive older individuals possibly due to an improvement in muscle strength.

Key Words : Flexibility · aerobic training · resistance training · combination training · elderly.

32. **Exercise Therapy for Low Back Pain: A Systematic Review Within the Framework of the Cochrane Collaboration Back Review Group.**
    Spine. 25(21):2784-2796, November 1, 2000.
    van Tulder, Maurits PhD *; Malmivaara, Antti MD, PhD +; Esmail, Rosmin MSc ++; Koes, Bart PhD [S]

Abstract:

Study Design : A systematic review of randomized controlled trials was performed.

Summary of Background Data. Exercise therapy is a widely used treatment for low back pain.

Objectives : To evaluate the effectiveness of exercise therapy for low back pain with regard to pain intensity, functional status, overall improvement, and return to work.

Methods s The Cochrane Controlled Trials Register, Medline, Embase, PsycLIT, and reference lists of articles were searched. Randomized trials testing all types of exercise therapy for subjects with nonspecific low back pain with or without radiation into the legs were included. Two reviewers independently extracted data and assessed trial quality. Because trials were considered heterogeneous with regard to study populations, interventions, and outcomes, it was decided not to perform a meta-analysis, but to summarize the results using a rating system of four levels of evidence: strong, moderate, limited, or none.

Results: In this review, 39 trials were identified. There is strong evidence that exercise therapy is not more effective for acute low back pain than inactive or other active treatments with which it has been compared. There is conflicting evidence on the effectiveness of exercise therapy compared with inactive treatments for chronic low back pain. Exercise therapy was more effective than usual care by the general practitioner and just as effective as conventional physiotherapy for chronic low back pain.

Conclusions : The evidence summarized in this systematic review does not indicate that specific exercises are effective for the treatment of acute low back pain. Exercises may be helpful for patients with chronic low back pain to increase return to normal daily activities and work.

33. **The association between flexibility and running economy in sub-elite male distance runners.**
Medicine and Science in Sports and Exercise. 28(6):737-743, June 1996.
Craib, Mitchell W.; Mitchell, Vicki A.; Fields, Karl B.; Cooper, Theresa R.; Hopewell, Regina; Morgan, Don W.

The purpose of this study was to examine the association between nine measures of limb and trunk flexibility and **running economy**. Within a week prior to running economy assessment, and after 10 min of jogging at 3.13 m[middle dot]s-1, 19 well-trained male sub-elite distance runners underwent two complete sets of lower limb and trunk flexibility assessments. Runners then completed two 10-min running economy assessment sessions on consecutive days at 4.13 m[middle dot]s-1 following two 30-min sessions of treadmill accommodation at 4.13 m[middle dot]s-1. Intraclass correlation coefficients indicated that the repeated flexibility measurements were highly reliable([horizontal bar over]X R = 0.92 +/- 0.09), as were the two running economy appraisals (R = 0.99). Correlational analyses revealed that **dorsiflexion** (r = 0.65) and standing hip rotation (r = 0.53) were significantly (P <= 0.05) associated with the mean aerobic demand of running, such that runners who less flexible on these measures were more economical. Although speculative, these results suggest that inflexibility in certain areas of the musculoskeletal system may enhance running economy in sub-elite male runners by increasing storage and return of elastic energy and minimizing the need for muscle-stabilizing activity.

34.   **Continuum of Cardiovascular Performance Across a Broad Range of Fitness Levels in Healthy Older Men**
Circulation. 1996;94:359-367.

Steven P. Schulman, MD; Jerome L. Fleg, MD; Andrew P. Goldberg, MD; Jan Busby-Whitehead, MD; James M. Hagberg, PhD; Frances C. O'Connor, MPH; Gary Gerstenblith, MD; Lewis C. Becker, MD; Leslie I. Katzel, MD; Loretta E. Lakatta, BSN; Edward G. Lakatta, MD

the Gerontology Research Center (J.L.F., F.C.O., E.G.L.), National Institute on Aging, and the Division of Gerontology (A.P.G., L.I.K., J.M.H., L.E.L.), University of Maryland School of Medicine and Geriatrics Research, Education and Clinical Center, Veterans Administration Medical Center, Baltimore; the Divisions of Geriatric Medicine and Gerontology (J.B.-W.) and Cardiology (S.P.S., G.G., L.C.B.), The Johns Hopkins Medical Institutions; and the Center on Aging (J.M.H.), University of Maryland, College Park, Md.

Correspondence to Edward G. Lakatta, MD, Gerontology Research Center, Laboratory of Cardiovascular Science, 4940 Eastern Ave, Baltimore, MD 21224.

Background Although it has become clear that habitual exercise in older individuals can partially offset age-associated cardiovascular declines, it is not known whether the beneficial effects of exercise training in older individuals depend on their prior fitness level.

Methods and Results Ten sedentary men (S), age 60.0±1.6 years (mean±SEM), who were carefully screened to exclude cardiac disease underwent exercise training for 24 to 32 weeks, and eight age-matched endurance-trained men (ET) stopped their exercise training for 12 weeks. All underwent **treadmill** exercise and rest and maximal cycle exercise upright gated blood pool scans at baseline and after the lifestyle intervention. Before the intervention, the treadmill maximum rate of oxygen consumption (O2max) was 49.9±1.9 and 32.1±1.4 mL·kg-1·min-1 in ET and S, respectively. During upright cycle exercise at exhaustion, although heart rate did not differ between groups, cardiac index, stroke volume index, ejection fraction, and left ventricular contractility index (systolic blood pressure/end-systolic volume index) all were significantly higher, and end-systolic volume index, diastolic blood pressure, and total systemic vascular resistance all were significantly lower in ET versus S. After the partial deconditioning of ET men, O2max fell to 42±2.2 mL·kg-1·min-1, and training of S increased O2max to 36.2±1.6 mL·kg-1·min-1. Training of S had effects on cardiovascular function that were similar in magnitude but directionally opposite those of detraining ET. All initial differences in cardiovascular performance at peak work rate between S and ET were abolished with the intervention. Across the broad range of fitness levels encountered before and after change in training status (O2max of 26 to 58 mL·kg-1·min-1), cardiac index, stroke volume index, end-systolic volume index, ejection fraction, and the left ventricular contractility index were all linearly correlated with O2max.

Conclusions Exercise training or detraining of older men results in changes in left ventricular performance that are qualitatively and quantitatively similar, regardless of the initial level of fitness before the intervention.

Key Words: aging • exercise • cardiac volume

35.   Long-term Effects of Varying Intensities and Formats of Physical Activity on Participation Rates, Fitness, and Lipoproteins in Men and Women Aged 50 to 65 Years
Circulation. 1995;91:2596-2604.

Abby C. King, PhD; William L. Haskell, PhD; Deborah R. Young, PhD; Roberta K. Oka, DNSc; Marcia L. Stefanick, PhD

From the Division of Epidemiology, Department of Health Research and Policy, and Stanford Center for Research in Disease Prevention, Department of Medicine (A.C.K.); the Division of Cardiovascular Medicine, Department of Medicine (W.L.H.); and Stanford Center for Research in Disease Prevention, Department of Medicine (D.R.Y., R.K.O., M.L.S.); Stanford University School of Medicine, Palo Alto, Calif.

Correspondence to Abby C. King, PhD, SCRDP, 730 Welch Rd, Suite B, Palo Alto, CA 94304-1583.

Background : Although exercise parameters such as intensity and format have been shown to influence exercise participation rates and physiological outcomes in the short term, few data are available evaluating their longer-term effects. The study objective was to determine the 2-year effects of differing intensities and formats of endurance exercise on exercise participation rates, fitness, and plasma HDL **cholesterol levels** among healthy older adults.

Methods and Results : Higher-intensity, group-based exercise training; higher-intensity, home-based exercise; and lower-intensity, home-based exercise were compared in a 2-year randomized trial. Participants were 149 men and 120 postmenopausal women 50 to 65 years of age who were sedentary and free of cardiovascular disease. Recruitment was achieved through a random digit-dial community telephone survey and media promotion. All exercise occurred in community settings. For higher-intensity exercise training, three 40-minute endurance training sessions per week were prescribed at 73% to 88% of peak treadmill heart rate. For lower-intensity exercise, five 30-minute endurance training sessions per week were prescribed at 60% to 73% of peak treadmill heart rate. Treadmill exercise performance, lipoprotein levels and other heart disease risk factors, and exercise adherence were evaluated at baseline and across the 2-year period. Treadmill exercise test performance improved for all three training conditions during year 1 and was successfully maintained during year 2, particularly for subjects in the higher-intensity, home-based condition. Subjects in that condition also showed the greatest year 2 exercise adherence rates (P<.003). Although no significant increases in HDL cholesterol were observed during year 1, by the end of year 2 subjects in the two home-based training conditions showed small but significant HDL cholesterol increases over baseline (P<.01). The increases were particularly pronounced for subjects in the lower-intensity condition, whose exercise prescription required more frequent exercise sessions per week. For all exercise conditions, increases in HDL cholesterol were associated with decreases in waist-to-hip ratio in both men and women (P<.04).

Conclusions : While older adults can benefit from initiating a regular regimen of moderate-intensity exercise in terms of improved fitness levels and small improvements in HDL cholesterol levels, the time frame needed to achieve HDL cholesterol change (2 years) may be longer than that reported previously for younger populations. Frequency of participation may be particularly important for achieving such changes. Supervised home-based exercise regimens represent a safe, attractive alternative for achieving sustained participation.

Key Words: exercise • lipoproteins • cholesterol • aging • risk factors.

36. A randomized outcome evaluation of group exercise programs in long-term care institutions

Journals of Gerontology Series A: Biological Sciences and Medical Sciences, Vol 54, **DA Lazowski, NA Ecclestone, AM Myers, DH Paterson, C Tudor-Locke, C Fitzgerald, G Jones, N Shima and DA Cunningham**

The Centre for Activity and Ageing, The University of Western Ontario, London, Canada. lazowski@julian.uwo.ca

Background: Physical activity programs in nursing homes typically consist of seated, range of motion (ROM) exercises, regardless of resident abilities. The Functional Fitness for Long-Term Care (FFLTC) Program was designed not only to maintain ROM, but also to improve strength, balance, flexibility, mobility, and function. In addition, it was tailored to meet the needs of both high and low mobility residents.

Methods: The feasibility and efficacy of the FFLTC Program were evaluated with 68 residents (mean age 80) from five institutions. Persons were classified as low or high mobility and randomized into either the FFLTC program or a seated ROM program. Classes were conducted in groups of 4 to 10 residents by trained facility staff for 45 minutes, three times per week.

Assessments at baseline and 4 months consisted of mobility, balance, gait, flexibility, functional capacity, and several upper and lower extremity strength measures.

Results: Attendance averaged 86% for the FFLTC and 79% for the ROM classes. Four months of exercise led to significant improvements in mobility (16%), balance (9%), flexibility (36%), knee (55%), and hip (12%) strength for the FFLTC group. Shoulder strength was the only improvement found for the ROM group. The ROM group significantly deteriorated in some areas, particularly hip strength, mobility, and functional ability.

Conclusions: Institutionalized seniors, even those who are physically frail, incontinent and/or have mild dementia, can respond positively to a challenging exercise program. The FFLTC program demonstrated clear benefits over typical, seated ROM exercises. Moreover, with minimal training, the program can be safely delivered at low cost by institutional staff and volunteers.

37.   **Effects of one year of resistance training on the relation between muscular strength and bone density in elderly women**
       Br J Sports Med 2000; *34*:18-22

E C Rhodes1, A D Martin1, J E Taunton2, M Donnelly3, J Warren3 and J Elliot3
1.   School of Human Kinetics, University of British Columbia, Vancouver, British Columbia, Canada
2.   Allan McGavin Sports Medicine Center
3.   STAT Unit, Vancouver Hospital and Health Sciences Center, Vancouver
       Correspondence to: Dr E C Rhodes, School of Human Kinetics, War Memorial Gymnasium, University of British Columbia, Vancouver, BC V6T 1Z1, Canada.

Objectives : There is a paucity of long term studies on exercise training in elderly women. The purpose of this study was to investigate the effects of one year of progressive resistance exercise (PRE) on dynamic muscular strength and the relations to **bone mineral density** (BMD) in elderly women.

Methods : Forty four healthy sedentary women (mean age 68.8 years) volunteered for this study and were randomly assigned to either an exercise group or a control group. The exercise group were involved in three one hour sessions a week for 52 weeks of supervised PRE to strengthen the large muscle groups of the body, while the control group were instructed to continue their normal lifestyle. The exercise circuit included three sets of eight repetitions at 75% of one repetition maximum focused on the large muscle groups. BMD was measured by dual energy **X-ray absoptiometry** (Lunar DPX) at the lumbar spine and at three sites in the proximal femur. Other selected parameters of physical fitness were also measured.

Results : Statistical analyses (analysis of covariance) showed significant strength gains (p<0.01) in bilateral bench press (>29%), bilateral leg press (>19%), and unilateral biceps curl (>20%). No significant difference between groups was evident in body weight, grip strength, flexibility, waist to hip ratio, or the sum of eight skinfolds. Significant relations (p<0.05) were recorded between dynamic leg strength and the BMD of the femoral neck, Ward's triangle, and the lumbar spine.

Conclusions : Significant strength changes, after one year of PRE, were evident in elderly women, and the muscle increases may parallel changes in BMD; however, correlation coefficients were moderate.

Key Words: strength training; muscular strength; bone density; elderly.

38. **High-Intensity Strength Training of Patients Enrolled in an Outpatient Cardiac Rehabilitation Program.**
   Journal of Cardiopulmonary Rehabilitation. 19(1):8-17, January/February 1999.
   Beniamini, Yael PhD *++; Rubenstein, Joel J. MD ; Faigenbaum, Avery D. EdD [S]; Lichtenstein, Alice H. DSc *+; Crim, Marilyn C. MD, PhD *

   Purpose : This randomized controlled study assessed whether adding a program of high-intensity strength training (80% of maximum) to an outpatient cardiac rehabilitation program would be a safe and effective means of improving muscle strength and body composition.

   Methods : Thirty-eight cardiac patient volunteers (29 men and 9 women) were randomized to either high-intensity strength training or flexibility training added concurrently to a 12-week outpatient cardiac rehabilitation aerobic exercise program. Muscle strength, local muscle endurance, joint flexibility, maximum treadmill tolerance time, and body composition were measured before and after completion of the training.

   Results: The strength-trained patients (n = 18) had greater increases in mean strength (90 +/- 19% versus 9 +/- 4%, P < 0.0001) and local muscle endurance (20 versus 6 times, P < 0.0001), and decreases in mean perceived exertion for lifting the initial one repetition maximum load (11 +/- 1 versus 15 +/- 1, P < 0.001) when compared with flexibility-trained patients (n = 16). The strength group lost more body fat (2.8 +/- 2.0 versus 1.3 +/- 2.0 kg, P < 0.01), tended to gain more lean tissue (1.5 +/- 2.3 versus 0.5 +/- 1.2 kg, P < 0.10), and had greater improvements in treadmill time (2.3 +/- 1.3 versus 1.2 +/- 1.0 minute, P < 0.02) than did the flexibility group. Improvements in joint flexibility were similar for each group. None of the subjects had evidence of cardiac ischemia or arrhythmia during the training sessions.

Conclusions. Medically supervised high-intensity strength training is well tolerated when added to the aerobic training of cardiac rehabilitation programs and allows patients to aggressively gain the strength and endurance they will need to complete daily living tasks at lower perceived efforts. Strength training also reduces cardiac risk factors by improving body composition and maximum treadmill exercise time.

39.   **Physical fitness related to age and physical activity in older persons.** *Medicine & Science in Sports & Exercise.* 30(3):434-441, March 1998. *Van Heuvelen, Marieke j. G.; Kempen, Gertrudis I. J. M.; Ormel, Johan; Rispens, Piet*

Objective: This study investigated physical fitness as a function of age and **leisure time physical activity** (LTPA) in a community-based sample of 624 persons aged 57 yr and older.

Methods: LTPA during the last 12 months was assessed through personal interviews. A wide range of physical fitness components was measured using performance-based tests.

Results: Physical fitness was associated with the interaction age by LTPA in only a few components, in a gender-specific way, with generally larger differences in fitness between active and less active persons with increasing age. All LTPA, including low intensity LTPA, is positively and age-independent associated with most physical fitness components.

Conclusion: The importance of LTPA typically participated in by the general population lies not so much in the delaying of the motor aging process but rather in a general, age-independent, positive effect.

40.   **The Effect of Endurance Training on Parameters of Aerobic Fitness** *Sports Medicine*, Volume 29, Number 6, 1 June 2000, pp. 373-386(14). **Jones A.M.1; Carter H.2**

Endurance exercise training results in profound adaptations of the cardiorespiratory and neuromuscular systems that enhance the delivery of oxygen from the atmosphere to the mitochondria and enable a tighter regulation of muscle metabolism. These adaptations effect an improvement in endurance performance that is manifest as a rightward shift in the 'velocity-time curve'. This shift enables athletes to exercise for longer at a given absolute exercise intensity, or to exercise at a higher exercise intensity for a given duration. There are 4 key parameters of aerobic fitness that affect the nature of the velocity-time curve that can be measured in the human athlete. These are the maximal oxygen uptake (O), exercise economy, the lactate/ventilatory threshold and oxygen uptake kinetics. Other parameters that may help determine endurance performance, and that are related to the other 4 parameters, are the velocity at O (V-O) and the maximal lactate steady state or critical power. This review considers the effect of endurance training on the key parameters of aerobic (endurance) fitness and attempts to relate these changes to the adaptations seen in the body's physiological systems with training. The importance of improvements in the aerobic fitness parameters to the enhancement of endurance performance is highlighted, as are the training methods that may be considered optimal for facilitating such improvements.

Key Words: Aerobic exercise; Endurance training; Exercise performance

41. Therapeutic value of exercise training in Parkinson's disease.

Medicine & Science in Sports & Exercise. 31(11):1544, November 1999.

Reuter, Iris; Engelhardt, Martin; Stecker, Klaus; Baas, Horst

Purpose: The objective of this study was to investigate the influence of an intensive exercise training on motor disability, mood, and subjective well-being in parkinsonian patients.

Methods: The study was designed as an open long-term pilot trial over 20 wk. Sixteen slightly to moderately affected idiopathic **parkinson**ian patients (PD) were included. An intensive standardized exercise training was performed twice weekly over 14 wk in all patients. Evaluations were performed before the start of the study (exam. 1), after 7 wk (exam 2), 14 wk (exam 3), and 20 wk (exam 4/long-term effect). The test battery included: 1) basic motor test (BMT) [test for muscle strength, flexibility, and coordination]; 2) **Unified Parkinson's Disease Rating Scale** (UPDRS) and **Columbia University Rating Scale** (CURS) for PD-specific motor disability; and 3) registration of psychometric data by **Mini Mental State** (MMS) for dementia and the **Adjective Mood Questionnaire of Zeersen** (AMQZ) and Sickness Impact Profile (SIP) for subjective well-being.

Results: UPDRS [SIGMA] score (P < 0.0001), CURS [SIGMA] score (P < 0.0001) and BMT [SIGMA] score (P < 0.0001) improved significantly by exercise training. Six weeks after termination of the training program, the majority of the patients had lost only minor components of their regained motor skills. There was no significant change in cognitive function during the study. The results of open interviews referring to subjective well-being were confirmed by the AMQZ and SIP. As an unexpected side effect, dyskinesias seemed to be better controlled.

Conclusion: Motor disability as well as mood and subjective well-being can be clearly improved by intensive sports activities in early to medium stage PD patients. A sustained ongoing benefit outlasting the active training period for at least 6 wk can be achieved but the exact duration of this benefit is open.

42.   **Exercise for Patients with Fibromyalgia: Risks versus Benefits**
Current Rheumatology Reports 2001, 3:135-140
S. R. Clark, K. D. Jones, C. S. Burckhardt, and Robert Bennett, MD, FRCP

Although exercise in the form of stretching, strength maintenance, and aerobic conditioning is generally considered beneficial to patients with fibromyalgia (FM), there is no reliable evidence to explain why exercise should help alleviate the primary symptom of FM, namely pain. Study results are varied and do not provide a uniform consensus that exercise is beneficial or what type, intensity, or duration of exercise is best. Patients who suffer from exercise-induced pain often do not follow through with recommendations. Evidence-based prescriptions are usually inadequate because most are based on methods designed for persons without FM and, therefore, lack individualization. A mismatch between exercise intensity and level of conditioning may trigger a classic neuroendocrine stress reaction. This review considers the adverse and beneficial effects of exercise. It also provides a patient guide to exercise that takes into account the risks and benefits of exercise for persons with FM.

43.   **Inheritance of physical fitness in 10-yr-old twins and their parents.**
Medicine & Science in Sports & Exercise. 28(12):1479-1491, December 1996.

Maes, Hermine H. M.; Beunen, Gaston P.; Vlietinck, Robert F.; Neale, Michael C.; Thomis, Martine; Eynde, Bavo Vanden; Lysens, Roeland; Simons, Jan; Derom, Catherine; Derom, Robert

This study focuses on the quantification of genetic and environmental sources of variation in physical fitness components in 105 10-yr-old twin pairs and their parents. Nine motor tests and six **skinfold** measures were administered. Motor tests can be divided into those that are performance-related: static strength, explosive strength, running speed, speed of limb movement, and balance; and those that are health-related: trunk strength, functional strength, maximum oxygen uptake, and flexibility. The significance and contribution of genetic and environmental factors to variation in physical fitness were tested with model fitting. Performance-related fitness characteristics were moderately to highly heritable. The heritability estimates were slightly higher for health-related fitness characteristics. For most variables a simple model including genetic and specific environmental factors fitted the observed phenotypic variance well. Common environmental factors explained a significant part of the variation in speed components and flexibility. Assortative mating was significant and positive for speed components, balance, **trunk strength**, and cardiorespiratory fitness, but negative for adiposity. Static strength, explosive strength, functional strength, and cardiorespiratory fitness showed evidence for reduced genetic transmission or dominance. The hypothesis that performance-related fitness characteristics are more determined by genetic factors than health-related fitness was not supported. At this prepubertal age, genetic factors have the predominant effect on fitness.

44. **Aerobic Fitness, Not Energy Expenditure, Influences Subsequent Increase in Adiposity in Black and White Children**
PEDIATRICS Vol. 106 No. 4 October 2000, p. e50

Maria S. Johnson*, Reinaldo Figueroa-Colon, Sara L. Herd, David A. Fields, Min Sun, Gary R. Hunter, and Michael I. Goran*

From the * Department of Preventive Medicine, Institute for Prevention Research, University of Southern California, Los Angeles, California; and Department of Nutrition Sciences, University of Alabama at Birmingham, Birmingham, Alabama.

Background : Low levels of energy expenditure and aerobic fitness have been hypothesized to be risk factors for **obesity**. Longitudinal studies to determine whether energy expenditure influences weight gain in whites have provided conflicting results. To date, no studies have examined this relationship in blacks or whether aerobic fitness influences weight gain in white or black children.

Methods : One hundred fifteen children, 72 white (55 girls and 17 boys) and 43 black (24 girls and 19 boys) were recruited for this study. Aerobic fitness, resting, total, and activity-related energy expenditure and body composition were measured at baseline. The children returned annually for 3 to 5 repeated measures of body composition. The influence of the initial measures of energy expenditure and fitness on the subsequent rate of increase in adiposity was examined, adjusting for initial body composition, age, ethnicity, gender, and Tanner stage. Because 20 children did not attain maximum oxygen consumption, the sample size for the combined analysis was 95.

Results : Initial fat mass was the main predictor of increasing adiposity in this cohort of children, with greater initial fat predicting a higher rate of increase of adiposity. There was also a significant negative relationship between aerobic fitness and the rate of increasing adiposity (F1,82 = 3.92). With every increase of .1 L/minute of fitness, there was a decrease of .081 kg fat per kg of lean mass gained. None of the measures of energy expenditure significantly predicted increasing adiposity in white or black children.

Conclusions : Initial fat mass was the dominant factor influencing increasing adiposity; however, aerobic fitness was also a significant independent predictor of increasing adiposity in this cohort of children. Resting, total, or activity-related energy expenditure did not predict increasing adiposity. It seems that aerobic fitness may be more important than absolute energy expenditure in the development of obesity in white or black children. **energy expenditure**, fitness, longitudinal, obesity.

45.   Resistance exercise decreases skeletal muscle tumor necrosis factor in frail elderly humans

The FASEB Journal. 2001;15:475-482.

Jeffrey s. Greiwe1, Bo Cheng1, Deborah C. Rubin, Kevin E. Yarasheski and Clay F. Semenkovich2

Departments of Medicine and Cell Biology and Physiology, Claude D. Pepper Older Americans Independence Center, Center for Cardiovascular Research, Washington University School of Medicine, St. Louis, Missouri 63110, USA.

2Correspondence: Washington University School of Medicine, Box 8046, 660 S. Euclid Ave., St. Louis, MO 63110, USA. E-mail semenkov@im.wustl.edu.

Skeletal muscle protein and function decline with advancing age but the underlying pathophysiology is poorly understood. To test the hypothesis that the catabolic cytokine tumor necrosis factor alpha (TNF-) contributes to this process, we studied the effects of aging and resistance exercise on TNF-expression in human muscle. Using in situ hybridization, TNF- message was localized to myocytes in sections of skeletal muscle from elderly humans. Both TNF- mRNA and protein levels were elevated in skeletal muscle from frail elderly (81±1 year) as compared to healthy young (23±1 year) men and women. To determine whether resistance exercise affects TNF- expression, frail elderly men and women were randomly assigned to a training group or to a nonexercising control group. Muscle biopsies were performed before and after 3 months. Muscle TNF- mRNA and protein levels decreased in the exercise group but did not change in the control group. Muscle protein synthesis rate in the exercise group was inversely related to levels of TNF- protein. These data suggest that TNF- contributes to age-associated muscle wasting and that resistance exercise may attenuate this process by suppressing skeletal muscle TNF- expression.

Key Words: cytokines • sarcopenia • aging • lipoprotein lipase.

46. **Randomised controlled trial to compare surgical stabilisation of the lumbar spine with an intensive rehabilitation programme for patients with chronic low back pain: the MRC spine stabilisation trial**
BMJ 330:1233 ,28 May, 2005.

Jeremy Fairbank, consultant orthopaedic surgeon1, **Helen Frost**, research fellow2, **James Wilson-MacDonald**, consultant orthopaedic surgeon1, **Ly-Mee Yu**, statistician3, **Karen Barker**, director of physiotherapy research1, **Rory Collins**, professor4, for the for the Spine Stabilisation Trial Group.

1 Nuffield Orthopaedic Centre, Oxford OX3 7LD, 2 University of Warwick, Division of Health in the Community, Coventry CV4 7AL, 3 Centre for Statistics in Medicine, Oxford OX3 7LF, 4 Clinical Trial Service Unit and Epidemiological Studies Unit, Radcliffe Infirmary, Oxford OX2 6HE.

Correspondence to: J Fairbank jeremy.fairbank@ndos.ox.ac.uk

Objectives : To assess the clinical effectiveness of surgical stabilisation (spinal fusion) compared with intensive rehabilitation for patients with chronic low back pain.

Design : Multicentre randomised controlled trial.

Setting 15 secondary care orthopaedic and rehabilitation centres across the United Kingdom.

Participants : 349 participants aged 18-55 with chronic low back pain of at least one year's duration who were considered candidates for spinal fusion.

Intervention Lumbar spine fusion or an intensive rehabilitation programme based on principles of **cognitive behaviour therapy**.

Main outcome measure : The primary outcomes were the Oswestry disability index and the shuttle walking test measured at baseline and two years after randomisation. The SF-36 instrument was used as a secondary outcome measure.

Results : 176 participants were assigned to surgery and 173 to rehabilitation. 284 (81%) provided follow-up data at 24 months. The mean Oswestry disability index changed favourably from 46.5 (SD 14.6) to 34.0 (SD 21.1) in the surgery group and from 44.8 (SD14.8) to 36.1 (SD 20.6) in the rehabilitation group. The estimated mean difference between the groups was −4.1 (95% confidence interval −8.1 to −0.1, P = 0.045) in favour of surgery. No significant differences between the treatment groups were observed in the shuttle walking test or any of the other outcome measures.

Conclusions : Both groups reported reductions in disability during two years of follow-up, possibly unrelated to the interventions. The statistical difference between treatment groups in one of the two primary outcome measures was marginal and only just reached the predefined minimal clinical difference, and the potential risk and additional cost of surgery also need to be considered. No clear evidence emerged that primary spinal fusion surgery was any more beneficial than intensive rehabilitation.

47. Water-based exercise improves health-related aspects of fitness in older women.

Medicine & Science in Sports & Exercise. 34(3):544-551, March 2002.

Takeshima, Nobuo; Rogers, Michael E.; Watanabe, Eiji; Brechue, William F.; Okada, Akiyoshi; Yamada, Tadaki; Islam, Mohammod M.; Hayano, Jyunichirou

Purpose: The purpose of this study was to determine the physiological responses of elderly women to a well-rounded **exercise program performed in water (WEX)**.

Methods: The participants (60-75 yr of age) were randomly divided into a training (TR) group (N = 15) and a control group (N = 15). The TR group participated in a 12-wk supervised WEX program, 70 min[middle dot]day-1, 3 d[middle dot]wk-1. The WEX consisted of 20 min of warm-up and stretching exercise, 10 min of resistance exercise, 30 min of endurance-type exercise (walking and dancing), and 10 min of cool-down exercise.

Results: The WEX led to an increase (P < 0.05) in peak O2 (12%) and O2 at lactate threshold (20%). Muscular strength evaluated by a hydraulic resistance machine increased significantly at resistance dial setting 8 (slow) for knee extension (8%), knee flexion (13%), chest press (7%) and pull (11%), shoulder press (4%) and pull (6%), and back extension (6%). Vertical jump (9%), side-stepping agility (22%), trunk extension (11%), and FEV1.0 (7%) also increased significantly. There was a significant decrease in skin-fold thickness (-8%), low-density lipoprotein (LDL) cholesterol (-17%), and total cholesterol (-11%). There were no significant changes in these variables in the control group.

Conclusion: These results indicate that WEX elicits significant improvements in cardiorespiratory fitness, muscular strength, body fat, and total cholesterol in older adult women. Water-based exercise appears to be a very safe and beneficial mode of exercise that can be performed as part of a well-rounded exercise program.

48. Etiology and modification of gait instability in older adults: a randomized controlled trial of exercise

*J Appl Physiol,*Vol. 90, Issue 6, 2117-2129, June 2001

Jeffrey M. Hausdorff1, Miriam E. Nelson2, David Kaliton1, Jennifer E. Layne2, Melissa J. Bernstein2, Andrea Nuernberger2, and Maria A. Fiatarone Singh2,3

1 Gerontology Division, Beth Israel Deaconess Medical Center, and Division on Aging, Harvard Medical School, Boston 02215; 2 The Exercise Physiology, Nutrition, and Sarcopenia Laboratory, Jean Mayer United States Department of Agriculture Human Nutrition Research Center on Aging at Tufts University, Boston, Massachusetts 02111; and 3 School of Exercise and Sport Science, University of Sydney, Lidcombe, Australia.

Increased gait instability is common in older adults, even in the absence of overt disease. The goal of the present study was to quantitatively investigate the factors that contribute to gait instability and its potential reversibility in functionally impaired older adults. We studied 67 older men and women with functional impairment before and after they participated in a randomized placebo-controlled, 6-mo multimodal exercise trial. We found that 1) **gait instability** is multifactorial; 2) **stride time variability** is strongly associated with functional status and performance-based measures of function that have previously been shown to predict significant clinical outcomes such as morbidity and nursing home admission; 3) neuropsychological status and health-related quality of life play important, independent roles in gait instability; and 4) improvement in physiological capacity is associated with reduced gait instability. Although the etiology of gait instability in older persons with mild-moderate functional impairment is multifactorial, interventions designed to reduce gait instability may be effective in bringing about a more consistent and more stable walking pattern.

Key Words: muscle function; aging; plasticity; exercise; dynamics variability.

49. Aerobic and anaerobic power responses to the practice of taekwon-do
Br J Sports Med,35:231-234, 2001.

A F Melhim

Department of Exercise Science, Faculty of Physical Education, Yarmouk University, PO Box 5040, Irbid 21163, Jordan

Correspondence to: Dr Melhim ayedm@hotmail.com

Background : Practising the martial art of **taekwon-do** (TKD) has been proposed to have beneficial effects on cardiovascular fitness as well as general physical ability. Furthermore, TKD masters and participants have promoted TKD as a total fitness programme. Research studies substantiating this, however, seem to be lacking, perhaps because TKD is recognised more as a method of self defence than a fitness programme.

Methods : Nineteen TKD practitioners with an average age of 13.8 years and 10.4 months of TKD training experience were recruited to participate. Measurements included resting heart rate, aerobic power, anaerobic power, and anaerobic capacity.

Results : Paired t test analysis showed no significant differences in either resting heart rate or aerobic power after training. However, significant differences were observed in anaerobic power and anaerobic capacity (p = 0.05). The increases in anaerobic power and anaerobic capacity were 28% and 61.5% respectively.

Conclusion : The practice of TKD promotes anaerobic power and anaerobic capacity, but not aerobic power, in male adolescents.

Key Words: taekwon-do; poomses; VO2MAX; anaerobic power; anaerobic capacity.

50. **Pulmonary rehabilitation**
    Chest, Vol 113, 263S-268S, 1998.
    DA Mahler
    Section of Pulmonary and Critical Care Medicine, Dartmouth-Hitchcock Medical Center, Lebanon, NH, USA.

There has been a resurgence of interest in pulmonary rehabilitation mainly because the prevalence of COPD has increased, scientific studies document consistent benefits (increased exercise endurance and reduced **dyspnea**), and thoracic surgeons recognize that preoperative and postoperative conditioning enhances the results of lung volume reduction surgery and lung transplantation. Although education and psychosocial/behavioral interventions are important components of a multidimensional program, exercise training of the upper and lower extremities is essential to achieve the described improvements. Current programs vary considerably in the frequency, intensity, and duration of exercise reconditioning. Two "key" questions relating to pulmonary rehabilitation are as follows. What is an appropriate training intensity? How should patients monitor the training intensity? Maintenance exercise programs and the development of home- or community- based programs will be important future developments.

51. **The effects of exercise on falls in elderly patients. A preplanned meta-analysis of the FICSIT Trials. Frailty and Injuries: Cooperative Studies of Intervention Techniques**
    The Journal of the American Medical Association, Vol. 273 No. 17, May 3, 1995
    M. A. Province, E. C. Hadley, M. C. Hornbrook, L. A. Lipsitz, J. P. Miller, C. D. Mulrow, M. G. Ory, R. W. Sattin, M. E. Tinetti and S. L. Wolf
    Division of Biostatistics, Washington University School of Medicine, St Louis, MO 63110, USA.

Objective : To determine if short-term exercise reduces falls and fall-related injuries in the elderly.

Design : A preplanned meta-analysis of the seven Frailty and Injuries: **Cooperative Studies of Intervention Techniques** (FICSIT)—independent, randomized, controlled clinical trials that assessed intervention efficacy in reducing falls and frailty in elderly patients. All included an exercise component for 10 to 36 weeks. Fall and injury follow-up was obtained for up to 2 to 4 years.

Setting : Two nursing home and five community-dwelling (three health maintenance organizations) sites. Six were group and center based; one was conducted at home.

Participants : Numbers of participants ranged from 100 to 1323 per study. Subjects were mostly ambulatory and cognitively intact, with minimum ages of 60 to 75 years, although some studies required additional deficits, such as functionally dependent in two or more activities of daily living, balance deficits or lower extremity weakness, or high risk of falling.

Interventions : Exercise components varied across studies in character, duration, frequency, and intensity. Training was performed in one area or more of endurance, flexibility, balance platform, Tai Chi (dynamic balance), and resistance. Several treatment arms included additional nonexercise components, such as behavioral components, medication changes, education, functional activity, or nutritional supplements.

Main Outcome Measures : Time to each fall (fall-related injury) by self-report and/or medical records.

Results : Using the Andersen-Gill extension of the Cox model that allows multiple fall outcomes per patient, the adjusted fall incidence ratio for treatment arms including general exercise was 0.90 (95% confidence limits [CL], 0.81, 0.99) and for those including balance was 0.83 (95% CL, 0.70, 0.98). No exercise component was significant for injurious falls, but power was low to detect this outcome.

Conclusions : Treatments including exercise for elderly adults reduce the risk of falls.

52. Cardiovascular fitness, cortical plasticity, and aging
PNAS, vol. 101, no. 9, 3316-3321, 2004.
Stanley J. Colcombe *, Arthur F. Kramer *, Kirk I. Erickson *, Paige Scalf *, Edward McAuley, Neal J. Cohen*, Andrew Webb*, Gerry J. Jerome , David X. Marquez , and Steriani Elavsky

*The Beckman Institute, Neuroscience Program, and Departments of Psychology, ¶Kinesiology, and ||Electrical and Chemical Engineering, University of Illinois at Urbana-Champaign, Urbana, IL 61801.

Cardiovascular fitness is thought to offset declines in cognitive performance, but little is known about the cortical mechanisms that underlie these changes in humans. Research using animal models shows that aerobic training increases cortical capillary supplies, the number of synaptic connections, and the development of new neurons. The end result is a brain that is more efficient, plastic, and adaptive, which translates into better performance in aging animals. Here, in two separate experiments, we demonstrate for the first time to our knowledge, in humans that increases in cardiovascular fitness results in increased functioning of key aspects of the attentional network of the brain during a cognitively challenging task. Specifically, highly fit (Study 1) or aerobically trained (Study 2) persons show greater task-related activity in regions of the prefrontal and parietal cortices that are involved in spatial selection and inhibitory functioning, when compared with low-fit (Study 1) or nonaerobic control (Study 2) participants. Additionally, in both studies there exist groupwise differences in activation of the anterior cingulate cortex, which is thought to monitor for conflict in the attentional system, and signal the need for adaptation in the attentional network. These data suggest that increased cardiovascular fitness can affect improvements in the plasticity of the aging human brain, and may serve to reduce both biological and cognitive senescence in humans.

Abbreviations: CFT, cardiovascular fitness training; MFG, middle frontal gyrus; SFG, superior frontal gyrus; SPL, superior parietal lobule; IPL, inferior parietal lobule; ACC, anterior cingulate cortex; fMRI, functional MRI; RT, reaction time; HR, heart rate.

To whom correspondence should be addressed. E-mail: a-kramer@s.psych.uiuc.edu.

53. **Resistance exercise training reduces hypertriglyceridemia in HIV-infected men treated with antiviral therapy**
J Appl Physiol 90: 133-138, 2001.

Kevin E. Yarasheski1, Pablo Tebas2, Barbara Stanerson1, Sherry Claxton1, Donna Marin2, Kyongtae Bae3, Michael Kennedy2, Woraphot Tantisiriwat2, and William G. Powderly2

1 Division of Metabolism, Endocrinology and Diabetes, 2 Division of Infectious Diseases, and 3 Department of Radiological Sciences, Washington University Medical School, St. Louis, Missouri 63110

Hypertriglyceridemia, peripheral insulin resistance, and **trunk adiposity** are metabolic complications recently recognized in people infected with human immunodeficiency virus (HIV) and treated with highly active antiretroviral therapy (HAART). These complications may respond favorably to exercise training. Using a paired design, we determined whether 16 wk of weight-lifting exercise increased muscle mass and strength and decreased fasting serum triglycerides and adipose tissue mass in 18 HIV-infected men. The resistance exercise regimen consisted of three upper and four lower body exercises done for 1-1.5 h/day, 4 days/wk for 64 sessions. Dual-energy **X-ray absorptiometry** indicated that exercise training increased whole body lean mass 1.4 kg (P = 0.005) but did not reduce adipose tissue mass (P = NS). Axial proton-magnetic resonance imaging indicated that thigh muscle cross-sectional area increased 5-7 cm2 (P < 0.005). Muscle strength increased 23-38% (P < 0.0001) on all exercises. Fasting serum triglycerides were decreased at the end of training (281-204 mg/dl; P = 0.02). These findings imply that resistance exercise training-induced muscle hypertrophy may promote triglyceride clearance from the circulation of hypertriglyceridemic HIV-infected men treated with antiviral therapy.

AIDS; metabolic complications; progressive resistance exercise training; muscle protein mass; lipid metabolism; magnetic resonance imaging

54. **Does strength training inhibit gains in range of motion from flexibility training in older adults?**
Med Sci Sports Exerc. 27(10):1444-9, 1995.
Girouard CK, Hurley BF.
Department of Kinesiology, University of Maryland, College Park 20742, USA.

Thirty-one untrained men between the ages of 50 and 74 (61 +/- 6 yr, mean +/- SD) were studied to compare the effects of strength and flexibility (SF) training, flexibility only (FO) training, and no training (inactive control group) on shoulder and hip range of motion. Fourteen of these subjects volunteered to participate in an SF training program three times per week for 10 wk. Ten others participated in an FO training program during this same time period, and the remaining seven subjects agreed to serve as an inactive control group by not participating in any regular exercise. The SF training consisted of a 3-min warm-up on a stationary bike, approximately 30 min of heavy resistance strength training, and about 10 min of static stretches performed before and after each training session. Maximal oxygen uptake (VO2max), percentage of body fat, and muscular strength (three-repetition maximum and **peak isokinetic torque**) were assessed before and after training for the SF group. Shoulder abduction, shoulder flexion, and hip flexion were measured with a universal **goniometer** in all groups before and after the training period. The FO training consisted of the identical warm-up and stretching exercises used in the SF training but without strength training. The results indicate that the FO group increased its range of motion in shoulder abduction to a significantly greater extent than the SF group (P < 0.001), and none of the changes in range of motion for the SF group was significantly different than the changes in the control group.

55.   Exercise training and heart rate variability in older people.

Medicine & Science in Sports & Exercise. 31(6):816-821, June 1999.

Schuit, Albertine J.; Van Amelsvoort, Ludovic G. P. M.; Verheij, Ton C.; Rijneke, Rob D.; Maan, Arie C.; Swenne, Cees A.; Schouten, Evert G.

Purpose: Heart rate variability (HRV), a characteristic that is potentially increased by physical activity, has been associated with incidence of cardiac events and total mortality. Since the incidence of cardiac events among older people is high and their physical activity levels and HRV are generally low, it is important to investigate whether regular physical activity can modify HRV in this age group. The purpose of the study was to investigate the effect of regular physical activity on HRV in older men and women.

Methods: In a randomized controlled trial, the effect of six months' training on HRV was investigated in a group of 51 older men and women (67.0 +/- 5.1 yr). The training group gathered three times per week for 45 min supervised training.

Results: At the end of the intervention period, HRV was higher primarily during the day. During daytime, the SD of all normal intervals (+6%) as well as the low frequency component (+15%) and the very low frequency component (+10%) of HRV were significantly increased ($P < 0.05$) as compared with the control group. Effects of training were most pronounced in subjects inactive in sports at baseline.

Conclusion: This study demonstrates that regular physical activity increases HRV (specifically in the very low and low frequency components) in older subjects. Hence, in older subjects, physical training may be an effective means to modify positively a factor that is associated with increased incidence of cardiac events.

56.   Older Women's Beliefs About Exercise Benefits and Risks

The Journals of Gerontology Series B: Psychological Sciences and Social Sciences 55:P283-P294 (2000)

Sandra O'Brien Cousinsa

a Faculty of Physical Education and Recreation, University of Alberta, Edmonton, Canada

Daily physical activity is advocated by various federal health agencies for reducing many of the health risks affecting old age, but older women are generally not heeding the message. The Health Belief Model proposes that sedentary living occurs when people believe that the risks of exercising exceed the benefits. To clarify the beliefs that act as incentives and barriers to more active living, the author asked 143 independent-living women aged 70 and older to respond to open-ended questions on their beliefs about benefits and risks for 6 fitness activities: brisk walking, aquacize, riding a bike or cycling, stretching slowly to touch the toes, modified push-ups from a kneeling position, and supine curl-ups. Content analysis organized perceived risks into 19 categories and perceived benefits into 6 categories providing original data on the conceptions that older women hold about the utility of various types of physical activity. Respondents generally recognized broad health benefits to fitness activities, but beliefs about risks were strong, anatomically specific, and sometimes sensational in description. The findings suggest that many older women feel physically vulnerable, are unsure about their actual risks and benefits in exercise settings, and, in the face of that uncertainty, report medical reasons why they should be excused from fitness-promoting exercise.

57.   The Impact of Stretching on Sports Injury Risk: A Systematic Review of the Literature.
Medicine & Science in Sports & Exercise. 36(3):371-378, March 2004.
Thacker, Stephen B. 1; Gilchrist, Julie 2; Stroup, Donna F. 3; Kimsey, C. Dexter Jr. 3

Purpose: We conducted a systematic review to assess the evidence for the effectiveness of stretching as a tool to prevent injuries in sports and to make recommendations for research and prevention.

Methods: Without language limitations, we searched electronic data bases, including MEDLINE (1966-2002), Current Contents (1997-2002), Biomedical Collection (1993-1999), the Cochrane Library, and SPORTDiscus, and then identified citations from papers retrieved and contacted experts in the field. Meta-analysis was limited to randomized trials or cohort studies for interventions that included stretching. Studies were excluded that lacked controls, in which stretching could not be assessed independently, or where studies did not include subjects in sporting or fitness activities. All articles were screened initially by one author. Six of 361 identified articles compared stretching with other methods to prevent injury. Data were abstracted by one author and then reviewed independently by three others. Data quality was assessed independently by three authors using a previously standardized instrument, and reviewers met to reconcile substantive differences in interpretation. We calculated weighted pooled odds ratios based on an intention-to-treat analysis as well as subgroup analyses by quality score and study design.

Results: Stretching was not significantly associated with a reduction in total injuries (OR = 0.93, CI 0.78-1.11) and similar findings were seen in the subgroup analyses.

Conclusion: There is not sufficient evidence to endorse or discontinue routine stretching before or after exercise to prevent injury among competitive or recreational athletes. Further research, especially well-conducted randomized controlled trials, is urgently needed to determine the proper role of stretching in sports.